# THE GREAT
# TURNING

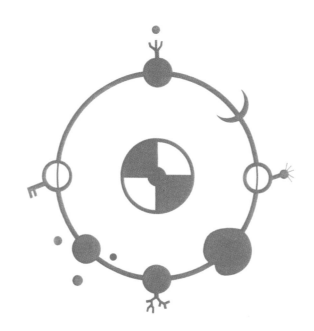

## MICHAEL GREEN

*The Barbury Castle Formation*

# THE GREAT TURNING

*Crop Circles and their Message to Humanity*

## MICHAEL GREEN

edited by Mary Coales

The Squeeze Press

First Published 2023
Copyright © James Michael George Insley Green 2023

Published by The Squeeze Press
An Imprint of Wooden Books Ltd
Glastonbury, UK

A CIP catalogue record for this book is available
from the British Library.
ISBN-13: 978-1-906069-27-8

Designed and typeset by YouCaxton
and Wooden Books Ltd, UK.

Printed and bound by
Dream Colour Printing, China.

www.woodenbooks.com

the
SQUEEZE
PRESS

*Dedicated to the Council and Membership of
the Centre for Crop Circle Studies
who faithfully served and supported the organisation
in one capacity or another during its existence.*

*Founders and research members of the Centre for Crop Circle Studies*

**Back row:** *Richard Andrews, George Wingfield, Leonie Starr,
Michael Green, John Michell, Professor Archie Roy, Ralph Noyes*

**Middle row:** *Christine Green, Alick Bartholomew*

**Front row:** *Busty Taylor, Barbara Davies, Maria Bartholomew,
Richard Beaumont, Beth Davis*

https://www.youtube.com/watch?v=2MN1zl43y50

Also by Michael Green (Henry James Michael Green),
architect, archaeologist, historian and psychic

Books:

*Godmanchester* (1977). Cambridge: The Oleander Press

*Historic Clapham* (2008). Stroud: The History Press

*Durovigutum: Roman Godmanchester* (2018).
Compiled, collated and edited by Tim Malim. Oxford: Archaeopress Publishing

Numerous book chapters and articles on crop circles, see Bibliography, and contributions to
various magazines and journals, including the *Illustrated London News*,
*The Archaeological News Letter*, and the *Proceedings of the Cambridge Antiquarian Society*

# On Michael Green

Obituary by Andy Thomas, author and lecturer on unexplained mysteries:

https://www.truthagenda.org/2018/02/01/michael-green-1932-2018/

I first visited Stonehenge in my teenage years and was completely taken over by the significance of the site. I have since visited sites on five continents, investigating the energy fields which I found I was sensitive to. Years later, the Crop Circle phenomenon appeared primarily in Wiltshire. I heard of a Michael Green organising an event at Winchester. I attended, giving a short presentation revealing certain links to my previous earth energy investigations. Within a few days I was appointed scientific advisor to the newly formed 'Centre for Crop Circle Studies.' I worked closely with Michael, and, despite the fact we approached the topic from opposite ends of the cultural spectrum, he from the arts and I from the scientific end, we immediately established a very strong rapport.

We set out to analyse crop formations scientifically. A key objective was to establish the respectability of our findings. I suggested that a formative electrical discharge to ground would enhance the nitrate level within the crop. Michael submitted crop samples to the UK Agricultural Test Laboratory. The results were startingly positive! Michael's initiative had revealed the true nature of the phenomenon. We had found a significant link to the ancient concept of a conscious cosmos.

Our collaboration continued for many years. Michael's legacy establishes the true nature of man's interaction with the cosmos. I will always remember him with high regard for his abilities and dedication, as indeed will many other followers.

James Lyons
Chartered Engineer, Academic Researcher in energy technology, co-author, *The Energies of the Crop Circles*, 2019.

I first met Michael Green in 1998 after listening to one of his lectures. Little did I know that the direction of my life would change thereafter and result in my present involvement in the crop circle phenomenon. He opened a new and fascinating world for me of learning, investigation and research. His enquiring mind appealed to me and, having been born with one myself, it was a joy to learn more and more. Green was an avid pursuer of knowledge in many different but inter-connected fields; as an academic, his interests spread far and wide, concentrated mainly around ancient sites, ancient customs and theology to name but a few.

This long awaited book will reveal his vast knowledge and his quest for more. The reader will not be disappointed.

Lucy Pringle
Author, aerial photographer, researcher and world-wide lecturer on crop circles. Co-author, *The Energies of the Crop Circles*, 2019.
www.lucypringle.com

I remember Michael's contribution to the study of the crop circles through the CCCS, and his own initiatives in the early days of the phenomenon, to be both erudite and profound.

His academic approach, which attempted to discern meaning from the early symbols and signs with reference to theosophical studies and even earlier cultural references, both inspired and interested me. He also managed to balance this more intellectual appreciation and investigation with an equally grounded and practical one in the fields themselves, devoted to clothing the phenomena in scientific attempts and measurement and interpretation. In this way he heralded and embodied the need to bring respectability and an academic and practical rigour to a phenomenon that otherwise demands to remain mysterious and to point to unanswerable questions.

Today's conscious technology movements, forging paths into a relationship with technology that becomes a bridge between intention and connection, would seem to be birthed from the early catalysts of the Crop Circle energies. These technologies enter more into the realms of Information Fields and Life Force Energy and so their expressions span Wellness, Free Energy and Agriculture. These are a trinity perfectly contained and conditioned in any crop circle!

The Crop Circles at once seem to help re-member and re-balance Mother Earth as they invite her to act as their canvas, and also to catalyse new currents in those who came close to admire and study them.

Michael was an important flag bearer and herald for this age, and we can see the work of himself and others from that time in the 90s bearing fruit in these pivotal times. The dramas we are witnessing are perhaps the mirror and counterpoint to the imbalances and lack of understanding that we collectively carry, at once helping to discharge the static and also to catalyse and direct an urgent and critical quickening of those who realise what they stand to lose from an AI technocracy that threatens to engulf our freedoms and sacred origins. Michael and the CCCS kept some of those origins alive and relevant for us.

Oliver Perceval

Architect, Co-founder of Orynoco Ltd. Author, *Quantum Gnosis, the Spirit of Science and our Journey Home*, 2007.

# Acknowledgements

The substance of *The Great Turning* is concerned with an interpretation of the geophysical crop circle phenomenon in the light of Theosophical concepts, and in particular the communications of Djwhal Khul through the channeller, Alice Bailey (1880-1949). In 1990, soon after the Centre for Crop Circle Studies (CCCS) had been founded, I visited the headquarters of the *Lucis Trust* (set up to promulgate the Bailey publications) in Whitehall, London, and spoke to Sarah McKechnie (Chairman) and her team. I explained the spiritual principles that I was following in connection with the possible link between the Bailey material and the crop formations. I am grateful for the interest and sympathy of the Lucis Trust, and the subsequent help over the next decade or so of members of their staff such as Helen Durant at the Lucis Press.

I am also deeply indebted for metaphysical material from other channellers such as Bob Armstrong, Isabelle Kingston, Paul Bura, Carol Cochrane and L. C.-H. Many friends and colleagues of the former CCCS have provided invaluable help and support in terms of fieldwork, pictorial and written material for this book, especially George Bishop, Beth Davis, Andrew King, Jim Lyons, Michael Newark, Margaret Novakovic, John Sayer and Richard Smith. The work of numerous aerial photographers has been invaluable. I am indebted to Mr Alec Down for illustrative material in connection with the Chilgrove pavement.

My wife Christine has been an active and sympathetic pillar of support in the genesis and production of this book. Lastly the work could not have been carried through without the dedicated secretarial and editorial skills of my Personal Assistant, Mary Coales, to whom I am profoundly grateful.

Michael Green

Under this text, prepared in 2008, Michael wrote, in manuscript: – 'there will necessarily have to be additions to this basic list.' One is Robert Stewart, for inspiration. Many others appear in the book. On Michael's behalf I thank them all, as he would have wished. Their names are in the Index.

I am myself grateful for generous help from Steve Alexander, Richard Beaumont, Anthony Cheke, Bob Croxford, Beth Davis, Chad Deetken, Marilyn Emmett, Andrew King, Nick Kollerstrom, Ulrich Kox, John Martineau, Ronnie O'Brien, David Parker, Lucy Pringle, Busty Taylor, Andy Thomas, Grant Wakefield, George Wingfield and Richard Wintle, and for the drawings of James Green for his father's book.

Many thanks to Martyn Campbell and Helen Christmas, who worked patiently with me on the images, particularly Michael's drawings, to bring them into the digital age, and especially to Christine Green.

Mary Coales, Editor, 2023

# Acknowledgement of permissions to use quotations

Every effort has been made to fulfil requirements with regard to reproducing copyright material. The author's heirs will be glad to rectify any omission at the earliest opportunity.

The editor is grateful to the following for the permissions to use quotations from the works listed:

The Lucis Trust, who hold the copyright for the Alice Bailey books (see Bibliography)

Bloomsbury Publishing Plc. © Cannon Johnson, P. (2005), 'The Neoplatonists and the Mystery Schools of the Mediterranean' in *The Library of Alexandria*, ed. Roy Macleod, I.B. Tauris, an imprint of Bloomsbury Publishing Plc.

Taylor and Francis. Castleden R. (1987). *The Stonehenge People: an exploration of life in Neolithic Britain 4700-2000 BC*. Routledge and Kegan Paul Ltd. Pages 236 and 239

White Crow Books. Cummins, G. (2012). *The Road to Immortality*

Solange de Mailly Nesle. *Astrology: History, Symbols and Signs*. (1981)

Janice Delgado. Delgado, P. and Andrews, C. (1990). *Crop Circles: the Latest Evidence*. Bloomsbury

Faber and Faber. Eliot, T. S. (1936). 'Usk', in *Collected Poems*. 1909-1935

The Society of the Inner Light. Fortune, D. (1976 and 1995 editions). *The Cosmic Doctrine*

Carcanet Press, Manchester, UK, by kind permission. Robert Graves' 1950 translation of *The Transformations of Lucius, otherwise known as the Golden Ass*. By Lucius Apuleius. Penguin Books

for Shambhala Publications. *What makes you not a Buddhist*. © 2007 by Dzongsar Jamyang Khyentze

Quoted with the author's permission. Kingsley, P. (1999). *In the Dark Places of Wisdom*. The Golden Sufi Centre

Reproduced with permission of the Licensor through PLSclear. Kirk, G.S., Raven, J.E. and Schofield, M. (1983). *The Presocratic Philosophers*. © Cambridge University Press

From *Reading Buddhist Art: An Illustrated Guide to Buddhist Signs & Symbols* by Meher McArthur, © 2002. Reprinted by kind permission of Thames & Hudson Ltd., London

From *An Introduction to Islamic Cosmological Doctrines: Conceptions of Nature and Methods Used for its Study by the Ikhwan al-Safa, al-Biruni and Ibn Sina* by Seyyed Hossein Nasr, © 1978. Reprinted by kind permission of Thames & Hudson Ltd., London

Dr Seyyed Hossein Nasr. *Ideals and Realities of Islam*. (2000)

Welbeck Publishing Group (previously Carlton Books). Derek and Julia Parker. (1983). *A History of Astrology*. London: Andre Deutsch

Robert J. Stewart. (1985). *The Underworld Initiation: a Journey towards Psychic Transformation*. Wellingborough: The Aquarian Press

Reproduced with permission of the Licensor through PLSclear. Toynbee, J.M.C. *Art in Britain under the Romans*. © Oxford University Press 1964

The Permissions Agency, LLC, Rights Agency

# CONTENTS

# FOREWORD

*The stars are like letters that inscribe themselves at every moment in the sky. Everything in the world is full of signs. All events are coordinated. All things depend on each other. Everything breathes together.*

Plotinus, fourth century AD

As Michael recounts – about the synchronicity of events which overtook his life – there was a calling and he responded ('*the attractor factor*'). As an archaeologist and ancient historian he had a deep, intuitive knowledge of the ancient world and its practices. He perceived that the symbols/mandalas appearing as crop formations were a communication from a Cosmic Intelligence revealing the Nature of Reality and the Unity of everything, all religions stemming from the One Divine Imagination, as evinced through the Ancient Timeless Wisdom. These fields encompassed a multiplicity of information about Consciousness, including sound and vibration, mathematics, geometry, quantum physics. They were symbols of a spiritual reality in which both Heart and Mind were invited to engage - indeed Fields of Transformation.

Why were the crop formations appearing at this particular moment in Time? Are they/were they portents of a new world order? In an increasingly digital technological age of scientific materialism, with its disconnect from the Source, from Nature, from ourselves, where there is massive information without illumination, how could the Cosmos communicate? Word and language were increasingly debased, devoid of truth and meaning, religion divisive, prophets ignored, so universal symbols/mandalas were elected.

Which quality each of the researchers, whether mystics or scientists, drawn to the phenomenon shared, was an enquiring Mind, a discerning intellect, courage and perseverance, and an ability to speak, write and disseminate the information being conveyed, as well as learning to engage with an often humorous but patient Intelligence with an imperative message to Humanity - to Be Awake and fully Conscious - to recognise its creative role within Nature, to take up its part in the divine Dance of the Cosmos.

One of the earliest formations, the Barbury Castle tetrahedron in 1991, represented a sequence in the evolutionary history of this planet - Spirit infusing Matter, the Dance of Life, and the Great Turning and eventual ascension of Humanity.

This book is about Michael's theophanic view of the Universe, the nature of Deity, the structure of the Cosmos, and the relationship between Deity and Man, as well as his own personal revelatory journey, which I was privileged to share, from 1989 to his death in 2018.

Christine Green

London 2023

*YET SOME THERE BE THAT BY DUE STEPS ASPIRE*
*TO LAY THEIR JUST HANDS ON THAT GOLDEN KEY*
*THAT OPES THE PALACE OF ETERNITY:*
*TO SUCH MY ERRAND IS ...*

Milton

*Comus 12-15*

# INTRODUCTION

*"Know that you are being guided and taken, your footsteps leading pathways of Light. The opening of the mind to the Higher Consciousness of the Cosmos with the Earth and its Beings of all levels is your task: a pioneer in virgin territory. You will find that a deeper understanding will come with the writing of your works, so in fact you will be channelling more that is held within yourself, the knowledge that is within you. For you are of the ancient ones, the ones who came before the coming of man. You are of the stars, thus you have the knowledge within."*

The Archangel Michael, 'Lord of the World' 16.6.1990

This channelling by Isabelle Kingston to me in 1990 was a formidable commission. Since 1990 various mediums have mentioned this project in similar terms. Most significantly Michael in 1989 (through Bob Armstrong) stipulated that the book must be relevant for this age.

## CROP CIRCLES

The catalyst for this book was the crop circle phenomenon at the close of the twentieth century. Although these strange occurrences had been recorded since the seventeenth century, their sudden florescence in earnest in 1990 coincided with the realisation by a small group of investigators that this was not a mere freak weather phenomenon, but something much more significant. It appeared to be a sophisticated communication process, the product of a non-human Intelligence of a high order. Mandalic symbolism seemed to be used, but the complex pictograms seemed ancient and obscure. Fortunately, when an Inspector of Ancient Monuments, I had made a special study of prehistoric symbolism, lecturing on it at the London Institute of Archaeology. I recognised symbols familiar to ancient man

about the nature of Deity, the spiritual character of the Cosmos and the role of mankind. The crop circle phenomenon really is about the 'meaning of life and everything', now conveyed by a Cosmic Intelligence, in simplistic terms 'God'.

## THE ANCIENT WISDOM

How does such mandalic material relate to systems of belief and thought, both ancient and modern? The most direct line seemed to lead to that numinous body of material described as 'Secret', 'Perennial', 'Timeless' or 'Ancient' Wisdom. I shall use the term *Ancient* Wisdom throughout.

What then is this strange corpus of information from the distant past and how does it connect to later religious thought? The Hellenist, Megan H. Williams, traced its origins to the ideas of Pythagoras (sixth century BC) which, together with 'Stoic ethics, Platonic metaphysics, and Aristotelian logic and natural science were fused into a comprehensive, eclectic system ... This philosophy had profound religious tendencies: amongst its central concerns were *personal ethics and lifestyle issues such as diet, the quest for knowledge of the gods in this life and the fate of the soul after death* [my italics]. Like the founder of this philosophical school, the Pythagorean initiate was expected to be an individual of mysterious, charismatic, even magical or semi-divine powers – not only a learned man but an avatar of divine wisdom.' (Williams, M.H. 2000, p. 35)

The sophisticated, secretive Pythagorean-Platonic system would have had a very limited intellectual, or even spiritual, appeal to the *intelligentsia* of the Ancient world. It was by nature *exclusive*, whereas the system I am promoting in this book is *inclusive* and comes with a sense of urgency that it should reach the mass of humanity at this time.

Looking at the western system of the Druids and their successor traditions, there is an interesting and perhaps more apposite definition of the Ancient Wisdom related by the mystic David Conway. As a fourteen year old boy in rural Wales in the earlier part of the last century, he had an out-of-body experience in which he met his spiritual Master on Domen Bedwyr. The unnamed mentor explained: '... where the occult path I had set out on is intended to lead us. It is a path, he told me, that to begin with conducts us into our innermost being, enabling us to rediscover the true self that lives deep within us ... Through it we are able to perceive a wider, more beautiful reality whose own selfhood, while not the same as ours, is no different from it in essence. Thanks to this we and everything outside us, the totality of manifested being, are brought into conscious and loving union with the causeless cause of that phenomenal existence which is but the creative and personal manifestation of the one, unmanifest, uncaused and self-existent God ... This elevated state, attained by dint of our efforts, cannot but hasten the day when the karmic debt requiring us to incarnate again and

again is finally redeemed. In due course will follow the consummation of the entire world ... and we, with our human stage behind us, will be free to continue our progress, watching new worlds come and go, until at last the youngest of these transcends its becoming, and, in company with us, reconciles its new-found being with the non-being that is God. *Factum est*. The Great Work is completed.' (Conway 1985, pp. 180-182)

This is the essence of the Ancient Wisdom, which is aimed at the redemption of not just a few initiates, or those of a particular faith, but of all humanity and created life. This study is an expansion of the ideas set out by Conway's Mentor, brought to fruition under the Cosmic Laws of Thought and beautifully illustrated by the mandalic crop formations.

The teaching of the Ancient Wisdom appears like threads of gold in most religious systems – sometimes the weave is dense, sometimes not.

Elements can be found in the Vedic and Taoist belief systems in Asia developed as Zoroastrianism and Buddhism. In the West the ancient Egyptian and Babylonian systems carrying such ideas were transmuted into Hermeticism, Kabbalism, Judaism and Gnosticism. The teaching of the Buddha, Jesus Christ and Mahomet are central to the message of the Ancient Wisdom, but not necessarily as expressed in the World Faiths that grew out of their teaching.

In its most developed form, however, the Ancient Wisdom is to be found in the Theosophist (*Knowledge of God*) movement, originating in the East, particularly Tibet, but finding its most profound expression in England and America during the late nineteenth century. The flood of spiritual knowledge from this source was channelled material – communications through mediums from discarnate entities.

## PARANORMAL SOURCES

Six sources provided the basic channelled information for this book:

*Alice Bailey* between 1919 and 1949 channelled Djwhal Khul, a former Tibetan mystic.

*Dion Fortune* in 1923 and 1924 channelled 'a Lord of Hermetic Wisdom', to whom I allude as the 'Greater Master.'

*Bob Armstrong* channelled various Entities.

*Paul Bura*, in the early 1990s channelled Juez (Chapter 1), Joeb, who had had a former life as a British priest in the first century AD, and other Entities.

*Isabelle Kingston* (between 1989 and 1993) and *L. C.-H.* (between 1998 and 2007) channelled messages from the Archangel Michael concerning the production of this book.

As a child I was aware of my psychic abilities, which included memories of previous lives and meetings with Beings from the Cosmos. In adulthood I was conscious, in my better moments, of being 'guided and taken' to use the archangel's expression, along unconventional spiritual paths to enable me to produce this book.

As Dion said, speaking of herself, but also for me and others in this context: 'Those who trained me, take pupils. The way to Them is the old, old path of renunciation and initiation; I did not find Them by chance, but followed the track marked out through the Mysteries of all ages and races. By fulfilling the conditions I had to fulfil, others can experience what I have experienced ...' (Fortune 1995, p. 9) I hope that those who read this book will also find the answers to the 'meaning of life and everything' that I started to seek all those long years ago.

## THE GREAT TURNING

My title, *The Great Turning*, is taken from a communication that R.J. Stewart had many years ago with a discarnate guardian at Les Monts Grantez burial mound overlooking St Ouen's Bay on the Island of Jersey. (Stewart 1985, pp. 262-266) Within the mound is a megalithic passage grave (*allée couverte*), which opens into a chamber tomb at its western end, off which opens, in turn, a smaller chamber to the north. (Hawkes 1937) This is a tomb-type which appears to date to the mid fifth millennium BC. When excavated in 1912 the chambers had several inhumation burials accompanied by animal bones. The exception was a single adult skeleton sitting upright against the stone menhirs of the passage. This being was probably the 'Earth-man' or 'Stone-King' who had been buried alive (voluntarily) within the tomb and was psychically earth-bound, acting as a psycho-pomp and spiritual guide for the people of his clan. Stewart saw him as an older man, very brown, with curly hair and black beard, and spiral cheek tattoos. His eyes appeared like large black stones, due to the visual effect of tattooing or colouring around the deep eye sockets. He wore clothing made of skins, a tight tunic, and trousers tied around with sinews.

The Stone-King's view of the space-time continuum was very different from our own. 'On attempting to convey the meaning of the flow of time, the response from the King was the equivalent of: *there is no line of such a shape. There is only turning until you are inside the earth. From the little turning to the great turning that is inside the little turning. Inside the great turning is earth-peace.*' (Stewart 1985, pp. 265-266) The image conjured up by this is that of the oldest of global mandalas, sometimes known as the Trojan Maze, but in the ancient mind representing in symbolic form an image of the Earth Goddess. It occurs as a petroglyph not only in the Mediterranean world but also in Western Europe. In the British Isles its best known example is from Tintagel, Cornwall, reproduced here. (0.1) The three outer turns (the Little Turning) represent the progressive stages of human corporeal development, physical, emotional and mental: whereas the four stages of the inner turns (the Great Turning) leading up to the centre (earth-peace) constitute the stages of spiritual development, which are sometimes described as 'initiations', but should equally be regarded as 'expansions of consciousness.' (See Bailey 1922a), p. 15.) The final stage takes the person on the spiritual path out of our system, a form of apotheosis, and is correctly described as 'earth-peace' for that individual by the Stone-King. The Trojan Maze thus sums up the principles of the 'Way of Life' for humanity on the spiritual Ascension Process, the core theme of this book.

*0.1* ***The Tintagel Maze***
*Petroglyph on metamorphic slate bedrock, Rocky Valley, Tintagel, Cornwall (OS SU073894). Date unknown*

# 1. THE ROAD TO SILBURY HILL

*It is strange to be here. The mystery never leaves you alone.
Behind your image, below your words, above your thoughts, the
silence of another world waits.*

John O'Donohue
*Anam Cara: Spiritual Wisdom from the Celtic World*

In August 1994 I received a phone call from an American interested in the crop circle phenomenon, the late Jon Erik Beckjord. He had read an article of mine in *The Circular* magazine, the journal of the Centre for Crop Circle Studies, and wanted to know the meaning of life and everything. However it had to be snappy, he said, because he was on a pay phone! I duly tried to explain the principles of the Ancient Wisdom in three minutes flat, but Erik cut me short. "The man on the Manhattan bar stool wouldn't understand that," he said. As indeed he would not. A conventional Judaeo-Christian background, indeed probably that of any of the great current belief systems in the western world today, is no preparation for the mind-boggling quantum leaps of perception needed to understand the Ancient Wisdom and the nature of Ultimate Reality.

This book has its genesis in Erik's not unreasonable demand: the need for a succinct, clear presentation of the great truths about the nature of Deity, the structure of the Cosmos and the relationship of both to mankind – set out in digestible form for the man on the Manhattan bar stool, known in Britain as the man on the Clapham Omnibus.

But how had all this begun, what had it to do with crop circles? Indeed how had I got myself involved in the first place?

## STONEHENGE (1.1)

It began at Stonehenge, the great prehistoric megalithic monument in southern England, on a summer morning in the late 1960s. At the time I was a professional architect

**1.1 Stonehenge**
*The summer solstice at dawn*

and archaeologist with a former British government department, the Ministry of Works, whose successors are English Heritage and Historic England. I had been lecturing for some years at the Institute of Archaeology, amongst other places, on prehistory with special reference to the religious beliefs of ancient man. My job at Stonehenge was to officiate with one of the Under-Secretaries of State over the summer solstice proceedings. In those days there was tight security, barbed wire, searchlights and police dogs, but none of the unpleasantness of later years.

Beyond the wire were the 'flower children', the first fruits of the New Age, sitting in a haze of pot. A happy expectancy hung around throughout the night as the crowds drummed, had sex and generally enjoyed themselves. As a grey dawn broke and the rising sun nudged its way over the Heelstone, the modern Druids pattered out in their white wellies to carry out rites invented by a Welsh clergyman in the nineteenth century.

What struck me then was the wholly bogus nature of the occasion, with the possible exception of the expectancy of the hushed hippies beyond the wire. Standing by the Altar Stone in the centre of the stone circle I made a silent vow to try and find out the true nature of the beliefs and rituals of the prehistoric worshippers.

## GLASTONBURY

I continued my studies and journeys. The latter took me to the West Country and Glastonbury.

Around 1986 I met Palden Jenkins at Glastonbury, and became involved with the Oak Dragon and Rainbow Circle camps, with which he was associated. The principal camp leaders were ladies with roots in the *Wicca*

traditions, practical systems of shamanism and magic. They showed me, beyond any doubt, that in the right circumstances, with compatible people using ancient and effective mantras, magical ritual and healing really does work at a beneficial level. I shall never forget how the Vedic rain-making ceremony of the Five Sacred Fires resulted in a torrential downpour out of a clear sky, which ceased as soon as the rite was over. I made many friends, some of whom would take a leading part in the great rite on Silbury Hill described later in this chapter, and the founding of the Centre for Crop Circle Studies.

One winter afternoon at this time I was in Watkins central London bookshop looking desperately, as ever, for intellectual bedrock to provide systemic underpinning of my occult experiences. An attractive woman (not a staff member) asked me what I was looking for, and stated that everyone at a certain stage on the spiritual path should study the communications of Djwhal Khul. She took me to a shelf housing the collected writings of Alice Bailey. My guide then left the premises: I sometimes wonder who she was.

## CHANNELLING AND MEDIUMSHIP

In my study of the Ancient Wisdom this material was a revelation. Alice Bailey (1880-1949) was an upper-class English woman who believed she channelled a Tibetan Master, Djwhal Khul, during the earlier part of the twentieth century. Assiduous in transcribing this information while conscious, she produced some twenty volumes, the longest of which runs to 1,300 pages. (*A Treatise on Cosmic Fire*, 1925)

For many people channelling poses insuperable problems. Does it really constitute communion with discarnate spirits, or is it merely another *persona* of the medium giving voice or, worse, just a cynical fraud? Only wide experience of mediums and their discarnate entities can give an eventual clue. Does the channelled material check with other information to which the medium could have had no possible access? Is it consistently lucid, spiritual and informative; or does it conceal some hidden agenda of which the medium may not be fully aware? Certainly the medium's intelligence, vocabulary and spiritual state are crucial factors. If judged only as another spiritual voice the Bailey material is extraordinary when compared with the formidable corpus of the Ancient Wisdom over two thousand years. It bears a family resemblance to the output of Helena Petrovna Blavatsky, which is usually regarded, with that of her disciples such as Steiner, as the basis of the Theosophical movement.

My first serious brush with authentic mediumship occurred at an Oak Dragon camp in 1987. Bob and Loni Armstrong were making a video of camp life. It rapidly became clear that Bob was an exceptionally gifted medium with unusual psychic powers. My concern was to gather information about the beliefs and rites of prehistoric man, which was of relevance to my work with English Heritage. However, Bob's channelled communicators had something else on their minds.

## WORLD ECOLOGICAL CRISIS

I already knew that the human and ecological crisis at the end of the twentieth century would call forth a corresponding reaction from those of the human race sensitive to the situation. The Theosophical movement itself was a response to the great shift of human consciousness at the end of the nineteenth century. At a simpler level an inchoate yearning for cosmic help had given rise in the late 1980s

to the Harmonic Convergence Movement, a transatlantic, New Age campaign. Such cosmic help was felt to be necessary due to the critical condition of the Earth, *Gaia*, the global Entity. The process of poisoning the earth, the seas and the atmosphere had reached an advanced stage by the end of the twentieth century. The possibilities of recuperation, even then, were so limited, due to the progressive destruction of such features as the rain forests, that very soon an irreversible situation would be reached. A frightening deterioration of the climate would decimate mankind with the real possibility that the earth would be unable to support human life. The growing enlightenment of mankind to those issues was taking too long and was still too limited in its effect to avert the coming catastrophe.

As it was put to me at the time by various Entities channelled through Bob Armstrong and others, a drastic initiative was needed, to raise the consciousness of mankind globally, and bring a special level of enlightenment to world leaders in relation to their handling of environmental matters. The energy to be introduced, which the Communicators described as the 'White Energy', would not directly repair the damage to, say, the ozone layer, but would stimulate levels of concern and knowledge enabling mankind to do this for himself. Many political parties, economic organisations and spiritual groups would be directly affected in a positive way. However, not all would be sweetness and light. The White Energy would "seek out the dark places of earth" and there would be conflict, which would manifest itself at both human and natural levels.

The nature of the White Energy, its source, dynamics and method of release, was explicitly set out, and was corroborated from a number of different sources. Three great Forces of Energy would be involved. A positive energy of love would be released from the esoteric force centre of Sirius, which is the 'heart centre' of a great cosmic Entity of whom our own solar system forms another centre. The involvement of the Sirian energy was supposed to be evidenced by the presence of this star in the sky at dawn, together with the moon, on the day of the summer solstice when the rite was to be carried out.

The Sirian force would then be stepped down through certain other energy systems at solar and terrestrial level towards a particular sacred site in England. Sacred sites on earth are the 'acupuncture points' of Gaia, and are planned as connection or transformer points providing access to other levels of consciousness. The energy of Gaia, which might be described as 'intelligent creation', would rise to meet the Sirian force at the chosen sacred site. There was a difficulty, however, because all such sacred sites are now closed by their Guardian Spirits due to the corrupting influence of mankind. It was here that the human element was to come into play, for it was the commission of those designated for this work to open up the chosen sacred site, so that the two energies could blend and release the White Energy. The human group at the site would act as living transformers who would enable the Guardian to unlock the way through the use of certain ancient formulae, which had been set out in great detail. Once the White Energy had been released from the first site it would spread out like a great invisible tidal wave to wake the other 'acupuncture points' of Gaia all over the globe. The rite or Work was designated for a particular site, date and time to ensure optimum conditions for success. It was programmed for the summer solstice of 1989, giving us a year to prepare.

## SILBURY HILL (1.2)

I was then offered the opportunity to gather together the group responsible for the rite, prepare them and lead the Work. It was a momentous challenge. Although my earlier experience in the field of ritual magic led me to believe that I had both the motivation and skill needed, there were serious factors to be considered. First, and most important, was this rite spiritually sanctioned by, what I might call, the global management of planet Earth, and if so were I and the team the right people to do it? Although so specific in other respects, the Armstrong communications were vague about these crucial matters. Then there was the possible risk to the participants, made more uncertain by the unpredictable side-effects of the Energy released.

It was up to me to decide. There was a risk, but the challenge of climate change was so great that I felt the Work should go ahead, so long as the participants were clearly aware of what was at stake. The group to be called for the rite had strict instructions, channelled by Bob Armstrong, which indeed hold for all the Work of White Magic. 'They who enter into this Work should be united in their purpose and come in cleanliness of spirit. You must not enter into this Work with any purpose that will flatter your vanity, create for you wealth or in any way enhance your acceptance as a being. You must enter humbly, with the Divine Light, and with the sole purpose of helping mankind.'

The choice of suitable individuals who would provide a balanced group and work well together fell to me. It was a most difficult task, and involved a number of training and selection sessions. Eventually twenty two people were gathered together, a very heterogeneous group representing every strand of the New Age. In

1.2 **Silbury Hill from the air**, with crop circles below

retrospect it may be significant that Bob and Loni Armstrong refused to attend, although Bob had channelled most of the instructions for the rite. Isabelle Kingston, a Wiltshire mystic, took Bob's place as channeller. Her communicant was Michael, spiritual Lord of the World.

I selected Silbury Hill in Wiltshire as the venue. One important practical reason was to ensure privacy, since the mound was normally closed to the public. I had to get official permission from English Heritage and the police. It was also central to the area where most of the participants lived. However, the overriding reason for my choice was its character and use in prehistoric times. This huge Bronze Age mound, the largest in Western Europe, dates by radio-carbon to c. 2400 BC, with a small round mound which was later considerably enlarged by a series of chalk cones, one on top of the other to give a stepped appearance. (Parker Pearson 2005, p. 61) The original shape was a pyramid with rounded corners. With its facing of chalk clunch blocks (only later covered with earth), it must have borne an extraordinary resemblance to the Ancient Egyptian stepped pyramid at Saqqara built slightly earlier (after 2630 BC). Exhaustive archaeological excavations in the 1960s and earlier found no evidence that it was used as a burial mound. The official archaeological position in 2007 was that the purpose of Silbury Hill remained enigmatic, despite ongoing investigations. (Scarre 2007, p. 116)

However, I believe the real purpose of Silbury Hill, and similar places, was to provide a communication platform where priests and shamans of the prehistoric world could consult extra-terrestrials (see Note), and I use the word advisedly. I spoke to one such in June 1994 on the top of Cissbury Ring, Sussex, when I was with a crop circle group where Paul Bura was the channeller. The Entity Juez claimed to be a messenger from Sirius: "It has been a long time since we have communicated here, a long time ... I am not of human form, but similar: Sirius, the Dog Star." (Juez was evidently a Paschat, a life form from that star system, who we know from other evidence were humanoid beings of leonine form, and whose images have survived from the Palaeolithic period in various ancient cultures. (1.3) I know he was a Paschat, because he actually gave a leonine roar before speaking! (I have it on tape.) Paul was greatly upset by this Paschat prologue!) "Beings such as we are surround the Earth, giving inspiration and support to all those who seek the Light. We have been around for a long time, during great civilisations upon this Earth. I am a spokesman."

It is worth listening to the very apposite message of Juez to the leaders of the crop circle movement in 1994. "I understand your frustration concerning the corn circles – but the frustration will continue, because of those who will not accept ... You have to accept that power comes from circles. The reason that they are here is because your Earth now needs to change. The knowledge of this we have known for thousands of years and we have hinted at it through various mediums and channels for so long, so long. DO NOT PLACE SUCH IMPORTANCE ON THE PROOF! ...You will have proof with the corn, but who will really believe you? You can turn the world upside down and they will not believe you ... The circles are here to help with this so-called 'rising of the Earth'. She must rise up now and join us. She is like a child to us in space, a jewel and she is waiting to flourish, to become who she really is and take you all with her. It is such a journey – such a fantastic journey! – and you are part of that journey and you must ride

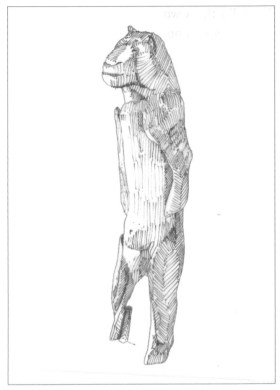

1.3 'Sirian Avatar'
*Ivory figurine of lion-man from Hohle Fels cave, Germany, c.38,000 years old*
*Ulm Museum*

with her. You understand what I am saying to you? You must ride with her and keep the love of God, whatever you conceive that energy to be, in your heart and keep it alive ... And the beauty will continue. Lights in the sky. More corn circles ... You say they are miracles – yes we ARE miracle workers – but there are limits. We cannot change the mind of Man. He must do that. You, my friends here, all changed to what you were, and it is only the beginning of vast changes." (Bura 2000, pp. 122-123)

The Sirius group, as it called itself, gathered on the top of Silbury Hill for the ceremony at dawn on 20.6.1989 (20th June 1989)*. The solemn rites of purification, protection and invocation were carried out. The key invocation, one of the most powerful of the ancient mantras of planet Earth, is worth quoting in part in its English translation:

*'Let the Lords of Liberation issue forth.*

*Let Them bring succor to the sons of men.*

*Let the Rider from the secret Place come forth,*

*And coming, save.*

*Come forth, O Mighty One.*

*Let the souls of men awaken to the Light.'*

*(Bailey 1957, p. 249)*

I am told that numinous figures were seen behind me as leader of the rite, but I did not see them myself. However what we all saw was a great plume of white light rise from the surface of Silbury Hill, which was reflected across the landscape in the dawn light. (1.4)

## THE WHITE ENERGY

I do not know what we expected, but the collapse of the Russian communist state and the apartheid regime in South Africa, and the social uprising in China (Tiananmen Square) – all occurring later that year, was a profound shock. We were told that as the White Energy moved eastward round the globe, its power would diminish, so that the American continent would be virtually unaffected.

What is one to think now about this extraordinary event and its aftermath? Of course no political or social analyst, let alone a scientist, could possibly accept any correlation between the rite on Silbury Hill and the later events of 1989. How could a group of amateur occultists, however well intentioned, carrying out a ceremony, possibly affect the course of world events? And yet something

extraordinary occurred on the summit of Silbury Hill on that beautiful summer morning of 1989.

It is true that there has been exponential growth in global awareness of the ecological plight of the planet since 1989, which was the prime purpose of the Silbury Hill rite in the minds of the celebrants. However, notwithstanding the political liberation of Eastern Europe and South Africa, the plight of the Third World and the rampant greed and violence of the leading world powers today is worse than ever.

One of the first shocks after the rite was the discovery that the star in the sky presiding over the ceremony was not Sirius at all, a system

*1.4 'The White Energy'*
*Silbury Hill, Wiltshire, summer solstice 1989*

of cosmic spirituality, but Aldebaran, a quite different matter and one of great significance to an occultist.

The star system Aldebaran is the 'eye' of the constellation Taurus, and symbolises an esoteric dichotomy. At one level it is the eye of spiritual illumination, but at another it is the stimulator of human desire and greed. As Djwhal Khul puts it: 'Today we see the wilful dash of the lower nature of humanity, embodied in the forces of aggression, and the purposeful progress of those people and peoples who seek, even if without full understanding, to work out the plans of God, proceeding in spite of each other ... hence the critical situation now to be found. The question is: will the Bull of desire or the Bull of divine illumined expression succeed?' (Bailey 1951, p. 378)

My view now is that the Sirius group were the unwitting pawns of a climactic confrontation between the forces of Light and Darkness. The latter may have designed the rite to stimulate the lower nature of humanity, whereas the former may have restructured it so that mankind could experience a transformative vision to save the planet. Perhaps the result was something of both, but we will never know. What is crystal clear to me, however, is that no members of the group have the right to claim any responsibility for the perceived outcome of the Silbury Hill rite, whatever their personal feelings.

On the evening before the solstice rite when an advance party arrived on the summit to lay out the ceremonial mandala, it was to discover a crop circle swirled into the rough grass at the top: the first and only occasion it ever occurred here. Around the hill that summer were groups of circles, in quintuplet patterns. It may be significant that shortly before the

first quintuplet appeared near Silbury Hill, in July 1988, a motorist in the vicinity had seen a 'constant beam of white light which stretched from the clouds to the ground' nearby. (Meaden 1989, p. 55)

Later that summer Silbury Hill was surrounded by crop formations in the fields on every side.

*\* All dates in this book are on the United Kingdom model – day, month, year.*

## NOTE

*LOCI CONSECRATI*

*Harvest Hills.* Silbury Hill is the largest in north-west Europe of a number of extremely big mounds (not apparently burial mounds), sited in the vicinity of prehistoric communities, which may have been used as communication-locations with celestial Beings. Clifford Hill beside the River Nene is 85 ft high (as opposed to the 131 ft of Silbury Hill). Lewes Mount is 43 ft high and stands on the floor of the Ouse beside what was a tidal lagoon in the Neolithic period. Merlins Mount at Marlborough is 50 ft high and is now covered in trees. Hatfield Barrow beside the River Avon was 'excavated to destruction in 1818 by Colt-Hoare and Cunnington, who were confused to find not a trace of a burial; Colt-Hoare concluded that the mound was a 'Hill Altar or a *locus consecratus.*' (Castleden 1987, p. 239) In a thoughtful summary about this class of monument Rodney Castleden concludes that these mounds 'were designed to stand for all eternity' as an expression of ancient communities' relation with the

*1.5 'Pleiadean Avatar'*

Visitation at the Portsmouth Temple
of Spiritualism, 23.11.1996

*1.6 'Pleiadean Stele'*

Megalithic monolith c.3500 BC from Rocher
des Doms, Avignon, Vaucluse, France

Cosmos and as *'machines for sustaining it'* (my italics). (Castleden 1987, p. 236) However, since all oral tradition of the precise nature of that relationship has been lost, and no recording of the form of that communication process would seem to have survived, their function might appear inscrutable, except for one remarkable case.

*Les Stèles d'Avignon.* On 23.11.1996 I gave a talk in Portsmouth on 'Star Child: crop circles and world change'. I am told I was joined by a Being (invisible to myself and most of the audience) who was sketched on the spot by a Mr P. Ryder. (1.5) I recognised the Entity from the sketch as one of the Communicators

from the Pleiades star cluster, similar to Juez mentioned above.

These humanoid Beings are lesser Avatars sent by the solar systems of our local solar group, (*Archon*, see Chapter 16) to help humanity. The incident brings me to the one firm case where such Beings not only communicated with prehistoric man but where stelae survive recording their identity and cosmic source.

The place was the Rocher des Doms near Avignon (Vaucluse), France, in the ancient territory of the *Aedui*. On one of the stelae from here, now in the Musée Lapidaire, Avignon (1.6 and 1.7), the facial representation on one side bears a close resemblance to the Pleiadean

Being as recorded at Portsmouth: long straight hair framing a pointed face with large eyes, a long nose, and tight pursed mouth which doubles as one ray of an eight-pointed star, indicating that the Entity is a stellar Being. On the reverse of the stone is a star map clearly and recognisably that of the Pleiades. (See Gagnière and Granier 1963, pp. 45, 46.) One of the largest of the holes represents the most prominent star of the Pleiades stellar cluster, *Alcyone*, a

significant star in our local solar group, the source of these Entities. It is fortuitous that the *Aedui* shamans had the psychic, perceptive ability to record this information about their cosmic visitor(s), without which we should ever be uncertain about the nature of the possible communicants at Silbury Hill and at similar *loci consecratis*.

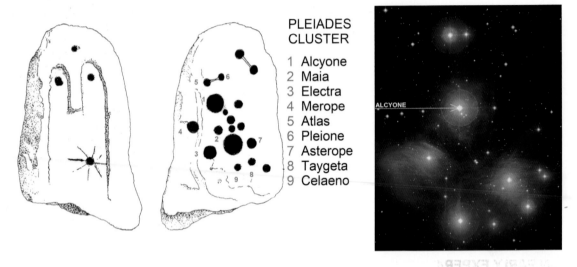

PLEIADES CLUSTER

1 Alcyone
2 Maia
3 Electra
4 Merope
5 Atlas
6 Pleione
7 Asterope
8 Taygeta
9 Celaeno

ALCYONE

1.7 *Rocher des Doms monolith*, with Pleiades star map on reverse, compared with photograph of the Pleiades

# 2. THE CROP CIRCLE PHENOMENON

*While the true is Godlike, it does not appear directly.*
*We must divine its reality from its manifestations.*

Goethe

## PART 1 - THE CENTRE FOR CROP CIRCLE STUDIES

While I was lecturing in London in 1989 on prehistoric symbolism and its possible meaning the late Ralph Noyes, in the audience, mentioned that these symbols had been appearing as crop formations in the English countryside in recent years. Further enquiries drew a blank. He and I therefore decided to set up our own organisation, the *Centre for Crop Circle Studies* (CCCS), to be run on an investigative basis using scientific method and with a remit to publish the results openly.

### AN EARLY EXPERIENCE – THE A34 FORMATION

My next encounter (after the Silbury rite) with a crop formation was on 24.6.1990. My wife and I had been attending a conference in Oxford organised by Dr Terence Meaden purporting to explain that the crop circle phenomenon was a natural weather effect produced under the lee of hills by warm air creating a plasma vortex effect. It was pointed out that several circles had already occurred in flat fenlands, and when Busty Taylor, the aerial photographer, showed the complex crop formations that had occurred in England that year, it was clear that the plasma vortex theory was 'busted'. Even the specially-invited Japanese scientists began to laugh, and the conference ended in uproar.

As we drove south from Oxford late for a family engagement, Christine said, after a thoughtful silence, "I would like to find our own crop formation so we can make up our own minds." Literally, as she spoke, a vast formation appeared on the other side of the road, nearly 140 ft long in the centre of a cornfield sparkling in the morning sun. It was a critical moment. Should we pretend this hadn't happened to us and drive on? We did a U turn on the A34 road, and climbed over the fence in our best clothes.

The crop inside the formation had been carefully swirled and bent over to the ground, not damaging the stalks, and in the centre of the two great circles it was spun and woven into a complex carpet. The formation was pristine, the ground was still hot, and the electromagnetic charge which hung over the formation made one's skin prickle. Two big circles were connected by a narrow track, on each side of which were two boxes. Across the higher circle was a pair of ring segments, like haloes. We were stunned. Christine went to the haloed circle and in a meditational state communicated with the Divine Feminine Energy, non-judgmental and loving, behind the phenomenon. I struggled to record the physical structure of the formation.

[The circle was still warm and 'throbbing', the centre a raised complex interwoven 'basket'. I sat two-thirds of the way out to the perimeter and was contemplating the damage we were doing to the planet when an unexpected diaphanous blue non-judgmental Loving Presence enveloped me. (Christine Green)]

This beautiful but strange experience brings into sharp focus some of the more interesting but disturbing features of this extraordinary phenomenon. First, it is real. Unlike almost any other paranormal occurrence, it has a physical existence, which can be experienced and recorded before the crop is cut at the end of the growing season. Second, it is a genuine paraphysical phenomenon, or certainly was in this case. Yes, of course there have been many hoaxes since 1990, but the scientific research work of the CCCS has enabled us with a fair degree of accuracy to distinguish between the genuine, geophysical phenomenon and human 'land-art'. Third, there is clearly an intelligence of a high order behind it. The formation which we experienced that day was an image of the Solar Logos, discussed in Chapter 15. Last, the phenomenon is highly interactive with the minds and feelings of those human beings who are prepared to take seriously these miracles in the fields, for miracles they are.

It is these features about the phenomenon that make the political and religious establishments of western society profoundly uneasy, when they think about it at all.

## HISTORICAL PERSPECTIVE

The phenomenon is not new. English scientists in the late seventeenth century were examining and reporting on quite complex crop formations in St Giles' Field, Oxford. Robert Plot in his *Natural History of Staffordshire* (1686) attributes such phenomena to the action of whirlwinds (2.1), a hypothesis not far off the mark. (Chapter 17) During the next two hundred years there were spasmodic reports of formations in southern England.

*2.1 **The earliest recorded grass formations in England**
Later seventeenth century. Three formations in St Giles' Field, Oxford, and whirlwind at Offley Hay, Stafford. Published by Robert Plot in The Natural History of Staffordshire (1686)*

In British farming communities there were many accounts during the twentieth century, which first attracted press attention in the 1960s and 70s and were attributed to the activities of flying saucers. In the 1980s the phenomenon became more complex, with simple circles being replaced by elaborate groupings of circles, and other shapes. (Wilson, T. 1998, pp. 8ff.) Internationally, formations were reported across Northern Europe, in Russia, in the paddy fields of Japan and the grain prairies of Canada and the USA. In the southern hemisphere, some of the earliest recorded incidences were in Australia and New Zealand. Serious international interest was aroused by the publication of *Circular Evidence* in 1989 by Delgado and Andrews. There had been an average of about 10 formations a year in the UK in the three preceding years. The huge surge of crop circle activity in the next decade or so resulted in over 50 formations annually, with a peak of around 200 in 2000 in the UK.

Wilson's *The Secret History of Crop Circles* (Wilson, T. 1998) traces the international history of the phenomenon from the seventeenth century to 1980 with updating to 1997, demolishing any claims that it is exclusively a recent phenomenon.

## HOAXING

Many readers by now, (if not earlier) will be thinking 'But *surely* the whole phenomenon is man-made, as the hoaxers claim?' Based on the evidence, the answer is a categorical *No*. The hoaxing 'explanation' was first seriously sprung on the world at *The Cerealogist* magazine's first Annual Conference in September 1991 at Glastonbury, when the now defunct *Today* newspaper introduced two local Hampshire men, Doug Bower and Dave Chorley, who claimed (initially) to have made all the crop formations over the previous thirteen years.

George Wingfield exposed their spurious claims, (Wingfield 1991-2, pp. 3-6) but it was not until 1999 that I made a comprehensive study of Doug and Dave's hoaxes in 1991 and earlier. This was possible thanks to scientific and visual evidence for genuineness established in 1995. (See parts 2 and 3 of this chapter.)

The scientists and investigators in 1990 were perhaps naive not to anticipate that such paranormal occurrences, if widely accepted as genuine, would have profound consequences for the religious and political establishments at a global level, from which there was likely to be a backlash. Indeed, one of the hoaxing activists made a recorded remark in 1992 which confirmed this: "There are a number of agencies throughout the world which have taken an interest [in the phenomenon]. It involves several countries ... we have support at the highest level. *It is potentially a very explosive phenomenon ... trying to bring about changes in world consciousness*" [my italics] "There are those of us who would like to see this new trend stopped." (Green, Michael 1999b, p. 24)

By the early 1990s what might be termed 'the opposition' had already recognised the potential transforming capacity for humanity of the phenomenon and the dangerous consequences for the existing world order. The backlash was devastating. Large teams of hoaxers were recruited in 1990-1 and the landscape of southern England was flooded with man-made formations. Attempts were made to penetrate and break up the groups of serious crop circle investigative bodies, and a global propaganda campaign was put in hand suggesting that the whole phenomenon in England up to 1991 was a crude hoax by a couple of local lads who had fooled scientists and investigators. The truth, however, was that we were and are up against a highly professional conspiracy, extremely well-funded and organised.

## THE CENTRE FOR CROP CIRCLE STUDIES (CCCS)

The CCCS was founded in April 1990 'in the belief that the crop circle phenomenon offered remarkable challenges to understanding which would only be met by drawing on a wide range of insights and expertise in many different fields. The principal objective of the CCCS was to encourage this interdisciplinary approach and to ensure that it was sustained by sound research and reliable information.' These were the founding principles set out by the then president, the late Professor Archie Roy, and incorporated in our constitution.

During the subsequent fifteen years, and through various changes of fortune, the core group of the organisation as represented by the Council and its research officers faithfully endeavoured to follow these principles of rational, objective research, whether scientific or metaphysical. However, times change, both in terms of the phenomenon itself and the structure of the CCCS as a research body.

In the early years, thanks to the efforts of Ralph Noyes (then Secretary of the Centre) and colleagues on the CCCS Council, the organisation achieved a membership of over 1000, with local branches countrywide and overseas, and a scientific research capacity efficiently organised by the late Montague Keen. Extensive international hoaxing propaganda from 1991 on led to a rapid fall in membership until 2005 when it was just over 100, a 90% drop.

Almost from its foundation the CCCS had difficulties with its research aims, an intractable mixture of the scientific and the metaphysical. The situation was exacerbated by the heterogeneous make-up of membership and council. The problem as I put it in 1993 was the difficulty 'of scientific work in a field where the parameters are so uncertain and external financial support practically non-existent ... What exactly are we looking for in conventional scientific terms, and why? Are we using the type of methodology which is going to produce the sort of results on which we can build a programme of investigation, which will stand up to critical examination?' (*The Circular* (1993) Volume 4, Number 1, p. 7)

However the really critical question if scientific work of any kind was to be done was how to distinguish between man-made formations and genuine or 'geophysical' ones. Although 'Project Argus' in 1992 (an independent American scientific exercise organised by Michael Chorost) established differences between the two types of formations, no overall diagnostic system was established. This came only in summer 1995 under the inspired leadership of a new CCCS scientific officer, James W. Lyons BSc, MSc, CEng, MIEE (Jim), who organised the testing of a relatively small number of formations by the national research body, the Agricultural Development and Advisory Service (ADAS). Testing for the presence of nitrate (see part 2 of this chapter) showed that it was clearly possible to make this distinction scientifically.

As important, however, was the discovery that, from the air, each type of formation (already separated on the basis of the scientific criteria) showed distinctly different physical construction characteristics. This in turn enabled nearly all formations from the late 1980s to be classified as either man-made or geophysical. (See part 3 of this chapter.) This was the great breakthrough that *bona-fide* researchers had been looking for for years.

In 1996 various factions within the CCCS attempted to close it down. Whatever their motives, the result was the breaking away of many former branches under dominant personalities to become commercially-orientated New Age organisations. Most of these jettisoned rational research in favour of an uncritical acceptance of the phenomenon whether genuine or man-made – an approach encouraged by those concerned with merchandising activities.

The CCCS was refounded in 1997, but with straitened finances, a smaller membership and consequently a curtailed research capacity. Nevertheless research programmes continued at both scientific and metaphysical levels, published in The Circular and The Cereologist magazines.

The CCCS from the beginning did tests and experiments seeking to establish the mechanics of the circle-making force. (See parts 2 and 3 of this chapter for Jim Lyons' research.) The implications at a para-scientific, metaphysical level are covered in Chapter 17 in connection with the crop circles at Sibson, Cambridgeshire.

When UK crop formations were assessed for genuineness in 2004 on the basis of the scientific and visual evidence, it was shown that even by 1991 49% were man-made, rising to 74% in 1995 and 86% in 2003. (2.2)

Since almost all formations were man-made by 2005 the CCCS's primary raison d'être had ceased to exist, and it was dissolved in that year.

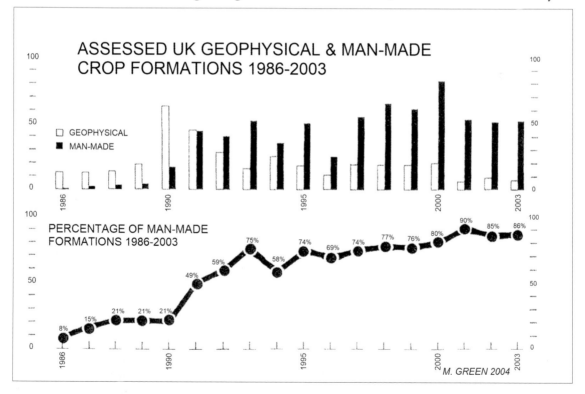

*2.2 The Rise in United Kingdom Man-Made Crop Formations 1986-2003*
*Numbers and percentages of geophysical and man-made formations between 1986 and 2003,*
*assessed by combining ADAS's scientific testing with visual evidence*

## THE INTELLIGENCE BEHIND THE PHENOMENON

However it was the evidence for *Intelligence* that emerged in the 1990s that was troubling scientists and researchers. It looked as if we were in communication with Beings from other levels of reality, namely the Intelligences of the non-human agencies of this planet and those outside our system.

To our growing excitement in 1990 and 1991 it became clear that now the non-human Crop Circle Makers had our attention, we were being treated to a crash course in the basic principles of the Ancient Wisdom: namely the origins of the Cosmos, the structure of God, the agencies of Deity, the nature of Mankind and the relationship between them. Each educational stage, starting with simple basic truths, was beautifully and economically elaborated. Conceptual elements were introduced and then assembled in mandalic form.

The subject matter of these mandalas is fascinating. Careful reference has been made to every stage of human development and knowledge. The shamanistic concepts of primitive man appeared early on, followed by reference to classical Hermetic beliefs (the Barbury Castle formation in 1991) (Chapter 15), and even the most advanced scientific thinking of today (the Mandelbrot formation of 1991). (Chapter 11 part 2)

It is noticeable that specific symbolism related to current belief systems, Christianity, Islam, Judaism and Buddhism, for example, has largely been passed over in favour of older, more universal systems, the Indo-Aryan, Vedic and Semitic concepts of Asia and Europe, and the proto-Taoist symbolism of the Far East.

When challenged to communicate in *writing*, the Crop Circle Makers obligingly produced the Milk Hill inscription of 1991. (Chapter 3) This inscription is of particular importance since it is the only instance of a written response to an explicit request, 'Talk to us.' The answer pointed directly and irrevocably to DEITY as the author and creator of the crop circle phenomenon. All that follows in this book is based on this premiss.

## PART 2 - THE SCIENTIFIC EVIDENCE

Possibly the most important scientific work done on crop circles was the series of tests done by Jim Lyons with the Agricultural Development and Advisory Service (ADAS, then part of the Ministry of Agriculture, Fisheries and Food), in 1995.

The writer and Jim published the results in a paper – Soil Tests by the Agricultural Development & Advisory Service, in *The Cerealogist* #17 (1996, pp. 6-8).

Jim Lyons, a professional engineer, became the Scientific Research Officer of the CCCS in 1994, following the resignation, after sterling service, of Montague Keen. Jim had a special interest in the new physics concerning the subtle energies in nature, and was already a noted crop circle researcher, with publications in *The Cerealogist* (Lyons 1995a, p. 11) and *The Circular* (Lyons 1993a, pp. 18-20; Lyons 1993b, pp. 23-24; Lyons 1994, pp. 16-18). Jim's general theory was that:

'... the fundamental hypothesis [is] that the process of formation ... is essentially geophysical in nature and therefore strongly related to processes occurring naturally in the earth's biosphere. The most likely process involves strong vertical electrostatic fields interacting with low-impedance points on the earth, these being at the cross-over of energy lines on the earth's energy grid. This is known to be the effect involved in lightning strikes on the earth's surface...' (Summary Statement of ADAS and other 1995 Crop Circle Tests published in *The Circular* #23, pp. 6-7)

Under normal circumstances, nitrogen and oxygen in the atmosphere remain separate, but lightning causes them to combine, and fixes nitrogen in the soil in the form of nitrate, $NO_3$. $NO_3$ combines with other elements in soil, making it accessible to plants for the production of amino acids.

Jim's hypothesis was that the strong electrostatic fields described above, whilst forming the crop circles, also fixed nitrogen in the soil in the form of nitrate. Since the effect of this would be clearly present in the vicinity of the crop and soil it should be possible to analyse for it post the event. Soil tests for nitrate were accurate to within 5% and could be carried out cheaply.

Normally, crops draw up nitrate from soil in a steady but not dramatic process. Jim set out to discover whether there would be dramatic changes in soil nitrate in crop circles.

In the spring of 1995 I approached ADAS in Cambridge, with the support of the CCCS Council, to test Jim's theory on a range of formations. In the end soil samples from 18 formations were tested. The tests were carried out 'blind' at the ADAS research laboratory in Wolverhampton. I am grateful to ADAS for supplying the sampling protocol and equipment.

I personally supervised the operation throughout the summer, and would like to put on record my thanks especially to those who carried out the sampling, digging holes in the rock-hard soil in the hot summer, which was extremely arduous, and my indebtedness to Dr Mike Fowley, to David Yarham, the then head of the plant clinic, for facilitating and monitoring the research at Cambridge, and to Dr John Evans, head of the UK laboratory services at Wolverhampton.

Testing concentrated on nitrate (Nitrate/N, or $NO_3$) levels ($CaSO_4$ extract) mg/l, in soil samples taken from within the crop circles, with control samples taken from nearby. Considerable natural variation across a field can be expected for nitrate, depending, for example, on the degree to which plants have taken it up in their immediate locality. Rainfall and the solution of nitrate can also be a factor, but fortunately the summer of 1995 was the driest in living memory, with no appreciable rain in the growing season, and consequently unusually stable growing conditions.

Results from 12 of the formations were set out on a bar chart. (2.3) ADAS provided information on the normal (mean) variation of soil nitrate, which was 20%. Formations with fluctuations substantially above the norm were inferred to be of geophysical origin. The numbers along the base of this chart relate to the individual formations in illustrations 2.4-2.6, where the plans and figures for each were set out in diagrammatic form.

The detailed results, with comments by ADAS, were reported in *The Cerealogist* (see reference above). A summary description of the 18 sites is provided here.

1. Southease, East Sussex (8.5.95) Oilseed rape
   ADAS Ref. 95006253 (second sampling 14.7.95).

2. Newington, Oxon (9.7.95) Wheat
   ADAS Ref. 95004511 (sampled before 14.7.95).

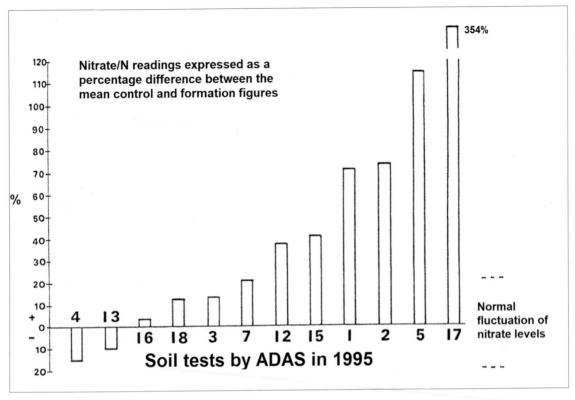

*2.3 Nitrate-Nitrogen readings in 1995 at randomly chosen crop formation sites in the UK*

3. Alfriston, East Sussex (31.5.95) Barley
   ADAS Ref. 95003618 (sampled 1.6.95)
   Man-made formation.

4. Telegraph Hill (nr. Winchester), Hants
   (12.6.95) Barley
   ADAS Ref. 95003885 (sampled before
   28.6.95) Man-made formation.

5. East Grinstead, West Sussex (29.6.95)
   Wheat
   ADAS Ref. 95004322 (sampled 29.6.95).

6. Pentlow, Suffolk (test formation, before
   12.7.95)
   ADAS Ref. 95004470
   Man-made formation.

7. Beckhampton, Wilts (29.5.95) Barley
   ADAS Ref. 95003251 (sampled 4.6.95).

8. Bratton Castle (nr. Westbury), Wilts
   (early June 95) Barley
   ADAS Ref. 95004512 (sampled 28.6.95).

9. Litchfield, Hants (6.7.95) Wheat
   ADAS Ref. 95004523 (sampled 12.7.95)
   Man-made formation.

10. West Stowell, Wilts (25.6.95) Wheat
    ADAS Ref. 95004531 (sampled 28.6.95)
    Man-made formation.

11. Wandlebury (nr. Cambridge), Cambs
    (mid July 95) Wheat
    ADAS Ref. 95004795 (sampled 24.7.95 by
    ADAS – but results not received)
    Man-made formation.

12. Roundway Hill (nr. Devizes), Wilts
    (20.7.95) Wheat
    ADAS Ref. 95005422 (sampled 26.7.95).

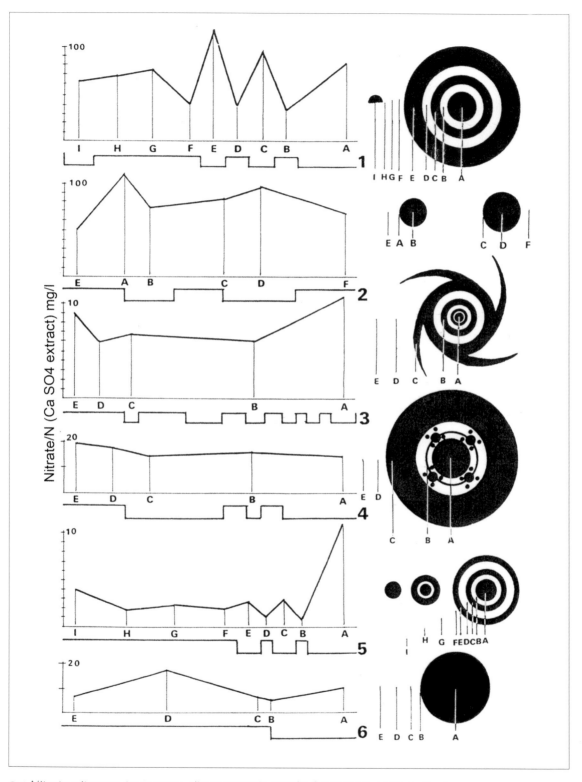

*2.4 Nitrate-nitrogen tests 1995, diagrammatic results for individual formations*

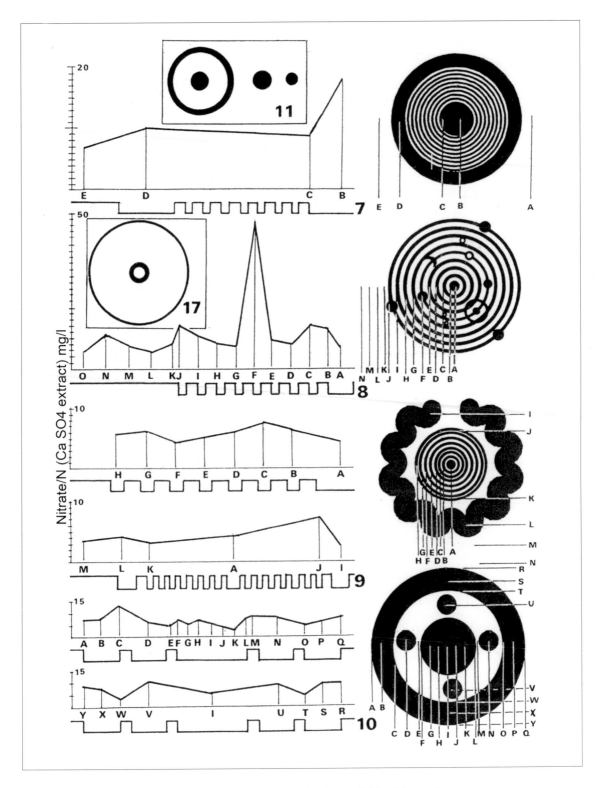

2.5 Nitrate-nitrogen tests 1995, diagrammatic results for individual formations

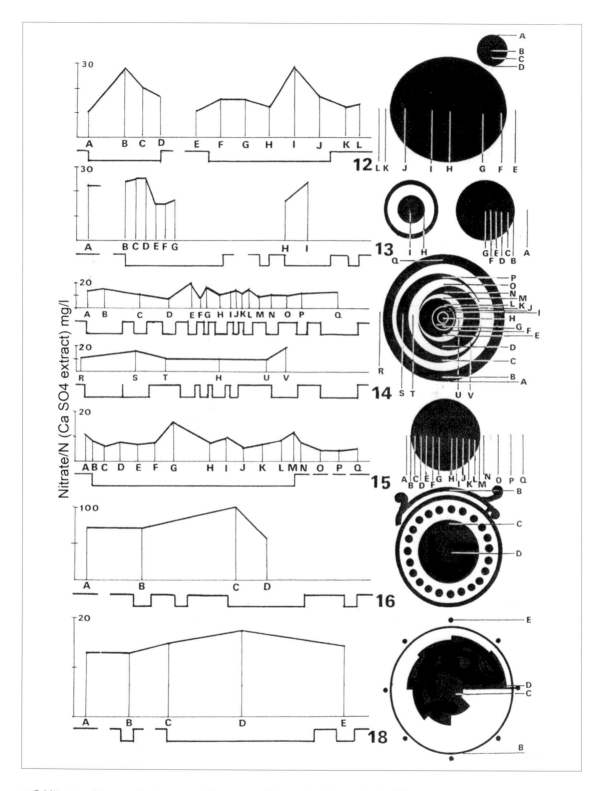

*2.6 Nitrate-nitrogen tests 1995, diagrammatic results for individual formations*

13. Kirkton of Culsalmond, Grampian (late July 95) Wheat
    ADAS ref. 95006007 (sampled 26.8.95)
    Man-made formation.

14. Warnford, Hants (mid July 95) Wheat
    ADAS Ref, 95005424 (sampled 2.8.95)
    Man-made formation.

15. Woodhouse Eaves, Leics (mid July 95) Wheat
    ADAS Ref. 95005448 (sampled 30.7.95).

16. Arreton Manor, Isle of Wight (22.7.95)
    ADAS Ref. 95005559 (sampled 4.8.95)
    Man-made formation.

17. Sibson, Cambs (26.7.95) Barley
    ADAS Ref. 95005678 (sampled before 21.8.95)
    Jim Lyons comments: "Although only two samples were taken from the single formation near Peterborough, the central figure exceeded the control by over 350%."

18. Stockbridge Down (nr. Andover), Hants (mid July 95) Wheat
    ADAS Ref. 95007732 (sampled before 16.7.95)
    Man-made formation.

At the time I thought that where a tested formation had the hallmarks of being man-made it was likely that other formations of a similar character might be similarly suspect. On this basis it would appear that a high proportion of the formations from Wiltshire and Hampshire were man-made in 1995. However, the important feature that emerged from this research exercise was that it now appeared possible to distinguish on scientific grounds between geophysically-created (i.e. genuine) and man-made formations.

Ideally, scientific testing would have been carried out annually thereafter, but for various reasons, political and financial, this was not to be. However, the 1995 work laid the basis for later distinguishing between the genuine article and the fake by using *visual* evidence. Those formations which tested positive for genuineness in 1995 all exhibited a *spiral* form of construction, and the fakes were built up of *rings*. This fact, and the significance of the difference, dawned on us only gradually. In the following years I was able to look back over pictures of formations going back to 1986, and assess how many of them could confidently be diagnosed as genuine, as shown in illustration 2.2. In part 3 of this chapter I reprint two papers published in 1998, describing this dawning realisation.

# PART 3 - THE VISUAL EVIDENCE

## INTRODUCTION

To describe the assessment of the visual evidence for authenticating the crop formations, I can do no better than reprint here the paper I published on the subject in 1998 – 'Spirals and Rings'.

Also in that year I published an account of the Beltane Torus formation. A few crop circle investigators, myself and Jim Lyons included, were privileged from time to time to be provided by the non-human Agency behind the phenomenon with tailor-made formations designed to answer pressing research problems. The Beltane Torus which appeared between 4.30 am and 5.30 am on the morning of 4.5.1998 was such a case, and was specifically aimed at Jim Lyons' research area of bio-energy fields. The tailpiece to my paper, provided by him, discusses the method of creation of this very distinctive formation, and by extrapolation, others.

In Chapter 17, on the series of formations at Sibson, Cambridgeshire between 1990 and 2001, I go into more detail on the processes by which genuine geophysical formations are created.

## SPIRALS AND RINGS

[From Green, Michael 1998a in *The Circular* #31, 1998, May, pp. 44-46]

For those of us who are still concerned to clearly distinguish between man-made and geophysical formations the position would appear (as it has been over the last five years) depressingly intractable. Indeed there is a noisy faction within the croppie community that maintains that even to try and make this distinction is an irrelevance. It is not. The genuine article is perhaps the most important paraphysical phenomenon of this generation: a permanent metaphysical event capable of intelligent study on a world-wide scale, which shows clear evidence of nonhuman intelligence. Past metaphysicians of earlier generations would have given their eye teeth for the opportunity to study such a phenomenon. As a research organisation the CCCS has a constitutional obligation to do everything in its power to make the crucial distinction between the genuine article and artefacts produced by hoaxers.

Hard scientific evidence, not to mention careful fieldwork, from a small number of formations each year suggests that they are of geophysical origin and not hoaxes. Furthermore the long history of the phenomenon and its geographical spread indicates that this is, and continues to be, a genuine phenomenon. However it is necessary to concede that such is the proficiency of the hoaxing fraternity today that it is difficult in many cases to be sure whether any particular formation is man-made or not. The fact of the matter is that only a tiny proportion of the 200 odd formations each year in this country are thoroughly examined in a scientific diagnostic fashion. ADAS after intensive field and laboratory work managed to examine less than 10% of the formations in 1995. Dr Levengood in his laboratory in Michigan covers even less and since 1995 has been dealing with only a very small number of British formations. The results of such laboratory work, which is necessarily slow and painstaking, take months, sometimes years, to be made public. Furthermore specialist research often using protocols which are rarely understood by a lay public (even when published, which is not always the case), is a highly subjective matter. Levengood works entirely on his own and the same is true of most other specialists. As regards fieldwork, there are very few individuals around with the necessary skills and expertise who have the opportunity to examine formations in fresh condition. In most cases in Wiltshire and Hampshire the physical structure of formations is trampled, beyond any hope of useful ground research, by enthusiastic croppies within hours of being reported on the internet. Other forms of research are even more controversial. Dowsing for example may be central to a future understanding of the function of subtle energy fields that are the formative agency behind the mechanics of the phenomena. However as a technique it is highly subjective and individualistic. It is totally unacceptable to the scientific community and many leading crop circle investigators.

What has been needed for years is a simple diagnostic technique accessible to anyone with a pair of eyes and an open mind. Notwithstanding the value of scientific laboratory and field research, I believe that we have such a diagnostic technique, indeed it has been literally staring us in the face for years.

Ironically the clue came from the title of Jim Schnabel's book, *Round in Circles,* that clever exposé of the croppie community by a confessed hoaxer and *agent provocateur.* Looking at the excellent photo of the 1997 Winterbourne Bassett formation [2.7 Author's note: the article as first published wrongly cited the circle as being at Headbourne Worthy.] on the cover of the Sussex Circular for July 1997, it struck me forcibly that the structure of the circles was quite different from those of formations which had occurred in the years before 1990. The early formations are characterised by a spiral whorl form whereas the Winterbourne Bassett formation and many others of recent years show a structure of neat uniform rings, rather like tree rings.

The CCCS scientific theorist Jim Lyons, has kindly provided a description of the principle behind spiral crop flow, which is the characteristic feature of geophysical (i.e. not man-made) crop formations.

*'Work so far has indicated a strong relationship to the Earth's geomagnetic field, particularly as regards columnar vortices (cf. Weak stationary tornadoes) that display both microwave and ionised EM fields. The bifurcations of these vortices generating nested toroidal fields are believed to be responsible for the patterns created. Formation shapes together with crop flow can be predicted to a limited extent using this model. The underlying energy source is believed to be related to vacuum state energy which is currently under intense study in several branches of physics. This energy is seriously being suggested as that involved in the effects of sonoluminescence, remarkably similar to the luminosity effects seen near crop formations and indeed earthquakes.*

*If a wave flows around the Torus; once in a poloidal plane to once in a toroidal plane, this is termed a winding ratio of one. For a Torus having no centre hole, this gives a projected pattern on the ground, which is in fact a cardiod pattern, the main section of the Mandelbrot. In general, the combined poloidal and toroidal flows move at around 10 ft sec giving rise to a pressure wave of around 15 lbs per square inch. The plasma formed has around $10^{15}$ electrons per cubic metre at a temperature of 2000 ° C for a fraction of a second (figs 1 and 2). [2.8 and 2.9]*

*The bifurcation processes of vortex breakdown where toroids form within toroids give rise to a large variation in possible patterns. The latest work on generalised toroids*

2.7 **Man-made crop formation**, *identified by parallel stripes Winterbourne Bassett, Hampshire, 1.6.1997*

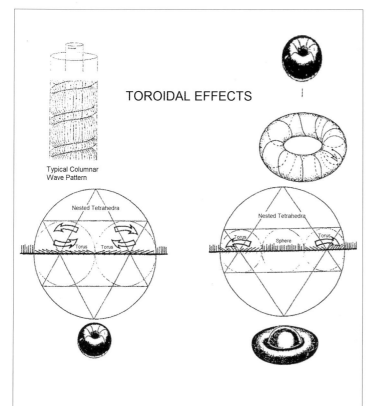

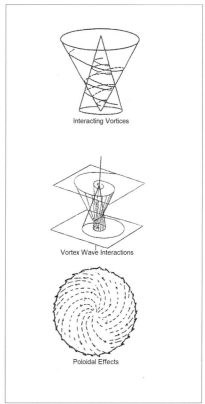

*2.8 Spiral crop flow as a **toroidal** effect*

*2.9 Spiral crop flow as a **poloidal** effect*

*termed scroll waves suggests that even more complex patterns can be generated from a very simple code sequence of bifurcations. These ideas indicate that the potential for pattern creation is way beyond that we have seen so far.'*

Early crop circle investigators were well aware of this effect even if they were ignorant of the laws of physics that lay behind it. The pattern of the crop is clearly recorded for example at the formation at Headbourne Worthy in 1986 by Terence Meaden (*The Circles Effect and its Mysteries.* 1989 fig 7, p. 18). In 1997 notable crop formations whose spiral form is clearly evident from the air photos are those at Lane End Down and Upham, both in Hampshire.

The first generation of hoaxers, Doug and Dave and the Wessex Sceptics class of 1992,

were equally aware of the importance of the spiral form as an indicator of genuineness. Indeed Stanley Morcom, one of the CCCS's most scrupulous investigators, was interrogated several times by the hoaxers to discover exactly how formations were made. Small grapeshots were easy enough using a spiral layout as Jim Schnabel demonstrated at Montague Keen's farm in July 1993. '*Schnabel then offered to demonstrate the art of making grapeshot....Schnabel did two demonstrations and then it was my turn. The result – an exquisite Pringle Peak (photographs to prove it) though it made me feel extremely dizzy*' (Lucy Pringle, The Bluffer's Bluff is Called' *The Circular* Issue 14). Hoaxers usually have the central part of a large man-made formation spiralled before reverting to a series of rings.

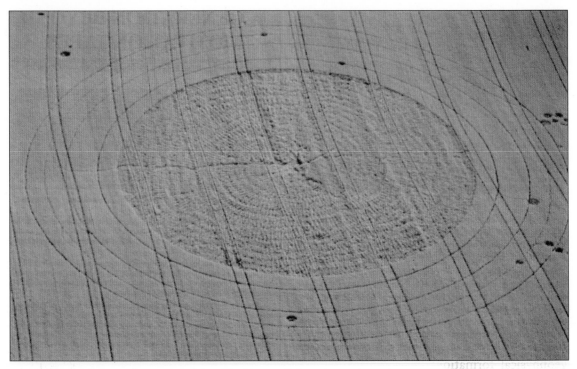

*2.10* **Man-made crop formation**, *identified by radial push-marks*
*Bishops Cannings, before 19.5.1990; outer ring added before 27.5.1990*

So where do the rings originate? In 1992 Ken Brown, one of the most assiduous investigators of man-made formations drew attention to the presence of concentric rings as the hallmark of hoaxed circles. In the case of the Bishops Cannings ringed circle of 1990 [2.10] each ring was characterised by regular push-marks from the use of a board to flatten the crop, giving a radial appearance to the layout of the formation (Brown K *The Fake that Grew a Ring The Cerealogist* 1992 no 7). Boards, which were very much the trade-mark of the Doug and Dave era, were replaced after the 1992 Hoaxing Competition by the use of light plastic garden rollers which became *de rigueur* for the Schnabel generation of hoaxers. Indeed he used one at Montague Keen's meeting in 1993, and Adrian Dexter is shown sporting a roller in connection with the creation of the Soil Association crop logo in

1995 (*The Cerealogist* No. 15). The fact of the matter was that the board and string method had become too cumbersome, whereas a roller was quick and efficient in poor light and when time was at a premium (fig. 3). [Not included here.]

The Soil Association logo shows off the level of proficiency that had been achieved in 1995 by the leading hoaxers, and they have improved their techniques since then. The tell-tale marks of rollers have been carefully smoothed out in this formation to give an even flow of crop. However such attention to detail is only really possible in daylight conditions and working at a leisurely pace, as was the case here.

However, although the use of a roller is not particularly noticeable on the ground, from the air the paths are all too evident whether as concentric rings or straight paths. It should be emphasised that the geophysical formations do not show such features, so evident for example in the 'Circular Saw' formation at Barbury Castle or the 'Ring Quintuplet' at Headbourne Worthy in 1997. (The latter, incidentally being the only one of the season which shows clear evidence of having been produced by a board or stalk-stomper)

Where does this leave the 1997 formations in general terms? There were aerial photos of some 42 formations out of about 130 reported from the UK: i.e. about one third of the total (the smaller circles and formations away from Wiltshire and Hampshire are rarely photographed from the air). Some 23% of formations are shown on the photos as having spirals of the type characteristic of the geophysical formations, 40% are ringed and 37% are indecipherable. It may be significant that a high proportion of the ringed formations appear over weekends!

Clearly we need to look back carefully over all the earlier formations and above all, to try in future to improve the quality and coverage of aerial photos of formations.'

## 'THE (BELTANE) TORUS FORMATION 1998

[From Green, Michael 1998c in *The Circular* #32, 1998, September, pp. 16-17]

This formation [2.11] appeared in a field of Canola (Oilseed Rape) during the early hours of 4th May 1998 at a location midway between West Kennet Long Barrow and Silbury Hill in Avebury CP, Wiltshire (OS ref, SU 413679) [Amended to SU103679 (Ed.)]. It is possibly one of the most important formations to have been put down in recent years, and has already been the subject of a technical study by Jim Lyons, a copy of which is appended herewith.

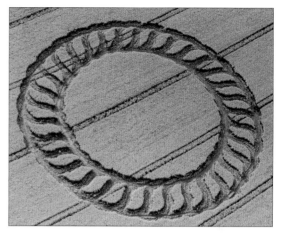

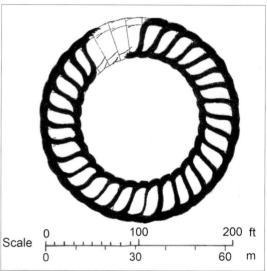

*2.11 The 'Beltane Torus'*
*West Kennet, Wiltshire (OS SU103679), between 4.30 am and 5.30 am, 4.5.1998*

These notes, therefore, are not concerned with its scientific parameters, but are to establish its authenticity as a geophysical crop formation and to introduce the *Dramatis Personae* involved.

## TONY CRERAR (TONY CRERAR OF LLANDRINDOD WELLS, POWYS)

On the night of 3rd/4th May Tony Crerar, a photographer taking time-exposure photographs, had positioned himself just off the A4 (the main road which runs East-West between the Barrow and Silbury Hill) adjacent to the Sanctuary, (another ancient monument very close by). His avowed purpose to capture some views of moonset and sunrise. The Sanctuary is almost exactly one mile east of the rape field, which later had the Torus formation, and overlooks it. He took up position at about 2300 hours on the 3rd and was actively moving around until about 0300 hours on the 4th. The photo exposure was set to operate between 0230 and 0300 hours covering an area facing due West with Silbury Hill central to the picture, and the rape field slightly off camera to the left.

Crerar reported that the night was fine, still and cold. The lights of the only car that passed along the A4 during this time were recorded on the moonset photograph. Between 0300 and 0400 hours Crerar relaxed in his car, awake but not watching the area. At about 0430 hours, he drove West past the rape field and says that he did not see any formation in the half-light at that time. At 0530 hours he returned driving East and the Torus formation was in position.

Shortly afterwards he went into the formation and reports that it was in pristine condition. His report of its geometry is included as an annexe to this paper.

### MR & MRS MICHAEL SHILLING

The three members of the Shilling family from Calne (Wiltshire) were out in the area listening to the dawn chorus on the morning of 4th May. Mrs Shilling reports that they drove past the rape field at 0430 hours and no formation was seen, but on returning at about 0545 hours it was clearly visible in the field.

They visited the Torus at about 0600 hours and were probably [amongst] the first people to do so. Mrs Shilling says that not only was

the formation in excellent condition, but that there were no signs of human disturbance or foot prints in the heavy dew and moist ground, although they themselves could not avoid leaving marks behind them.

The independent testimonies of Crerar and the Shillings therefore establish (in my mind) that the formation appeared within a time frame of an hour between 0430 and 0530 hours. It also establishes that it was in undamaged condition with no evidence of human activity, a point confirmed by Francine Blake who inspected the formation at a slightly later stage during the morning. The only damage she noted was around the entry to the formation.

### PETER SØRENSEN

This American investigator, temporarily resident at Alton Priors (Wiltshire), visited the formation at about 1000 hours on the morning of the 4th. There were already a number of people wandering about the Torus at that time. He reported that the base of the rape stalks were crushed and crumpled, and that many of the stems were broken some 18 inches (45cm) from the ground. He reports that the stems were "scraped". The condition of the rape was indicative (to him) of a man-made origin for the formation.

### FRANCINE BLAKE

A Wiltshire crop circle investigator, Francine Blake, took a team of BBC Wiltshire Sound Unit for an interview within the formation at 0800 hours on 5th May. There was a serious malfunction of the equipment that corrected itself once they had moved 150ft away (50m) from the formation. On returning to the Torus the same problem re-occurred. At 1100 on the same day an ITV Bristol television unit visited the formation with Francine. On playing back the interview the pictures and sound were found to be severely distorted and could not be used for the scheduled programme.

## HELENEIA BRIERLEY

This well-known psychic from Essex visited the formation some days after it had appeared. Her channelled communication reported that the formation had appeared just before dawn on 4th May and took between 3 and 5 seconds to make. She also spoke of a visionary effect of spirals of energy "like worms" interweaving to make the formation, which was intelligently created by forces from our own planetary system.

## SUMMARY

The overwhelming impression gained from these various independent testimonies is that the Torus formation of 1998 is a true, geophysical event and not man-made. In its early state it was evidently in immaculate condition with no evidence of human activity. Unfortunately the numbers of visitors attracted by the Internet reports quickly reduced the formation to the damaged condition reported by Peter Sørensen by the mid-morning of the 4th. The well-authenticated camera and radio malfunctions due to the remnant electro-magnetic field are of particular interest, and indeed to be expected in genuine geophysical formations.

## ACKNOWLEDGEMENTS

I am indebted for first-hand reports about this formation to: Francine Blake, Heleneia Brierley, Tony Crerar, Mrs Shilling and Peter Sørensen.

## ANNEXE BY TONY CRERAR

Here [2.11, bottom] is a reconstruction of the design of the formation drawn by standard draughting methods. I have left a section unfinished to display the minimum construction points and arcs, which support this design. The construction features around the rim would be obliterated by the laying of the rape plants, but the centre would not. I could not discern any marks in the centre of the formation nor could I detect any tracks pushed through the crop towards the centre.

With a design demanding such high level symmetry as this, it is difficult to see how the basic form, two concentric circles, could be drawn so accurately without using a pegged line located at the centre. Even an experienced draughtsman could not expect to draw this design to that standard by free-hand sketching on paper. If a vehicle were used, locking the steering to make the two rings, traces of access should be evident on the tramlines — unless the vehicle was very large with high axles. Such a vehicle would have to be directed from the ground to complete the segments, by someone carrying good resolution construction lengths. These segments are of such regular symmetry that their construction points would need to have been found by calculation. These calculations are based on the correct diameters. Unless the designers could ascertain the diameters of the two main rings beforehand, they would have to make their calculations in the field after measuring the first two diameters first scribed. It would require a practiced crew to complete this design without discernible fluffs. It is difficult to imagine it being done in less than two hours.

It would appear that this design was executed without recourse to regular draughting techniques. This suggests that the feature was 'stamped' or stencilled into the rape from a previously created mould or master.

## SILBURY TORUS FORMATION BY JAMES LYONS, 24 MAY 1998

This formation which occurred on 4th May 1998 was by no means unexpected. In the light of work undertaken last year, it is becoming very clear how the formations are created by the underlying energy source extracted from the earth's geophysical field. The influence of the energies on electrical equipment near the formation again demonstrated how these magneto-gravitic fields can generate lingering anomalous effects, discernible by commercial electrical devices. What is even more intriguing, however, is the way we are beginning to see how coding for the geometry occurs. Our starting point in this article is the workshop I gave to the Wiltshire Group on 4th April. There, I explained the significance of the Torus Knot (see Issue 50) which occurred at Alton Barnes last year. Following on from this, I dared to make the suggestion that we would he seeing more Torus Knots that went a little further forward to show how the generating vortex flow would wind into a braiding pattern. [2.12A] A mere glance at the Silbury formation shows a braiding effect incorporated into yet another Torus Knot. Mathematically, the formation follows closely the outline shown in [2.12A]. Here we indicate the basic feature of the current formation, namely the requirement to circle twice around the toroid before returning to the start point. This effect is already well known in many fields of physics. The number of loops seen here – 7, indicating the knot's appearance when viewed from above, shows how the 2-D cross-section seen in the field yields the perceived pattern. In the real formation, we have 33 loops, we do not see the "underside" of the knot and clearly have a large central circle. The mathematics however is precisely the same having only differing constants and the equation for those

interested is simply $r = 1 + \cos(16.5.\theta)/5$, where 'r' is the radius of the formation and 'θ', the angular displacement around the formation. In [2.12B], it can be seen how the vortex bifurcation plot for the formation works. From the basic hemispherical energy bubble

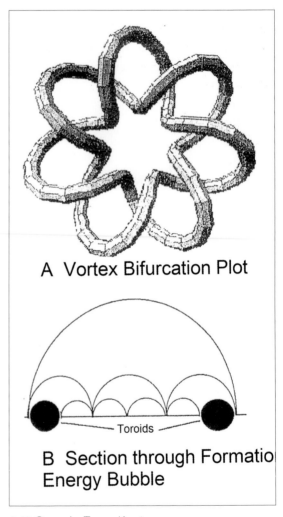

A Vortex Bifurcation Plot

B Section through Formatio Energy Bubble

*2.12 Sample Torus Knot*

over the formation there is first an asymmetric bifurcation creating a toroid enclosing a central circle (yang symbol). These toroids each in turn bifurcate to form nested toroids, the outer ones of which are energised creating those involved in the formation shape. They are shown in black and indicate that they exist partly above ground and partly below. The waves then flow around these toroids creating the final shape. The unknown at the moment is why 33 turns? It can be shown that this is harmonically related to a major tone on the diatonic scale but I feel there is something still more significant that we do not yet comprehend. The shape of the formation is elliptical displaying overall orthological dimensions of 222ft by 215ft (67m by 65m). The aspect ratio of slightly over 3% difference is in line with other measurements taken over the years and comes from the spiral winding shape of the outer toroid.

It is interesting to observe that this sort of topological shape is precisely the form that researchers in consciousness studies are investigating to explain the formation of thought patterns occurring in human bio-energy fields. Is it stretching the hypothesis too far to suggest that maybe the coding of our thoughts is carried out in precisely the same way that Nature employs to define the morphology of its creations, which clearly embraces the crop circle phenomenon?'

# 3. THE MILK HILL INSCRIPTION

*Senzar is 'the name for the secret sacerdotal language, or the "mystery speech" of the initiated adepts all over the world. It is a universal language, and largely a hieroglyphic cipher.'*

Djwhal Khul
Bailey 1922a, p. 224

## DISCOVERY

The crop formation which appeared on Milk Hill, central Wiltshire (OS SU097634) on 1 August 1991 is very important, since it is the only formation to my knowledge that has used archaic writing in textual form. Kevin Constant and a friend surveyed the formation before it was destroyed by the farmer, and contacted me on 18 August. The feature that most impressed them, indeed convinced them that this was a genuine, geophysical formation, was the treatment of the serifs at the top of the letters. These were not clearly visible on the aerial photos, but were observed on the ground to flow away to 'the thickness of a finger' into the crop – a refinement of detail wholly beyond the technical capacity of hoaxers at the time.

## ERIK BECKJORD

It appears to have been no accident that this unique formation appeared when it did. The American researcher, Erik Beckjord, whom we met in Chapter 1, took an interest in the crop circle phenomenon as a likely 'communication process'. He had published an article 'Having a go at decoding' in *The Circular* (1991 #2.2, pp. 13-15) in which he interpreted crop formation elements as glyphs similar to the Berber symbolic alphabet *Tifinag*, which he believed

had connections with ancient Norse letter forms. It was a remarkably perceptive insight.

One evening members of the CCCS Council were in the *Wagon and Horses* pub at Beckhampton, Wiltshire. We were discussing whether there was an Intelligence behind the phenomenon and how to contact it. Beckjord, who happened to be present, grew impatient with us and said he had permission to write TALK TO US in the crop of a local field. I remember it was pouring with rain as he sloshed his way up Hackpen Hill nearby to trample out his message.

A week later the Milk Hill inscription arrived, 3 miles away. (3.1) By coincidence Beckjord was up the hillside the morning after it appeared, but dismissed it as a reply to his peremptory demand since the answer had not come back in English! As the late John Michell, then editor of *The Cerealogist*, commented in a footnote to his magazine (1991-2 #5, p. 24): 'the obscurity of the response was no doubt in the interests of politeness.' This touches on a problem which is common to all such mandalic crop circle messages. If the communication is too simplistic it runs the risk of rejection by researchers as a hoax. In this case if a clear response had come back in the King's English using simple, non serif, letters it would have been dismissed

*3.1 **The Milk Hill Inscription** - Senzar Agriglyph*
*Crop formation at Stanton St Bernard, Wiltshire (OS SU097634), 1.8.1991*
*Author's transliteration and translation below*

out of hand by everyone as man-made. Some subtlety was clearly called for on the part of the geophysical crop circle makers, and indeed it has proved possible to attempt a translation of this message, as we will see below.

## THE STRUCTURE OF THE INSCRIPTION

We appear to have two words or phrases which should be read from right to left. Each word or phrase is separated by vertical spacers which also divide them from the 'determinative' symbols at each end of the inscription. In the ancient world such determinative symbols gave the general sense of the associated inscription. These particular determinatives (the Chinese *Bi* glyph), symbolise, quite simply, God.

The jade *Bi* disc appears as early as the fourth millennium BC in ancient China, and is still used as the astrological sign for the sun (The Light behind the Light) in the West. The symbolism is very subtle; the empty central space represents Spirit or the Unmanifested State of Deity, whereas the ringed shape (or disc) constitutes manifest form as an expression of Deity.

The words themselves are made up of square-letter glyphs constructed from right to left, and written in each case (following the flow of the crop formation) starting at the bottom right-hand corner. The general effect is as if they were copied from an original painted with a brush.

We are faced with an interpretative puzzle.

## THE IBERIAN SYLLABARY (3.2)

A clue to the translation of the Milk Hill inscription lies in Erik Beckjord's perception that its letter forms are related to the North African Berber script of *Tifinag/Tifineh*. I believe the source of this ancient script lies in a class of syllabary which developed in Iberia (present Spain) and North Africa from prehistoric times, the evidence for which would appear to be found in ancient and surviving Niebla, Libyan, Iberian, Imushagh, Berber and related scripts. (3.2) In Spain it appears in prehistoric and protohistoric contexts, and as a written system it was eventually incorporated in the medieval Kabbalistic tradition as the *Aiq Beker* system, and thence into mainstream medieval magic and alchemy.

## THE AIQ BEKER SYSTEM

This derivative system is described by Henry Cornelius Agrippa of Nettesheim in his seminal work *Three Books of Occult Philosophy*, first published in 1531. The edited and annotated version referenced here is by Donald Tyson. (Tyson 1995, p. 561)

This script is a branch of the medieval Jewish tradition and is known as *the Kabbalah of the Nine Chambers* or *Aiq Beker*, so called from the

IBERIAN AND NORTH AFRICAN SYLLABARIES

A Core glyphs (Agrippa 1531)
B Milk Hill formation 1991
C Niebla, Andalusia (Whishaw 1928)
D Libyan and Imushagh (Bates 1913)
E Levantine Iberian 425 BC (Gomez-Moreno 1962)
F Numidian-Tifineh (Jensen 1969)
G Berber (Jensen 1969)
H South Andalucian cave paintings, epi-paleolithic (Breuil and Burkitt 1929)

AIQ BEKER SYSTEM
(Kabbalah of the Nine Chambers)

| גלש | בכר | איק |
|-----|-----|-----|
| וסם | הנך | דמת |
| צץ | חפף | זען |

*3.2*

first six letters of the Hebrew alphabet that constitute it. (3.2) The Hebrew alphabet is written into the nine cells of a grid formed by two pairs of parallel lines that intersect at right angles, resulting in three letters in each cell (22 letters plus 5 final forms equal 27 letters). The framework grid itself, when disassembled, constitutes the basic structure of the letter forms.

However the Aiq Beker system, with its somewhat uncomfortable adaptation to the Hebrew alphabet, was only the last development of an ancient system by the medieval Jewish Kabbalists in Spain. The exploded 'letter-framework motif', like the scripts listed above, was derived from the earlier syllabary of the region, and, I believe, is the basis of the syllabic system of *Senzar*.

In Theosophist teaching the language and writing of *Senzar*, the mystery speech of the adepts, had its origin ultimately in Plato's lost civilisation of Atlantis, which, (see Whishaw E.M. 1997) had extensive trading and cultural relations with Spain before its disappearance beneath the ocean.

The square-letter forms and ancillary symbols can, I believe, be reassembled to form a phonetic system of consonants and vowels, which relates to that lost linguistic cipher.

## SENZAR

In fact Senzar, as defined above, is a relatively straightforward, semi-syllabic system. The letters and sounds, thanks to their survival in traditional North African cultures, can now be deduced.

Returning to the enigmatic Milk Hill inscription we have two words which have to be read from right to left. In my opinion their general sense is indicative, regardless of whatever language they may originally have formed a part. They are the names of God, or more likely, the name of God and a defining epithet as was commonly used in the ancient world.

The first name reads PH.E.H.TH.I. The closest parallel is the name of that most ancient of Egyptian deities, Ptah, the primeval Creator whose hieroglyphic inscriptions describe Him as being 'the Very Great God, who came into being in the earliest time, Father of fathers, Power of powers, Father of beginnings, and Creator ...'

The second name is E.A.E.CH.-CH.E. Again the closest parallel is not Ancient Egypt, but the oldest civilisation of all, Mesopotamia, where Ea-Enki was the God of Wisdom and lover of mankind, concerned with every aspect of human life.

Hence my transcription of the Milk Hill text is: 'The Creator, Wise and Loving.' Far from being a hoax then, the Milk Hill inscription is arguably one of the most important, explicit communications from the numinous levels of Ultimate Reality which the crop circle community has been privileged to receive in this age.

Indeed, it is clear from which 'Numinous Level' this inscription is derived, since its signature is to be found to the left and above the line of writing, clearly seen in the photograph. (3.1) The large circle with the smaller circle adjoining is the signature of our own Earth Logos. The larger circle represents the planet, the smaller one the moon.

# 4. THE COSMIC CONNECTION

*The slenderest knowledge that may be obtained of the highest things is more desirable than the most certain knowledge obtained of lesser things.*

Saint Thomas Aquinas

A celebrant of the Ancient Mysteries standing on the summit of Silbury Hill in Wiltshire, England at the dawn of the summer solstice in 1989 would have noticed something strange and new in the landscape. Emerging out of the golden mists that surrounded the mound were to be seen the intricate patterns of the crop circles in the fields below. (4.1) They had not been there a few days before, but now the four sets of quintuplets shone in the corn on both sides of the hill, together with a single circle on the very summit itself. The circle formations reflected the sun and the full moon in the sky together on that beautiful morning, with the star Aldebaran, the 'eye' of the constellation Taurus, glowing between them. Aldebaran, the Hebrew Aleph, God's Eye, (Hinckley Allen 1963, p. 385) was regarded in the ancient world as the leading star of the heavens, harbinger of Light, Illumination and Sound, and in Christian parlance, the Light of the World.

4.1 *'Quincunx' formations*, near Silbury Hill, Wiltshire
Top: 12.7.1989 (SU098688). Bottom: 16.7.1989 (SU097689)

Within the elaborate patterns of the major circle formations around Silbury and elsewhere were grouped smaller circles, or 'grapeshot', which looked like constellation patterns.

Strange phenomena round a mysterious prehistoric monument: these are not the subjective fantasies of an impressionable mystic or ufologist, but hard physical facts, a structural expression of metaphysical realities, if you like, in the landscape of Britain in the 1980s, and afterwards increasingly in other parts of the world.

## THE ANCIENT WISDOM

The sight of the crop circles at Silbury brought back memories of another morning half a lifetime ago when as a poor student the writer had been browsing through a second-hand bookshop at King's Cross, London, now long defunct. In a battered copy of Waring's classic study of prehistoric ornament (Waring 1870, p. 55) was an engraving of solar and stellar symbolism, which had formed patterns which decorated the sides of a small Venus shrine of Gallo-Roman date from Brittany, now lost, but of a type characteristic of second century AD *ex-votos* made in Gaul. (Green, Miranda 1991, p. 38) The elaborate concentric circles arranged singly and in quintuplet patterns bear a close resemblance to the configuration of the crop circles, but in the case of the Venus shrine are to be identified with the symbolism of the Celtic Tree of Life.

### The Celtic System

The circles of the Tree, the Welsh *cantrefi*, are analogous to the Kabbalistic *sefirot*. A *cantref* in Old Welsh means a canton or subdivision (literally a hundredth) of land, and was used in a metaphysical context to denote the seven states of consciousness (Conway 1985, p. 173),

which together with the primordial Trinity constitute the Ten, the Causal Consciousness of the Solar Logos, the god of our system. (Chapter 15) Likewise the *sefirot* are also ten, being 'containers, numbers, lights of the Attributes of God on the Tree.' (Halevi, Z'ev ben Shimon, p. 327) It was beginning to look as if the crop circle phenomena might relate to the symbolism of the Ancient Wisdom of north-west Europe.

### The Hellenistic and other ancient systems

The Ancient Wisdom, that great body of esoteric knowledge, deals with the nature of Deity, the origins of the manifested creation, God's expression in the natural world and His relationship with mankind on the Wheel of Life, where humanity finds its spiritual apotheosis. The teaching is profound, complex and scattered throughout the ancient and modern writings of the world. It shines like threads of gold in the tapestry of each great religious system. It vibrates with the timbre of their cultures, whether the *Sufis* of Islam, the *Kabbalists* of Jewry or the *Mystics* of Christendom, but the density of the weave is dependent on the quality of their spiritual systems.

'We can thus point to a line of succession from Pythagoras and the Mystery Schools of the first millennium BC, through the Neo-Platonist philosophy and the Hermetic-Cabalist tradition to the present day. The highest principle of Platonist philosophy was the exercise of intellect leading to *gnosis* and thus to wisdom ...' (Cannon Johnson 2005, p. 159) Indeed this is an identical state to that of the Buddhist who has 'achieved' Nirvana. 'When Siddhartha became enlightened, he became known as the Buddha. *Buddha* is not a person's name, it is the label for a state of mind. The word *buddha* is defined as one quality with two aspects: "accomplished one", and "awakened one". In other words, one who has purified defilements and one who has attained knowledge.' (Khyentse 2007, p. 98) This is a very rare condition for most members of humanity today or in the past, but it may become more common with mankind in the *New Age* of the future.

In the Hellenic world, Diogenes Laertius (third century AD), quoting Pythagorean traditions of the fourth century BC, lists four esoteric schools which had analogies with the Greek philosophic systems of the Ancient Wisdom. (Chadwick 1966, p. 64) These were: the *Magi* of the Persians, the *Chaldeans* of the Babylonians, the *Gymnosophists* of the Indians and the *Druids* of the Celts and Galatae. (Diogenes Laertius, *Lives of the Philosophers*, Book 1, preface) Each of these systems of the ancient Indo-Aryan world is a cultural branch of the Ancient Wisdom, of whom Ammianus Marcellinus (AD 330-391) singles out the Druids, who, being 'of a loftier intellect, and bound by the rules of brotherhood as decreed by Pythagoras' authority, were exalted by investigations of deep and serious study ...' (Chadwick 1966, p. 26)

If there is an idea which defines the Ancient Wisdom and in a sense separates it from most belief systems of today, it is the realisation of the principle of *Emanation*, which as Patricia Cannon Johnson states is a concept that 'has been much misunderstood. The Emanation principle is a theory of Creation. It refers to a Unity or Monad – the Eternally Existent, or Good – which, whilst indivisible within itself, yet emanates Creation – the Many or the All – by a process of multiplicity through a hierarchy of levels or dimensions from one state of being to the next. ... By a mystical process the Monad indwells the whole of its creation,

and all the levels of descent are regarded as equally holy. Man – and indeed all life – is a microcosm of the Cosmos. Manifested life is viewed as a final flowering of the harmonically differentiated levels of vibration which underlie the process of the One or the Good into phenomenal existence.' (Cannon Johnson 2005, pp. 145-6) Indeed much of what follows in this book is concerned with the *Emanation principle*, although defined in other terms.

Unlike some other traditions, however, the Druidic and earlier religious beliefs were never committed to writing. Apart from brief references by the classical writers, only the symbols, iconography and monuments of the prehistoric belief systems of north-west Europe have survived to give any hint of the character and complexity of their beliefs. Nevertheless it is necessary to relate this evidence of these lost systems to the patterns and structure of the crop circles, for they are closely related.

## CROP FORMATIONS: INVESTIGATORS AND ANCIENT SYMBOLS

*The strange character of the phenomenon*

In 1990 when I wrote the chapter 'The rings of time: The symbolism of the crop circles', (Green, Michael 1990) I already considered the phenomenon as some form of cosmic communication process. However, most of the other philosophers and scientists who formed the core of the newly-founded Centre for Crop Circle Studies (CCCS) did not share this view. Its study was approached in strictly scientific terms, initially as a freak weather effect in the 1980s by the meteorologist Dr Terence Meaden. The scientific approach of the CCCS was ably set out by Montague Keen in his paper *1991 – Scientific Evidence for the Crop Circle Phenomenon* (Keen 1992), and in an earlier study by another Council member, Pat Palgrave-Moore, *Crop Circle Classification*. (Palgrave-Moore, 1991) There was much criticism of this approach, and indeed, as recounted in Chapter 2, it was not until 1995 that means were discovered to distinguish scientifically between geophysical and man-made formations.

However, this was not in origin a natural physical phenomenon explicable by conventional scientific enquiry. As a physical fact in the landscape the phenomenon was real enough, unlike most paranormal phenomena, but there was increasing uneasiness amongst serious investigators, that its manner of operation was somehow uncanny and not really susceptible to conventional scientific inquiry. What gradually emerged in this writer's view was an extraordinary reversal of what scientifically is known as the *observer effect*. Far from merely studying the phenomenon, we the observers were being studied ourselves and contacted by a highly intelligent, non-human Agency, which was involving particular individuals for different functions.

The process appeared to operate as follows. An individual, not necessarily a countryman, had his or her attention drawn to the phenomenon by a single inexplicable circle appearing in a locality in the countryside with which he was familiar. Next, he would be brought into the orbit of others studying the phenomenon, or would read an account of it somewhere. Finally, and this is most important, a formation would appear tailored to catch his interest as relating to his particular background or training. A formation that could not be explained away as a freak weather effect: a formation that showed clear evidence of a non-human intelligence and an intimate knowledge of the human individual concerned being targeted. Many would-be investigators freaked out at this stage, but those who carried on would be drawn into the corporate study of the phenomenon, and would contribute according to their particular strengths, whether as a flier, a field investigator or surveyor, an analyst or a public relations communicator. Most of my colleagues who were seriously involved went through this sequence of events, but how was I personally affected?

In 1985 I was running an archaeological excavation at Godmanchester, Cambridgeshire, for English Heritage. While I was there the owner from a local farm (Wyboston Farm) came over to see me and asked me to come and look at an area near the farmhouse where a small circle had mysteriously appeared in a patch of chick peas. It clearly had nothing to do with archaeology, and was altogether very strange. As recounted in Chapter 2, it was when I was lecturing on prehistoric symbolism in 1989 that my attention was drawn to the crop circle phenomenon by Ralph Noyes, which led directly to my involvement with the founding of the CCCS in 1990. However it was not until I flew over the Silbury Hill area in 1989 and saw a formation of quincunx (quintuplet) design that I really woke up to the metaphysical significance of the phenomenon. As mentioned above, I had first seen such a design on a Gallo-Roman religious figurine in a book I had bought some years earlier in London.

### The Sun God figurine (4.2)

The figurine in question had been found in 1868 in an underground sanctuary or *souterrain* at La Tourelle, Quimper in Brittany. Much votive material was found including several hundred pipe-clay figurines of deities and

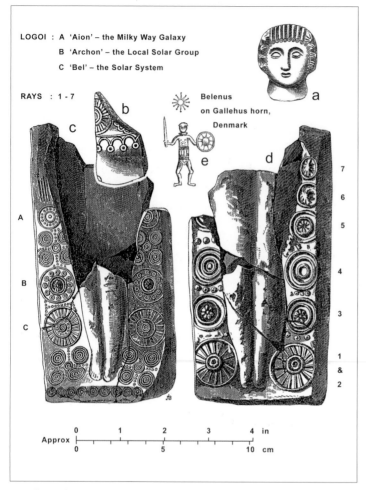

**4.2** *Cosmic Symbolism on a Romano-Celtic 'Apollo Belenus' Figurine*
*La Tourelle, near Quimper, Brittany*
*Second century AD*

animals. (Le Men 1868, pp. 308-309 including plates IV and V) This particular figurine, in contrast to others, was of a red fabric with a white slip, so that the different fragments could be confidently associated. The excavator identified the figure as that of the Celtic Apollo *Belenus* ('The Shining One'), which in view of the associated symbolism would appear to be correct.

The figure would appear to be naked except for a short cape or tunic (4.2b) decorated on the front with a solar symbol and a tasselled fringe of a type which had been introduced into Amorica (France) in the fifth century BC (Kruta and Forman 1985, p. 31), although the figurine itself would appear to be Roman, of the second century AD. A figure embossed on a ritual horn from Gallehus, Denmark (4.2e) dated at about AD 500, would appear to show an 'Apollo Belenus' figure with a similar solar symbol on its breast. (Gelling and Davidson 1969, p. 177)

The really significant aspect of this figurine is the decoration on the front and back, which makes it, perhaps, the most important of its kind ever found. This type of Romano-Celtic Deity, particularly the Venus figurines, is richly embellished with variants of cosmic symbolism. The front (4.2c) has two identical vertical panels on either side of the central figure, each of which appears to consist of three elements, separated by beaded divisions, which I would identify with three cosmic Logoi. (A *Logos* might be defined as the outward expression of any 'Emanation' of Deity, or an outer 'effect' of the Cause which is ever concealed. Thus, speech is the Logos of thought, aptly translated by the Latin *verbum* or 'word' in its metaphysical sense). (See Bailey 1922a, p. 220.) The upper register (4.2A) consists of a *Bi* symbol with an outer band with circles, representing the Logos of the Milky Way galaxy, *Aion*. The middle register (two concentric circles and the quincunx above) (4.2B) consists of the Septead (the seven Rays, see below) of our local solar group, *Archon*, whose solar systems are shown as rings on the band of the wheel. (For Aion and Archon see Chapter 16.) The bottom register (4.2C) comprises the Septead of our Solar Logos, *Bel*. The four Lords of the Elements (air, fire, earth and water) and the Archangel who controls them (whom the Archangel Michael describes as the Five) are depicted as a quincunx. This is the same quincunx which appeared as crop formations in the Wessex fields in the 1980s and later, and appropriately symbolises the physical functions of planet Earth. A particularly detailed rendering of the Solar Septead of the same design occurs on the back of a Belenus figurine from Rézé, Brittany and is reproduced by Miranda Green. (Green, Miranda 1991, p. 129, fig. 94)

On the back of the Tourelle plaque (4.2d, 1–7), again in paired strips on either side of Belenus, are the symbols of our planetary Septead in linear form, shown as circles beginning at the bottom. I have designated them in terms of their Ray identifications.

To introduce the Rays, as Djwhal Khul, through Alice Bailey, puts it: 'All manifestation is of a septenary nature, and the Central Light which we call Deity, the one Ray of Divinity, manifests first as a Triplicity, and then as a Septenary. ... The students of occultism ... may call these Beings the One Ray, demonstrating through the three major Rays and the four minor, making a divine Septenary.' (Bailey 1922a, p. 3) The three major Rays are the Rays of Aspect, the *Trinity*, and the four minor, the Rays of Attribute, the *Quaternio*. I refer to all the rays together as the *Septead*. The characteristics of the Rays of Aspect are:

Ray 1   Will or Power, the 'Father' aspect

Ray 2   Love-Wisdom, the 'Son' aspect

Ray 3   Active Intelligence, the 'Holy Spirit' or 'Mother' aspect.

More will be said in Chapter 5 about the Rays and the human psyche, and in Chapter 10 and later chapters as this complicated subject is explored.

The largest circle at the bottom with solar rays also doubles as a cosmic wheel, a symbol of Apollo's solar chariot, much in evidence on Gallo-British, Celtic coinage. The two symbols are virtually interchangeable. The wheel motif, however, goes further in Celtic religious thinking since its components comprise two essential elements of any Logoic manifestation: the inner Unmanifest state of Spirit (the hub) and the outer Manifest state between the hub and the outer ring or *felloe* of the wheel, designated here as Rays 1 and 2 respectively.

*A wheel on a Roman votive water pot*

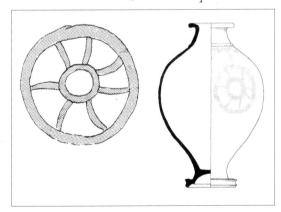

4.3 **Seven-spoked Celtic solar wheel** on a water jar from temple precinct of Abandinus Godmanchester, Cambridgeshire
Second century AD

The significance of this type of Celtic symbolism is especially clear as decoration on a water pot from the temenos of the god Abandinus from Durovigutum (Roman Godmanchester). (4.3) Here the outer band has seven spokes carefully delineated – an unusual number for any wheel – representing the Septead of the Manifest State of Deity. It is a reminder that the Seven Rays in manifestation in any Being are a product of the Second Ray or Christ Spirit, or Soul in the human context. 'All things came into being through him, and without him not one thing came into being.' (*John* 1:3) Other Celtic wheels with a four or eightfold spoke arrangement probably refer to the spiritual initiatory systems discussed later. It will be evident that the Celtic wheel symbolism is a direct reflection of the *Bi* symbolism of the East, and is evidence of the strong spiritual undercurrents of the Indo-Ayran movements across the ancient world. Returning to the Ray system of the Tourelle figure (4.2d), Ray 3 is another double ring with sevenfold petalled flower in the centre, again symbolising the manifest states of Deity. The other four represent Rays 4-7, the lower Rays (uppermost here) being shown as starred circles.

### The wisdom of the Druids

How is it that a modest figurine of the Celtic Sun God should be, like many of its kind, so rich in profound, esoteric symbolism? There is no doubt in my mind that we are looking at the last fruits of a long tradition of esoteric knowledge, which to the uninitiated would merely look like pretty decoration. We must return to the late classical writer, Ammianus Marcellinus, and his statement about the profound wisdom and high spiritual state of the Druids, for in this symbolism we hear the distant echoes of their teaching.

If the quincunxes at Silbury Hill in 1989 pointed the way towards an understanding of the crop circle phenomenon at that time, the sort of detailed interpretation set out above had not yet been reached. I was more concerned then to understand the significance of the relatively simple formations that had been appearing up to that date. The sections below based on my paper 'The rings of time', make clear my thinking in 1990.

Taking all these factors into consideration and bearing in mind the progressive elaboration of the phenomena since 1980, a tentative classification of formations up to 1990 can be put forward under six headings.

## CLASSIFICATION OF CROP FORMATIONS C. 1987-1990

First there were the basic circle types, of which there appeared to be at least seven. Second, these could be subdivided in certain cases into five or more subclasses by the addition of satellites, a process which became marked in about 1988. Third, there were the very small circles (grapeshot), not more than about 6 ft in diameter, which were forming increasingly complex patterns, both around the main circles and on their own. The configurations suggest possible constellation and other patterns. The fourth group which started in 1987 appear to be thematic formations representing certain cosmic principles. The fifth group which appeared in 1990 comprises symbolic figures of the Sun God (Solar Logos) and Earth Goddess (Earth Logos) and has a range of attributes illustrating their different functions. The sixth group, and the most spectacular, are great composite, non-symmetrical formations which bring together aspects of the previous group. The grapeshot patterns further define the source and nature of the energies involved at both a macrocosmic and microcosmic level.

It is proposed that if the main circles represent symbols of different types of cosmic energy and their subdivision in certain cases, the thematic formations represent certain cosmic principles.

## THE PLANETARY SYMBOLS

It seems inconceivable, at least to this writer, that such complex, symmetrical formations, which often have features added over several weeks, can be explained except as a consequence of intelligent activity. If indeed these are symbols, what do they refer to and how does this give a clue to their origins?

It occurred to certain research workers in this field, notably Busty Taylor and John Michell, that the circles bore some sort of generic resemblance to pre- and proto-historic symbolism occurring in the British Isles.

A remarkable discovery made some years ago at a Roman villa in Sussex really began for the first time to break the metaphysical code of the circles. Villa II at Chilgrove, near Chichester, was excavated by Alec Down in the 1960s. (Down 1979) In an outhouse dating to the early fourth century AD a mosaic (4.4) had been constructed with a pattern of seven circles across the centre of the room and two additional circles near the doorway. Behind the main group of circles large patches of burning had partly damaged the mosaic in the late Roman period.

The Chilgrove circles are symbols of the planetary deities presiding over the days of the week. The sequence starts with *Saturn* – Saturday – at the south end (on the left in my illustration) (a circle with four lobes encircled by three rings),

followed by *Sol* – Sunday – (sun rays and a swastika pattern), *Luna* – Monday – (handled mirror), *Mars* – Tuesday – (convex shield), *Mercury* – Wednesday – (ring with central dot), *Jupiter* – Thursday – (a plain ring) and *Venus* – Friday – (a four-lobed centre with a

*4.4 Crop Circles as Planetary Deities*

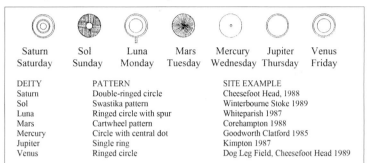

| DEITY | PATTERN | SITE EXAMPLE |
|---|---|---|
| Saturn | Double-ringed circle | Cheesefoot Head, 1988 |
| Sol | Swastika pattern | Winterbourne Stoke 1989 |
| Luna | Ringed circle with spur | Whiteparish 1987 |
| Mars | Cartwheel pattern | Corehampton 1988 |
| Mercury | Circle with central dot | Goodworth Clatford 1985 |
| Jupiter | Single ring | Kimpton 1987 |
| Venus | Ringed circle | Dog Leg Field, Cheesefoot Head 1989 |

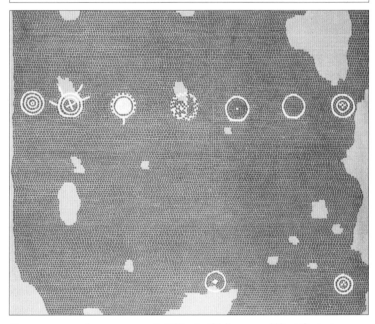

*Roman mosaic pavement, Villa 2, Chilgrove, West Sussex*
*Early fourth century AD*

double ring). The additional two circles at the east end of the room probably represent *Ceres* or Earth (circle with broad outer band), near a niche, and a circle representing the etheric or mystic centre which has two rings round a three-lobed centre. The latter can be taken to represent the Cosmos. In esoteric terms it symbolises the Unmanifest Deity, the Central Spiritual Sun (the Light behind the Light of the physical Sun). The three-lobed centre in this context represents the Primal Causal Triad of manifestation functioning within the Ring-Pass-Not which separates the inner Ring-Cosmos from the outer Ring-Chaos.

It would appear that the room was used for storing cult floats (*fercula*) dedicated to the various deities of the week, which were carried in religious processions (*pompa*). Paintings of *fercula* from Pompeii show them to have been of a light timber construction carried on the shoulders of the celebrants, rather like the images of Catholic saints, on a Roman feast day. The evidence of burning on the mosaic suggests that the stored floats were burnt in situ.

If the symbols of the planetary deities from Chilgrove are compared with the different types of crop circle, the resemblance in many cases is remarkable. (4.4)

Each planetary symbol has a long history stretching back into the prehistoric past in which the basic type survives, but differs in interpretation according to its cultural context. To take one example: the mirror of *Luna* symbolises at a superficial level the Moon reflecting the light of the Sun. At a deeper level it illustrates the principle of form or matter reflecting the illumination of the spiritual Sun; or again at the human level the dichotomy between the Soul and Personality.

## THE COSMIC SYMBOLS

From 1990 onwards the relatively simple crop circle formations of the early years were replaced by elaborate patterns of an entirely new type, which represent, in my view, certain cosmic principles of the Ancient Wisdom which were implanted in the matrix of human consciousness millennia ago and were recorded by glyph and symbol.

*The Cosmic Egg Type*

In June 1990 a strange variation of the circle with three rings appeared at Middle Warren, Longwood Estate, Chilcomb, Hampshire. The two inner rings are broken alternately to form quadrants. (4.5A)

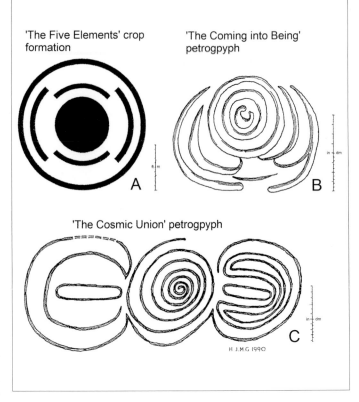

'The Five Elements' crop formation

'The Coming into Being' petrogpyph

'The Cosmic Union' petrogpyph

H J.M.G 1990

*4.5 **Cosmic Egg Symbols** A - Formation at Middle Warren, Longwood Estate, Chilcomb, Hampshire (OS SU529275), 6.6.1990. B and C - Stone initiation basin and kerbstone 5 petroglyphs from Knowth Passage Grave, County Meath, Ireland, c. 3100 BC*

The type is well known on petroglyphs from the Irish megalithic monuments. It represents the breaking apart of the Cosmic Egg, or the disintegration of the primal centre to form the elements of the manifested Cosmos. The process is shown on the side of the great stone initiation basin in the eastern chamber of the Knowth Passage Grave dating to c. 3100 BC. (Scarre 2005, p. 394a and Eogan 1986, p. 108) (4.5B) The theme is elaborated on another stone from Knowth (kerbstone 5). This shows in symbolic form the Sacred Marriage, with the *lingam* of the male principle of Spirit in the broken egg on the left-hand side, and its penetration into the female *vulva* of matter on the right-hand side in the other half of the egg. (4.5C) The resulting fertilisation produces the third element of the primal Trinity, the sacred child, the Son of Man, evidenced as a great spiral of cosmic energy between the male and female principles. The crop formation illustrates this principle. The eighteenth century Welsh mystic Iolo Morganwg expressed it thus: 'When God pronounced His name, with the word [*Logos*] sprang the light and the life ... And in the declaration was His Love, that is, coinstantaneously with it sprang like lightening all the universe into life and existence, co-vocally and co-jubilantly with the uttered Name of God, in one united song of exultation and joy – then all the worlds to the extremities of *Annwn*.' (Williams, J. 1862, p. 17) The cosmic orgasm, the 'big bang' in every sense of the word, was essentially threefold in structure: 'form and sound; and one unitedly with [these two] was life ... and in Life was God.' (Williams, J. 1862, p. 19)

It is significant that, within the ring-pass-not of the outer circle, the crop formation has split into five parts, a segment on each quarter, and a centre.

When the Hellenic philosopher Apollonius of Tyana asked the Brahmin sage Iarchas "of what the cosmos was composed", he was told "of elements". "Are there then four?" asked Apollonius. "Not four," said Iarchas, "but five." "And how can there be a fifth," said Apollonius, "alongside of water and air and earth and fire?" "There is the ether," replied the other ... "the stuff of which gods are made." (Conybeare 1912, pp. 307-308)

In the initial stages of any manifested system the unitary point of consciousness polarises to form a positive and negative duality (spirit on the one hand; form or matter on the other) which in turn synthesises to create a triplicity. Conceptually, this outcome is described as the Second Cosmic Logos, and in the ancient world was symbolised as taking place in an egg, the Cosmic Egg, whose breaking apart leads to formation of the Third Cosmic Logos.

*The Hazeley Down Crop Formation 3.8.1990 (4.6 and 4.7)*

In 1990 there was a series of geophysical crop formations illustrating these processes, culminating in the beautiful mandala on Hazeley Down, Twyford, Hampshire on 3.8.1990. It expresses the principles of *Cosmogenesis* or 'Coming into Being' as described above. Although its particular reference may be to the Solar Logos, judging by the double halo at the top of the formation, I have included it here because the principles of numinous creation are basically the same at every level from the One to that humble unit, man. This was clearly understood in ancient Hermetic spirituality in the *Trismegistic Tractates*. The ancient alchemical formula encoded in the Emerald Tablet (*Tabula Smaragdina*) and attributed to Hermes Trismegistus neatly encapsulates this cosmic process:

*4.6 'Cosmogenesis'*
*Hazeley Down, Twyford, Hampshire*
*(OS SU497262), 3.8.1990*

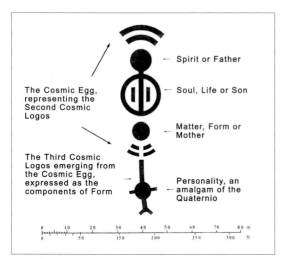

*4.7 'Cosmogenesis' or The Coming into Being*
*Hazeley Down, 3.8.1990*

'What is below is like that which is above; and what is above is like that which is below: to accomplish the miracle of the one thing. ... so all things are born of this one thing, by choice.' (Tyson 1995, p. 711)

The interesting feature of this formation is its clear reference in symbolic terms to the Cosmic Egg and thus to the Orphic first-born god *Phanes Protagonus* (cf. the Modena relief of Aion). (Chapter 16) The top and bottom of the Cosmic Egg are symbolically represented by double arcs, the bottom pair of which is fractured. Within the Egg is depicted a diagram of the structure of the Trinity of Deity. (4.7)

Within the separated double envelope of the Cosmic Egg (symbolised by the paired arcs top and bottom) lies the primal triplicity of, in Theosophic terms:

1.  *Spirit*. The Father and Initiator, who embodies the Spirit or Will aspect of any entity. Spirit and Soul are closely linked, as indeed are the Father and Son in Christian theology.

2.  *Soul/Life*. The Son, the Form-builder, who designs and energises the body which the Spirit must occupy. This element representing the Soul (Son) has a box in each semicircle. I believe this is a reference to the dual nature of this, Ray 2 in Theosophic terms, whose quintessential nature is Love-Wisdom. On the holistic principle, this also forms a duality; Spirit/Form, which is not synthesised until the third component comes into play.

3.  *Matter*, intelligently organised/Form. It is the means of expression and development of 'Spirit' and 'Soul/Life'. It is imbued by that essence of Deity, the Holy Spirit. It is an expression of the intellectual facet of Deity, ('Active Intelligence') and is the archetypal feminine or 'Mother' aspect in terms of its creative function.

Those two principles of Deity, Rays 1 and 2, Spirit and Soul/Life, are indissolubly linked, as is indicated in the Hazeley Down formation, but this is not the case with Matter on Ray 3, which is a new construct for each developmental phase of any entity, at whatever level. At the end of each phase it is destroyed to be replaced by a new model in due course.

The two boxes in the centre also indicate that this is the Second Cosmic Logos and that the process is a function of the second spiritual ether of the Cosmic Physical Plane. (Chapter 8)

The Cosmic Egg represents collectively the Second Cosmic Logos as developed from its Unmanifested State (the First Cosmic Logos). Emerging from the broken shell is the developed aspect or ideation of the Trinity in manifestation operating in the dense world of matter, the Third Cosmic Logos. I have termed this circled organism the Personality, which has emerging from it the four elements of the *Quaternio*, which the crop-circle makers have cleverly assembled to look like a stick figure – the human Monad, Man.

The formation is directed at humanity and its message is the sacredness of physical form and matter as an expression of Deity.

## LOGOI FORMATIONS

In that great *paean* by Chief Seattle of the Suquamish tribe to the American Senate in the nineteenth century these principles are beautifully set out:

"Every part of this earth is sacred to my people. Every shining pine needle, every sandy shore, every mist in the dark woods, every meadow, every humming insect. All are holy ... Will you teach your children what we have taught our children? That the earth is our

mother? What befalls the earth, befalls all the sons of the earth. ... All things are connected like the blood which unites us all. Man did not weave the web of life, he is merely a strand in it ... Our god is also your god. ... The earth is precious to Him."

'The Earth is our Mother' ... It is perhaps no accident therefore that it was at Chilcomb in 1990 that a new type of pictogram appeared which became common in later years right across the crop fields of southern England. I describe them here as *Logoi*, symbolic representations of Cosmic Entities of various grades and sexes who are the numinous 'Emanations' of Deity. The first to appear, on 23.5.1990, was in the Velpins Bank Plantation, Chilcomb, Hampshire – an image of the Earth Mother, *Gaia* Herself. (4.8)

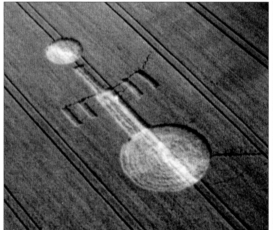

*4.8 The first 'Gaia' formation*
*Velpins Bank, Chilcomb, Hampshire (OS SU520286), 23.5.1990*

This goddess archetype had as innovatory features a dumb-bell shape of the body, consisting of two circles of different sizes partially linked by a path narrowing at the 'head' end. On either side of the figure were pairs of boxes. This was the first of an entirely new design and there were initially doubts about its authenticity. However, subsequent careful study of the aerial photos of the time, for example that illustrated here, by Beth Davis, suggest that the formation was made in two stages. The lower layer has the ring structure characteristic of man-made hoaxes, whereas the small upper circle is swirled and thus of geophysical origin. It appears that the upper circle, neck, and the four boxes (subtly splayed out to taper towards the head), were added by the geophysical crop circle makers. Crop circle investigators were so used to hoaxers adding bits and pieces to genuine formations, that it never occurred to us that the reverse might be true – a man-made formation to which geophysical additions had been made.

'Gaia' formations became a standard type in 1990, some of them man-made. Their symbolism will be discussed in Chapter 11. Other pictograms representing other Logoi, each bearing some defining symbol, occurred, particularly in the Chilcomb area in 1990. See Chapter 19.

## THE CONSTELLATION PATTERNS

During the early summer of 1990 complicated groups of formations, which I have called 'Triangles of Power', were created in Wiltshire. They were part of a battle between the forces of Light and Darkness, described fully in Chapters 19 and 20. The measures taken by the Light Workers – the geophysical crop circle makers – included the use of constellation patterns to invoke the Solar Logos.
*Stone Pit Hill, Bishops Cannings CP, Wiltshire (OS SU030650) on 19.5.1990*
*The Southern Cross, or 'Crux' Constellation* (4.9)

A complex pattern of small circles of between approximately 3 ft and 16 ft in diameter was added by the Light Workers to a negative-

energy-creating man-made formation, which had been placed on the Michael-Mary Line, possibly on the same night. (Noyes 1990, p. 93) (The great Michael-Mary Energy Line runs SW-NE across southern England from Cornwall to Norfolk, connecting energy centres of our living planetary ecosystem. It links with other energy lines to make up the geomorphic Energy Body of the Earth.) Careful study of the pattern from the survey drawing in Wolfgang Schindler's picture archive (privately published, Hamburg 1995) indicates that it is a star map of a particular

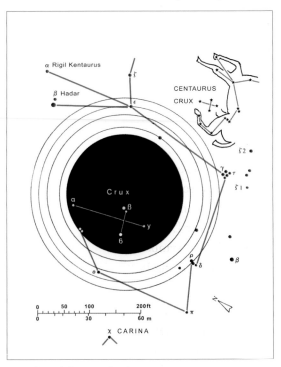

*4.9 'Crux' Constellation pattern*
*Stone Pit Hill, Bishops Cannings, Wiltshire (OS SU030650), 19.5.1990*

area of the southern skies, the constellation of *Centaurus*, the Centaur. However it is not this constellation, as such, which is important, but the small constellation which lies between the Centaur's feet and is actually marked out in the crop formation itself. This is the *Crux* constellation (the Southern Cross), which in the early historic period was visible to the civilisations of the Middle East and the Mediterranean, but which the process known as *precession* subsequently carried below the horizon in Europe. (Hinckley Allen 1963, p. 185)

The 'grapeshot' in the circle representing the stars of the *Crux* constellation are distinctly visible. The terminal of the short left arm has two small circles representing, respectively, the *Jewel Box Cluster* (NGC 4755) and *Beta Crucis* or *Becrux*. *Delta Crucis* forming the terminal of the right arm is also clearly visible. *Gamma Crucis* or *Gacrux* at the top of the cross is less easy to identify, although just visible. *Alpha Crucis* or *Acrux* at the bottom of the cross is almost invisible since it is caught up in a tramline.

The Southern Cross is not an equal-armed Celtic cross. It is a distinctive Christian Cross with a long southern arm, and this I think points to its importance in this context. So far as the Solar Logos is concerned, this Cross is the primary symbol for mankind today. If cosmic help is being invoked then it is that of the Christ Spirit of the Solar Logos.

The significance of the placing of this constellation pattern is thus evident. The Cross neutralises the negative energies of the man-made formation on the Michael-Mary Line, and is an invocation to the Solar Logos. *Upton Scudamore, Upton Scudamore CP, Wiltshire* (OS ST866472) on 2.7.1990

*The Boötes constellation pattern* (4.10 and 4.11)

The Forces of Darkness that summer also put down, through human agents, a further Triangle of Power, 18 miles away to the south west, but still on the Michael-Mary Line. This

*4.10 Upton Scudamore, Wiltshire (OS ST866472), 2.7.1990*

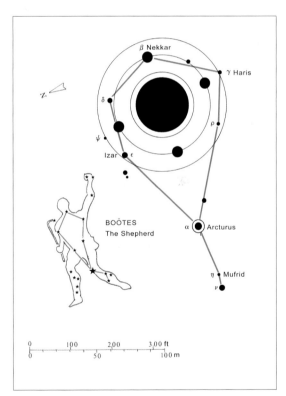

*4.11 'Boötes' constellation pattern*
*Upton Scudamore, 2.7.1990*

consisted of a tight little group of formations (none more than half a mile from each other) which were located at Upton Scudamore, Wiltshire. Although undoubtedly sequentially spaced, they all appeared on the same night of 2.7.1990.

It is a particular man-made formation, added to by the Light Workers, that is of interest in connection with this constellation pattern. This formation is a three-ringed quincunx, with the Earth Logos signature (a larger and a smaller circle, the smaller representing the moon) beside it. Arranged around the formation (but not in the central circle) is a pattern of ten 'grapeshot', which on careful examination proved to be the constellation pattern of *Boötes*. (4.11) Its pre-eminent star *Arcturus*, which is the brightest star north of the celestial equator (*Alpha Boötis*), is distinguished in the crop formation by being larger and having a ring. This star pattern is mostly of geophysical origin. The drawing, as in the case of the *Crux* constellation described above, is based on a careful plan by Wolfgang Schindler. The Light Workers reused one of the four man-made satellites for the star *Beta Nekkar*.

In the case of the *Boötes* constellation, the interest and significance lies in the history and attribution of the constellation in folklore and legend of the distant past. The name *Boötes* is of course the primary clue. To quote Hinckley Allen:

'The Italian **Boöte** and the French **Bouvier,** is transliterated from Βοώτης, which appeared in the *Odyssey*, so that our title has been in use for nearly 3000 years, perhaps for much longer ... The not infrequent title **Herdsman,** from the French Bouvier, also is appropriate, ... for **Pastor** the Shepherd, presumably is from the Arab idea of a *Fold* around the Pole or from the nearby flock in the Pasture towards the southeast ...' (Hinckley Allen 1963, pp. 92, 95)

There are other transliterations, but this I believe is the critical one following on with another biblical allusion to Jesus Christ, this time as the *Good Shepherd* as in "I am the good shepherd. The good shepherd lays down his life for the sheep. ... I know my own and my own know me." (*John* 10:11, 14) As in the case of the *Crux* formation, it is not only a symbol to neutralise the negativity of the Forces of Darkness, but also an appeal to the Christ Spirit of the Solar Logos.

## SIGNATURE SYMBOLS (4.12)

In 1990 it became clear that the Crop Circle Makers were actually signing the major formations. More is said later in this study, but I will here simply identify the three major types of signature symbols.

*4.12 The signatures of the Earth Logos (Ibez), the Solar Logos (Bel) and our Local Solar Group (Archon), respectively*

1. A large and small circle which I identify with our Earth Logos. At one level it might be considered a physical symbol of planet Earth and the Moon. However, in the light of the planetary and solar symbolism described later, it might be better viewed as the 'head and body' of the Earth Logos, *Ibez*.

2. A small and large ringed circle which I believe to represent our Solar Logos, *Bel*. The ring round the larger circle marks the achievement of the First Cosmic Initiation.

3. A small and large double-ringed circle which I believe is that of our local solar group, namely that Being whom I term *Archon*, who has achieved the Second Cosmic Initiation.

# 5. THE HUMAN MONAD: PSYCHIC STRUCTURE

*I am the tender voice calling away ...*
*I shine afar till men may not divine*
*Whether it is the stars or the beloved*
*They follow with rapt spirit.*

George William Russell (A.E.)
*Song and its Fountains, 1932, p. 108*

## SUMMARY

This chapter opens with my experience in the 1980s of *lucid dreaming* and the discovery of the Archetypes of my inner *personae*. The Indian term for such Beings is *Pitris*, and they showed me how they functioned, particularly through the dreamstate. They introduced me to some of the other intelligent entities who run my system. My conscious physical self was the *Personality*, beyond that again was my *Soul*, the spiritual interface between the *Form* aspect and the *Spirit*. In all there are seven principal Archetypes in the human system.

## THE INNER PERSONAE

It began in the early 1980s when I was travelling amongst the ancient classical sites of Turkey. Lucid dreaming is a strange experience where one is enabled to take a rational, active part in one's dreamstate, fully aware that it is a dream, and when awake to remember its substance. I was already familiar with the psychological work of Freud and Jung (particularly the latter) in terms of the autonomy of the Beings or Archetypes encountered in dreams. This knowledge enabled me to ask pertinent questions once I realised what was happening.

It quickly emerged that the human *persona* was a structured complex of living entities, of whom the upper echelons were intelligent, to a greater or lesser extent. These Beings operate at different levels, of which only those functioning at the lowest and most dense level of raw physicality are visually detectable. There is basically a sevenfold structure with infinite subdivisions ultimately working down to the physical atomic structure of the human corporeal system.

### The Pitris

There were four *personae* who ran my inner systems. I experienced them as an older and younger couple. They were fully conscious, intelligent entities, whose role as part of their own spiritual development was to manage my system of being, working to a higher entity, which might be termed my Soul.

Djwhal Khul describes in detail the origins and functions of such *Beings* whom he terms the solar and lunar *Pitris*. (Bailey 1925, p. 773) In the ancient world they were described as 'Lunar Lords' when they were concerned with the lower centres (or *chakras*) (see below) and Personality levels, or 'Solar Lords' when they were responsible for the upper, more cerebral or spiritual levels. The Indian, Sanskrit term *Pitr* can be translated as ancestors, not merely in terms of a remote bloodline, but as discarnate relatives who take an active interest in the spiritual progress of their descendants. In classical times the Roman world recognised such Beings as *Penates*, household gods and family ancestors who were worshipped at domestic shrines. The lunar *Pitris* are set in motion by the Soul at the beginning of the incarnation process, not merely that of a current life span of an individual, but all previous lives. They are thus in a very real sense 'ancestors' as defined above, who vivify progressively over many lifetimes the permanent atoms of the *energy bodies* of the human Monad – in turn, the causal (spiritual or buddhic), mental (or manasic), emotional (or astral) and physical bodies (the latter being a combination of the physical, the sacral and the etheric (which can be thought of as electromagnetic) energy body). These will be described and their functions explained in this and later chapters. Only then can the lunar *Pitris* begin their work and coordinate the substance of the conjoined physical/sacral/etheric body, and the bodies of the emotional, mental and causal membranes (the latter being the spiritual sheath of the Soul). Each body operates at a progressively finer vibration and forms an invisible sheath (but still detectable by dowsing and Kirlian photography, as identified by their different colour values). These sheaths form round the dense physical body, with the limits of the causal, spiritual or buddhic sheath being furthest away from the physical body. Each of my inner Entities or lunar *Pitris* was responsible for the working of one of my bodies:

*Older male*:  Causal Body
*Older female*:  Mental Body
*Younger male*: Emotional Body
*Younger female*: Physical Body.

These four *Pitris* can be seen as a direct reflection of the *Quaternio*, the four Rays of Attribute of our planet and the systems beyond.

If my *Pitris* were then counterparts of the four Rays of Attribute, where were the three Rays of Aspect in my system? As it gradually emerged, I, my conscious Personality, was Ray 3, the controlling aspect of form, who was expected to work closely with the four *Pitris* of my *Quaternio*. The other two Rays (1 and 2) were essentially angelic with overall command, and were working to form a closer and controlling link with my Personality. Ray 1, (my Spirit) I never consciously met in the dreamstate, and only on rare occasions Ray 2 (my Soul).

My lunar *Pitris* showed me many things. How they construct the framework, *personae* and background of my nightly dream sequences – all devised to balance the pressures of daily life. They showed me how objects, persons and landscape can be constructed by thought processes, and how difficult this is to carry out without considerable mental concentration and experience. They introduced me to other members of their team: lesser *Pitris* who operated specific areas of my metabolism and physicality. I remember being introduced to a *Pitr* whose responsibility was the functioning of my brain. She burst into a detailed, technical explanation of my cerebral functions – all this at 3 am. I must have yawned or shown some sign that I was not taking it in, and I remember that she was grievously offended! There were 98 or 104 other intelligent *Pitris* operating under their control – they could not remember the exact number.

All was going well in my terms, until one night I met a Being whom I had not encountered before in the dreamstate, and whom I now recognise to have been my Soul. This person was very much to the point. "If you go on asking the four *Pitris* silly questions and diverting them from their essential duties, I will put you in a position where you cannot ask any more questions." I took no notice and went on cross-questioning my internal *personae*. In due course, as warned, I lost the faculty of lucid dreaming. However, the *Quaternio* of *Pitris* still return on occasions when they need my conscious help in dealing with something in the mundane world, usually of a medical nature.

I have set down in outline my experiences of lucid dreaming and the important discoveries of my inner psychic management system because I believe it is a direct reflection of how other, higher states of cosmic management operate. This was a direct, personal experience. I am sure that every human individual has a similar structure of Beings with whom they are expected to work in a positive fashion by their higher spiritual selves, 'to accomplish the miracle of the one thing,' (Tyson 1995, p. 711) the 'One Thing' being, of course, *Spiritual Ascension*, whether that of a human being, a Planetary or Solar Logos, or even a Galactic Entity.

### Spirit, Soul and Personality

An essential distinction needs to be made at this point about the relationship between the Personality and Soul, and their higher counterpart, the Spirit. The *Spirit* has been defined as a Divine Spark (Reflection or Image) from the Deific Cosmic Fire. (Fortune 1976, p. 59) It is the Solar Angel who forms the focal point of every human being, and whose ultimate function is to enable the fully developed human organism to achieve its immortal destiny of attaining 'the consciousness of the higher self, and subsequently that of the Divine Spirit.' (Bailey 1922a, p. 64) The Spirit may also be described as the 'Indwelling Thinker' or 'Silent Watcher', and operates at a higher vibrational level which does not enable Him to control directly the lower functions of his being.

For the physical expression of the great work of human cosmogenesis to take place, the Spirit has to move to a lower gear and form another *persona*, that of the *Soul*. The Soul is a direct reflection of the character and characteristics of the Spirit, and in this sense it may be described as the *Logos* of the Spirit. As explained earlier, any *Logos* is the physical manifestation of a numinous spiritual Entity. The Soul may also be considered as the individualised or separated self, the Ego, which is defined as a 'conscious thinking subject.' (Oxford English Dictionary) Djwhal Khul elaborates about the Soul: 'The Ego, or the self-conscious Identity is in essence and in truth Love-Wisdom, but manifests primarily as intelligent consciousness.' (Bailey 1925, p. 684) The role of the Soul is to organise the components of the physical form and ensure their efficient operation. For this to be effected a further expression is required which I have termed the *Personality*, operating at a still lower vibrational level. 'The Ego synthesises or gathers in the life forces of the fourfold lower man' (Bailey 1925, p. 830), while at the same time engaging through its higher mental faculties with the Spirit. Or to put it another way, 'Matter is the vehicle for the manifestation of soul on this plane of existence; soul is the vehicle for the manifestation of spirit, and these three as a trinity are synthesised by Life, which pervades them all.' (Bailey 1922a, p. 223)

## THE HUMAN MONAD AS PREHISTORIC SYMBOLS

As far back as the fifth millennium BC, prehistoric petroglyphs were appearing in north-west Europe which conveyed spiritual teaching about the human condition. In particular this included material about the psychic structure of man, identifying the *chakras* (to use the Indian term) or *centres of force*, which I shall generally call *centres* in this book, and their relationship with the whole. Again it must be emphasised that these are two-dimensional diagrams trying to express transcendental concepts in symbolic form. The carvings are not of course annotated in any conventional sense, but usually there is sufficient detail to link the ideas conveyed with other known mandalic material, some of it very ancient.

*Idole des Pierres Plates*

The shamans and 'Stone-Kings' (see Introduction) of the ancient prehistoric world of north-west Europe must have had similar experiences to my lucid dreaming, or perhaps more direct communications on these matters. Certainly extraordinarily detailed information about the psychic structure of the human metabolism has survived as carvings on the standing stones of megalithic passage graves of the Morbihan region of Brittany dating from the fifth millennium BC. As in their counterparts in Ireland (see Introduction and Chapter 4), these sacred spaces had only a secondary use as tombs; their primary purpose was for spiritual teaching and initiation. The orthostats that line the passages and chambers are intricately carved with information about the nature of 'Ultimate Reality' as that ancient world perceived it.

The stone from the Pierres Plates Passage Grave (5.1 and 5.2) near Locmariaquer is one

5.1 **Stone 13, Pierres Plates Passage Grave**
*Locmariaquer, Brittany, fifth millennium BC*

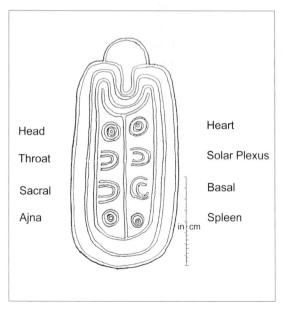

5.2 *The Centres of the human Monad*
*Stone 13 from the Pierres Plates Passage Grave*

of several from this site which have anthropomorphic entities symbolically depicted in a rectangular frame. The figure from stone no. 13 (Burl 1985, pp. 161-162) brings together a number of features of this type. It has the three envelopes of the psyche representing the physical, emotional and mental bodies. The rounded head symbolises the causal (spiritual) aspect. The curved shoulders carry a schematic necklace of authority with a central drop which acts as a division between the lower symbols.

The Pierres Plates carving is one of several decorated uprights from this passage grave, which appear to have in three other cases seven rings/cups divided into three and four by the central division. (Burl 1985, p. 160; Gagnière and Granier 1963, p. 41) On this basis these markings may be straightforwardly identified as the seven centres or chakras of the Divine/human Monad divided between the three Rays of Aspect and the four of Attribute. However this particular stone (Burl no. 13) has eight markings which are divided between rings and cups (i.e. solar symbolism) and double horns (i.e. lunar symbolism). The two upper rings and cups may perhaps be identified as the head centre (Spirit) and the heart centre (Soul). Three of the lunar centres have New Moons and may represent the throat, solar plexus and sacral centres. The fourth lunar symbol is that of the Old Moon, and represents in all probability the basal centre, that of carnal physicality. The two lowest, small ringed circles represent, I believe, the solar centres ajna, and spleen, of *Pranic* importance. The centres are discussed in detail in Chapter 6.

5.3 *'Earth Monad'*
*Carving on the underside of capstone of the north-east chamber of the Newgrange Passage Grave Ireland, c. 3200 BC*

### The Newgrange Capstone (5.3)

Another important petroglyph dealing in more detail with the same subject is carved onto the underside of the roof capstone of the north-east recess or initiation chamber of the megalithic Newgrange Passage Grave, Ireland. The carbon 14 evidence from this monument would suggest a date of c. 3200 BC. This capstone, which is covered with mandalic subjects, was probably reinstated here from some other feature of the earlier monument. As a consequence only part of the carving described here is visible. However, since there is a similar one immediately adjacent, we can postulate with some confidence that there was the same 'circle' arrangement here. The primary use of this recess was as an initiation chamber. Indeed the stone basin marked with the buttock positions of the initiate was found in situ.

I believe that this image represents the etheric structure of the Earth Logos in symbolic terms, which the human Monad copies on a minuscule scale. Three circles represent the 'head', but each is differentiated according to the number of haloes (including the initial circle). That on the left has three rings (Ray 3), that in the centre has 7 rings (Ray 1) and that on the right has 5 rings (Ray 2). The body comprises four rings or 'envelopes', which we have already identified from the centre outwards to be the physical, emotional, mental and causal bodies. These envelopes surround eight circles (the same number of symbols as on the *Idole des Pierres Plates*). One of the circles is ringed. The significance of this distinction may be in the fact that whereas the physical construct of the Earth is a transient vehicle for the Earth Logos, the Seven Spirits are eternal, as indeed they are in the case of the *Pitris* who are the physical creators of the human Monad. The principles of this ancient system are set out in the Vedic hymn *The Birth of the Gods* (Taittirīya Samhitā):

'The birth of the Gods ... in the primeval age ...

*as Being emerged from non-Being ...*

*Thence did divisions follow into existence*

*From the Infinite, [i.e. Spirit] Intelligence*

*was born.' [i.e. Form] 'Eight were the sons*

*of the Infinite born from Herself. With seven*

*she approached the Gods, Martanda she ...*

*brought forth for the sake of generation*

*and dissolution.'*

(Rig Veda Mandala 10 Hymn 72)

(For more on this see Miller 1985 and Daniélou 1985, p. 114)

As with other examples of prehistoric megalithic carving discussed in Chapter 4, this glyphic statement of the human psyche is amazingly spiritually perceptive. This is revealed knowledge imparted to the priesthood of these ancient peoples about numinous realities, as applicable today as then.

## THE CROP FORMATIONS

The geophysical crop circle makers have gone to some trouble to distinguish between these different and somewhat confusing aspects of the human psyche: namely the Solar and Lunar Lords (*Pitris*), the bodies, the centres and the different glands through which the centres vitalise the physical organs. (See the Alton Barnes 1996 and Fosbury 1997 formations, in Chapter 6.)

I turn now to the crop formations which appear to deal specifically with the psychic structure of the human Monad. Because of the complexity of our paraphysical constitution, the geophysical crop circle makers put down a series of formations between 1991 and 1998 dealing with different aspects, whose general sequence I have followed here.

I suspect that during this eight year period there were one or more formations put down every year in different parts of the country dealing with this momentous theme. Not all were necessarily identified, and some that might be regarded as statements about other aspects have been dealt with elsewhere in this study. Some small formations which may have had only a local significance have also been omitted.

*Goring Group, Oxfordshire and Berkshire,* July 1994

Three crop formations appeared in the Goring area of the South Midlands during the summer of 1994.

1. *Garsons Hill, Ipsden CP, Oxon* (OS SU647845). 10.7.1994, in wheat. This formation, which was concerned with the *initiations* which form part of the Ascension Process, is discussed in Chapter 9.

2. *Kingstanding Hill, Moulsford, Wallingford CP, Oxon* (OS SU567840). Earlier July (surveyed 16.7.1994), in wheat (5.4 and 5.5) Diameters and direction of flow, clockwise (cw) or anticlockwise (acw): (1) ring (acw), outer edge 199 ft, ring width 29 ft; (2) crescent (cw), outer diameter 199 ft. 8 circles: (3) 102 ft (cw); (4) 66 ft (acw); (5) 47 ft (cw); (6) 21 ft (centre acw – outside cw); (7) 15 ft (acw); (8) 7 ft 6 in (acw); (9) 4 ft 6 in (acw) and (10) 2 ft 6 in (acw).

3. *Shrill Down, East Ilsley CP, Berks* (OS SU491798). Surveyed 14.8.1994 by Anthony Cheke and Geoff Ambler, but probably laid down much earlier. Wheat? (5.6 and 5.7) Diameters and flow as 2. (6) Crescent, outer diameter 159 ft (acw), enclosing crescent in standing crop, outer diameter 84 ft. 5 circles: (5) 61 ft (acw); (4) 36 ft (cw); (3) 23 ft 6 in (acw); (2) 18 ft (acw), and (1) 15 ft (acw).

This beautiful and important group of formations was put down over 30 miles to the north-east of the main assemblage of crop circles in Wiltshire, no doubt with the intention that they should not be confused with those from Wessex, many of which were man-made in 1994.

*5.4 Kingstanding Hill, Moulsford, Oxfordshire (OS SU567840), early July 1994*

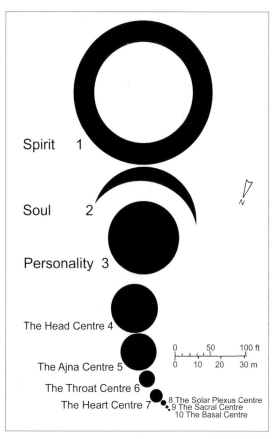

Spirit 1

Soul 2

Personality 3

The Head Centre 4

The Ajna Centre 5

The Throat Centre 6

The Heart Centre 7

8 The Solar Plexus Centre
9 The Sacral Centre
10 The Basal Centre

0   50   100 ft
0   10   20   30 m

*5.5 The Centres of the human Monad*
*Moulsford, early July 1994*

## THE CENTRES (OR CHAKRAS)

2. *The Moulsford formation* (5.4 and 5.5) carries the Ray 1 input of the group, concerned with the synthesis of Spirit and Matter, and the work of the Soul in the functioning human mechanism. Each element of the formation is carefully defined, and this, combined with the internal details, indicates that it is concerned with the function of the centres.

I deal in Chapter 6 with the significance and relationship of the human centres and the functioning of the *Antahkarana* in connection with the Alton Barnes formation of 1996. All that is necessary here is to tabulate the elements of the Moulsford formation. The triple aspects of the human Monad comprise:

1. Spirit symbolised as a ring of form or matter enclosing the unmanifested aspect of pure Spirit. As mentioned in Chapter 3, this critical aspect was represented by the *Bi* symbol in ancient China. This is the *Spirit* aspect of the human Monad.

2. The New Moon. The lunar crescent as the reflection of Spirit is shown as close to the ring of Spirit, and indeed appears to have the same diameter. This is the *Soul* aspect of the human Monad, and is characterised by Love-Wisdom.

3. The third aspect of the Monad is the polarity between Spirit and Matter. The circle which symbolises the third aspect is markedly larger than the rest of the circles and is set apart by some 20 ft from the remainder. This is the *Personality* aspect of the human Monad.

The remaining seven circles represent the seven centres, (the primary chakras), of the human Monad. They can be briefly tabulated as follows:

4. *The Head Centre* – seat of the Spirit

5. *The Ajna Centre* – interactive centre between the Spirit and Soul

6. *The Throat Centre* – seat of the Personality

7. *The Heart Centre* – seat of the Soul

8. *The Solar Plexus Centre* – Emotional focus

9. *The Sacral Centre* – Sexual focus

10. *The Basal Centre (Base of the Spine)* – Physical focus.

The circles representing the lower, essentially physical, centres, i.e. the heart centre (7), solar plexus centre (8), sacral centre (9) and basal centre (10) all had an anticlockwise crop flow. Circle 6, identified here as symbolising the throat centre, i.e. linked to the intelligence factor of mankind, had an anticlockwise movement of the crop in the centre which changed to a clockwise motion towards the outside of the circle. This is a most unusual feature, and was undoubtedly meant to symbolise the fact that whereas this is a physical organ, its source of inspiration is spiritual. The direction of the crop lay of the different features at the top of the formation alternated between clockwise (2, 3, and 5) and anticlockwise (1 and 4). Now this use of the flow to distinguish between radically different 'states of being' does not appear to work on the rather simplistic basis that clockwise = spiritual and anticlockwise = form, but rather that the change of direction of the flow represents a distinct change of consciousness compared with that of the element that went before.

The colossal variation in size between, say, the three lowest centres concerned with physicality and the others, reflects not only in general terms the infinitely greater importance of the higher centres, but also has, I believe, a mathematical application. This may refer not only to the higher vibration of the centres on the Upper Planes, but may also be linked in some way to the etheric structures of the various planes. (See Chapter 8 on the planes and ethers.) Djwhal Khul states that:

'... matter and ether are synonymous terms and that this ether is found in some form or other on all the planes, and is but a gradation of cosmic atomic matter, called when undifferentiated mulaprakriti' (i.e. undifferentiated substance) 'or primordial pre-genetic substance, and when differentiated by Fohat (or the energising Life, the third Logos or Brahma) it is termed prakriti, or matter.' (Bailey 1925, p. 118)

## THE ENERGY BODIES

3. *The East Ilsley formation* (5.6 and 5.7) fulfils the role of Ray 3, that concerned with form, or matter organised by Active Intelligence. As might be expected, it deals with the six *energy bodies* of the human metabolism, that aspect of the human Monad most directly concerned with physicality.

In metaphysical studies, the symbolism of the number 6 is most important. Djwhal Khul has somewhat to say on the subject:

'... six is the number of the great work of the period of manifestation, ... is ... the lower nature as far as man is concerned, and' (at one level) 'is all that which seeks to destroy the higher life, but also that which can be controlled and directed finally by the soul.' (Bailey 1951, p. 128) 'The goal of all the initiatory process is to admit mankind into realisation of and identification with the will and purpose

5.6 *Shrill Down, East Ilsley, Berkshire (OS SU491 798), early August 1994*

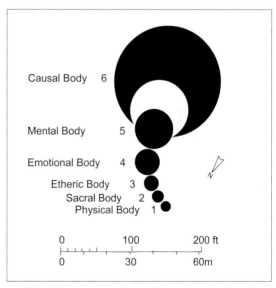

5.7 **The Energy Bodies of the human Monad** *East Ilsley, early August 1994*

of Deity. The number 6 is the number of form or of manifestation, which is the agent or medium through which this realisation comes and by which the consciousness is unfolded so that it can become the foundation of the higher process which is instituted at the third initiation.' (Bailey 1960, p. 79)

The three Goring formations thus have a common structure indicating a particular theme (the human Monad in this case), but the details vary considerably. The Ring, the symbol of Spirit, is found in both the Ipsden and the Moulsford formations, but is omitted at East Ilsley to be replaced by the lunar crescent, which here is the symbol of the Soul. This indeed is one of the clues to the interpretation of this formation.

The sixfold physical structure of the human Monad (including the invisible 'etheric' bodies) may be tabulated as follows starting with the smaller circles at the bottom of the formation. (5.7)

1. The *Physical Body* which is the template for all the structures of the human Monad, whether physical or etheric. 'So God created humankind in his image, in the image of God he created them.' (*Genesis* 1:27)

2. The *Sacral Body* is concerned with all aspects of sex and reproduction.

3. The *Etheric Body*. This is a structure operating at a higher vibrational level, but replicating the physical form. Circles 1-3 were anticlockwise, since they represent the basic physical structure of the human Monad.

4. The *Emotional Body*. For the generality of mankind this forms the centre of gravity or main focus. The direction of flow of the crop changes to a clockwise rotation.

5. The *Mental Body*. This is the seat of the Personality in advanced mankind. It is susceptible to 'soul energy', and this is symbolised by having the circle metaphorically 'gripped' by the crescent of the causal body formation.

6. The *Causal Body*. Above the mental body lies the *causal body*, the highest aspect of the 6-part structure of the human Monad. As its name suggests it is the source of the deepest motivation of the ordinary person. It is also the seat of the Soul, and this is symbolised by its crescent shape, since like the New Moon it reflects the light of the spiritual Sun of the Spirit. The Moulsford formation used the same symbol for the 'Soul'. The planned function of this body is to reflect the spiritual aspect of the human Monad. However, because the non-spiritual person is full of dark and worldly motivation, it influences the other five bodies adversely and thus seeks 'to destroy the higher life'. The Soul seeks to dominate the situation and pour the spiritual light of its 'crescent' into the bodies of the Monad.

The East Ilsley crop formation brilliantly illustrates this process by having the mental body 'gripped', as it were, by the pincers of the Soul, Who, if all goes well, will transform all the bodies of the human metabolism in the course of the spiritual Ascension Process.

The relationship and structure of the above energy bodies 1-6 are analysed in greater detail in connection with the Fosbury formation of 1997. (Chapter 6) As with the Moulsford formation, the relative sizes of the elements of the formation are likely to be of mathematical significance.

# 6. THE HUMAN MONAD: THE FUNCTION OF THE ANTAHKARANA

*Oh Lord ... I praise you, for I am fearfully and wonderfully made: wonderful are your works ...*

*Psalm 139:14*

## SUMMARY

This chapter looks in more detail at the psycho-physical make-up of the human Monad. The Alton Barnes formation of 1996 is in the form of a DNA Double Helix with sine waves. It is basically in the shape of the eastern *Antahkarana* with the Life, Consciousness and Creativity threads (*Sutratrama*). It is thus a demonstration of the union of the Triplicity of Spirit reaching through and down the psyche of the human Monad to bring about Spiritual Life. Each of the centres is discussed. This whole long process of death and renewal is an essential motor of spiritual growth, not merely in humanity but in all Beings throughout the Cosmos. The Fosbury formation of 1997 develops the theme of the *Antahkarana*, also a feature of the Birling formation of 1998, discussed in Chapter 7.

## THE ANTAHKARANA

In Chapters 7 to 10 we will consider aspects of the role of the human Monad in its destined progression in the spiritual Ascension Process. Such matters as the planes, the initiations and the basic composition of the human Monad are essentially *cosmic structures* that are already in place. The teaching of the crop circle phenomenon about building the *Antahkarana*, or 'Lighted Way', however, brings us to an area where the human Personality has a conscious role to play.

But first a definition: the *Antahkarana* term in classical Sanskrit means the *inner faculties*, (Daniélou 1985, p. 27) but it is indeed much more.

In metaphysical terms it may be defined as '*The path, or bridge,* between higher and lower mind, serving as a medium of communication between the two. *It is built by the aspirant himself in mental matter.*' (my italics) (Bailey 1922a, p. 215)

Djwhal Khul, as ever, has some apposite remarks to make on the subject:

'One of the points which it is essential that students should grasp is the deeply esoteric fact that this Antahkarana is built through the medium of a conscious effort *within consciousness itself*, and not just by attempting to be good, or to express goodwill, or to demonstrate the qualities of unselfishness and high aspiration ... It is all that, but *it is something far more*. Good character and good spiritual aspiration are basic essentials ... But

6.1 Alton Barnes, Wiltshire (OS SU114625), 17.6.1996

to build the antahkarana is to relate the three divine aspects. This involves intense mental activity; it necessitates the power to imagine and visualise, plus a dramatic attempt to build the Lighted Way in mental substance ... and the bridge of Living Light is a composite creation having in it:

1. Force, focussed and projected from the fused and blended forces of the personality.

2. Energy, drawn from the egoic body by a conscious effort.

3. Energy, abstracted from the Spiritual Triad.

It is essentially, however, an activity of the integrated and dedicated personality ... aided by the Soul.' (Bailey 1960, p. 467)

## THE ALTON BARNES FORMATION, 1996 (6.1 AND 6.2)

This was the first of two important formations in Wiltshire in 1996 and 1997 depicting in schematic form the structure of the human psyche. The beautiful linear formation found in the East Field at Alton Barnes, Alton CP, Wiltshire (OS SU114625) appeared on 17.6.1996. The aerial photo shows the spiral construction of the circles of the formation, indicative of a geophysical origin.

The formation attracted attention at the time due to its similarity to the familiar DNA double helix. It also represents *sine waves*. (Parrott 2002, p. 40) The formation thus has a recognisable scientific structure, but it also has a psychic format, the two almost certainly linked. It sets out some of the elements of the human Monad showing their interrelationships. The primary feature is the *Antahkarana*, which is depicted as three component elements or 'threads' (*Sutratrama*) (see illustration 6.2) namely:

1. The 'Life' thread (*Sushumna*), which is directly related to the will of the Monad or Father, who can thus 'reach the personality in a direct manner, and can arouse the basic centre, and with it blend, unify and raise the three fires.' (Bailey 1953, p. 183) This process is known in esoteric circles as raising the *Kundalinī* fire, but with the important *caveat* that this is strictly the work of the Spirit and not that of the Personality. (*Kundalinī* = 'the coiled-energy').

2. The 'Consciousness' thread (*Pingala*), which equates with the Mother aspect (matter intelligently organised), and is concerned with the vivification of form.

3. The 'Creativity' thread (*Ida*), which equates with the Son or Soul aspect whose primary quality is Love-Wisdom.

The *Antahkarana* is thus nothing less than the union of the Triplicity of Spirit reaching through and down the psyche of the human Monad to bring about Life, Quality and Appearance. Thus does the Spiritual Monad grip the human Personality, through the psychic structure of the body, to achieve eventual ascension and apotheosis of His human Monad. The *Kundalinī* is thus an expression of the active power (*Sákti*) of the One, which in the microcosm of the human Monad expresses itself initially as a dormant energy, coiled like a serpent. However, when awakened by the human Monad, it will destroy the illusion of matter, permitting the crossing beyond the five spheres of manifestation to achieve spiritual liberation.

The other striking feature of this formation, apart from its overall pattern, is the multiplicity of circles, 89 in all, varying in size from 50 ft to 3 ft in diameter. These represent in schematic and symbolic form the centres of the human Monad. The centres are not physical organs, but 'whirlpools of force that swirl etheric, astral and mental matter into activity ...' (Bailey 1925, p. 167) Each comprises 'three concentric interblending whorls or wheels' whose rotation, with the spiritual development of the human Monad, is intensified to become 'scintillating radiation, a "wheel turning upon itself" in four dimensions'. (Précis from Bailey 1934, p. 362)

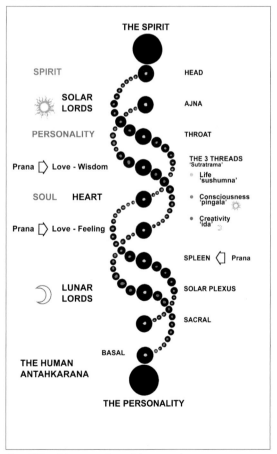

6.2 *'The Human Antahkarana'*
*Alton Barnes, 17.6.1997*

These spheres of fire or pure life force form 'the body of fire' which eventually is all that is left, first to man in the three worlds, and later to the Monad. This is the 'imperishability' of 1 *Corinthians* 15:53 'and is the product of evolution, of the perfect blending of the three fires, which ultimately destroy the form.' (Bailey 1925, p. 166) For the individual on the spiritual path, it is the natural product of personal 'purification, conformity to rule, and an aspiration that brooks no hindrance and that ceases not for pain.' (Bailey 1934, p. 363) The centres in turn vitalise the physical organs of the body through different glands as indicated below.

'The etheric body is a body composed entirely of lines of force and of points where these lines of force cross each other and thus form (in crossing) centres of energy ... and where great streams of energy meet and cross, as they do in the head and up the spine, you have seven major centres.' (Bailey 1953, p. 72) 'When the form is destroyed there is left this intangible spiritual body of fire, one pure flame, distinguished by seven brilliant centres of intenser burning. This electric fire is the result of the bringing together of the two poles and demonstrates at the moment of complete at-one-ment, the occult truth of the words "Our God is a Consuming Fire" (*Hebrews* XII 29).' (Bailey 1925, pp. 166-167)

In the crop formation the Spirit and Personality are symbolically represented by 50 ft diameter circles at the ends of the 660 ft long figure. They are interlinked by ten 30 ft diameter circles which represent the seven major centres together with three lesser centres which I have selected as being of special significance. The *Pingala* and *Ida* threads are made up of swirling lesser centres varying in size from 20 ft to 3 ft in diameter, totalling 77. Djwhal Khul states that there are 7 major centres, 21 lesser centres and 49 smaller centres (see Bailey 1953, p. 72), giving a total of 77 centres, the same (apart from the central 10) as in the formation.

We turn now to the ten centres forming the spine of the Alton Barnes formation. I have followed in my drawing the traditional arrangement of the seven centres (chakras), with the head centre at the top. I have also inserted three other lesser but important centres at relevant positions. These brief notes below hardly do justice to the complexity of this subject, which is covered in detail by Djwhal Khul in the various works transcribed by Alice Bailey.

Of the seven, three centres reflect directly the threefold nature of the Monad, namely

6.3  6.4

*Examples of Celtic heads from the fourth century BC, showing the Ajna Centre physically expressed as the two lobes of the pituitary body. Left, obelisk from Pfalzfeld, Germany. Right, stele from Holzgerlingen, Germany*

the head centre (Spirit, Will or Power), the heart centre (the Soul or Ego characterised by Love and Wisdom), and the throat centre (the Personality characterised by Active Intelligence). The other centres are primarily concerned with the physical, mental and emotional bodies (as described earlier, see also the following formation at Fosbury).

*The Head Centre* is the seat of the Monad, its reflection in the Soul and its interpreter the Mind. It registers purpose and corresponds to the electrical fire of the solar system. It is dynamic in character. Its dense physical externalisation is the pineal gland in the head.

*The Ajna Centre* is to be found between the eyebrows. It relates the Monad to the Personality through the Soul acting 'as a screen for the radiant beauty and the glory of the spiritual man.' (Bailey 1953, p. 147) It is thus closely related to the throat centre which constitutes its further expression as creative activity. Its physical expression is the two lobes of the pituitary body. This gland has esoterically 96 'petals' or units of force, and may thus be the seat of corporeal intelligences of the human Monad mentioned earlier in this book. It reflects the dual aspect of the Monad: spiritual will (*Atma*) and spiritual love (*Buddhi*). Prehistoric, particularly Celtic, iconography sometimes depicted deities with this centre symbolised as two 'balloons' on either side of the head, something that would have been visible to the etheric vision of the shaman. The relief head on the obelisk from Pfalzfeld, St Goar, Germany (6.3) dating to the fourth century BC (Rheinisches Landesmuseum, Bonn), is a good example. (Raftery 1990, p. 47) The stone figure with Janiform head from Holzgerlingen, Württemberg (6.4) of similar date is another example. (Württemberg Landesmuseum, Stuttgart) (MacCana 1970, p. 58)

*The Throat Centre* synthesises the life of the Personality and connects to the mental plane. For the vast majority of advanced people at this time, the throat centre is the most developed since it is concerned with the intellectual processes which constitute the 'beginning of wisdom' for mankind. As such it has been regarded as the first spiritual initiation: a point where there is a general coordination of the physical, emotional and mental capacities of the individual. However, amongst the 'older' Souls of our system, this is where the Third Initiation takes place: where buddhic intuitive wisdom is the determining factor that signifies admission to the Spiritual Path. (See Chapters 8 and 9.) The throat centre is specifically the organ of the 'Word' or *Logos*, where the spiritual person expresses the concepts of the Soul, behind whom stands the Monad. The physical organ of the throat centre is the thyroid gland, which in itself is of great importance in balancing the physical metabolism of the human body.

*The Heart Centre* is the seat of life and constitutes the highest principle which expresses itself through man. It 'corresponds to the "heart of the Sun" and therefore to the spiritual source of light and love.' (Bailey 1953, p. 156) As such it is the seat of the Soul. It is the organ for the distribution of planetary spiritual energy poured out via the Soul into the heart centre of all humanity on the spiritual path after the Second Initiation. This brings about the critical regeneration of humanity through love. The physical organ is the thymus gland, which, when working in balance with the pineal gland of the head centre and the adrenal glands of the basal centre, helps govern and direct the spiritual person so that the divine purpose is achieved.

*The Solar Plexus Centre* is the seat of the emotional life of the human Monad. It is a lower reflection of the heart centre in the sense that the individual might have 'feelings' about something or somebody, but the person acting from the heart centre would actually get on and *do* something positive about the situation. It is the aim of the Soul working through the ajna centre to raise the centre of consciousness of the human Monad from the solar plexus centre to the heart centre. In the words of Djwhal Khul: 'He *must* transmute desire into aspiration.' (Bailey 1953, p. 170) The physical organ of this centre is the pancreas operating in conjunction with the liver and stomach. Ordinary humanity is centred here.

*The Sacral Centre.* A necessary distinction needs to be made at the outset between *sacral*, i.e. pertaining to the *sacrum*, a physical structure in the abdomen, and the other meaning of the word, *sacred*. The sacral centre is in the area of the sacrum, and controls the sex life of the human Monad. It is, as might be imagined, a powerful centre for the generality of mankind. At a higher level it corresponds to the creative aspect of the physical sun 'the source of vitality, and the life-giving agent on our planet.' (Bailey 1953, p. 176) It is primarily concerned with the gestation and organisation of matter, and as such forms a Triangle of Force with the spleen (the organ of *Prana* – see below) and the basal centre (the life-force of the human Monad). The gonads or sexual organs are the physical expression of the sacral centre.

As Djwhal Khul emphasises: 'sex is, in reality, the instinct towards unity; first of all, a physical unity.' It is also 'the urge to union with the divine' (Bailey 1953, p. 180), a metaphor or aspiration at a spiritual level towards that greater unity between the physicality of the Personality and the numinous of the divine Monad.

*The Basal Centre* (the centre at the base of the spine) is, in the words of Djwhal Khul, 'above everything else, controlled and governed by the Law of Being ... where spirit and matter meet.' (Bailey 1953, p. 181) As the essential life-force of the human Monad it thus has a close relationship with the heart centre, the seat of the Soul, by whom it is ultimately awakened and transformed by linkage along the *Sushumna* path. The physical organs associated with this centre are the adrenal glands, whose secretions produce 'animal courage and resistance to shock.' (Bailey 1957, p. 119)

These then are the seven primary centres of the human Monad which the clairvoyant can see as fiery wheels situated in or around the physical body (the head and spine particularly). The Alton Barnes formation in 1996, however, has ten centres along its spine (not including the two large circles at the top and bottom). The three remaining ones are those concerned with the admission of *Prana* (Life Energy) to the human metabolism. This is of critical importance at this time when humanity is facing great challenges to its physical and spiritual survival. This physical vitality, essential for the corporeal and higher development of mankind, has as its source the nuclear energies of the Sun, both in its physical form and as the 'Light behind the Light'. Djwhal Khul alludes to the three centres which receive the solar force but without going into any great detail. (Bailey 1925, p. 98)

The three centres form a dynamic triangle which only in this and future ages will begin to be fully activated:

1. The apex of the triangle is a centre which I have termed that concerned with '*Love-Wisdom*'. It is 'between the shoulder blades; this centre is between the throat centre and the heart centre in the spinal column, but nearer the heart than the throat.' (Bailey 1934, p. 433) Its input into the human system is that concerning the higher centres, and in particular the *Manas* principle (intelligence) of the higher (abstract) mind and the lower (concrete) mind, together with the altruistic love principle, the distinctive quality of the Logos of our solar system.

2. The second aspect of the *Prana* input is that which I have termed the '*Love-Feeling*' centre, which is focussed above the diaphragm. It is concerned with stimulating the emotional life, the will-to-good of the human Monad, and raising these aspirations for their practical activity in the heart centre. However the solar plexus centre which is already over-active amongst humanity has ensured that the love-feeling centre had been effectively in abeyance until now.

3. The *Spleen* centre is the third component of the *Prana* input, that which is most vitally concerned with the input of Life Energy into the human Monad. The physical organ has been described as 'a ductless gland of irregular form ... situated at the cardiac end of the stomach in man ... [which] serves to produce certain changes in the blood.' (Oxford English Dictionary) The spleen until now has been the most active source of *Prana* for mankind since working in conjunction with the physical organ of the heart 'it pervades the entire physical body through the medium of the blood stream, for "the blood is the life".' (Bailey 1942, p. 62)

In conclusion it should be emphasised that the centres as they have been enumerated above have three main functions:

'First, to vitalise the physical body.

Second, to bring about the development of self-consciousness in man.

Third, [most important of all] to transmit spiritual energy and sweep the entire man into a state of spiritual being.' (Bailey 1934, p. 285)

## THE FOSBURY FORMATION, 1997 (6.5 AND 6.6)

The (relatively) straightforward teaching set out in the Alton Barnes formation of 1996 was taken a step further the next year. The new formation concerning the human Monad appeared in wheat on 5.8.1997 adjacent to Fosbury Fort (Wiltshire) near Vernham Dean, (Hampshire) (OS SU325562).

This was a complex linear formation with adjuncts set within a curved path outline indicating that it should be viewed as a unitary, discrete entity (i.e. a *Monad*). The formation appears to show how the human *Antahkarana* operates, vivifying the four 'energy bodies' of the human metabolism, and their relationship to certain key centres.

Within the outline, the *physical body* is symbolised by a group of three circular units at the base of the formation. It attempts in symbolic form to illustrate the structure which Djwhal Khul describes as being 'triple in design' (Bailey 1950, p. 152). 'In the human body ... we have an underlying, interpenetrating vital body which is the counterpart of the physical ... It is an energy body and is composed of force centres and nadis or force threads.' (Bailey 1934, p. 500) The *nadis* are the counterpart of veins in the human body and convey electromagnetic energy derived from the *Pingala* and *Ida* threads passing down through the centres, as described in the Alton Barnes formation of 1996. Since these energies ultimately derive from the centres concerned with the admission of *Prana*, they may be described as essentially solar in origin.

The dense physical body balances the etheric body at the base of the formation. If the etheric body is the left hand circle, the right hand circle complex represents two closely linked units separated by the crescent moon. If the overall right-hand circle symbolises the physical body, the inner circle clasped by the moon represents the sacral body, the unit concerned with sexual reproduction (see sacral centre). The moon, yes, symbolises form, but elsewhere the crop circle makers have used the new moon image to depict the Soul. Here the Soul clasps one of the essential functions of the human Monad

– the necessity to carry on the species. It is significant that the ringed circle to which the lower circles feed in is also lunar, again emphasising the close function of the Soul in the physical unit. But the lunar symbolism does not end there, since it represents the *old moon*, because the physical vehicle is ultimately subject to decay and death.

The remainder of the formation above the physical body consists of four elements: the other three bodies of the human Monad; the two groups of conjoined centres; the *Pingala* and *Ida* threads swinging from side to side of the formation (B and C); and the *Sushumna* thread running vertically through the middle (A).

*The Emotional Body* is an important body of the triad (i.e. the mental body, the emotional body and the physical body) that makes up the lowest unit of the human Monad, namely

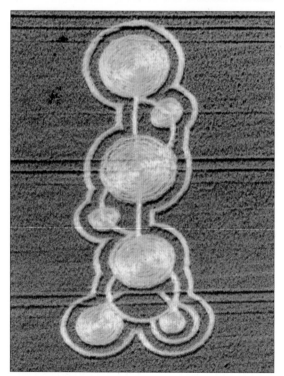

6.5 *Fosbury Fort, near Vernham Dean, Wiltshire (OS SU325562), 5.8.1997*

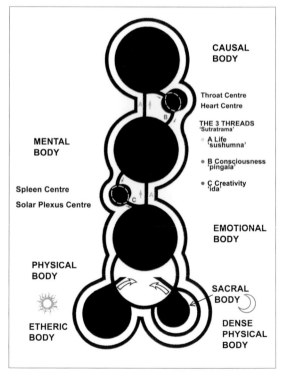

6.6 *'The Human Antahkarana'*
*Fosbury Fort, 5.8.1997*

the Personality. Important because it is the focus of activity for most of humanity, and for the person on the spiritual path the 'desire vibration' (its most characteristic feature) has to be eliminated and 'selfish inclination transmuted into spiritual aspiration.' (Bailey 1922b, p. 98) The emotional body is closely linked to the physical body, as indeed is shown in the Fosbury formation where it overlaps and dominates the lower ringed circle.

The *Ida* thread conveying 'creativity' (C) enters the circle in the upper left-hand corner where it is shown as passing through and conveying the energies of two conjoined centres to the emotional body. As might be expected, one of these centres is that of the solar plexus, conveying the physical energies: the other is the spleen centre conveying the solar *Prana* energies.

*The Mental Body* 'is the vehicle of the intelligent energy of will that is destined to be the dominant creative aspect' for mankind in the future. (Bailey 1942, p. 8) As such it is the transmitter of soul energy which, functioning properly, is 'the organ of relationship to all other human races.' (Bailey 1954, p. 126) The consequence for the individual is that the *Antahkarana* between the higher mind and the mental sheath is built. In other words it becomes 'a transmitter of the thoughts and wishes of the Solar Angel [the Soul], and should act as the agent for the Triad.' (i.e. the lower three bodies) (Bailey 1925, p. 1103)

The *Pingala* thread conveying consciousness (B) enters the circle in the upper right-hand corner where it is shown as passing through and carrying the energies of two conjoined centres to the mental body. One of these is obviously the throat centre, which is concerned with intelligence and represents the highest centre of the Personality. The other is the heart centre, the seat of the Soul.

*The Causal Body*, the highest of the circles depicted in the Fosbury formation, is in many respects the most important in terms of its spiritual significance for the individual. It is 'causal' in the sense that being the 'seat' of the Spirit, it is the originator of the Personality aspects of the human Monad (the lower self, the physical plane man) set out in the lower structures of the crop formation. Unlike, say, the etheric body, it does not take up the shape of its physical counterpart, but is essentially a formless container of two vital aspects, the Soul (*Buddhi*) and the Higher Mind (*Manas*), together reflecting the third, higher aspect, Spiritual Will (*Atma*). Djwhal Khul says: 'The Causal Body is a collection of permanent atoms, three in all, enclosed in an envelope of mental essence.' (Bailey 1922b, p. 30)

The crop formation shows the causal body as linked both to the consciousness thread (*Pingala*) and to the life thread (*Sushumna*), the latter running vertically down the figure with the mental, emotional and physical bodies in alignment. It is therefore evident that the Fosbury formation represents in symbolic form the perfected, spiritual human Monad. In the case of average man, who is not on the spiritual path, there is a discontinuity between the mental body and the causal body. The bridging of this gap in etheric matter, so that the *Kundalini* fire of spiritual ascension can rise, has to be achieved by an act of will on the part of the person on the spiritual path. As the aspirant cleanses himself and seeks the higher good through obedience to the spiritual laws and service to his fellow man, so he automatically builds the *Antahkarana* in mental matter. It is a critical development for the individual, for without it there can be no spiritual progress.

# 7. THE HUMAN MONAD: THE MODES OF BEING

*'Therefore be full of joy, O pilgrim on the Way towards enlightened Being, for gain and loss are one; darkness and light eternally reveal the True; love and desire eternally invoke the Life. Naught disappears but pain. Nothing remains but bliss, – the bliss of knowledge true, of contact real, of light divine, the Way to God.'*

Djwhal Khul from the 'Old Commentary'

Bailey 1942, pp. 33-34

## SUMMARY

First we study the formation at East Dean in West Sussex which appeared at the same time as the Goring Group in Oxfordshire, and is closely related to the formation from East Ilsley, Berkshire. (Chapter 5) It shows the energy bodies of the human Monad, which I treat in terms of successive 'modes of being'. Each individual has five 'sheaths' or psychic 'envelopes', one for each 'body', which are successively discarded during the Ascension Process. At the end of this long process the human Monad stands free of the need to take any further physical forms as it moves into higher spiritual realms.

We have seen how each individual is, essentially, *a sum of parts*: a complex group of living Entities carefully structured and organised. In Chapter 5 the components are described in detail. In Chapter 6 we saw how this human organism is so interrelated that the spiritual *Ascension Process* can be facilitated. In this chapter we consider the Birling formation from North Kent in 1998, in effect a summary of the teaching concerned with the psycho-physical structure of the human Monad, and how each centre (chakra) is not only a psychic organ but also an experiential state, or 'mode of being' which is encountered in the Ascension Process.

## THE EAST DEAN FORMATION, 1994 (7.1 AND 7.2)

*East Dean (S.B. (Sussex Branch of the CCCS) ref. 94.08) West Sussex* (OS TQ896136). 23-24.7.1994, in barley.

Diameters in feet. Direction of flow all anticlockwise. The largest element was a ringed circle (1-3) 128 ft to the outer edge of the ring. Circles: (4) 84 ft, (5) 62 ft, (6) 38 ft and (7) 21 ft. To these were added various grapeshot several days later, of uncertain origin. The largest of the grapeshot, south of circle 7, 5 ft in diameter, appears to be geophysical and associated with circle 7.

There are five main elements to this formation, and on this basis alone it could be postulated that we are dealing with five 'bodies' of the human Monad, namely:

Physical Body – (including the sacral body) – circle 7

7.1 *East Dean, West Sussex (OS TQ896136), 23/24.7.1994*

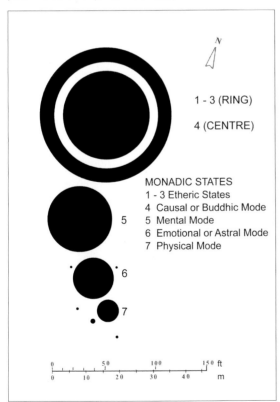

1 - 3 (RING)

4 (CENTRE)

N

MONADIC STATES
1 - 3 Etheric States
4 Causal or Buddhic Mode
5 Mental Mode
6 Emotional or Astral Mode
7 Physical Mode

7.2 **The Modes of Being of the human Monad** *East Dean, 23/24.7.1994*

Etheric Body – possibly grapeshot adjacent to circle 7

Emotional Body – circle 6

Mental Body – circle 5

Causal Body – composite circle 1-3 and 4.

However, as indicated above, I wish to consider this formation as a statement about the 'modes of being' which are encountered by the human Monad as part of 'the force of evolution which drives the Ego [Soul] to progress through the cycle of reincarnation back to union with his kind.' (Bailey 1925, p. 583)

I therefore intend to treat this formation as a paradigm of *change* for the human Monad and regard the process as developing 'modes of being' rather than 'bodies'. The Greater Master discusses in some detail this necessary progression (Fortune 1976, pp. 119-123), which He describes as *the Law of the Seven Deaths*. As emphasised elsewhere in this study, this is a fundamental key process in the development of the One, and all Monads at every level of the Cosmos.

As the Greater Master puts it: 'Life, having evolved beyond the capacity of lowly forms to give it expression, builds itself higher forms ... It is only by the abandonment of the simpler form that life could enter the more complex, though the consciousness that is in the plane of the simpler form sees therein a tragedy because it cannot conceive the higher life and it sees its own passing prefigured; but the consciousness which is of the higher life sees the birth of a new manifestation and rejoices, for it sees the further expression of its potentialities.' (Fortune 1976, p. 119)

In Chapter 8 I describe more fully the progressive development of the human Monad which can be summarised here.

First, the *Physical Mode* (Level 7, the lowest monadic state). (This includes the etheric body – see above.) This is essential for the Monad since it holds the greatest potential for spiritual development due to the life-experience function of its environment, which includes the sacral functions or procreation. All seeking spiritual development on planet Earth will have as many lives as is necessary to achieve this aim – reincarnations which involve a multitude of different experiences and challenges.

Death on the physical plane necessarily involves the destruction of the physical body and separation from the husk or shell of the etheric body. If a 'natural' death is involved the process takes about three days. This stage of departure for many is often described like passing through a dark tunnel with a light at the far end where are gathered together loved ones who have come to greet the departing spirit. Since the old etheric body carries within it the memories of the life just past (and indeed previous lives), these are passed to the Soul and the new etheric form, and have given rise to the expression 'All my past flashed before my eyes' as part of the death experience. At this stage also the emotional, mental and causal bodies are released from the physical form, and can be psychically seen as issuing from either the solar plexus centre (in the case of the generality of mankind) or the head centre (in the case of spiritual persons). As the old etheric shell carries with it the memories, or more accurately the mental habits, of its former state, this sometimes takes the form of a ghost literally repeating the habits of a lifetime. In my home in London the invisible etheric shell of a former Victorian servant girl waits outside her bedroom door at the top of the stairs. Every morning at dawn she can be heard going downstairs to light the former kitchen fires in the basement, something she did every day of her working life. In time the etheric shell will dissolve as the old memory habits fade. A new etheric body is constructed in the border zone between the physical and emotional (or astral) planes. (Chapter 8)

Next, the *Emotional or Astral Mode* (Level 6). In its new state on the emotional (or astral) plane, also called the 'Summerland', the Personality has a new etheric body, but carries with it the old (formerly invisible) emotional body, which now becomes the new physical sheath. This can be a major problem for some. A kind, decent person in life on the physical plane will have automatically constructed a healthy, attractive emotional body. However those individuals who have lived selfish, disagreeable lives full of violence and hatred will emerge in the 'Summerland' with an unpleasant, diseased emotional body which is all too obvious to those around them. These need immediate attention from those amongst the Wise who specialise in the healing of such, usually in the lower *ethers* (see Chapter 8) of the emotional plane.

Jane Sherwood, a medium who had lost her husband during the First World War in 1916, discusses in some detail the working of the emotional plane. Sherwood had three communicants. The one that concerns us here is Andrew, her former husband. Andrew speaks of the new existence: 'The astral [the emotional body] is usually undeveloped at first, often diseased and seldom under ego [Soul] control. The next process, that of the maturing and discarding of the astral will therefore be delayed until maturity is reached.

So the era of our existence on the astral planes is usually the longest term of the whole cycle. It seems to me that the purifying and perfecting of the emotional body is our main task here. Eventually, when this is completed, the astral substance will be cleansed and cured, the body well formed and controlled by the ego and the man as astral being will enjoy a supremely happy maturity. This, after a longer or shorter time, will pass into a gradual decay, or rather, gradual transformation, into the next order of being. Then the mature and beautiful astral body will be left behind but before this ... it will have passed on to the ego the essence and meaning of its whole long existence with all the poignant variety of its emotional experiences throughout this cycle of living.' (Sherwood 1969, pp. 177, 178)

This fascinating 'take' by Andrew on the purpose of the emotional plane is, I believe, a necessary corrective to the descriptions by the Ascended Masters such as Djwhal Khul, who, having passed through this mode of being aeons before, tend to regard it as a place to be got through as quickly as possible before the greater challenges of the later initiations.

Then, the *Mental Mode* (Level 5). The pattern and sequence of spiritual development should now be clear. Each transference to a higher mode of being constitutes effectively a new initiation, a discarding of the outer form of the previous mode and the adoption of the next sheath of the Personality. With the discarding of the old emotional body and associated etheric form, the Personality again passes to a higher level, where a new etheric body is created and the Personality takes on as its physical sheath the mental body. Other features of this existence are described in Chapter 8 in relation to the Baverstock formation.

This is the last of the strictly physical states, which Andrew describes as the 'fourfold being of man.' Andrew could not give first hand information about modes of being beyond the emotional.

This is the problem with those Personalities on the physical or emotional planes (unless they have reincarnated from one of the higher planes). Because they mix with Personalities all at the same level of development, it is very difficult to perceive the bigger picture beyond their own plane of existence. A friend and colleague of mine in the CCCS, Montague Keen, died in 2004. At a séance in America a year or two later he returned to say that they were "as confused about the crop circle phenomenon over here" (i.e. the emotional plane) "as ever we were on Earth."

The *Causal or Buddhic Mode* (Level 4). This marks the big break in the development of the human Monad, to be described in some detail under the Ascension Process. (Chapter 8) This is the 'Breaking of the Image' and the transformation of the Personality which is now fully absorbed by the Soul or Ego. It is the Third Initiation, where the mental body as a distinct separate sheath disappears and is incorporated in the causal membrane, the sheath of the Soul. The human Monad is beginning to approach the Fourth Initiation and is on course to become a Master of Wisdom.

Djwhal Khul throws an interesting sidelight on the intellectual development of the human Monad as he passes through these different modes of being. He likens it to an educational process where initially at the physical and emotional levels the human being is groping through *the Hall of Ignorance*. The next stage is *the Hall of Learning* where 'knowledge' is acquired. (Bailey 1922a, p. 10)

The causal or buddhic mode on Level 4 he likens to the cosmic university or '*Hall of Wisdom*'. 'When he has passed through that school he will graduate with his degree as a 'Master of Compassion.' (or Wisdom) (Bailey *Ibid.*) Wisdom he defines as the 'intuitive apprehension of truth apart from the reasoning faculty, and the innate perception that can distinguish between the false and the true, between the real and the unreal. It is more than that, for it is also the growing capacity of the Thinker to enter increasingly into the mind of the Logos ...' (Bailey 1922a, p. 11)

Above the causal or buddhic are etheric states covered later in this study.

These deaths and rebirths of the different modes of being may seem confusing in a condensed narrative, but are utterly necessary for spiritual development. Hundreds of years may pass for the human Monad in any particular mode of being, punctuated by brief spells in human form on the physical plane to gain further experience in some field or settle some karmic debt. Death is an essential factor in this process, not only for the human Monad but for all other living forms in the Cosmos. The Greater Master says: 'Learn to trust death. Learn to love death. Learn to count upon death in your scheme of things ... for thus you will learn to build the bridge between life and death so that it shall be trodden with increasing ease. ... Thus shall the bridge be built that leads beyond the veil. Let the chasm between the so-called living and the so-called dead be bridged by this method that men may cease to fear death.' (Fortune 1976, p. 120)

## THE BIRLING FORMATION, 1998 (7.3 AND 7.4)

An important crop formation apparently concerned with the human psyche appeared around 4.7.1998 near the village of Birling, North Kent (OS TQ677619). In plan the formation consists of three lines of rings and circles connected by paths of variable width. The central ring, which has a small central grapeshot, is connected by paths to two sets of circles.

*The septenary structure* was discussed in Chapter 5. 3 rings and 4 circles would normally be taken to refer to the Ray structure – the three Rays of Aspect and the four Rays of Attribute. Although in the most general sense this distinction applies here, there are features pointing to a particular cosmic meaning.

The elements of the formation have well-established metaphysical connotations and can be categorised as follows:

1. Plain circles, which symbolically in this context represent single 'points of consciousness.'

2. Rings, which represent in metaphysical terms what might be termed group consciousness or corporate form.

3. The ring disc with a hole in the centre (the *Bi* disc) which has been used by the non-human crop circle makers as a symbol for Deity.

The Birling mandala can be visualised as a highly schematic and simplified diagram of human psychic energy fields and their connections.

In each ring there is a *triadic pattern of energy points*, (established by dowsing by Jim Lyons and the writer), with each point or centre having a separate intelligent existence (see 7.4, inset squares). In each set of three points there is:

A. A crossover point of geophysical energy lines (energy centre), symbolising the initiating power of the Spirit.

B. A geometric centre (*the Jewel in the Lotus*), symbolising the creative Force.

C. A vortex centre of the spiralled crop flow (structural centre), symbolising the formative energy.

The energy points uncannily constitute the three levels of *Atma*, *Buddhi* and *Manas*:

A. The Will Aspect (*Atma*)

B. The Love-Wisdom Aspect (*Buddhi*)

C. The Intelligence Aspect (*Manas*).

The upper ring of the formation symbolises the Spirit, the Angelic Intelligence that energises the Spiritual Triad. In this ring the three energy points lie within six feet of each other and form a triangle.

Normally the individual has little or no direct connection with A and B, but increasingly as the spiritual path is followed a process of contact, eventually leading to assimilation, is achieved.

The middle ring represents the Soul, which is the interface between the spiritual, non-corporeal aspects of the human Monad and the manifested faculties of the Personality, which it has the responsibility for creating and transmuting. In the case of the human Monad this Being operates through the conscience, the God within.

Linked to the middle ring by paths are four circles symbolising what Djwhal Khul calls 'permanent atoms', and also *Pitris*, the angelic or devic Intelligences that preside over the functions of the energy bodies of the human psyche, and are answerable directly to the Soul. (See Chapter 5.)

The lower ring represents the Personality of the human Monad.

*The Antahkarana.* Linking the three rings is a path, wide between the 'Personality' and 'Soul' and narrowing between the 'Soul' and

*7.3 Birling, North Kent (OS TQ677619), 4.7.1998*

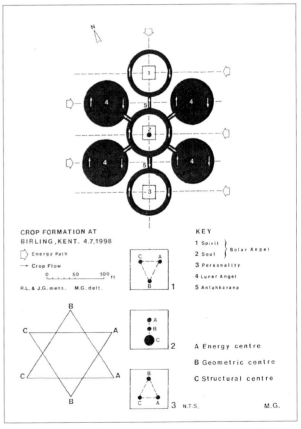

*7.4 Energy pattern mandala of the human Monad, showing the human psychic energy fields and their connections*
*Birling, 4.7.1998*

'Spirit'. This, interestingly, is the clue to the metaphysical interpretation of this formation. The path is emblematic of the *Antahkarana*, the 'Lighted Way' which connects in progressive stages the lower states of consciousness with those of the higher. As the threefold *Kundalini* energy it rises, empowering the various centres of the Personality, Soul and Spirit.

This very real process, required it is said of every individual, is beautifully expressed in what Djwhal Khul describes as the 'Old Commentary':

'The Solar Orb shines forth in radiant splendour. The illuminated mind reflects the solar glory. The lunar orb rises from the centre to the summit, and is transformed into a radiant sun of light. When these three suns are one, Brahma breaks forth. A lighted world is born.' (Bailey 1934, p. 98)

This figuratively means that when the conjoined Soul (symbolised as the Solar Orb) and Personality (the lunar orb) are firmly linked to the Spirit, only then can the creative power of this Solar Angel be fully manifested, and the spiritual human being move on to greater things. The Indian *Bhagavad Gita* expresses it thus: "Though I am Unborn, the Soul that passes not away, though I am the Lord of Beings, yet as Lord over My nature I become manifest, through the magical power of the Soul." The rings of the crop formation can thus be seen in terms of the ancient symbolism as varying, ascending levels of human consciousness.

The 'Old Commentary' reminds us that the process of apotheosis, for it is nothing less, applies (with considerable differences of degree and scale) to the greater cosmic powers also, and in particular to the presiding spirit of our own planetary system, the Earth Logos.

The great difference between the human and planetary Monads is that whereas the spiritual *Antahkarana* connections in the former are only beginning to be developed, in the latter they are effectively complete.

The pattern of energy centres in the three rings was extraordinarily interesting. The upper circle energy points (1 in the diagram) form an inverted triangle, those of the lower circle (3) form an isosceles triangle and in the centre circle (2) they form a line, a metaphorical *Antahkarana*.

Now when the process of apotheosis eventually takes place in the human being and the three circles become one sphere, the energy points form a six-pointed star (the Seal of Solomon). This constitutes a merging of the subjective life and the objective form overshadowed by the Love-Wisdom aspect of the Soul (the *Buddhi* principle). As Djwhal Khul expresses it:

'This is the higher expression ... of the six-pointed star, formed of two interlaced triangles. A replica of this fundamental triangle and of this symbol of energy, with its inflow and distribution, is to be found in the relation of the three higher centres in the human being – head, heart and throat – to the three lower centres – solar plexus, sacral centre and the centre at the base of the spine.' (Bailey 1960, p. 69)

Thus the Birling formation from Kent is a beautiful and deeply significant mandala indicating both a spiritual process currently being speeded up in mankind, but also perhaps constituting a call to those who are ready to allow this process to take place in their own psyche.

# 8. THE HUMAN MONAD: THE ASCENSION PROCESS

*He mingled with the multitude. I saw their brows were crowned and bright.*
*A light about the shadowy heads, a shadow round the brows of light.*

George William Russell (A.E.)
*Song and its Fountains 1932*

## SUMMARY

We have considered the physical and psychic make-up of the human Monad in Chapters 5-7, and how humanity's psychic structure is organised to enable the human Monad to take the spiritual path for which its system is designed. In Chapters 8 and 9, perhaps the most important in this book in terms of the projected spiritual future of the human race on this planet, we look at the stages and nature of the Ascension Process. There is also a Note on the Egyptian 'Book of the Dead'.

In this chapter two important crop formations are considered. The extraordinary Baverstock formation of 1991 might be regarded in some respects as the equivalent of the Kabbalistic *Ladder of Jacob*, and related to the Theosophic chart, *The Constitution of Man*. The Cowdown formation of 1995 is concerned with the same momentous process, but is designed in a simpler mandalic form.

## THE BAVERSTOCK FORMATION, 1991 (8.1 AND 8.2)

It is not clear whether the diagram of *The Constitution of Man* appearing in *Initiation, Human and Solar* (Bailey 1922a, p. xiv) and in later volumes, (for example Bailey 1925, p. 117) was material directly channelled by Djwhal Khul to Alice Bailey, or taken from one of the theosophical treatises of the time. However the crop formation which appeared in early August 1991 at Baverstock, Wiltshire (OS SU032337) is sufficiently similar to the diagram for the connection to be made.

This (effectively) multi-dimensional diagram is set in the context of the *seven planes* of our solar system. These can be described as states of consciousness, through which the human Monad needs to pass to reach apotheosis, starting with the physical plane and ascending to the logoic plane of Deity. They are each divided into seven sub-planes or *ethers*. The planes of our solar system follow the basic structure of those elsewhere in the Cosmos. See later in this chapter for a fuller description.

The tabulation of the planes and ethers on the left hand side of my diagram (8.2) was not of course depicted as such in the landscape, but is based on the Bailey chart. Because space was needed to insert the different parts of the structure of the human Monad within the framework of the seven planes, this formation was exceptionally long (about 150 yards), as was noted at the time by field investigators.

The basic psychic structure of man is threefold, and starts on the second plane, the *monadic* plane.

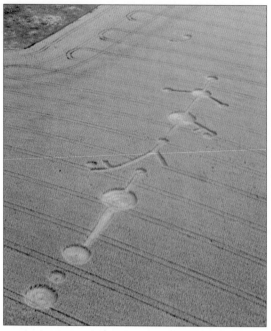

8.1 Baverstock, Wiltshire
(OS SU032337), early August 1991

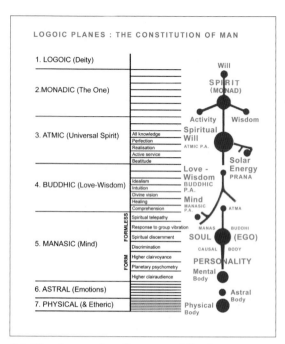

8.2 *The Ascension Process of the human Monad.* Baverstock, early August 1991

1. *The Monad or pure Spirit*, the 'Spark of God' 'is only contacted in the final initiations, when man is nearing the end of his journey and is perfected.' (Bailey 1922a, p. xv) This Being consists of three aspects:

*Will* (or Power), the 'Father' aspect.

*Wisdom* (characterised by the dual qualities of 'Love-Wisdom'), the 'Son' aspect.

*Activity* (or Active Intelligence), the 'Holy Spirit' (or 'Mother') aspect.

These three aspects are depicted in the crop formation as a three-armed figure with a central circle which represents the unified Monad itself. The *Will* aspect is situated in the first ether of the monadic plane, the other two are shown on the seventh ether, essentially that of manifestation. The Monad nucleus is shown in the fifth Ether, which on the buddhic plane (see diagram) is that of 'Divine Vision'.

2. *The Soul or Ego.* This too is shown as a triple figure, but with more detail than in the Bailey diagram. It reflects at a lower level of vibration the essential structure of the Monad with which it is directly connected. The large circle is the *Spiritual Will* or *Atmic* 'permanent atom' as Djwhal Khul terms it. (Bailey 1925, pp. 515-517) An arm extended from this circle holds in its embrace that essential gift from the Solar Logos to all its life forms, namely *Prana*. The Spiritual Will operates from the central ether of the third plane, that of *Atma* or universal spirit. There is then a break in the linear line of the formation as the aspects of form, however tenuous, begin to be reached. The Heart aspect of the Soul operates from the first ether of the fourth or buddhic plane. Djwhal Khul describes this permanent atom as essentially 'Intuition', which is true. I, however, would define it as 'Love-Wisdom', its predominant quality.

Below the buddhic permanent atom are two branches. One has no defining circle, but I believe functions to clasp, so to speak, the lower figure operating at the manasic (mental) plane level. The other to the left is shown as receiving the element of *Manas* (intelligence) operating at the first ether of the manasic plane. This is subtly different from the Bailey diagram where it is shown as integral to the Soul (which is also true). *Manas* was a gift to our solar system from another centre of *Archon*, that located in the constellation of Draco. (Bailey 1925, p. 795-6) The significance of this connection is discussed in greater detail in Chapter 19. The atmic, buddhic and manasic aspects of the Soul (all permanent atoms) are thus carefully located in their correct positions on the planes.

However, the three permanent atoms of the Soul or Ego also come together to function in the causal body of the human Monad, on the manasic plane. Both the Bailey diagram and this crop formation show the centre of gravity of the Soul or Ego figure to be located on the third ether, that of 'Spiritual Discernment'. However, the location of the components differs between the two sources. In the Bailey diagram all three permanent atoms are shown as on the third ether of the manasic plane. In the formation, the atmic (spiritual will) permanent atom is shown at the Head end of the figure relating to the bottom or seventh ether of the buddhic plane, that of 'Comprehension', with the other two permanent atoms (*Manas* and *Buddhi*) on the third ether of the manasic plane. This element, representing the Soul within the causal body, is shown as separated from the features both above and below. It is I think significant that the Soul is shown

on the manasic (intelligence) levels rather than in the buddhic (Love-Wisdom) focus, perhaps because it is this aspect of the physical body with which the Soul has most contact. Indeed this is clearly indicated in the Baverstock formation. 'The Ego [Soul] begins to make its power felt in advanced men, and increasingly on the Probationary Path until by the Third Initiation [see below] the control of the lower self by the higher is perfected, and the highest aspect begins to make its energy felt.' (Bailey 1922a, p. xv)

3. *The Personality*. This third aspect of the human Monad is depicted in the formation as a line of three circles. The mental body is shown as operating on the seventh ether of the manasic plane. Although it is close to the Soul, there is a definite discontinuity which has to be bridged as described later in this chapter. 'The aim of evolution is therefore to bring man to the realisation of the Egoic aspect and to bring the lower nature under its control.' (Bailey 1922a, p. xv) The emotional body and the physical body (which includes the etheric body as we have seen), are centred respectively in the sixth (emotional or astral) and seventh (physical) planes.

The Baverstock formation is thus exceedingly important in that it not only delineates the total structure of the human Monad in a summary form, but also highlights the problem of discontinuity between the various elements which the Ascension Process has to surmount. Lastly it should be noted that this formation is signed, (see 8.1, top left of the formation) as was the case with most of the more significant mandalic crop formations. The glyph is that of the Sixth Lord of the Great Council of planet Earth, Varuna (see Chapter 12), whom I equate with the Archangel Gabriel.

## THE LOGOIC PLANES AND ETHERS

Two Masters of Wisdom, namely Djwhal Khul and the 'Greater Master' channelled by Dion Fortune in 1923 and 1924, together with those communicating through Helena Blavatsky, have provided the most valuable compilation on this abstruse subject. Of special interest is the material provided by the discarnate Soul of F.W.H. Myers (*Obit.* 1901), classical lecturer at Trinity College, Cambridge in 1865 and a co-founder of the Society for Psychical Research, communicating through Geraldine Cummins between 1924 and 1931.

This structure of the concrete and numinous worlds is implicit in the communications of the geophysical crop circle makers.

*Level 7: The Physical Plane*

The physical plane relates to the human Monad before death, and the higher planes are closely tied up with the Monad after death. The series of subdivisions or ethers can be categorised in seven stages from the highest level down as follows:

1st Ether – Atomic

2nd Ether – Sub-atomic

3rd Ether – Super etheric

4th Ether – Etheric

5th Ether – Gaseous

6th Ether – Liquid

7th Ether – Dense.

These seven subdivisions are to be found on all the seven planes of our system.

Every ether on every plane is associated with a particular sense or medium through which the Soul and Personality comes in contact with his environment. The five senses of the physical plane in descending order of importance are:

1st Ether – Smell

2nd Ether – Taste

3rd Ether – Sight

4th Ether – Touch, feeling

5th Ether – Hearing.

The two lowest ethers (sixth and seventh) are esoterically ' "below the threshold" and concern forms of life beneath the human.' (Bailey 1925, p. 187)

However, for those who have passed on, the apparent solidarity and normality of our physical state is an illusion, more unreal than what we might think of as the numinous states which are the hard realities of the other worlds. Myers termed the physical plane *Penia*, perhaps derived from the Latin *poena* meaning punishment, or more likely in the Ciceronian sense of *hardship*. It may be significant that Iolo Morganwg (quoted in Chapter 4) describes this state as the Circle of *Abred* (*Ab* = from, *rhed* = a course. Old Welsh). Morganwg described it as the circle of inchoation or 'beginnings' in which 'are all corporal and dead existences ... and man has traversed it.' (Williams, J. 1862, p. 223 and p. 171)

The 'Greater Master' sought to set out the human spiritual experience in terms of the bigger picture of cosmic development:

'The aim of a universe is to raise every atom to Cosmic level ... whereby it can continue its own evolution.' (Fortune 1976, pp. 68-69) 'Each succeeding wave of evolution penetrates deeper into the "form" aspect of the universe; renders it more complex in its organisation; brings it a stage further in the development of that perfect balance of forces which it seeks to reach as a whole, and when the entire manifested universe reacts as a whole it is fully self-conscious.' (Fortune 1976, p. 89) 'For each lesson they learn they teach to the Logoidal Consciousness ... when they have been out to the uttermost plane and returned ... they have given their final message to the Logoidal Consciousness.' (Fortune 1976, p. 79) 'The forthsending and returning of an evolutionary life swarm conveys the same harvest of experiences to the Logoical Consciousness as the Individuality of a man receives from the incarnation of a Personality.' (Fortune 1976, p. 89) 'Elaboration means differentiation, and differentiation means personality.' (Fortune 1976, p. 75)

In the other states beyond this material existence the human Personality in its etheric body may receive teaching, advice, even stimulus, but only in the tough, incarnate conditions of human physical existence is it really possible to make actual spiritual progress. The opportunity is short and passing in each life. Little else is of any real consequence – wealth, possessions, social standing or fame. In the Islamic canon of teaching by Jesus Christ is the saying: "The world is a bridge. Cross this bridge but do not build upon it." (Khalidi 2001, saying 99, p. 106)

*Level 6: The Emotional or Astral Plane, or 'Hades'*

This plane includes the next stage for the human Personality after death, that which has been termed *Hades* by Myers. 'Immediately on the dissolution of the body there comes a brief period of seeming disintegration, a temporary dislocation of those parts which make you one. ... For me Hades was a place of rest, a place of half-lights and drowsy peace. As a man wins strength from a long deep sleep, so did I gather that spiritual and intellectual force I needed during the time I abode in Hades.' (Cummins 2012, p. 9) Thus Myers speaks of his own death experience and that place or state on the frontiers of two lives, on

the borders of two worlds. Other Personality types, depending on their spiritual state, may have different experiences, not all necessarily benevolent. In this state not only is there complete severance with the former physical body, but also the structure of the etheric body associated with it. 'Each individualized consciousness lives to die and dies to live. It is only by death that we can reap the fruits of life.' (Fortune 1976, p. 119) The new 'physical body' is the former emotional sheath on the emotional plane.

The new etheric body, a finer configuration of its earthly counterpart, enters a dream-state which for most takes on the form of the physical world with which he is familiar. This is the 'Summerland', already mentioned, where the Personality, 'freed from the limitations of the flesh, has far greater mental powers, and can adapt the memory-world to his taste. He does so unconsciously, instinctively choosing the old pleasures, but closing the door to the old pains.' (Cummins 2012, p. 9)

The upper five senses associated with the ethers of the emotional plane are:

1st Ether – Emotional idealism

2nd Ether – Imagination

3rd Ether – Clairvoyance

4th Ether – Psychometry

5th Ether – Clairaudience.

As on the physical plane, the two lowest ethers concern forms of life beneath the human.

Depending on the character of the human Personality built up over the period of a lifetime, or perhaps many lifetimes – whether he be 'spirit-man', 'soul-man' or 'animal-man' – so the time spent in the 'Summerland' is short or long. 'After a while this life of pleasure ceases to amuse and content him. Then he begins to think and long for the unknown, long for a new life. He is at last prepared to make the leap in evolution and this cloudy dream vanishes.' (Cummins 2012, p. 18)

The move to the next level, the manasic (mental) plane, is a huge step, leading to different paths being taken by different Personalities. Animal-man usually chooses to reincarnate again on the physical plane where he can experience its gross delights.

### Level 5: The Manasic or Mental Plane

The manasic level is also known as the Plane of Colour or *Eidos* (perhaps a compound of the Latin *aedes* = sacred place and *dos* = dowry or quality gift). The transition to this state represents another major step, indeed a 'death' for the soul-man who is seriously contemplating the spiritual path. The etheric body of the sixth plane is replaced by a finer etheric form leading to progressively more subtle forms as the ethers are ascended. The emotional body is discarded and replaced by the mental body, which now becomes the outer sheath.

The setting of the manasic plane is a world which is the original of the Earth – planet Earth as it was meant to be. There is a certain similarity, a correspondence between the appearances of nature and the semblance of this luminiferous plane. 'Flowers are there; but these are in shapes unknown to you, exquisite in colour, radiant with light. Such colours, such lights are not contained within any earthly octave, are expressed by us in thoughts and not in words.' (Cummins 2012, p. 24)

The seven senses associated with the ethers of the manasic plane are:

1st Ether – Spiritual telepathy

2nd Ether – Response to group vibration

3rd Ether – Spiritual discernment

4th Ether – Discrimination

5th Ether – Higher clairvoyance

6th Ether – Planetary psychometry

7th Ether – Higher clairaudience.

Morganwg describes this plane and the two following as the *Circle of Gwynvyd* (the Circle of Felicity) 'where all things spring from Life, and man shall traverse it in heaven', or again, 'in which are all animated and immortal beings.' (Williams, J. 1862, p. 171, p. 223) It is in these realms that the Personality at last has direct contact with the Soul, and prepares to take the Third and Fourth Initiations in its final reincarnations on Earth. As Morganwg poetically puts it: 'The three necessities of man in Gwynvyd: godliness; love; and light; and from the three proceed all power, all knowledge and all everlasting joy, and hence all goodness without cessation, without end.' (Williams, J. 1862, p. 371) For the soul-man this is an entirely new experience. It is still a physical world, but one controlled by thought. Whilst much of the basic structure in the 'Summerland' is created for its residents by those who come from the upper planes – seemingly angelic, Myers describes them as 'the Wise' – on this plane the Personality begins the serious business of creative thought, 'must struggle and labour, know sorrow but not earth sorrow, know ecstasy but not earth ecstasy.' (Cummins 2012, p. 24) Both are of a spiritual kind. Not all therefore is sweetness and light, since ancient karmic conflicts with other Personalities need to be finally resolved.

For it is at this stage on the fifth plane that the Personality has to come to terms with what is termed the *Group Soul*. Each human Monad, to enable it to achieve its own necessary development, has to experience many lives or reincarnations. Each of these has produced a Personality, but all bound through the Soul to the one Monad. As Myers puts it: 'Many Soul-men do not seek another earth life, but their spirit manifests itself many times on earth and it is the bond which holds together a group of souls, [Personalities in my terminology] who, in the ascending scale of psychic evolution, act and react upon one another.' (Cummins 2012, pp. 29-30) They are able to do this with facility since by thought they are able to share each other's minds and past experiences in previous lives.

One of the most serious inhibiting problems with such a range of Personalities, many of whom were exceedingly devout in their day, is an unwillingness to pool and develop the quality of Love-Wisdom, freed of the associated trappings of their reincarnation experiences: 'he [the Personality] may, if a certain section of that group-soul be in a fixed mould, take upon himself its shape and remain within it for aeons of time. ... For instance, a fanatical Buddhist or very devout Christian may be held within the groove of his earthly beliefs. ... For it means ... dwelling in an intellectual chrysalis ...' (Cummins 2012, p. 31) 'they must learn how to escape from such a prison if they are to make further progress.' (Cummins 2012, p. 32) These remarks apply equally to all fanatical adherents to religious beliefs, or the scientific materialism of the modern age.

Thus it is on the manasic plane that the different Personality identities, expressing many different life experiences over past ages, need to collaborate and coordinate a Group response, and thus contribute in forming that particular essence or quality which will become the distinguishing contribution of any particular Monad. It can be, and usually is, a critical, confrontational phase in which the Group becomes an esoteric 'burning ground'.

'The fusing love of the Soul is absent ... It is blocked and intercepted by group conditions, and until there is at least some united will to take *together* what is needed in order to shift the life of the group to higher levels of awareness ... on buddhic [Love-Wisdom] levels, the technique of transference will not be committed to the group.' (Bailey 1960, p. 219)

As Djwhal Khul puts it elsewhere, they need to develop 'the consciousness of the group in which they themselves find place.'... 'This objective might be defined as ability to vibrate synchronously with the greater unit of which it is a part.' (Bailey 1925, p. 450, p. 1132)

To turn again to the Baverstock formation (8.2), it is the circle representing the combined forces of the *Manas-Buddhi* aspect of the Soul, which occupies the third ether, that has the major responsibility for indirectly cajoling these fractious elements of the Personality aspects into forming a functioning unit, so that the next great shift of consciousness can take place. It is noticeable that it is the *Atma* (Will) aspect of the Soul, at the junction of the fourth and fifth planes, that needs to push the coordinated Group Soul over the gap that takes its operation into the buddhic plane.

*Level 4: The Buddhic or Intuitional Plane*

The characteristics of this plane are the qualities of the Second Ray, namely Love-Wisdom. Myers describes this stage, which is reached through another death and rebirth, as the *Plane of Flame*. The concept of purification, indeed destruction, is also conveyed in Djwhal Khul's description of the Fourth Initiation as the Crucifixion or the Great Renunciation. 'This is the last veil between him and a conception of existence without form. He must free himself before he can go up another rung of the ladder, and freedom can only come through the deliberate process called "The Breaking of the Image".' (Cummins 2012, p. 33)

Myers sums up the functions of the Group Soul in its final stages on the buddhic plane as follows: 'For the spirit must gather a harvest of experience in every form [representatives of living creatures in varying states of evolution]. Gradually these intelligences evolve and merge. The experience necessary to the spirit is completed when all the souls [Personalities] necessary to the design have reached this [fourth] plane. Once they become sensible of their oneness and their individuality they may go forward to the [third] plane. There is, then, a breaking of the threads, a casting away of the dross of emotional experience, a sifting and changing on the part of all these [Personalities]. They pass once more into Hades and review, in that state, all that now lies behind them.' (Cummins 2012, pp. 35-36)

The Greater Master is even more succinct. 'The Fifth Death is the death of the Personality.' (Fortune 1976, p. 121) 'It is the farewell to appearance, to form as a necessity, to colour, to feeling as a certainty, as a condition of life.' (Cummins 2012, p. 33) The heart is now sufficiently pure and loving. 'He would no longer love with the personal love that loves a person, but with the higher manifestation of love which itself is Love and loves no person or thing but is a state of consciousness in which all is embraced.' (Fortune 1976, p. 121) 'The intellect [is now] sufficiently stable to stand the strain of *knowing*.' (Bailey 1922a, p. 88) Much intellectual work has to be engaged in before the initiate or *adept*, as he is technically called, is ready for the Fourth Initiation. It is this congruence and lifting of the qualities of affection and knowledge to that of love and wisdom that are the determining qualities of this plane.

The senses associated with the ethers of the buddhic plane are:

1st Ether and

2nd Ether – The nature of these realms of abstraction is revealed after the Fourth Initiation.

3rd Ether – Idealism

4th Ether – Intuition

5th Ether – Divine vision

6th Ether – Healing

7th Ether – Comprehension.

'He can contact ... the Master with Whom he is linked and with Whom he has worked consciously for a long time ...' The Personality and the Soul prepare to merge. 'By the time the fourth initiation is taken the initiate has mastered perfectly the fifth sub-plane' [the manasic plane] ... 'His buddhic vehicle can function on the two lower sub-planes [ethers] of the buddhic plane.' (Bailey 1922a, p. 89) [The Ethers of 'Healing' and 'Comprehension'] 'When man has attained the consciousness of the buddhic plane, he has raised his consciousness to that of the Heavenly Man [the Earth Logos] in whose body he is a cell. This is achieved at the fourth Initiation, the liberating initiation.' (Bailey 1925, p. 121) It is not until after this initiation, which occurs on the atmic plane, that the adept can become a Master of Wisdom.

In considering the hard decisions and irrevocable break with the past that mark the transference to the atmic plane, it may be useful to look again at the Baverstock formation. It will be noted that there is a gap at the junction of the projected planes 3 and 4, which I believe marks the point where the Personality needs to make the final decision to bridge this gulf to attain communion, indeed identity with, the Spiritual Will aspect of the

Soul, shown on the fourth ether of the atmic plane.

*Level 3: The Atmic Plane*

This is the plane of the *Atma*, the Soul or Logoic aspect of the Universal Spirit or divine Monad. In the Baverstock formation, this, the largest circle of the mandala, is identified as representing the spiritual will or atmic permanent atom. (8.2) It presides over the third, fourth and fifth ethers whose principal qualities are 'All Knowledge', 'Perfection' and 'Realisation', attributes of that human entity whose Personality and Soul are now to coalesce at the Fourth Initiation. 'The initiate is now functioning as a soul-infused personality, and therefore the three aspects of that personality are nothing more or less than agents of the soul, and thus are progressively responsive to the inflow of triadal energy.' (Bailey 1960, p. 598)

Myers describes this plane as that of *White Light*. 'Light, though composed of many colours, is colourless' (Cummins 2012, p. 37), or in the words of Djwhal Khul: 'When the light of the seven Rays is blended with that of the seventh Ray, then light supernal can be known.' [It] 'involves the Atmic plane'. Or again: 'he is being given his first opportunity to work with Light under the inspiration of the Will.' (Bailey 1955, pp. 370, 378) He begins to learn and practice not only as a 'creator' but also as an agent of destruction of the astral substance or phenomena 'for which he is not individually responsible but which is nevertheless related to the group or nation with which he is by birth or inclination affiliated.' (Bailey 1955, p. 379)

Every ether on each of the seven planes is a progressively higher and higher reflection of each of the five senses of the physical plane. 'Sight' on the third ether of the physical plane

has now the attribute of 'realisation' on the atmic plane. Another transformed sense is that of hearing which on the buddhic plane demonstrates as 'comprehension'. 'On the Atmic Plane this perfected hearing is seen as beatitude. Sound, the basis of existence; sound, the final unifier; sound therefore realised as the *raison d'être*, as the method of evolution, and therefore as beatitude.' (Bailey 1925, p. 192)

The ethers of the atmic plane, where the quality of beatitude is shown on the lowest or seventh ether are as follows:

1st Ether and

2nd Ether – The nature of these realms of abstraction is revealed after the Fourth Initiation.

3rd Ether – All knowledge

4th Ether – Perfection

5th Ether – Realisation

6th Ether – Active Service

7th Ether – Beatitude.

So when exactly, in terms of the planes, does the Fourth Initiation take place in the Ascension Process of the adept? This occurs, I believe, at the time of the Fifth Death (the transference from the buddhic plane to the atmic plane), although the process of preparation begins long before. The occasion is marked by the complex ceremony so graphically described by Djwhal Khul. (Bailey 1922a, pp. 112 ff.)

'After the fourth initiation not much remains to be done ... the matter of the higher sub-planes of the buddhic [plane] is coordinated. ... He becomes adept in the significance of sound and colour, can wield the law in the three worlds [physical, emotional, mental] and can contact his Monad with more freedom than the majority of the human race can contact their Egos [Souls]. He is in charge, also, of large work, teaching many pupils, aiding in many schemes, and is gathering under him those who are to assist him in future times' [if he stays to help humanity on planet Earth]. (Bailey 1922a, p. 90)

Three Monadic forces of energy flow into the initiate or Master of Wisdom after the Fourth Initiation. First, 'Light' operating under the Will or Ray 1 aspect; secondly, 'Sound' operating under the Activity (Active Intelligence) or Ray 3 aspect, and the third and, arguably, the most important input of the Monad is that found on Ray 2 – Love-Wisdom. Now it will be noted that in the diagram of the Baverstock formation, this aspect of the Spirit or Monad is shown only as 'Wisdom'. The spiritual 'corporate management' of planet Earth known as the 'Hierarchy' reflecting this greater Source, 'brings into activity the quality to which man has erroneously given the name of "love". This emphasises the sentimental aspect and signifies to the majority, very largely, simply the sentimental and emotional aspect, which is entirely of an astral nature. Pure reason, which is the supreme characteristic of the Members of the Hierarchy, will ever express itself in right action and right human relations, and that will manifest – when present – what love in reality is. *Pure love is a quality or effect of pure reason.*' (my italics) (Bailey 1950, p. 69) In the words of the Greater Master:

'The aim of evolution is to make all things one, and upon the planes of manifestation there are but two things which make all things one – Death and Love … Whoso loves, however dim may be his concept of Love, is manifesting a unification, and unification is the goal of Evolution. God is One. Love makes one – therefore it is truly said "God is Love". Whosoever expresses Love, brings

Spirit, which is One, into manifestation. To be separate is to be dead. Therefore choose Love and live.' (Fortune 1976, p. 133)

The atmic plane is thus another place of decision-making, and these decisions are painful at a certain level. Hence George William Russell's reference to the 'shadows round the brows of light' in our chapter head. The Fourth Initiation concerns the loss of individuality as an independent entity. But there are two, if not three, further initiations on this and the monadic plane, which involve a determinative choice of spiritual direction which is irrevocable and determines the cosmic future of the human Monad.

*Level 2: The Monadic Plane*

This represents the final planetary stage of the development of the human Monad when the Personality, Soul and Spirit finally come together as an indivisible unity, a stage marked by the Fifth Initiation. In the Baverstock formation the threefold structure of the Spirit fills the monadic plane, with the Second and Third Rays of 'Wisdom' and 'Activity' filling the lower ethers, and the First Ray, 'Will' on the first ether. The focussed concentration of this Trinity is on the fifth ether, which on the buddhic plane is that of 'divine vision', appropriate I believe in this case.

'When the latent fire of the personality or lower self blends with the fire of mind, that of the higher self, [the Soul] and finally merges with the Divine Flame [the Spirit] then the man takes the fifth Initiation in this solar system, and has completed one of his greater cycles. When the three blaze forth as one fire, liberation from matter, or from material form is achieved.' (Bailey 1925, p. 47)

'The purpose of the [second] plane of being might be described as "the assimilation of the many-in-one," the unifying of all those mind-units I have called souls, within the spirit. When this aim has been achieved, the spirit which contains this strange individualised life passes out Yonder and enters into the Mystery, thereby fulfilling the final purpose, the evolution of the Supreme Mind.' (Cummins 2012, p. 37) 'Now, on this level of consciousness pure reason reigns supreme. Emotion and passion, as known to men, are absent. White light represents the perfect equanimity of pure thought. Such equanimity becomes the possession of the souls who enter this last rich kingdom of experience. They bear with them the wisdom of form, the incalculable secret wisdom, gathered only through limitation, harvested from numberless years, garnered from lives passed in myriad forms. Knowledge of good and evil and of what lies beyond good and evil now belongs to them. They are lords of life, for they have conquered. They are capable of living now without form, of existing as white light, as the pure thought of their Creator. They have joined the Immortals.' (Cummins 2012, p. 37)

'It will be seen then that the essence of evolution is unification; and the manifestation of the unificatory principle upon the planes of manifestation is Love. Whether that love be intellectual sympathy on the plane of the concrete mind, or physical unity on the plane of matter, Love in all its aspects is the symbol of the Logos as One.' (Fortune 1976, p. 133)

*Level 1: The Logoic Plane*

Djwhal Khul briefly describes this plane as being that of 'Divine Consciousness. This is the awareness of the whole on the highest plane of our planetary manifestation.' (Bailey 1960, p. 463) The Greater Master states: '... he is born into consciousness of the Individuality, ... perceiving the "face of his Father which is

in Heaven".' (Fortune 1976, p. 121) But even these, the Masters of Wisdom, fall silent in their attempts to describe the human Monad's vision of God. Iolo Morganwg describes this state as *'the Circle of Ceugant'* (i.e. the Circle of Infinity), where there is nothing but God, of living or dead, and none but God can traverse it.' (Williams, J. 1862, p. 171) 'Man's primal loyalty is to the One – Unity. "Loyalty" is hardly the correct word to use as the One is a Law – no other type of existence is possible; in It we live and move and have our being.' [See also the Holy Bible: "In him we live and move and have our being." (*Acts* 17:28)] 'It is, however, very necessary to understand that the One – the Logos – is actually the becoming manifest of the Unmanifest; It is Unity not because It is concentrated or limited but because it is undifferentiated.' (Fortune 1976, p. 154)

Thus the dynamics of the heavenly state ensure that the state of changeless *nirvana* changes for the human Monad (and all Monads) as a new cycle of development begins. Djwhal Khul sums it up as follows: 'The work of evolution, being part of the determination of Deity to express divinity through form, is necessarily, therefore, the task of *revelation*, and as far as man is concerned, this revelation works out as the growth of soul evolution and falls into three stages:

1. Individualisation ... Personality

2. Initiation ... Ego [Soul]

3. Identification ... Monad.' (Bailey 1942, p. 8)

This then is the great cycle of 'Coming into Being' of which we are all part, the subject of this chapter following the teaching of the Baverstock formation in 1991 concerning the seven planes of our solar system and their part in the development of the human Monad. But as Djwhal Khul reminds us:

'Our seven planes – the mastery of which is our idealised spiritual goal – are after all only the lowest cosmic plane, the cosmic physical plane. From the cosmic angle, the Masters are only beginners, and even our deeply desired initiations (from the first to the sixth) are simply preparatory initiations for those to be taken later on upon the Way of the Higher Evolution.' (Bailey 1960, p. 390) Or again: '... avoid the concept that the attainment of the highest initiation upon this planet marks the end or the consummation of a great or final stage. It only marks only the beginning of significance.' (Bailey 1960, p. 203)

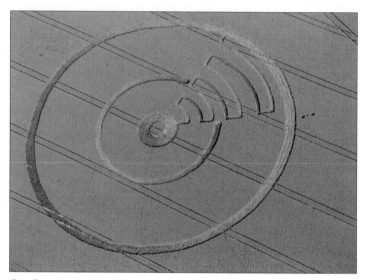

8.3 *Cowdown, Andover, Hampshire (OS SU375435), 19.6.1995*

## THE COWDOWN FORMATION, 1995 (8.3 AND 8.4)

*The Cowdown formation (Goodworth Clatford CP) Andover, Hampshire (OS SU375435) on 19.6.1995, in wheat*

Dimensions in feet, clockwise (cw) or anticlockwise (acw): outer ring 260 ft diameter, 8 ft 6 in wide (acw); inner ring 130 ft diameter, 6 ft wide (acw); central ring 37 ft 6 in diameter, 10 ft wide (acw). The special feature of the formation is the 'septile' segment with seven ring segments, 3 ft wide (alternately cw and acw), alternately connected. Nick Kollerstrom identified some special mathematical properties in connection with this formation. 'An image of what I'll call the septile angle, i.e. one-seventh of a circle: fifty one and a bit degrees, appeared in 1995 (Cow Down, Andover, 19th June). Seven "bars" comprised the segment ... Lastly, we are startled to note that the inner circle has one-seventh the area

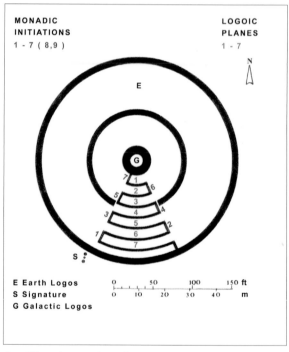

8.4 *The Ascension Process, the Initiations and Planes. Cowdown, 19.6.1995*

of the main, outer, circle, its radius being $\sqrt{7}$ of the larger one.' (Kollerstrom 2000, p. 3)

There are triple linear grapeshot circles on the south side with 4 ft, 2 ft, and 4ft diameters, evidently a signature. Amongst the range of signatures, from both on and off planet, which were accompanying important crop formations by this stage in 1995, this glyph is unique. I believe it to be that of the Sirian Logos, and a reference to the binary solar system of *Canis Majoris*. Sirius is one of a group of solar systems closely associated with our own, both systems being centres of that Being whom I call *Archon*. Esoterically the Sirian Logos is on the cosmic manasic plane and is thus closely associated with *Manas*, and by extension the regulation of ordered cosmic activity under the Sirian Law of Karma. (See Chapter 18.)

This elegant formation is quite unlike anything that had occurred previously. In 2000 I identified it as a statement about the spiritual initiations in relation to the Earth and Solar Logoi (Green, Michael 2000b, p. 16, fig. 4), an interpretation which I still believe to be fundamentally correct. I also associated the form with the Cosmic Laws.

The design of the formation is closely related to the *Third Cosmic Law, the Law of Economy*, as identified by the design of the Sibson formation (see Chapter 18), which appeared on 23.7.90. This is the law which orders the material and spiritual evolution of the Cosmos 'to the best possible advantage and with the least expenditure of force. [It] carries all onward, and upward and *through*, with the least possible effort, and with the proper adjustment of equilibrium, and with the necessary rate of rhythm.' (Bailey 1925, p. 568) Nowhere is this more true and apposite than in the case of the procedures that attend the apotheosis of mankind. Thus, by signatorial association and symbol, the Cowdown formation points to the Ascension Process of the human Monad.

The segment delineating this process is 'septile' because planet Earth operates on the *seventh (Physical) Ray* of our solar system, which in turn is related to the seventh Ray of Archon. The outer two rings of the formation effectively form the *Bi* disc symbol of the Earth Logos. The broad space between the rings, symbol of form or matter, is left open so as to illuminate the sequence of spiritual initiations for the human Monad. The spiritual 'formless' space in the centre has 'one-seventh the area of the area of the main, outer, circle' because the logioc plane is the uppermost of the Seven of our system. (See Baverstock formation diagram, 8.2.)

In my study in 2000 I identified the innermost ringed element (also a *Bi* symbol) as representing the Solar Logos. However, bearing in mind what I now know about the sequence of initiations of the human Monad, I believe now that this is the symbol of the Central Spiritual Sun of our galaxy, whom I call Aion.

If each arc represents a planetary plane on which the human Monad demonstrates a 'mode of being', each connecting arm to the next plane represents an initiatory experience which carries him to the next arc or plane.

The outer margins of the crop formation, from which, in symbolic terms, humanity has evolved as a physical entity, are esoterically '"below the threshold," and concern forms of life beneath the human altogether. We have a corroborating analogy in the fact that the two earliest root-races in this round are not definitely human, and that it is the third root-race which is really human for the first time.' (Bailey 1925, p. 187)

Djwhal Khul is presumably referring to two such sub-human species as *Homo erectus*

(c. 1.9-0.1 million years ago) and *Homo neanderthalensis* (400,000-30,000 years ago) which have a different DNA structure to present day humanity. *Homo sapiens* emerged from Africa about 60,000 years ago. (Renfrew and Bahn 2012, p. 157)

The two lowest ethers of the physical plane relate perhaps to etheric senses found in the animal world and sub-human species: possibly a heightened sense of hearing (seventh ether) and physical awareness (sixth ether).

Iolo Morganwg likened this outer ring to the *Circle of Abred* (Old Welsh - 'Mortality' or 'Beginnings') in *Annwn* (Old Welsh - the 'abyss', or the 'lowest level of mortality') which had to be traversed at the very beginning of the Ascension Process.

The four outermost ring segments are in the ring which represents form or matter of the Earth Logos. They indicate the first four initiations, on the physical, emotional, mental and spiritual levels. By the Fifth Initiation, the human Monad, by now a Master of Wisdom, is an enlightened member of the spiritual planetary teams and begins to move away from planetary service (if that is his destiny), firstly with the Solar Logos (Sixth Initiation) then Archon (Seventh Initiation) and finally Aion (Eighth Initiation), our Galactic Logos. The Ninth Initiation (the Refusal) is that in which the human Monad passes beyond our galactic system altogether. The last two initiations (8 and 9) are swallowed up, so to speak, by the Central Spiritual Sun of our galaxy.

The earlier 'modes' of development for the human Monad can take immense periods of time, but become shorter as the initiate progresses, all of which is indicated in the design of the formation.

To conclude this chapter, a word on the human Monad from Apollonius of Tyana, arguably the greatest mystic and spiritual Teacher (apart from Jesus Christ) in the early years of the Christian era:

"There is no death of anyone, but only in appearance, even as there is no birth of any, save only in seeming. The change from being to becoming seems to be birth, and the change from becoming to being seems to be death, but in reality no one is ever born, nor does one ever die. It is simply a being visible and then invisible; the former through the density of matter, and the latter because of the subtlety of being – being which is ever the same ..." (Mead 1901, p. 149)

---

NOTE

## THE ANCIENT EGYPTIAN BOOK OF THE DEAD

*The Fields of Peace* (*Sekhet-hetepet*). The ancient Egyptian texts on the Afterlife as it concerns humanity are gathered together under the title '*Chapters of Coming Forth by Day*' (*reu nu pert em hru*), rendered as *The Book of the Dead*. The scope of this material, which is directly related to the matter of this book, is too complex and substantial other than to be briefly noted here. It shows in its own terms and symbolism an extraordinary insight into the 'modes of being'.

The vignettes in the *Papyrus of Ånhai* (BM EA10472/5) is a particularly good example dating from the Twentieth Dynasty (c. 1100 BC) and is generally identified as *Spell 110*. It is concerned with the emotional plane, the first to be encountered after death. The sheet (8.5) is divided into four registers and should be read from left to right in each case. A hieroglyphic inscription runs along the top of each panel

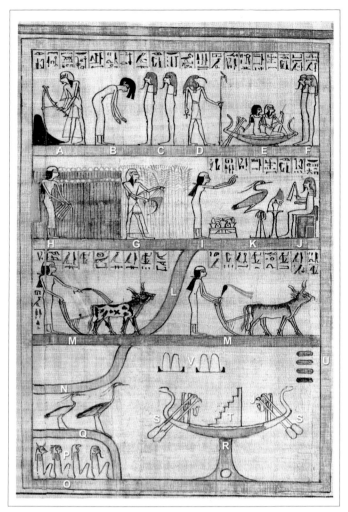

**8.5 *The Coming Forth by Day***

*The Fields of Peace. Papyrus of Ånhai, Spell 110. Twentieth Dynasty, c.1100 BC. London, British Museum EA10472. Sheet 5*

referring to the subject matter of the vignette. The fourth or lowest register appears to be missing most of these annotations.

*Register 1* (Top). Ånhai's husband (A) is constructing a mound of earth, probably over her grave. Ånhai (B) with her back to him, bows to her two mummified parents (C), one of whom is 'her mother Neferitu.' To be met at the point of death by loved ones, particularly family, is normal. The first stage is that in-

between state sometimes described as *Hades*. The dead woman is then led forward by the god Thoth (D), Ibis-headed, who holds the symbol of life (*ankh*) in his right hand and a sceptre of lordship in his left. He is called here 'The Lord of Divine Words'. Elsewhere in the *Chapters* 'The Word' (*hu*) is to be identified with the Soul, who leads the discarnate Personality forward into the next stage. The following scene (E) shows Ånhai and her husband, who by now has joined her in death, rowing a boat across the river (the classical Styx) to *the Fields of Peace* (*sekhet-hetepet*).

Ånhai is again met by her deceased parents (F), shown as mummies, who will help them settle in to a place which will be similar to that which they have left behind on the banks of the Nile. The hieroglyphic text reads 'Here begin the Chapters of the Fields of Peace, and the Chapters of Coming Forth by Day; or going into or coming out from the *duat* ['place of transformation'], of coming to the Fields of Reeds (*sekhet aaru*).'

*Register 2.* Ånhai and her husband are now living in the Fields of Peace where two kinds of cereal are growing: wheat which is being reaped by the husband (G), and behind him red barley in which stands Ånhai (H) following behind with a rush basket. This register ends with Ånhai standing by the side of a table of offerings (I) with her hands raised in adoration before a seated god, who is here described as the representative of 'the gods, the Lords of the *duat*' (J). Before him, on a table, are a libation vase and a lotus. The lotus is significant since it is the symbol *par excellence* of the four elements of creation (Lamy 1981, p. 10), and thus, by extension in this context, of the four Sons of Horus. Between Ånhai and the Deity is perched what is described as the *bennu*-bird, regarded as the Spirit (*akh*) of the deceased, which is now coming into prominence at this stage of her spiritual journey (K). This is alluded to in the accompanying hieroglyphic text 'Of being in the Fields of Peace, the mighty city' [see below], 'the Lady of Winds, of becoming a Spirit.' The 'Lady of Winds' is perhaps Ånhai's new, spiritual, name.

*Register 3.* This panel continues the functions of life in the Fields of Peace with a field divided into two by a stream (L) on each side of which Ånhai is seen ploughing with a yoke of oxen (M). The husband by this stage appears to have moved out of the picture. The hieroglyphic commentary of this register reads 'Of ploughing there; of reaping there; of making love there; and of doing everything even as a person doeth upon the Earth.' It continues "May I come therein, and may my soul follow after me [and obtain] divine food. May I plough therein and reap therein, even I the singer of Amen, Ånhai, triumphant."

*Register 4.* The lowest register has groups of symbols referring to the whole process of passing through the four lowest planes (4-7). On the left hand side are two islands. The upper island (N) is the 'birthplace of the god of the city' which in a symbolic sense refers to the rebirth of Ånhai as a cosmic spiritual being once past the fourth plane. The lower island (O) contains the figures symbolising the four lowest planes which have been traversed. These are the four Sons of Horus, and represent from left to right (P):

Plane 7.  *dua-mwt-f* with dog or jackal head
         Physical plane

Plane 6.  *kebeh-senuef* with falcon's head
         Emotional plane

Plane 5.  *hâpi* with baboon's head
         Mental plane

Plane 4.  *imset* with human head
         Buddhic or intuitional plane.

Ånhai's Personality has by the end of this process been absorbed by the Soul (*ba*) and the Spirit (*akh*) represented by the *bennu*-birds (Q) which face the barque (R) which will take her onward to the three planes beyond. On the moored barque are four oars, two at the bow and two at the stern, which represent respectively the solar and lunar *Pitris* of the human Monad, which are aspects of the Sons of Horus. In the centre of the barque is an erection of seven steps, symbolising the whole initiatory process of the seven planes (T).

The fourth register also has two further groups of symbols representing the different aspects of the Ascension Process in its lower fourfold structure. In the right-hand top corner there are four pools or lakes (U), here unidentified, but in the *Papyrus of Nebseny* (BM EA9900, sheet 17) they are given the names of minor deities for spiritual purification: "I have plunged into the lakes of *tchesert*: behold me, for all filth has departed from me." These lakes may be regarded as symbolic of the spiritual 'deaths' between each plane, but more particularly of the increasing levels of purification required as part of the initiatory process.

The last group of symbols in the fourth register represent four granaries (V). Again they are unannotated here, but their significance becomes clear from another vignette. In the *Papyrus of Ani* (BM 10470, 35) there is something equivalent which is described as providing food for the Spirits. It is possible that the four granaries in the Ånhai papyrus represent the provision of suitable sustenance at each level of development of the human Monad.

*The Pyramid Texts*

The concepts of sequential development in the Afterlife as set out in the *Chapters of Coming Forth by Day*, with specific reference to this Papyrus of Ånhai, is a core theme in the oldest of such collections, *The Pyramid Texts*. This compilation of religious writings was inscribed inside the burial chambers of nine royal tombs of the late Old Kingdom. The earliest set is in the Fifth Dynasty pyramid of Unas (c. 2350 BC) and the latest in the Eighth Dynasty pyramid of Ibi (c. 2150 BC). The texts comprise nearly a thousand individual utterances – spells, prayers and longer passages – although no pyramid contains a complete set. They concern the king's resurrection into the Afterlife and his destiny among the gods. The various utterances were probably composed at different periods and almost certainly reflect in origin an oral tradition. (Wilkinson 2005, p. 197)

The thoughts behind the particular vignettes emphasised here in the Papyrus of Ånhai are beautifully illuminated in Utterances 610 and 670. (Faulkner 1969)

'You have gone, but you will return, you have slept, [but you will awake] you have died, but you will live ...'

'Betake yourself to the waterway, fare upstream ... travel about Abydos in this spirit-form of yours which the gods commanded to belong to you; may a stairway to the Netherworld be set up for you to the Place where Orion is.'

Travel on the Waterway of Life carrying the human Monad ever onward and upward is a constant motif in the Otherworlds, equivalent to the concept of the Ascension Process, so frequently quoted in this book. The Fields of Peace are bordered and traversed by such a waterway in the Papyrus of Ånhai.

Abydos, ancient city of *Abedju* and the premier religious centre of the early Egyptian dynasties, was the numinous point of departure for the travelling human Monad, whereas the constellation of Orion (identified with Osiris, the god of resurrection) is the preordained destiny of the human Monad. This is due to the link that the constellation has with the star Sirius. Sirius, the Second Ray of Love-Wisdom of Archon, is the ultimate destiny of most of spiritual humanity. Djwhal Khul speaks of the importance of Sirius: 'This being the solar system of love-wisdom, or of astral buddhic development, the ... Path [to Sirius] includes the larger number of the sons of men ... [who] pass to the sun Sirius there to undergo a tremendous manasic stimulation, for Sirius is the emanating source of manas.' (Bailey 1960, p. 426) This marks their transition from being a *Lord of Compassion* to a *Master of Wisdom*, essentially a product of the Fifth Initiation.

For further reading see E.A. Wallis Budge's *The Book of the Dead* (1989 Arkana Edition of the 1899 Kegan Paul, Trench, Trubner publication), and John H. Taylor, ed. (2010). *Journey through the Afterlife, Ancient Egyptian Book of the Dead*. London: British Museum Press.

# 9. THE HUMAN MONAD: THE INITIATIONS

*... it shall be*

*A Face like my face that receives thee; a Man like to me,*
*Thou shalt love and be loved by, for ever: a Hand like this hand*
*Shall throw open the gates of new life to thee! See the Christ stand!*

R. Browning (1812-1889)

*Saul*

## SUMMARY

In this chapter we continue our study of the Ascension Process and look in more detail at the *initiations*. We start with the Cherhill crop formation of 1993, a symbol of spiritual *accord* or *benison* to the Ascension Process by the Galactic and Solar Logoi. The protracted process of the Nine Initiations covering many lifetimes and huge 'expansions of consciousness' is illustrated by the Ipsden crop formation of 1994.

This lengthy process is necessary to ensure that every facet of the human Monad's character is correctly tuned, since the electromagnetic vibration rate of his metabolism has to be transformed. The spiritual qualities brought to fruition during the Ascension Process are based on certain *divine principles* which our Earth Logos demonstrates through the structure of His name. These are Love, Wisdom, Obedience and Purity, which are related here to stages of the Ascension Process. We close with the Ascension Process as described by Poemandres in the *Trismegistic Tractates* of the *Hermetica*.

## THE COSMIC ACCORD

*The Cherhill formation, Wiltshire, August 1993* (9.1 and 9.2)

This important formation appeared to the north of Cherhill Hill, Cherhill CP, Wiltshire (OS SU042697) in the early morning of Sunday 8.8.1993. The exact time can be estimated as 3.30 am when the local dogs and foxes barked. This has occurred on other occasions when formations produced high electromagnetic transmissions affecting nearby animals. The formation was competently surveyed by Paul Vigay and Andy Hillis, also by M. Jackson on the day. The writer also examined and photographed it, both from the air and the ground. Balls of light were recorded hovering near it. Vigay and Hillis noted that a 'higher' than average radiation count was obtained in this formation: 'outside the count was 8-15 micro sieverts per minute, whilst inside a reading of 34 micro sieverts was detected.' Both this scientific evidence and the visual character of the formation indicate that it is a genuine, geophysical event.

The formation has a linear plan with two components at the north end, subtly separated

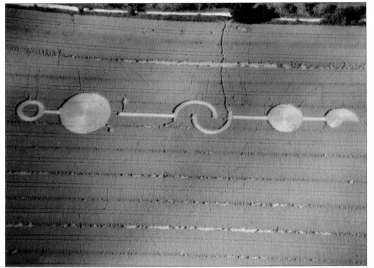

9.1 Cherhill, Wiltshire (OS SU042697), 8.8.1993

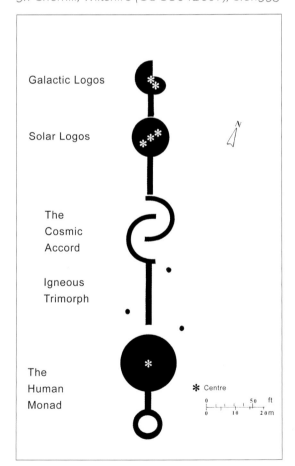

Galactic Logos

Solar Logos

The Cosmic Accord

Igneous Trimorph

The Human Monad

* Centre

9.2 *The Cosmic Accord*
Cherhill, 8.8.1993

from each other and the centre by a single row of standing stalks. At the other end is a dumb-bell formation comprising a ringed circle and a larger circle, well separated from the central pathway and the rest of the formation. The striking features are the two half-rings which appear to clasp each other in the centre. Between the dumb-bell and the clasp are three small circles.

There is no doubt in my mind that this formation is a simplified expression of 'good intent' on the part of the Galactic Spiritual Lords to the human Monads of planet Earth. Djwhal Khul speaks of the hierarchy of governing Souls which is an 'embodiment of the will aspect of the Logos – the will to good, the will to love, the will to know, the will to create.' (Bailey 1942, p. 245)

The northernmost element has a nautiloid shape, anticlockwise, with two spiral centres. The Pearly Nautilus (*N. pompilius*) has a cosmic significance since it symbolises the structure of our spiral galaxy. The Avatar to the Meso-american civilisations, Quetzalcoatl, who taught his people to make flower sacrifices rather than kill human beings, wore an image of the Nautilus round his neck. He whom I term *Aion*, the Central Spiritual Sun of our galaxy, uses this image as his numinous symbol. The two centres of this element are not just the two foci of the half circles; they say something significant about the essential status of this Cosmic Entity, Who operates on the Second Cosmic Plane (Bailey 1922a, p. 175), but also has in essence the dual aspects of Rays 1 and 2, where the One is expressed as Two.

The central pathway leading south out of the Nautilus element has a row of standing stalks at its junction with the next element, indicating its connection with, but separation from, the circle which forms the next element and which represents, I think, our Solar Logos. This anticlockwise element has three separate centres, which are again highly significant. Here the 'One is expressed in the Three', which is also the number of the cosmic plane on which our Solar Logos operates. Then there is a further pathway, essentially a cosmic *Antahkarana*, until it reaches the centre where again it is separated from the half ring by a single row of standing stalks.

At the southern end of the formation, aligned but separated from it by a 10 ft gap, is the element which I believe symbolises the human Monad, or more particularly Humanity. The southernmost feature is ringed, representing the spiritual aspect of the Monad; the upper feature, a large anticlockwise circle, represents the 'form' aspect of the Monad.

Between this southernmost element and the centre are three small circles forming an isosceles triangle straddling the formation, a symbol of *Agni*, Lord of Fire. (See Chapter 12.) This symbolises both the spiritual triadic make-up of the human Monad, and its connection with the Central Spiritual Fire of the Galactic Logos. 'At the fifth initiation the great secret which concerns the fire or spirit aspect is revealed to the wondering and amazed Master, and He realises in a sense incomprehensible to man the fact that all is fire, and fire is all.' (Bailey 1922a, p. 174)

## THE PLANETARY INITIATIONS

Three crop formations appeared in the Goring area of the South Midlands during the summer of 1994. The Garsons Hill, Ipsden,

Oxfordshire, formation is considered here. (9.3 and 9.4)

*9.3 Garsons Hill, Ipsden, Oxfordshire (OS SU647845), 10.7.1994*

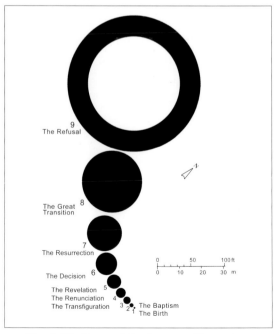

*9.4 **The Initiations of the human Monad** Garsons Hill, 10.7.1994*

It is my perception that this formation is concerned with the Ascension Process, and in particular the initiations. The other formations of this group, at Moulsford and East Ilsley, were considered in Chapter 5 in connection with the centres and bodies, respectively, of the human Monad.

*Garsons Hill, Ipsden CP, Oxon* (OS SU647845), between 5 am and 6 am, 10.7.1994, in wheat

Diameters in feet: (1) 3 ft, (2) 6 ft, (3) 11 ft, (4) 14 ft, (5) 21 ft, (6) 32 ft, (7) 52 ft, (8) 90 ft, and (9) ring outer edge 201 ft, ring width 31 ft. 8 circles according to Wolfgang Schindler. The CCCS database for 1994 states that there were 9 circles (*The Circular* #19, p. 21), i.e. 8 circles and a ring. Establishing the exact number of circles is important at a metaphysical, interpretative level. Unlike the formations from Moulsford and East Ilsley, which were carefully surveyed by Anthony Cheke and Geoff Ambler, not only do we not have the exact dimensions for most of the different features, except for circles 8 and 1, but we lack some details of the lay which would have provided critical additional information.

The Ipsden formation, from its position in the triangle at Goring, may be identified as referring to the 'Will' aspect (Ray 1 energy). There are nine elements of diminishing size, of which the largest is the ring or *Bi* symbol of Deity. The significance of the ninefold structure is emphasised by Djwhal Khul in terms of the threefold structure of Cosmic Life generally:

'Each of these three is also triple in manifestation, making therefore

a) the nine Potencies or Emanations,

b) the nine Sephiroth,

c) the nine Causes of Initiation.

These, with the totality of manifestation or the Whole, produce the ten (10) of perfect manifestation, or *the Perfect MAN*. [my italics] ... A human being is equally triple, manifesting as Spirit, Soul and Body, or Monad, Ego and Personality.' (Bailey 1925, p.4) The Greater Master, channelled by Dion Fortune comments as follows on this momentous theme: 'Ten is the Number of forces in manifestation for our universe, but nine is the Number of the Cosmic force which called that universe into being when that force is manifested on the first plane.' (Fortune 1976, p. 64)

The thrust of the Goring group of formations concerns the human Monad and its essential character and future, the Ipsden formation representing its highest aspect. Djwhal Khul is quite clear about the true nature of the human Monad. 'Man is *in essence* divine,' or to put this stupefying statement in its context: 'Each human being is an incarnation of God.' However: 'No Being can become a God without passing through the human cycles [briefly set out in Chapter 8], he represents also God in that He is a triplicity, being three in one, and one in three' (Bailey 1925, p. 809), and hence the numerological significance of the Ipsden formation.

So what precisely do those elements of the formation *mean* since they are clearly highly significant in symbolic terms? Returning to the earlier statement by Djwhal Khul about the ninefold structure of Cosmic Life, he selects three examples, the 'Potencies or Emanations', the 'Sephiroth' and the 'nine Causes of Initiation'. The great Cosmic Lords of the first two categories, although having some differential 'standing', could not possibly be represented as having the colossal differences in status shown in the elements of the Ipsden formation.

What we are looking at is the clearest possible statement of the Ascension Process of the human Monad in terms of the progression of initiatory experiences. (9.4) These critical 'expansions of consciousness' consist of a 'total possible nine initiations which confront developing humanity' (Bailey 1950, p. 90), each of which is of progressively more importance than the previous one.

*The First Initiation* ('The Birth'). The Soul begins to gain control over the physical appetites of the physical body of the Personality.

*The Second Initiation* ('The Baptism'). The Soul begins to gain control over the 'desire nature' of the emotional body of the Personality.

*The Third Initiation* ('The Transfiguration'). The development of the spiritual, intellectual faculties of the Personality.

*The Fourth Initiation* ('The Renunciation'). The absorption of the perfected Personality by the Soul or Ego. The initiate by this stage has mastered the physical, emotional and mental planes and is able to handle the lower ethers of the buddhic plane of Love-Wisdom.

*The Fifth Initiation* ('The Revelation'). If the previous four initiations represent the preparatory stages for the human Monad in the Ascension Process, the Fifth Initiation constitutes a spiritual 'coming of age', indeed it is deemed 'to correspond to the First Cosmic Initiation ... that of "entered apprentice".' (Bailey 1922a, p. 18) The Personality-Soul becomes an enlightened member of the Planetary Team under the Earth Logos. In the Ipsden formation all the lower circles up to this point are anticlockwise. Once the human Monad has completed the course of spiritual development on planet Earth, the remaining elements of the formation are laid down in alternating directions, symbolising 'changes of direction or function' required in the higher initiations.

*The Sixth Initiation* ('The Decision'). The Master of Wisdom at this point decides which of the Seven Paths of spiritual service he will follow, all except one of which lie outside our planetary system. The circle marking this point in the Ipsden formation has a clockwise rotation marking the transition to becoming a functioning cell of the Solar Logos.

At the time of the Sixth Initiation, the initiate has to face the choice of one of Seven Paths. But before any one of those Paths can be trodden 'a man must be a Master of the Wisdom, he must be a Brother of Compassion, and he must be able, through intelligence and love, to wield the law.' (Bailey 1922a, p. 185) As might be expected, this is not an absolutely free choice, but is determined by the sum total of past Personality/Soul orientation, experience and commitments. 'All these seven Paths lead either to the cosmic astral plane or to the cosmic mental plane, according to the decision made at the Sixth Initiation. Upon the cosmic astral plane there is no glamour, but instead a great vortex of energy – the energy of pure love – under the domination of the Law of Attraction.' (Bailey 1960, p. 399) Only one path is concerned with Earth Service, 'that keeps a man linked to the Hierarchy which is pledged to the service of our planetary scheme.' (Bailey 1925, p. 1244) The other six paths involve work either beyond our planetary system, or within a broader framework which incorporates it.

'At the sixth initiation, the initiate, functioning consciously as the love-aspect of the Monad, is brought ... into a still vaster recognition ... He thus makes his conscious contact with the solar Logos, and realises within himself the Oneness of all life and manifestation. This recognition is extended at the seventh initiation.' (Bailey 1922a, p. 118) He is then able to pass from the limits of our solar system to that greater Being of which our solar system forms part, whom I term Archon. This, the Initiation of Decision, is the point where he makes his final choice of Cosmic Path. 'Thus by a graded series of steps is the initiate brought face to face with Truth and Existence ... His faith for ages is justified, and hope and belief merge themselves in self-ascertained fact. Faith is lost in sight, and things unseen are seen and known.' (Bailey 1922(i), 118) As St Paul puts it: 'For now we see in a mirror, dimly, [Greek - in a riddle] but then we will see face to face. Now I know only in part; then I will know fully, even as I have been fully known. And now faith, hope and love abide, these three; and the greatest of these is love.' (*1 Corinthians*, 13:12-13)

*The Seventh Initiation* ('The Resurrection'). The human Monad, by this stage functioning as a fully spiritual being with its three components, Personality, Soul and Spirit fully conjoined, begins to operate within the orbit of that greater Being, Archon.

*The Eighth Initiation* ('The Great Transition'). In the Ipsden formation there is another change of direction in the flow of the crop to a clockwise direction, for this marks the point where the human Monad, as a Master of Wisdom and fully conversant with the Lords and life of our local solar systems, becomes part of the Being of the Galactic Logos, Aion.

*The Ninth Initiation* ('The Refusal'). The great ring at Ipsden, involving another change of flow of the crop to an anticlockwise direction, marks the last great expansion of consciousness of the human Monad. The ring, the *Bi* symbol, representing Deity, marks the call of the Cosmic Monad to the human Monad

to a state perhaps even beyond that of service. It is *the refusal* because He is aware of all that needs to be done to save humanity, and indeed what He could do for our Earth Logos. 'This appeal is so strong that the Initiate – because His heart is on fire with love – is tempted to go back upon His decision and stay upon the planet with Those World Saviours Who have chosen the Path of Earth Service. This He may not do, and in the sight of the assembled Initiates He makes His refusal and "does His whole duty as He journeys to the sacred Feet of the ONE WHO stands at the end of His chosen Path".' (Bailey 1960, p. 736)

'Through the Planetary Logos at the final great initiation flows the power of the Solar Logos, and He it is Who reveals to the initiate that the Absolute is consciousness in its fullest expression ...' (Bailey 1922a, p. 92)

In this pedestrian recital of the great initiations of the human Monad it is difficult to convey the momentous import of the spiritual initiations as great stages of human evolution – not even the majesty and excitement of such an occasion. However the Irish mystic, George William Russell, envisioned such a ceremony as follows:

'There was a hall vaster than any cathedral, with pillars that seemed built out of living and trembling opal, or from some starry substances which shone with every colour, the colours of eve and dawn. A golden air glowed in this place, and high between the pillars were thrones which faded, glow by glow, to the end of the vast hall. On them sat the Divine Kings. They were fire-crested. I saw the crest of the dragon on one, and there was another plumed with brilliant fires that jetted forth like feathers of flame. They sat shining and starlike, mute as statues, more colossal than Egyptian images of their gods, and at the end of the hall was a higher throne on which sat one greater than the rest. A light like the sun glowed behind him. Below on the floor of the hall lay a dark figure as if in trance, and two of the Divine Kings made motions with their hands about it over head and body. I saw where their hands waved how sparkles of fire like the flashing of jewels broke out. There rose out of that dark body a figure as tall, and glorious, as shining as those seated on the thrones. As he woke to the hall he became aware of his divine kin, and he lifted up his hands in greeting. He had returned from his pilgrimage through darkness, but now an initiate, a master in the heavenly guild. While he gazed on them, the tall golden figures from their thrones leaped up, they too with hands uplifted in greeting, and they passed from me and faded swiftly in the great glory behind the throne.' (A.E. 1965, pp. 35-37)

I understand that this momentous occasion is that of the initiate at the end of his development in our system, and is a vision of the Eighth Initiation where he ascends to Communion with the Galactic Logos.

The Tibetan, Djwhal Khul, must be allowed to have the last word on this momentous theme: 'One attainment leads to another; out of the lower kingdoms man has emerged, and (as a result of human struggle) the kingdom of God will also appear. The bringing in of that kingdom is all that truly concerns humanity today, and all living processes in mankind are bent towards preparing each individual human being to pass into that kingdom.' (Bailey 1960, p. 738)

How then does the ambitious aspirant achieve the process of initiation, that deeply desired result of spiritual achievement and ascension? Djwhal Khul, as ever, is particularly to the point: 'Students must get rid of the idea that if they are "very good and altruistic"

suddenly some day they will stand before the Great Lord. ... Goodness and altruism grow out of realisation and service, and holiness of character is the outcome of those expansions of consciousness which a man brings about within himself through strenuous effort and endeavour.' (Bailey 1922a, pp. 92-93) It is the product of what the New Age calls 'inner work' developing the mental body and controlling the emotional body. He thereby becomes sensitive to the vibrations of the Soul, the aspirant's Master and his fellow men – feeling 'the joys and pains and sorrows of those he daily contacts; he feels them ... and yet he is not incapacitated thereby.' (Bailey 1922a, p. 93)

The spiritual Ascension Process of the human Monad is thus a two-way process. It is the Soul, with the Spirit of the human Monad behind Him, that determines each step of the Way for His incarnated Personality. As Jesus Christ said: "No one can see the kingdom of God without being born from above." (*John* 3:3) During any incarnatory experience when the conditions are right, the Soul will stimulate the Personality to take a further step along the spiritual path. John Wesley's 'conversion' in 1738 is a classic example. He was directed to go to a particular Meeting House in London where by listening to a certain passage of scripture he felt his heart *strangely warmed*, and later considered that his true spiritual life began from that moment. (Rowell, Stevenson and Williams 2001, p. 287)

So what are the conditions that the Soul looks for in the Personality before the next step can be taken? We are told that the name of the Earth Logos is *Ibez*, named after four great Avatars or 'world saviours' who came to planet Earth in the first millennium BC. Each Avatar embodied a particular 'divine principle' (Bailey 1934, p. 379), and these can be deduced from their respective characters and teaching:

JESUS (Christ) c. 6/5 BC - c. 30/33 AD. *Love*

BUDDHA (Gautama Siddhartha) c. 563-483 BC. *Wisdom*

ELIJAH (The Tishbite) ninth century BC. *Obedience*

ZARATHUSTRA (Zoroaster) sixth century BC or earlier. *Purity*.

It will be evident that these spiritual qualities for their full and permanent development may require a lengthy period of time in terms of reincarnations and stages of the Ascension Process. Indeed, as reflecting the higher qualities of each virtue, it is clear that the structure of the initiatory process would gradually take an individual through each stage: the emotional state (*love*) – to the mental state (*wisdom*) – to the buddhic state (*purity*). The virtue that governs and colours all is that of *obedience*; a matter of following not merely a written code of behaviour imposed from outside, but also the inner promptings of conscience which is the voice of the god within. Indeed for spiritual progress there must be a corresponding urge for improvement, for spiritual change, at a Personality level. Thus the golden thread of the *Antahkarana* is built and maintained between the highest and lowest centres of the human Monad.

Now all this is at odds with most religious systems today, which teach that the individual has only one life to complete the entire spiritual process, or else is damned. This is not the teaching of the Ancient Wisdom as we have seen throughout this study. There is however an urgent need for each life or incarnation, as far as its human circumstances permit, to fulfil its spiritual potential. Indeed this is the prime purpose of our Earth Logos for humanity, when: 'He decided to create this planet of ours for strictly redemptive purposes.' (Bailey 1955, p. 223)

But how was this to be achieved, for the bulk of humanity as opposed to a few 'super saints' of whatever faith? The first syllable of the planetary name of the Earth Logos is 'I' (Jesus), and for a very good reason. In the past 'World Saviours and Workers' have traditionally promoted abstract ideas or laws in their teaching about the numinous nature of God and what is required of humanity. By incorporating Himself as a human being, the Soul of the Solar Logos (the God of our system) introduced a different system altogether, namely that of a personage with Whom a personal relationship could be achieved. This immediately opened up the possibility of a close connection with Deity not possible through the intellectual assimilation of mere abstract ideas. Or to put it another way, it introduced the concept of *love* as part of the dual quality of 'Love-Wisdom', so often discussed in this study. As Jesus Christ himself said: 'Very truly, I tell you, anyone who hears my Word and believes Him who sent me has eternal life, and does not come under judgement, but has passed from death to life.' (*John* 5:24)

The whole duty of the human Monad that it might fulfil its karmic destiny eventually, is thus summed up in the teaching of Jesus Christ.

**THE HERMETIC MESSAGE**

Perhaps the most sublime communication from the ancient Hellenistic world is that covered in the *Hermetica*, material concerned with Theosophy and Gnosis. The most profound of these voluminous writings of Hermes Trismegistus is that entitled '*Poemandres, the Shepherd of Men*', of which the late G.R.S. Mead, the authority on this corpus of material, writes that it 'not only belongs to the most important type of the Trismegistic literature, but is also the most important document within that type.' (Mead 1906, Volume 2.1.1, p. 20)

When asked "Who art thou?", Poemandres describes Himself as "Man-Shepherd" (Ποιμάνδρης), "Mind of all-masterhood" (ὁ τῆς αὐθεντίας νοῦς), Who, on the basis of the name and epithet alone, may be identified with the Solar Logos. I have earlier referred to this material (Chapter 4) under the *Trismegistic Tractates*, and I suggest that it was a vision of the Egyptian priest Nechepso, c. 150 BC. Orthodox scholarship, however, would date the *Hermetica* rather later, indeed to the early centuries AD.

Poemandres, amongst other important material, discusses the Ascension Process through the planes or modes of being, from a deific point of view. The 'ascended masters' of the Ancient Wisdom have much to say about *Gnosis*, spiritual knowledge or wisdom as an essential ingredient of this process. However, from the Solar Logos' point of view, even more important for the human Monad is spiritual *obedience* and *purity*. This section is worth quoting in full since it deals in turn with the seven modes of being of our own planetary system, and the eighth which moves into the orbit of the Solar Logos. The planes, which are here called *zones*, are numbered from the bottom upwards. Each stage, punctuated by an initiation, is seen by the Logos as a process of ridding the human Monad of undesirable character traits and habits.

'25. And thus it is that man doth speed his way thereafter upwards through the Harmony.

To the first zone he gives the Energy of Growth and Waning; unto the second [zone], Device of Evils [now] de-energized; unto the third, the Guile of the Desires de-energized; unto the fourth, his Domineering Arrogance, [also] de-energized; unto the fifth, unholy Daring and the Rashness of Audacity, de-energized; unto the sixth, Striving for Wealth by evil means, deprived of its aggrandisement; and to the seventh zone, Ensnaring Falsehood, de-energized.' (Mead 1906, Volume 2.1.1, pp. 15-16)

Notwithstanding the somewhat archaic terminology, it can be seen how, beginning with the physical state in the first zone, the Personality is forced to shed at each stage, first bodily and emotional sins, and then intellectual and spiritual ones as it moves upwards.

'26. And then, with all the energizings of the Harmony stript from him, clothed in his proper Power, he cometh to that Nature which belongs unto the Eighth, and there with those-that-are hymneth the Father.

They who are there welcome his coming there with joy; and he, made like to them that sojourn there, doth further hear the Powers who are above the Nature that belongs unto the Eighth, singing their songs of praise to God in language of their own.

And then they, in a band, (τάξει) go to the Father home; of their own selves they make surrender of themselves to Powers, and [thus] becoming Powers they are in God. This the good end for those who have gained Gnosis – to be made one with God.' (Mead 1906, Volume 2.1.1, pp. 16-17)

Although this material may have seemed strange to the scholars and those who transliterated the text down the centuries, the gist of it should now be clear. The strange use of the word 'band', for example, (also translated 'order' or 'group'), troubled earlier commentators. Walter Scott translates this section as 'each in his turn' (i.e. the men who have ascended to the eighth sphere) 'mount upward to the Father.' (Scott 1992, p. 53) However, as we have seen in Chapter 8, it is only on the fifth plane that the various Personalities from previous lives of the human Monad have to cooperate, indeed coordinate their spiritual response, before they can go forward as a group or 'band' to the buddhic plane.

Poemandres ends this profound dissertation with a spiritual challenge as applicable to the writer, and reader of this book, as it was to the priest Nechepso over two thousand years ago.

'Why shouldst thou then delay? Must it not be, since thou hast all received, that thou shouldst to the worthy point the way, in order that through thee the race of mortal kind may by [thy] God be saved?' (Mead 1906, Volume 2.1.1, p. 17)

# 10. THE HUMAN MONAD: THE LOGOIC RAYS, COLOURS, SOUND AND NAMES.
# THE JEWEL OF THE LAW

*"All paths meet at the centre. The many become the seven and the eight. From point to point the lines converge. They stretch from point to point. The outer square, the circle of the One and the point of unity are seen as one, and the Master passes on His way."*

Bailey 1955, p. 275

## SUMMARY

The miscellany of subjects in this chapter deals with aspects of the natural world which reflect qualities of the Cosmic Logoi in their relationship with mankind. It is also concerned with the expected behaviour of the human Monad on the spiritual path. The crop formation in 1994 at East Dean, West Sussex, appears to relate to the Seven *Ray* structure of Deity, indeed the generic make-up of any spiritual being, including man, 'made in the image of God.' Turning to *colour*, the crop formation in 2003 at Burham, Kent, does not of course show differentiated colours, but, as a simulacrum of the Solar Logos as a Star of David, it depicts the colourific structure of the spectrum, whose individual colours are analysed in terms of the Ray structure. The important point about the colour spectrum is that it represents the DNA

*10.1 The East Dean Group, West Sussex, 24.7.1994*
*Left, OS TQ897132, Right, OS TQ896136*

structure of the Solar Logos as a living Entity, and by extension the Planetary Logoi also. Logoic *sound* is closely related to colour value as an aspect of vibration. It is important because a proper understanding of the laws of vibration actively promotes healing and spiritual growth. The different sorts of *names* of the Cosmic Logoi are considered and the dangers of knowing or using them, illustrated by a personal experience. The last crop formation considered here is that of 1994 at Berwick Bassett, Wiltshire. The extraordinary symbolism of this formation with a claw holding a ball is a direct reference to the Buddhist concept of the *Jewel of the Law* where the Jewel held by the dragon comprises the Seven Laws of Soul or Group Life. Each of the Seven Laws is briefly considered since they are in effect the essential guidelines for spiritual humanity.

Chapter 10 is thus a *coda* to what has preceded it about the human Monad, and also an introduction to the wider realms of the Cosmos which follow in Chapters 11-14.

**THE LOGOIC RAYS**

*East Dean Group, West Sussex, July 1994* (10.1)

As we have seen, the Goring group of formations of 1994 concerns important aspects of the human Monad. That same summer a further group of two similar formations appeared 60 miles away at East Dean in West Sussex. (Thomas 1996, pp. 64-66)

I believe that the East Dean group of formations deals not so much with the human Monad in isolation but with its relationship to the Earth Logos. The two formations lay within half a mile of each other and were comprehensively recorded by members of the former Sussex Branch (S.B.) of the CCCS. The East Dean formation (S.B. ref. 94.08)

*10.2 East Dean, West Sussex (OS TQ897132). 24.7.1994*

RAYS OF ASPECT
1  Will or Power
2  Love-Wisdom
3  Active Intelligence

RAYS OF ATTRIBUTE
4  Harmony, Beauty and Art
5  Knowledge or Science
6  Abstract Idealism and Devotion
7  Organisation

10.3 **The Seven Rays**
*East Dean, 24.7.1994*

(7.1), which I believe to refer to the modes of being, was discussed in Chapter 7.

*East Dean (S.B. ref. 94.07) West Sussex* (OS TQ897132) on 23-24.7.1994, in wheat (10.2 and 10.3)

Diameters in feet. All features anticlockwise except (6) which was clockwise. Ring (1) outer diameter 185 ft. Ring width 28 ft. Outer edge of standing crescent (2) 130 ft. Inner circle (3)

100 ft. Circles (4) 68 ft, (5) 50 ft, (6) 24 ft and (7) 20 ft. The threefold structure of the Monad is evident, with the outer *Bi* ring of Ray 1, the crescent in standing crop Ray 3 and the inner circle representing Ray 2.

I have used the term 'Rays' because I believe this may be the theme of this formation. Other aspects of this subject will be covered in material dealing with the Earth and Solar Logoi. At this point I only wish to tabulate in simple format the essentials of this difficult subject, which is bound up with the processes of physical creation as an aspect of the 'development' of Deity.

To quote again from the Welsh mystic Iolo Morganwg:

'When God pronounced His name, with the word sprang the light and the life ... the springing of the light ... / | \ in three columns, ... and in the rays of light the vocalization – for one were the hearing and seeing; one unitedly the *form* and sound; and one unitedly with the form and sound was *life*, and one unitedly with these three was *power*, which power was God the Father' (my italics). ... 'Thus was the voice, that was heard, placed on record in the symbol, and meaning attached to each of the three notes:- the sense of O was given to the first column, the sense of I to the second or middle column, and the sense of V to the third; whence the word OIV ... it was by means of this word that God declared His existence, life, knowledge, power, eternity and universality. And in the declaration was His love ...' (Williams, J. 1862, pp. 17-19)

There are a number of Deific aspects which emerge from this extremely important Celtic teaching, and can only be touched on here:

1. The Rays of Light
2. The Sound or Creative Word
3. The Name of God.

'All manifestation is of a septenary nature and the Central Light which we call Deity, the one Ray of Divinity, manifests first as a Triplicity, and then as a Septenary ... The synthetic Ray which blends them all is the great Love-Wisdom Ray, for verily and indeed "God is Love".' (Bailey 1922a, p. 3) Each Ray conveys a different dynamic power characteristic of Deity in terms of electro-magnetic energy, colour, sound and quality as expressed in human Monadic consciousness.

| Rays of Aspect | | | |
|---|---|---|---|
| Ray | Energy | Quality | Colour |
| 1. | Will or Power (Father aspect) | Dynamic purpose | Red |
| 2. | Love-Wisdom (Son aspect) | Love | Blue |
| 3. | Active Intelligence (Holy Spirit/ Mother aspect) | Intellect | Yellow |
| Rays of Attribute | | | |
| 4. | Harmony, Beauty and Art | Harmony | Orange |
| 5. | Knowledge or Science | Discrimination | Green |
| 6. | Abstract Idealism and Devotion | Devotion | Violet |
| 7. | Organisation | Structure | Indigo |

These names are simply some chosen from amongst the many, and embody different aspects of force by means of which the Logos manifests. (See Bailey 1922a, p. 224.)

As we have begun to see in Chapter 5, any spiritual being, including man, also relates to the Rays of Aspect as follows:

Ray 1 – Spirit

Ray 2 – Soul

Ray 3 – Personality.

The basic qualities of the Rays of Attribute (the *Quaternio*) can be expressed as:

*10.4 Burham, Kent (OS TQ735621), 12.7.2003*

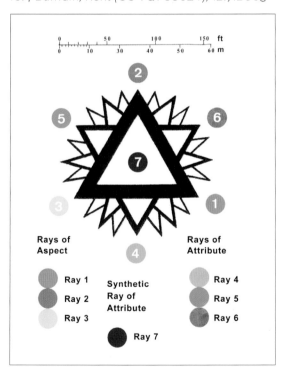

*10.5* **Colour and the Seven Rays**
*Burham. 12.7.2003*

Ray 4 – Spiritual/Buddhic aspect

Ray 5 – Mental aspect

Ray 6 – Emotional aspect

Ray 7 – Physical aspect.

## THE LOGOIC COLOURS

The colour spectrum is important because an understanding of colouration in terms of the qualities of the Rays helps explain the organic structure of the Monadic manifestation. The range of colours particularly associated with our Solar Logos is well known, being those associated with the rainbow, which is a spectrum of sunlight refracted through raindrops. From white solar light come the colours of red, orange, yellow, green, blue, indigo and violet – seven in all – in order of the decreasing wavelength or increasing frequency of electromagnetic energy.

*The Burham formation, Kent, 2003 (10.4 and 10.5)*

One of the most helpful of crop formations which would appear to throw light on the matter of colour was a solar mandala which appeared close to the Pilgrims' way near Burham, Kent (OS TQ735621) on 12.7.2003. The core of the formation is an ancient Semitic symbol, the Seal of Solomon (Star of David), which has more direct esoteric significance. (See comments by Djwhal Khul on the 6-pointed star in connection with the Birling formation of 1998, in Chapter 7.)

If the three primary colours of red, blue and yellow are applied to mark the apexes of the large uppermost triangle, they may be seen to represent the primary aspects (or Rays of Aspect) of the Solar Logos as follows:

Ray 1 (red) – *Will or Power*

Ray 2 (blue) – *Love-Wisdom*

Ray 3 (yellow) – *Active Intelligence.*

The secondary colours (the Rays of Attribute) mark the apexes of the lower triangle, and form intermediate colours between the primaries:

Ray 4 (orange) – *Harmony, Beauty and Art* between Ray 1 (red) and Ray 3 (yellow)

Ray 5 (green) – *Knowledge or Science* between Ray 2 (blue) and Ray 3 (yellow)

Ray 6 (violet) – *Abstract Idealism and Devotion* between Ray 2 (blue) and Ray 1 (red).

However there is a seventh Ray (indigo), which forms the numinous centre of the diagram and informs all the other Rays. It is this Ray, I believe, which is particularly associated with the physical organisation of matter, the end product in a way of the contribution of all the other Rays, which at the same time is supportive of them. (Bailey 1953, p. 181) It illustrates the close symbiotic relationship between 'Spirit' and 'Matter', this being represented *per se* by the basal centre of the human Monad. 'This basic centre is the point where, under the evolutionary law, spirit and matter meet, and life is related to form.' (Bailey 1953, p. 182) It is important to view the colour system as a vibrant *structure*. Djwhal Khul is particularly clear about this:

'The seven colours may be regarded as a band ... circling and continuously shifting and moving through the planes back to their originating source ... These seven bands of colour emanate from the synthetic Ray. The indigo sub-ray of the indigo Ray forms the path of least resistance from the heart of densest matter back again to the source. The bands of colour form a circulating ring which, moving at different rates of vibration, passes *through* all the planes, circling down and up again.' (Bailey 1922b, p. 211) 'The true *indigo* is the blue of the vault of heaven on a moonless night. It is the culmination, and at the

attainment by all of synthesis, the solar night will supervene. Hence the colour corresponds to what the sky nightly proclaims. Indigo absorbs.' (Bailey 1922b, p. 212)

Now the colourist familiar with the conventional colour circle will notice that the colour *purple* which is a synthesis of red and blue is missing. Indeed it has been replaced by *violet*, which is not a true synthesis of these colours. Interestingly in the colour spectrum, violet lies at the far end of the spectrum beyond indigo, almost as if it is a later addition. Why should this be so? Djwhal Khul refers to 'loathsome purple' and describes it as one of the 'involutionary colours.' 'They are the offspring of night, esoterically understood. They are the basis of glamour, of despair and of corruption, and must be neutralised by the pupil of the Great Ones by the admission of the colours connected with light.' (Bailey 1922b, pp. 209-210) In short the colour purple is associated in some way with 'cosmic evil' and the 'Dark Brotherhood.' I suspect, and it is only a suspicion, that the colour purple, demonstrating a particular Ray, was that of one of the 'fallen angels' of our system. Consequently it had to be completely removed from the spiritual spectrum of colour values of the Solar Logos.

Djwhal Khul was very reticent to say much, or indeed anything of any consequence, about how the colour spectrum related to the Rays – to the point of contributing misleading information which he described as 'blinds' at the time. The reason for this became evident in a communication on 28.8.1920, published in *Letters on Occult Meditation* in 1922. He is speaking about the bands of colour mentioned in the previous paragraph:

'These coloured rings do not follow a straight unimpeded course, but interweave in a most curious manner, blending with each other, absorbing each other in stated cycles, and grouping themselves in groups of threes or fives, yet ever moving onwards. ... Three major lines of colour should be portrayed as forming the lattice work ... with the four other colours interweaving.' (Bailey 1922b, p. 212)

Does this sound somehow familiar? Of course it does – Djwhal Khul is visualising what is effectively DNA, and not just any DNA, but that of the Solar Logos as a living Entity, and by extension, that of the Planetary Logoi also.

Back in 1920 this would not have meant very much to anyone, but the discovery of how deoxyribonucleic acid occurs in combination with protein in the chromosomes, which contain the genetic instructions for the fabric of life – all of which was discovered in 1953 – casts an entirely different light on the subject. Like DNA there would appear to be two chains (sugar and phosphate in DNA), recognised in occult studies as representing Ray 1 (red) and Ray 3 (yellow). As with DNA the chains are twisted round each other in the form of a double helix and held together by bonding (hydrogen in DNA), which could be equated with Ray 2 (blue) energies. The four nitrogenous bases which are arranged in a regular structure, and provide in code the genetic information in DNA, are paralleled by the four subsidiary colours of the spectrum, which are arranged in different patterns.

No wonder Djwhal Khul stated: 'it is not yet permissible to give out the esoteric significance of these colours, nor exact information as to their order and application. The dangers are too great ...' (Bailey 1922b, p. 212) For this reason the writer must also remain silent about any further information on this topic.

## LOGOIC SOUND

We start with a categorical statement by Djwhal Khul. 'It is a truism to say that sound is colour and colour is sound ... remember always that all sounds express themselves in colour. When the Logos uttered the great cosmic Word for this solar system, three major streams of colour issued forth, ... so giving us the seven streams of colour by which manifestation becomes possible.' (Bailey 1922b, p. 205) Which brings us back to the 'Coming into Being' statement by Iolo Morganwg quoted earlier in this chapter, which makes the same point.

Vibration and sound are thus essential ingredients of the creative process: *'Vibration* or initial activity, *light*, or activity taking form and animating form, *sound*, the basis of differentiation and the source of the evolutionary process, and *colour* the sevenfold differentiation – thus is the work carried on.' (Bailey 1925, p. 329) Or in the words of the Greater Master: 'The prime activity is MOVEMENT. The second activity is LIGHT. The third activity is SOUND.' (Fortune 1976, p. 19)

The science of Cymatics, the study of sound waves and their interaction with physical substances, has been the special field of study of Freddy Silva. (Silva 2002)

Returning to the subject of the Rays: 'each of the seven rays emits its own sound, and in so doing sets in motion those forces which must work in unison with it.' (Bailey 1936, p. 8) On the creative (and destructive) uses of vibration and sound, I will say only that I perceive there is a relationship between the different sizes of the East Dean formation elements and the tonal values of the sounds of the Seven Rays.

A closing word from Djwhal Khul: 'the method employed in the utilisation of colour and sound in healing, in promoting spiritual growth, and in esoteric construction on the physical plane, will be based on the laws that govern the mental body, and will be forms of meditation. Only as the race develops the dynamic powers and attributes of thought ... will the capacity to make use of the laws of vibration be objectively possible.' (Bailey 1922b, p. 251)

## THE NAMES OF GOD

Every organism in the Cosmos has its own true name, which is so constructed as to reflect the character, indeed inner make-up, of the Being concerned. This is why in occult studies it is perceived that the adept who knows the true name of any entity (and has the appropriate knowledge and strength) has power over it, since in theory he can control its inner workings. Thus it is that great Entities, in particular, have also a 'call name' for general use, and an 'epithet' which is a general description of the Entity and also alludes to Its primary character or quality. The Archangel Michael (Mikhael or Mikkel), the 'Soul' or 'Logos' of planet Earth, Lord of the World and head of its Great Council, has a name of two elements, MIKHA meaning 'like unto' and EL meaning 'God'. The matter is further complicated in that, say in the case of the Seven Great Lords of the Great Council of planet Earth, each great religious system has its own nomenclature for these Beings, reflecting their perceived character and duties. I understand that to use even the 'call name' is dangerous since the Entity concerned will be tempted to respond, which could destroy the ordinary disciple.

In the 1970s I used to stay regularly at Cannes in the south of France with a friend, and visit the Lérins islands off the coast, named after the Celtic god Lir, cognate with Varuna, the Indo-Aryan god of water and the sea. I located the area where the ancient shrine of the Deity had been on the Ile St Marguerite, and would sit listening to the wind in the pines and meditate on that ancient world. On one occasion I and a friend were there in February at the time of the great Celtic spring festival of *Imbolc*, and I was physically summoned to attend. However the weather was foul, the ferries were not working and I did not go. That night, in our ground floor hotel room facing out to sea, we had a visitation. A great storm came up and blew in the French windows of our room. The next morning we went out to see the damage. There was a path of destruction about 30 ft wide running straight up from the Mediterranean to our hotel room. This event taught me a sharp lesson. I had not consciously used the deific names in any summoning or form of ceremony, but I was aware of Who they were in a place where They had once been held sacred, and this was enough to ensure a response. The Devic world is desperate to establish communication with human *sensitives* who in some sense are on their 'wavelength', with possible dangerous consequences for the human Monad.

There is also the added complication that, say in the case of the Seven Rays or Aspects of Deity, they effectively constitute great Offices of State, certainly in the Councils of the Solar and Earth Logoi. Suitable spirits from all over our galaxy hold these posts for a determined period before moving on. The more senior of Them are in post for aeons of time during any one of the great cycles or *manvantaras* (periods of activity or manifestation). All these office holders have, of course, their own titles, which Djwhal Khul has been at pains to set out. (Bailey 1922a, pp. 37–49)

For all these reasons it is inevitable that there

is a measure of inconsistency in nomenclature in this study. I am permitted to use only the 'epithets' of the Cosmic Lords. Coming from the Christian tradition I would have liked to use only the names of the Archangels of our Solar and Planetary systems as established in the teaching of the Judaic/Christian/Islamic systems, and indeed these will be set out in the appropriate place. But the names of some of these Angelic Beings are now very obscure, and I have tended therefore to use the Indo-Aryan names of these Lords, where it appears to be more appropriate.

The name of God as described in the Old Testament, which I understand is that of the One, the 'one Boundless Immutable Principle; one Absolute Reality' (Bailey 1925, p. 3) has been clearly given for use by mankind. When Moses (c. thirteenth century BC) received his commission to be the deliverer of Israel (*Exodus*, 3), the Almighty, who appeared to him in the burning bush, communicated the name which he should give as credentials of his mission: 'And God said to Moses I AM WHO I AM.' (*ehyeh ăsher ehyeh* in ancient Hebrew) He said further: 'Thus you shall say to the Israelites, "I AM has sent me to you."' The etymological reading of this latter expression would be *Yahăveh* (Jehovah), which is of course an epithet only, but containing the three sacred syllables of the Threefold Nature of Deity YAH-ĂV-EH.

As we have seen, this threefold structure is also found in the three creative Rays of light and the sound that accompanies them. Djwhal Khul describes this process as follows:

'*The Logoic Breath ... First plane ... the Sound A*

This is the first etheric appearance of a solar system upon the atomic sub plane of the cosmic physical plane. The seeds of life are all latent ...

*The Logoic Sound ... Second plane ... the Sound AU*

This is the body of the solar system in the second ether. This ... is the archetype plane. The seeds of life are vibrating or germinating. The seven centres of energy are apparent ... the form is now potentially perfect.

*The Logoic Triple Word ... The Third Plane ... the Sound AUM*

The body of the solar system in substance of the third etheric plane is seen, and the three function as one. The triple energy of the Logos is co-ordinated, and nothing now can hinder the work of evolution.' (Bailey 1925, pp. 926-7)

## THE JEWEL OF THE LAW

*The Berwick Bassett formation, 1994* (10.6, 10.7)

One of the last formations of the 'human Monad' type of 1994 appeared in mid July under the lee of Hackpen Hill below Berwick Bassett Down (OS SU117737 approx) in wheat. It is recorded as being over 350 ft long. The formation was planned by Wolfgang Schindler from aerial and ground photos by Mike Hubbard and others.

The formation appears to summarise the essential teaching of this group of formations, with special emphasis on the initiations of the human Monad. The signature, a large and small circle to the side, is that of the Earth Logos.

The three smaller circles of the main formation are well spaced out and gradually increasing in size, symbolising the early initiations concerned with the coordination of the physical (1), emotional (2) and mental faculties (3).

The largest circle, representing the Fourth Initiation, the most important for the spiritual development of humanity at this time, is only slightly separated from the remaining group

*10.6 Berwick Bassett, Wiltshire
(OS SU117737), mid July 1994*

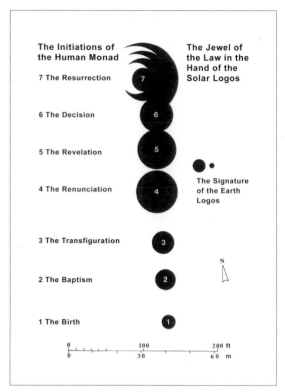

*10.7 **The Jewel of the Law**
Berwick Bassett, mid July 1994*

of three circles, which represent Initiations 5 to 7. The formation should be compared with the Cowdown formation of 1995, see Chapter 8, where the planetary initiations also end with the Seventh before being swallowed up in the Central Spiritual Sun of the Galactic Logos. (8.3, 8.4)

The special feature of the seventh circle, and thus by extension of the Seventh Initiation (the Resurrection) where the human Monad has developed as a fully integrated spiritual being, is that it is held in the embrace of a four-talonned claw. This ancient symbol is normally interpreted in Eastern traditions as a gift to humanity of some special, numinous quality. This is true, but it also represents, in my view, spiritual humanity's corporate offering towards the spiritual development of

the Logoi of our planetary and solar systems.

The claw and ball appears in ancient contexts in China and the Buddhist world. The temple-guardian Lion-dog (*shih-tzu-kou*) plays with a ball, symbol of the Buddhist Jewel of the Law. A dragon is generally depicted pursuing this jewel or pearl, which holds the premier position amongst the Eight Precious Things.

So what is so significant about this symbol of the Universal Law, emblem of the spiritual guardianship of sacred places?

The *Seven Laws of Soul or Group Life* are the essential guidelines for spiritual humanity. Corporately they represent the '*Jewel of the Law*', the gift to ascending humanity from the Solar Logos, and focus of His attention in His Dragon Aspect. See also Chapter 15, The Solar Logos as a Dragon of Wisdom.

The laws relate to the activity of conscious Souls (those who have already attained a measure of spiritual development, operating at or beyond the Seventh Initiation) in relationship to other soul-life at both higher and lower cosmic levels. They bear some relationship to the higher system, the *Laws of Thought* (see Chapter 17) as they relate to the solar system.

They have been described by Djwhal Khul as difficult and controversial, but with the thread of group love, understanding, relations and conduct to guide us. (See Bailey 1942, p. 87.) They are the necessary guidelines for any human Monad actively working in harmonious collaboration with any spiritual group on any Logoic Plane. They constitute perhaps for most of us that most difficult spiritual challenge which results in the subservience of the Personality for the greater good of the group.

These seven laws, with the essential *quality* of character that they produce in the adept, are, in brief, as follows:

1. The Law of Sacrifice – selflessness
2. The Law of Magnetic Impulse – devotion
3. The Law of Service – sympathy
4. The Law of Repulse – discrimination
5. The Law of Group Progress – inclusiveness
6. The Law of Expansive Response – spiritual freedom
7. The Law of the Lower Four – spiritual integration.

(See Bailey 1942, pp. 87 ff.)

'Owing to the major part which humanity has to play in the great scheme or Plan of God, this is the law which will be the determining law of the race. This will not, however, be the case until the majority of human beings understand something of what it means to function as a soul. Then, under obedience to this law, humanity will act as a transmitter of light, energy and spiritual potency to the subhuman kingdoms, and will constitute a channel of communication between "that which is above and that which is below." Such is the high destiny before the race.' (Bailey 1942, p. 112)

I cannot improve on this masterly summary by Djwhal Khul of the marvellous destiny envisioned by God for the human race. We are privileged indeed to receive such information in symbolic form at this critical hour for humanity. However it is not an automatic process. There are agencies at work in the world today actively striving against its achievement. It has to be worked out, so to speak, at the pit-face of human endeavour. We shall return to the claw and ball symbolism in Chapters 19 and 20 on the Triangles of Power in 1990 and 1991.

The Berwick Bassett formation is thus a fitting climax to the formations of 1994 conveying marvellous truths in symbolic form about the spiritual destiny and function of humanity in its wider cosmic setting.

# 11. THE EARTH LOGOS

*The Father, Spirit or Life, wills to seek the satisfaction of desire. The Mother or matter meets the desire and is attracted also by the Father. Their mutual response initiates the creative work, and the Son is born, inheriting from the Father the urge to desire or love, and from the Mother the tendency actively to create forms.*

Bailey 1936, p. 46

## PART 1 - THE EARTH AS A GODDESS

### SUMMARY

We start with a consideration of the *Gaia* crop formation which appeared at Chilcomb, Hampshire in 1990, the first of the humanoid-type formations showing different aspects of the Spirit of planet Earth. The Great Mother tradition is traced through history. Shrines from prehistoric sites of Old Europe show that the physical aspect of the Earth Logos was conceived of as female together with four Rays (4-7) of the Elements. This concept is supported by the different parts of the structure of the Chilcomb formation, which are similar to those of a goddess figurine from Skorba, Malta. This in turn is compared with the Kabbalistic mandala, the Ladder of Jacob, a refinement of the Tree of Life. The Gigantia temple on the neighbouring island of Gozo has provided an archaic inscription recording the prehistoric name of the goddess, **AIA.**

Part 2 covers the great Mandelbrot formation at Ickleton, Cambridgeshire, in 1991, which describes the Earth Logos in symbolic form. The Soul of planet Earth, the Archangel Michael, then describes His ancient names and functions. Finally, the mystical passage by the earliest Greek philosopher, Parmenides of Elea (early fifth century BC), is considered, in which he describes meeting the Great Goddess of planet Earth.

### THE GODDESS ARCHETYPE

*The Velpins Bank Plantation, Chilcomb, crop formation* (11.1, 11.2)

On 23 May 1990 a new type of pictogram arrived in southern England at Chilcomb, Hampshire. The innovatory features included the dumb-bell shape of the body, consisting of two circles of different sizes partially linked by a path narrowing at the 'head' end. On either side of the figure were pairs of boxes.

Although sharing features with the Solar Logos type, the symbolism suggests analogues with the Great Mother, the physical form of the Earth Logos. Early symbols of this type (11.3) appear in north-west Europe on Epi-Palaeolithic painted pebbles from Mas d'Azil, France (c. 9000 BC) and on cave paintings from Ciaque, Spain (c. 6000 BC). A stone figurine of c. 3500 BC illustrates the basic type in iconographic form. All such figurines consistently show the Great Mother in a timeless pose, holding her breasts as succourer of all terrestrial life forms, or as a worshipper.

The same sentiments are conveyed in the great hymn to Isis by Apuleius (second century AD) in the *Golden Ass*:

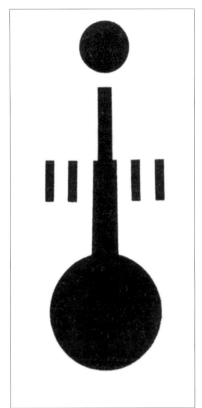

*11.2 **The Earth Logos***
*Chilcomb, 23.5.1990*

*11.1 **The first dumb-bell pictogram***
*Velpins Bank Plantation, Chilcomb,*
*Hampshire (OS SU520286), 23.5.1990*

'I am Nature, the universal Mother, mistress of all the elements, primordial child of time, sovereign of all things spiritual … the single manifestation of all gods and goddesses that are. … Though I am worshipped in many aspects, known by countless names, and propitiated with all manner of different rites, yet the whole round earth venerates me.' (Graves 1950, p. 228)

The stone figurine in illustration 11.3 belongs to a general type of fertility goddess in Europe and Asia which is derived from Late Palaeolithic prototypes. This fat naked woman is seated in the lotus position with crooked arms and hands holding her breasts. Its generalised shape bears a resemblance to the Chilcomb formation, and is helpful in identifying the components of the pictogram.

Although the general symbolism of the Chilcomb formation is clear enough, the detailed attributes are also worth careful examination. The rectilinear boxes, for example, mark the position of the folded arms of the Earth Goddess, but why should they be depicted in this form, and why four?

The rectilinear shape has always in the Ancient Wisdom represented manifested

*11.3 Exemplars of the Great Mother, the physical form of the Earth Logos*

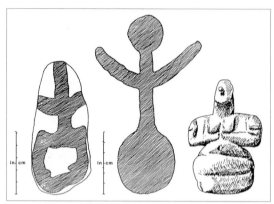

| Left | Painted pebble from Mas d'Azil, France (c. 9000 BC) |
| Centre | Cave painting from Ciaque, Spain (c. 6000 BC) |
| Right | Helladic stone figurine (c. 3500 BC) |

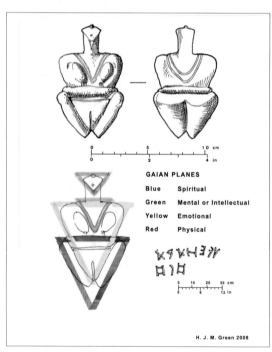

GAIAN PLANES

| Blue | Spiritual |
| Green | Mental or Intellectual |
| Yellow | Emotional |
| Red | Physical |

H. J. M. Green 2008

*11.4 Skorba goddess, Malta (c. 4100 BC), illustrating the Gaian planes of being, and (bottom right) inscription from Gozo of the name of the goddess, early first millennium BC*

form, a balanced amalgam of air, fire, water and earth, the Elements. Here it appears to be a brilliant means of symbolising the four Elements as the creative aspect of the Great Mother, the role of Her arms and hands if you wish. I also identify the boxes as the *Quaternio*, or four Rays of Attribute, whose different functions give organised structure and direction to the management of the rest of the body.

At a deeper metaphysical level the crop formation symbolises, in simplified form, the structure of the Earth Logos as Gaia showing the four planes or modes of being:

1. *Physical*: the abdomen, lower body and sexual organs

2. *Emotional*: the upper body, solar plexus and heart

3. *Mental*: the throat (the throat centre being concerned with intelligence)

4. *Spiritual:* the head and upper spiritual centres, set apart from the rest of the formation.

## PREHISTORIC ICONOGRAPHY

### *The Skorba goddess, Malta* (11.4)

Other figurines from the Neolithic Mediterranean world convey important cosmic information. In 1993 the late George de Trafford, mystic and one-time resident of Malta, gave me a replica of such a goddess shortly before he died.

When the Skorba site, near Mgarr, western Malta, was excavated in 1960-63 an early Temple of the 'Red Skorba phase' was discovered. It has a carbon 14 date of 4100 BC. (Trump 1990, p. 44) In the basement rooms of the northern temple was found a group of broken goddess figurines, arguably the earliest from the island. My replica is a composite figurine showing all the essential features of the goddesses of this group.

The goddess is shown squatting with knees drawn up. Her dress has been rolled up to her waist, exposing her sexual organs. Her hands hold her breasts. Her head is thrown back with the mouth open in orgasmic ecstasy.

Esoterically the feature of greatest interest is that the head and body are delineated as a series of overlapping triangles, a feature commented on by the Dutch archaeologist, Veronica Veen. (Veen 1992, p. 40) When these triangles are plotted they can be seen to represent four isosceles triangles of varying size with apexes pointing downwards, of which the lower three overlap.

For the occultist these overlapping spheres or planes are of the greatest significance. In the esoteric lore of the *Kabbalistic Tree of Life*, one of the most important mandalas is the so-called *Ladder of Jacob*, possibly envisioned by a Jewish mystic in early medieval Spain. When I was a child I was taken in vision to a valley at dusk where hung a structure of living balls of light. It was three-dimensional and I walked between the singing spheres pondering what it might mean. Fifty years later I found out. What I saw was the *Tree of Life* and the balls of light that compose it are the ten *Sefirot* which in symbolic stylised form reflect the living essence of Deity at all levels of the Cosmos. Their analysis lies beyond the scope of this chapter, but see Chapter 12.

Returning to the Skorba figurine and its relation to the Ladder of Jacob, each of the four planes of Gaia has in terms of the Kabbalistic teaching its own 'tree' superimposed and overlapping the one below. In Kabbalistic terms, from the bottom up, they may be termed:

*Assiah* – the world of making (physical form)

*Yetzirah* – the world of formation (emotional)

*Beriah* –the world of creation (mental or intellectual)

*Atziluth* – the world of emanation (spiritual).

The critical feature is that each world or plane interacts with the one below, so that the Sefirot conveying the energy of Love-Wisdom (Second Ray), from whatever level, inform and lift the Beings of the lower level to the higher.

As with the Chilcomb crop formation and the stone figurine, the different physiological areas of the body can be identified with the Gaian planes of Being. The red triangle covers the basal centre and sexual organs. It represents the physical plane aspect. The yellow triangle includes the heart and solar plexus centres and represents the emotional plane. However it reaches down to include the sexual organs also. The green triangle represents the throat centre, but reaches down to include the heart also. This is the mental plane. Then, as in the crop formation, there is a break, with the spiritual aspect or buddhic plane being represented separately, which includes the head centre. Thus this little figurine of over 6000 years old demonstrates a profound understanding of the major mysteries of the Ancient Wisdom. Where did these ideas come from? A clue may lie with the name of the goddess.

In 1912, on Malta's neighbouring island of Gozo, two women visitors to the temple site of Gigantia (G'gantija) found an inscription on a flooring slab at the entrance to the inner sanctuary. It consisted of two lines of ten letters, seven in the first and three in the second. The letter forms are archaic Phoenician/Greek, and the inscription is written *boustrophedon*, i.e. the first line reads from to right to left, and the second left to right. This type of writing dates in the most general terms to the early part of the first millennium BC. Experts consulted at the time found the inscription too difficult to interpret. However this need not deter us in suggesting a name for the Deity worshipped in this temple. All authorities agree that it is the second line of three letters that carries the name of the Deity.

Although it is unlikely that the site was a functioning temple at the time the inscription was made, having been built in the later fourth millennium BC and abandoned c. 2400 BC (Zammit 1980, p. 6), it was evidently still regarded with veneration by the local islanders and associated with a particular Deity. It is this writer's belief that it is an invocation, the first line being along the lines of 'Hail good ...' A simple rendering of the second line would be in Greek H I H, where the H in the early Greek Ionic form was pronounced as a breathy version of 'aitch' – i.e. HĀIHĂ, or some similar name sound as heard from local inhabitants by the Greek/Phoenician suppliants. This is obviously cognate with AIA, the core syllable of Gaia. There is also an old Portuguese word for a maternal nurse, Ayah (ai-ă), which was widely used as an Anglo-Indian name for a nursemaid, and I think was much closer to the original name of the Maltese prehistoric goddess. This takes us to the Iberian peninsula and the spread of the Cardial Ware culture down the Mediterranean in the fourth millennium BC, which brought with it echoes of a sophisticated metaphysical belief system which I believe had its origins in the lost lands of Atlantis in the Horseshoe Archipelago west of the straits of Gibraltar, a subject for which sadly I have not room here.

## OLD EUROPE

Another important class of this prehistoric material comes from the area categorised by prehistorians as 'Old Europe', centred on the lower Danube valley in modern Bulgaria and Romania. The heyday of this distinctive Neolithic and Copper Age group of cultures was between 5000 and 3500 BC.

Clay figurines of the Earth Goddess are ubiquitous in domestic, funerary and religious contexts. (See various reference works by the late professor *emerita* of European archaeology, Marija Gimbutas, in the Bibliography.) Two shrine groups are particularly important: at Dumeşti, Romania (Cucuteni A3 culture, 4200-4050 BC) and Ghelăieşti, Romania (Cucuteni B1 culture, 3700-3500 BC). (Bailey, D.W. 2009, pp. 113-127)

The Dumeşti group was found in a bowl and consisted of twelve figurines, evenly paired between male and female, representing the dual aspects of six Entities. (*Ibid.*, p. 118) (11.5) The female figures are of special interest since each is decorated differently on the front of the body, representing Beings of the Rays of Aspect and Attribute, the latter as the four Elements. Both male and female are naked, except that the male figures wear a decorated belt and baldric over the right shoulder (except the 'Earth' elemental, who wears his over the left shoulder).

The Ghelăieşti group of figurines (*Ibid.*, p. 120) (11.6) was found in a model shrine, in the form of a pedestalled bowl. There were seven assorted figures, the Septead in fact. The distinguishing features of these male and female figures are their relative sizes, since they are all naked and undecorated.

If both groups are brought together they can be classified as follows in terms of the Ray structure, their decoration, and relative sizes.

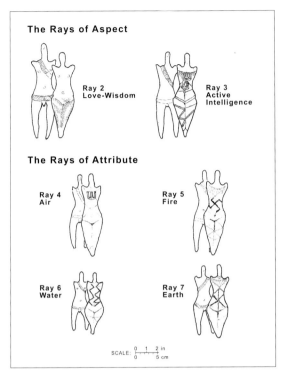

11.5 *'Ray' figurines*
*Dumeşti, Romania. Cucuteni A3, 4200-4050 BC*

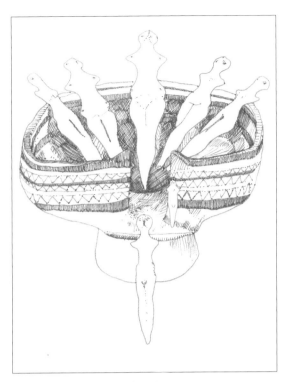

11.6 *The Septead of Old Europe*
*Shrine from Ghelăieşti, Romania. Cucuteni B3, 3700-3500 BC*

| Rays of Aspect | Dumeşti | Ghelăieşti |
|---|---|---|
| 1. Will or Power (Father) | | Small M |
| 2. Love-Wisdom (Son) | M/F (undecorated) | Medium M |
| 3. Active Intelligence (Holy Spirit/Mother) | M/F (composite) | Large F |
| *Rays of Attribute* | | |
| 4. Air | M/F (bird) | Medium F |
| 5. Fire | M/F (swastika) | Medium F |
| 6. Water | M/F (wave) | Medium F |
| 7. Earth | M/F (cross) | Medium F |

Of special interest is the small male figurine (1) from Ghelăieşti, on the front right of the bowl. In the Septead this represents the 'Spirit' aspect. It is small not because it is unimportant, but because this aspect of Deity is *remote* in terms of the experience of the priests and shamans of the Cucuteni B1 culture, who, a thousand years earlier, only recognised the Soul (Ray 2) as the spiritual aspect of Deity. The Personality (Ray 3) aspect of the Dumeşti culture is of great interest since the composite symbolism on the figure combines all the symbols of the Rays of Attribute (4-7), i.e.:

Breast – Bird (Air) – Ray 4

Diaphragm – Triangular spiral or swastika (Fire) – Ray 5

Legs – Wave (Water) – Ray 6

Abdomen – Cross (Earth) – Ray 7.

*11.7 The Elements*
*On the four sides of the Kermaria Stone,*
*Brittany, fourth century BC*

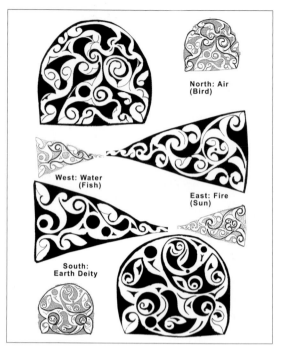

*11.8 The Elements*
*On the Turoe Stone, Ireland, (exploded view*
*from above, North upside down)*
*C. first century AD*

*Kermaria Stone, Brittany* (11.7)

An understanding of these symbols of the
Elements, each of which in ritual magic was
identified with one of the quarters (north,
south, east and west), comes from an interesting
source. Evidently across northern Europe,
prehistoric boundary stones (the equivalent of
the Greek *omphalos*) carry these symbols on
each of the four appropriate faces. That found
at Kermaria, Pont L'Abbé, Finistère near
Penmarc'h Point, Brittany (Kruta and Forman
1985, pp. 111-112), carries identical symbols
(except in the case of 'Water' – West) to those
marked on the figures of the Rays of Attribute
at Dumești, namely:

North – Bird (Air) – Ray 4

East – Swastika sun symbol (Fire) – Ray 5

West – Leaf (Water) – Ray 6

South – Cross (Earth) – Ray 7.

The leaf symbol refers to the fact that no
living thing can survive without water. The
Kermaria Stone dates from the fourth century
BC.

*Turoe Stone, Ireland* (11.8)

Another Celtic boundary stone of this type
comes from Turoe, County Galway, Ireland.
Within the La Tène curvilinear decoration
can be discerned:

North – Bird (Air) – Ray 4

East– Triskele sun symbol (Fire) – Ray 5

West– Fish (Water) – Ray 6

South – Head of Earth Goddess (Earth) –
Ray 7.

The Turoe stone dates to the first century
AD. (Kruta and Forman 1985, pp.114-115)

# PART 2 - THE MANDELBROT FORMATION 1991

*11.9 **The 'Mandelbrot' formation***
*Ickleton, Cambridgeshire (OS TL467413), 12.8.1991*

By far the most important crop formation providing an overall statement about the Earth Goddess, Aia or Gaia, was that which appeared near Ickleton, Cambridgeshire on 12.8.1991 in wheat (OS TL467413). (11.9, 11.10) In a sense it was a summation of the earlier Gaia formations, and led on to the more detailed statements about the Earth Logos, later in the decade, set out in Chapters 12 and 13.

It was the subject of a detailed investigation by my friend Beth Davis, who comprehensively measured and photographed it on the ground. Aerial photos were taken by David Parker and George Wingfield, who was also involved in the fieldwork. George contributed a chapter

(Wingfield 1992 'The Cipher of Chaos') in *Ciphers in the Crops* (Gateway Books 1992), edited by Beth Davis, in which she wrote her own chapter, 'The Ickleton Mandelbrot Formation.' (Davis 1992)

Its overnight arrival, set out in these accounts, and its pristine appearance, indicate beyond any reasonable doubt that this was a geophysical formation, notwithstanding the scepticism of mathematicians and scientists from nearby Cambridge University. (Davis 1992) This was in part due to the formation's similarity to the Mandelbrot Set, 'the most complex object in mathematics ...' (See Gleick 1987, pp. 221 ff. and plates between pages 114 and 115.) Benoit Mandelbrot discovered the Mandelbrot Set after years of exploring fractals on high powered computers. The consensus amongst scientists in 1991 was that 'It must be a hoax because it couldn't be anything else.' This blinkered mind-set was not shared by Mandelbrot himself, who on hearing of its discovery said he was "very pleased to hear of the theory taking *root* ... I don't think it is the work of extraterrestrials, I can't wait to see what the next one will look like." (*Sunday Telegraph*, pp. 25 ff. August 1991) At least the learned University men of Oxford in the early eighteenth century went to the trouble to examine the crop formations in the Oxford meadows, which is more than their Cambridge counterparts did in 1991 at Ickleton.

A year later, in August 1992, another Mandelbrot Set crop formation appeared, outside Oxford. Anthony Cheke took excellent ground photos of the formation, which was unfortunately never surveyed. The photos indicate that it was very similar to the Ickleton formation, and almost certainly of geophysical origin.

Beth Davis' Cerealogist report (Davis 1991, pp. 7-8) states: 'The formation had been created around a 'central' circle and node which displayed all the characteristics common to other [geophysical] crop formations. The ripened wheat was swirled in a clockwise direction and the bands, some 13 feet from the cleft, were expanded and deflected to fill the lobes [of the carotid central shape]. The outer band cut a clear edge in the corn and was swirled into the anticlockwise circles which were evenly arranged on the perimeter. The largest of these circles had a diameter of 17 feet and the smallest, which looked like nests, of less than 2 feet. They ornamented the large perimeter circles and pendant circle of 47 feet

diameter.' To the north of the formation '37 feet from the second pendant circle was a small 8-foot diameter circle which completed the formation.' Not quite in fact, because a quarter of a mile still further north, by a clump of woodland, was a small signature consisting of a small circle with an even smaller satellite (never properly recorded, but visible on aerial photos) which is the signature of the Earth Logos.

The article concludes: 'The Mandelbrot formation is a design of two recognisable symbols. One clearly is a symbol of our time (the first representation of a symbol of this type), and the other of primordial time. In form they are both symbols of infinity, and together they demonstrate the fusion of two apparently separate paths of human enlightenment. The scientific expression of a numerical paradigm, and the mystical concept of spiritual development; was its purpose to bring together the present day knowledge and beliefs of mankind?'

The Ickleton formation is not a straightforward copy of the Mandelbrot mathematical figure, if indeed such a thing were possible. The crop formation was an incomplete template of the design, without the solar flares. As Dr David Battison, a computer scientist at Cambridge, is reported to have said at the time: 'Solar flares, on the computer-produced designs, cannot be eliminated from the formula unless the design is artificially trimmed.' (Davis 1991, p. 7) It is in fact no less than an explicit statement about the spiritual energy construct of planet Earth, setting out not so much the different abstract influences in Her make up, but the Intelligences and Cooperative Groups that constitute Her Life Form, and their interrelationships.

*The Gaian Concept* (11.9)

The overall composition of the formation is a continuation of ancient concepts of the planet personalised as a naked female figure squatting on Her haunches, where β represents the head, the circle 2 the upper part of the body (including the throat), and the cardiac-shaped formation 3 the lower part of the body. The various groups of circles arranged around the periphery of the formation are of different sizes and this is a helpful reference to the identities of the different Individuals and Agencies which we have already begun to identify as part of the make-up of planet Earth. Their detailed analysis follows in Chapters 12 and 13.

Following the numbers and letters on illustration 11.10, the basic structure is as follows:

**LOGOS**

1 Spirit or Father
2 Soul or Son
3 Personality or Holy Spirit/Mother

**RAYS OF ASPECT**

α Will or Power
β Love-Wisdom
γ Active Intelligence

**RAYS OF ATTRIBUTE**

A Spiritual/Buddhic
B Mental
C Emotional
D Physical

**CREATIVE HIERARCHIES**

1   MICHAEL
2   HANIEL
3   URIEL
4   GABRIEL
5   RAPHAELwith SANDALPHON
6   *Parāśakti* ('Management')
7   *Kriyāśakti* ('Executive')
8   *Jñānaśakti* ('Design')
9   *Mantrikaśakti* ('Supervisors')
10  *Icchāśakti* ('Trainers')
11  *Kundalinisákti* ('Craftsmen')
12  *Āditya* ('Workforce')

**H.J.M. Green 8.8.2008**
SURVEY BY BETH DAVIS 1991

11.10 **The Earth Logos**. *Planet Earth shown as Gaia, with its managers Ickleton Mandelbrot, 12.8.1991*

1. The small 8 ft diameter circle set above and apart from the main body of the formation represents the *'Unmanifest' Spirit* of the Planet, the Earth Monad. At the very centre of this circle the corn stalks were arranged as a square, indicating that although this Spirit is beyond form as we know it, He nevertheless has an etheric structure symbolised by His fourfold centre. In other respects His sevenfold structure is reflected in the Ray structure described below.

β. The small circle, 17 ft in diameter, symbolises the mental states of the Logos and represents the head. It forms the 'head' of the circle below (2), which may be regarded as the Soul of planet Earth, Who is personalised as the Archangel Michael, Lord of the World.

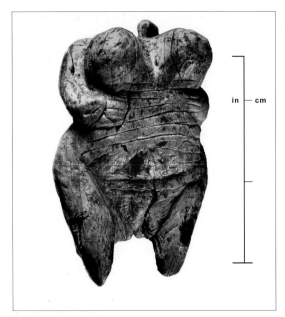

**11.11** *Gaian figurine of mammoth tusk ivory*
*Hohle Fels cave, Schwabia, Germany*

2. The large circle below the head, 47 ft in diameter, symbolises the upper part of the body, which, since it includes what is effectively the throat centre, is primarily concerned with the mental organisation of the body.

3. The large cardiac-shaped formation below circle 2 represents the lower part of the body, with emphasis on corporeal activity and sexual functions. The heart shape is also, of course, a reminder that such functions should be the product of Love. Mostly surrounding this cardiac formation are different sized circles symbolising the various 'managers' and 'agencies' which construct and maintain the form and functioning of planet Earth.

*Fertility Figurine from Germany* (11.11)

The humanoid symbolism of the Ickleton Mandelbrot formation should be compared with a small goddess figurine from a Palaeolithic site in Germany. The goddess was carved out of mammoth ivory and was found in 2009 at a deep level of the Hohle Fels cave in Schwabia. The carbon 14 date indicates that it is over 35,000 years old, and predates other similar fertility carvings by about 5,000 years.

Its characteristic features are grossly protruding breasts, swollen thighs and belly, and a greatly enlarged and explicit vulva. However its strangest feature is a disproportionately small head, which indeed is a notable feature of the Ickleton formation. Although to modern eyes the object is overwhelmingly sexual, indeed pornographic, to the ancient mind it may rather have emphasised fecundity, and those qualities of womanhood central to the propagation of the species, hence the small head and the downplaying of intellectual activity.

*The Great Council of Planet Earth and the Seven Ray Structure*

The make-up and identities of the Great Council of planet Earth are discussed in depth in the next chapter. Briefly, the Council consists of seven archangels – two triplicities of esoteric and exoteric archangels, with the Archangel Michael as Lord of the Council. Each archangel personifies a particular 'energy' or 'aspect' of the Earth Monad. In the Theosophic system, the Seven are divided into three Rays of Aspect (i.e. the fundamental aspects reflecting the threefold structure of the Monad Himself) and four Rays of Attribute, which are effectively a substructure of the Third Ray. Some care has been taken by the geophysical crop circle makers to set out the septenate structure of the Great Council as defined in the 'Ray system'. I shall follow it here (11.10) with the Greek letter forms alpha (α), beta (β), and gamma (γ) representing the Rays of Aspect and the

Latin letters A-D representing the Rays of Attribute. This complex system, touched on in earlier chapters, can be briefly summarised as follows:

*Rays of Aspect*

α. Will or Power (Father) – Ray 1

β. Love-Wisdom (Son) – Ray 2

γ. Active Intelligence (Holy Spirit/Mother) – Ray 3

*Rays of Attribute*

A. Spiritual/Buddhic aspect

B. Mental aspect

C. Emotional aspect

D. Physical aspect.

These represent the basic qualities of the *Quaternio* otherwise expressed respectively as Air, Fire, Water and Earth. Their functions are described in Chapter 14 'The Buddhas of Activity'. It is significant that the 'Son' (Love-Wisdom – β) aspect in the 17 ft diameter circles is placed as the head of the Soul, circle 2, effectively making it a buddhic figure in its own right – namely the Archangel Michael, whereas the 'Father' (Will or Power – α) aspect and the 'Holy Spirit/Mother' (Active Intelligence – γ) aspect are situated on either side of the planetary form (3). The four Rays of Attribute are symmetrically disposed also around the physical aspect of the planet.

*The Twelve Creative Hierarchies.* Regularly arranged around the figure are twelve tiny circles, 2 ft in diameter, which I identify as the 'Creative Hierarchies.' 'They are latent germs of force centres and manifest subjectively; they warm and vitalise groups of forms; they flower forth and express themselves through the medium of a form. ... These Hierarchies are all interrelated and are negative or positive to each other, as the case may be.' (Bailey 1951,

pp. 42-3) This is an important point since the energies balance each other across the figure and indeed the Rays of Aspect actually form an equilateral triangle.

The appearance of the Borstal Trimorph formation near Rochester, Kent in 1999 provided clues to the positions of the Creative Hierarchies on the figure (see Chapter 14, where more will be said about the Hierarchies). All that is necessary here is to tabulate their different corporate identities and types of energy:

1. *The Archangel Michael*, (Sanat Kumara). Synthesising energy

2. *The Archangel Haniel*, (Indra). Lord of Air and of Spiritual (Buddhic) Intelligence. (Ray 4)

3. *The Archangel Uriel*, (Agni). Lord of Fire. (Ray 5)

4. *The Archangel Gabriel*, (Varuna). Lord of Water. (Ray 6)

5. *The Archangel Raphael*, (Kshiti). Lord of Earth. (Ray 7) (*with the Archangel Sandalphon*). Lord of Earth. Planetary Energetics

6. *Parāśakti*, 'Management'. The Archangel Michael. The Angelic Lords of the Great Council

7. *Kriyāśakti*, 'Executive'. The Archangel Uriel. Responsible for production

8. *Jñānaśakti*, 'Design'. The Archangel Gabriel. Organisers of Spiritual, Mental and Physical evolution

9. *Mantrikaśakti*, 'Supervisors'. The Human spiritual Hierarchy (at all levels)

10. *Icchāśakti*, 'Trainers'. The Archangel Uriel. Organisers of intellectual development by the *Agnishvatas*, Solar Angels of the mental plane

11. *Kundaliniśakti*, 'Craftsmen'. The Archangel Gabriel. The management of the emotional plane under the *Agnisuryans* or water devas

12. Āditya, 'Workforce'. The Archangel Raphael with the Archangel Sandalphon. The Elemental work force of the Gaian corporate structure organised by the *Agnichaitan* fire devas.

The Creative Hierarchies 1-5 are effectively the 'private offices' or secretariats of the Individual named. They are staffed by advanced spiritual Beings, angelic or human, drawn from this and other systems. The Archangel Michael with over-reaching responsibility for the whole system has an input into all the Hierarchies. Other archangels may only handle one or two other departments.

The Creative Hierarchies of the *Solar Logos*, formerly also 12, are now 7. The upper five (The Liberated Hierarchies) were 'in their totality the subtotal of *manas*' (my italics) (Bailey 1925, p. 1197), and this having been achieved by the Solar Logos, (see Chapter 15) They have now moved out of our system. The upper five of the remaining Solar Creative Hierarchies have their planetary counterparts in the Buddhas of Activity, the primary agents for the creative processes on planet Earth. The lower two Creative Hierarchies of the Solar Logos 'deal with the display of physical energy; with the working out in the physical vehicle, of all divine purposes.' (Bailey 1925, p. 1207)

This important formation should be regarded as a preliminary statement about the hierarchical structure of the Beings of planet Earth, of which a more developed version was set out in the Borstal Trimorph formation of 1999 (Chapter 14). The Ickleton Mandelbrot formation was placed squarely on the Michael-Mary Line, discussed in Chapter 4 and elsewhere in this study.

The most important aspect of the formation, as was realised by John Michell, was that it was an attempted '*approchement*' to the scientific community using the Mandelbrot figure.

## THE ARCHANGEL MICHAEL

Finally in relation to the role of the Archangel Michael, I must quote what He said about Himself. The occasion was channelling by Isabelle Kingston on 27.10.1991 at Avebury. In the course of a long discussion about the crop circle phenomenon I asked Michael the following question:

"You are one of the Great Archangels, one of the Great Seven Manifested States of Deity in this Earth. First of all, – if it is possible; in relation both to the ancient Gods and the Theosophic system of numbers, – Who are You in these terms?"

The Archangel Michael replied: "I am the Infinity. I am known by many names. I am the One who comes. I am He who walks with the children. I am sometimes called Mars. I am sometimes called *Weed-hool-ah* (phon.) – *Vidyā-dhara*. You speak of numbers. (To) this I cannot relate, for I-am-Infinity."

[The *Vidyā-dharas* – the bearers of wisdom in the Hindu system, resemble men but have magic powers and change form as necessary. They are aerial spirits, generally benevolent. They live in the northern mountains (i.e. Shamballa) where they have cities and kings. The *Vidyā-dharas* are mentioned in Buddhist and Jain mythology. *Vidyā* = wisdom. *Dhara* = support or 'nourisher' of all physical life.]

Michael Green. "You have sometimes been equated with Mercury and the great energies of that Energy which protects mankind."

The Archangel Michael. "This is *Uh-hoor-ah* (phon.) – *Ahura*."

[*Ahura* of the Zoroastrian system is the equivalent of *Asura* used for the Supreme Spirit in the oldest parts of the Rig Veda.]

The Archangel Michael. "I am of many parts. I am in all. I am not limited ... as the Five. I am linked ... with the Mercury you talk of, but I am represented in but a small part [of the crop formations] being given to you, which represent the other Great Beings."

The 'Five' are the Buddhas of Activity whose composition and role is discussed in Chapter 14. The Archangel Michael has an overview and a directing role of this group of archangels who manage the planet, but is not strictly speaking One of Them. The centre of this group I believe to be Raphael (Ray 7) Who is responsible for the earth and all animal life.

It was clear from this transmission, and indeed others, that there are not hard boundaries in practice between the various Beings and their functions in our system. Elsewhere the Archangel Michael says: "By bringing the information that you seek, I find it difficult to separate what is in a sense a whole."

I stress again that the Archangel Michael is the Soul of planet Earth, and has direct access to the Spirit or Earth Logos, whom He calls 'Father'. This of course is comparable to the use of this term by Jesus Christ, the Soul of our solar system, for the Solar Logos. The corporate '*Personality*' of our planet called Aia or Gaia, and Michael Who is the '*Soul*', will be absorbed or become One with the '*Spirit*' or Earth Logos at a later stage of their development – to be precise when They achieve the Fifth Cosmic Initiation. The process is exactly comparable to the initiatory programme of the human Monad, described earlier in this study, but at an infinitely higher level.

Djwhal Khul uses slightly different terminology to describe these important relationships, but they are in all essentials the same:

'We have, in the larger issue, to consider the influence of the zodiac and the planets upon:

1. *The Spirit of the Earth*, the embodiment of the physical planet and the sumtotal of the form life in all the kingdoms of nature. These are the expression of the anima mundi or of the world soul.

2. *Humanity*, the individualised and finally initiated man. This is the embodiment of the human soul or ego, a differentiation of the world soul, which expresses itself as a personality (a correspondence to the spirit of the planet) and finally as a spiritual soul (a correspondence to the planetary Logos).

3. *The Lord of the Planet*, one of the great Lives or Sons of God, at present regarded as "an imperfect God" as far as our planet is concerned and yet, from the angle of humanity, perfect indeed.' (Bailey 1951, p. 113)

---

## NOTE

### THE MYSTICAL JOURNEY OF PARMENIDES OF ELEA TO THE GODDESS

One of the earliest and most outstanding of the pre-Socratic philosophers was Parmenides, born c. 515 BC. According to Plato, he visited Athens in 450 BC on the occasion of the Great Panathenaea. (Kirk, Raven and Schofield 1983, p. 239)

Parmenides has been credited with only a single 'treatise', which contemporaries and later scholars found obscure, although his 'arguments and his paradoxical conclusions had an enormous influence on later Greek philosophy.'(*Ibid.*, p. 241) In view of the importance of Parmenides' hexameter poem, the translation is included here in its entirety:

'The mares that carry me as far as my heart ever aspires sped me on, when they had brought and set me on the far-famed road of the god, which bears the man who knows over all cities. On that road I was borne, for that way the wise horses bore me, straining at the chariot, and maidens led the way. And the axle in the naves gave out the whistle of a pipe, blazing, for it was pressed hard on either side by the two well-turned wheels as the daughters of the Sun made haste to escort me, having left the halls of Night for the light, and having thrust the veils from their heads with their hands.

There are the gates of the paths of Night and Day, and a lintel and a stone threshold enclose them. They themselves, high in the air, are blocked with great doors, and avenging Justice holds the alternate bolts. Her the maidens beguiled with gentle words and cunningly persuaded to push back swiftly from the gates the bolted bar. And the gates created a yawning gap in the door frame when they flew open, swinging in turn in their sockets the bronze-bound pivots made fast with dowels and rivets. Straight through them, on the broad way, did the maidens keep the horses and the chariot.

And the goddess greeted me kindly, and took my right hand in hers, and addressed me with these words: 'Young man, you who come to my house in the company of immortal charioteers with the mares which bear you, greetings. No ill fate has sent you to travel this road – far indeed does it lie from the steps of men – but right and justice. It is proper that you should learn all things, both the unshaken heart of well-rounded truth, and the opinions of mortals, in which there is no true reliance. But nonetheless you shall learn these things too, how what is believed would have to be assuredly, pervading all things throughout.'

(Kirk, Raven and Schofield 1983, p. 243)

To those of us who have been privileged to have had similar experiences, the account is immediately recognisable as an 'initiation' occurrence of the type described in Chapter 9 for those individuals on the spiritual path, and to that extent is 'far indeed ... from the steps of men'. The horses and chariot represent the human metabolism and psyche which is so structured so as to enable the human Monad to make the desired spiritual journey, and the 'maidens' and 'daughters of the Sun' are the *Pitris* described in Chapter 5. The 'gates and great doors', so graphically described by Parmenides, are the initiation processes which, with determination and support, can be overcome. The Goddess to Whom all this is directed, and who waits at the end of the journey to greet the pilgrim, is the personification of the 'Personality' of planet Earth, experienced by Parmenides as a beautiful woman – the subject of this chapter.

Modern scholarship tends to regard Parmenides' account as merely 'an allegory of enlightenment, a translation from the ignorance of Night to the knowledge of Light' (*Ibid.*, p. 245) – it is all that, and much more. I am certain, having been that way myself, that it recounts a real visionary meeting with the Goddess when Parmenides was a young man. As real a meeting as Zarathustra had with Ahura Mazda on the banks of the river Dāityā (Oxus) somewhat earlier. (See Chapter 14.) The Goddess's words of greeting laid down the essential guidelines for Parmenides' spiritual and intellectual path, which he followed for the rest of his life. The translation of Her core admonition quoted above is slightly obscure, and perhaps better expressed in Kingsley's version:

'And what's needed is for you to learn all things: both the unshaken heart of persuasive Truth and the opinions of mortals, in which there's nothing that can truthfully be trusted at all. But even so, this too you will learn – how beliefs based on appearance ought to be believable as they travel all through all there is.' (Kingsley 1999, pp. 53-54)

The marriage of divine revelation with hard-won objective knowledge and experience – a premiss on which this book has been based – is as relevant today as it was two and a half thousand years ago.

Schofield states that Parmenides' ideas have nothing to do with the 'magical journey of the shamans', but this is precisely what they are concerned with. They are directly related to the spiritual search for cosmic revelation or *Gnosis*, which puts them in direct line of descent from Pythagorean metaphysics of a previous generation, and led on to the Hermetic traditions that followed.

# 12. THE PLANETARY HIERARCHY PART 1

*I saw the Lord sitting on a throne, high and lofty, and the hem of his robe filled the temple. Seraphs were in attendance above him; each had six wings: with two they covered their faces, and with two they covered their feet, and with two they flew. And one called to another and said: 'Holy, holy, holy is the Lord of hosts; the whole earth is full of his Glory.' ... And I said 'Woe is me! I am lost, for I am a man of unclean lips, ... yet my eyes have seen the King, the Lord of Hosts!'*

*Then one of the seraphs flew to me, holding a live coal that had been taken from the altar with a pair of tongs. The seraph touched my mouth with it and said: 'Now that this has touched your lips, your guilt has departed and your sin is blotted out.' Then I heard the voice of the Lord saying, 'Whom shall I send, and who will go for us?' And I said, 'Here am I, send me!' And he said, 'Go ...'*

Isaiah 6:1-9 (part)

## A VISION

It was dawn on Saturday 12.1.2008. The night's dreams had vanished and suddenly I was in a different reality, a visionary reality. The sun was rising to my left and I was standing on the edge of an abyss surrounded by my group of *Pitris*. On the other side of the abyss, some 300 ft away, were the Hosts of Heaven stretching from horizon to horizon. I could see only their white wings glistening in the dawn sunlight for 'with two they covered their faces, and with two they covered their feet ...' (*Isaiah* 6:2)

In the midst was the Archangel Michael waving and gesturing. His face was warm and kind, but I noticed it shimmered as if in a heat haze. No word was spoken on either side, but great encouragement and reassurance was

given for the work and traumas that lay ahead, and in particular the production of this book.

That is the only occasion that I have seen the Hosts of Heaven in a biblical sense, although I have spoken with Michael on many other occasions in the preparation of this work over the last quarter century and have seen Him from time to time at more intimate levels. For me, therefore, the Heavenly Host is not a mere abstract theological principle, but a living reality.

## THE PLANETARY ARCHANGELS

As I have already mentioned, there is a measure of inconsistency in the use of the Hierarchical names in this study. The Archangel Michael has always used his Judaic-Christian

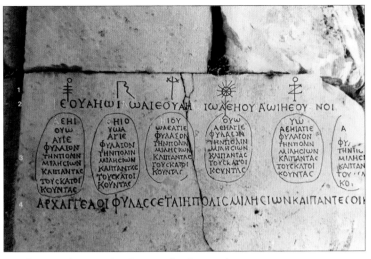

*12.1 Invocation to the Seven Archangels*
*Miletus, Turkey, north entrance of the Roman Theatre. AD 541*

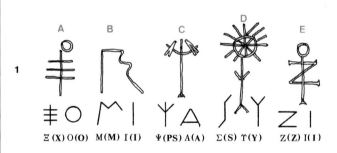

*12.2 Invocation to the Archangels, at Miletus*

nomenclature rather than that of the Eastern world, while at the same time being prepared to discuss other designations.

The Greater Master notes that 'Many who "work the Tree"' (i.e. are engaged in ritual magic) 'are inclined to try and get into touch with the God-Forces of the Sephiroth (using the god-forms of varying pantheons) whereas, in fact, there are certain archetypal powers of these Spheres that are better brought through by use of the Archangelic powers and forms.' (Fortune 1976, p. 152)

*Ancient nomenclature*

In the ancient world the names of the archangels were fairly well known in different forms, such as Papyrus No. 124 in the British Library, one of the oldest MS. sources extant. It is a Greek Magical Papyrus dating to the fourth or fifth century AD. (Betz 1996, p. 150) The names of the seven archangels translate as 'Michael, Raphael, Gabriel, Souriel, Zaziel, Badakiel, Syliel.' One of the most interesting is the invocation carved into the Hellenistic theatre entrance at the Asian city of Miletus, possibly in the sixth century AD, occasioned perhaps by the outbreak of plague in AD 541. (12.1) The Milesian formula, written out in illustration 12.2, comprises:

1. Symbols of each of the seven archangels (only five are still visible) in the form of acronyms

2. Magic formulae for each archangel separated by Greek vowels

3. An invocation to each archangel beginning 'O Holy One ...'

4. A composite prayer: 'Archangels, keep the city ...' addressed to the Seven Archangels for the preservation of the city and its inhabitants.

The prayer is made more powerful by the use of magic symbols (a whip symbolises Michael).

In medieval Kabbalistic lore the names of the archangels are listed under the diagram of 'the scale of the number twelve' collected by Agrippa of Nettesheim and first published in 1531. (Tyson 1995, pp. 294-295)

All these ancient lists differ in their nomenclature and spelling.

## THE TREE OF LIFE

*Occult transmissions.* The ineffable structure and relationships of the senior archangelic establishment of our Planetary Hierarchy have been set out in different ways down the centuries. One of the most valuable is the mandalic *Tree of Life* of Jewish Kabbalism which probably had its inspired origins amongst the mystical schools of the Diaspora, and is particularly associated with the teaching of Rabbi Nehuniah ben Hakanah (first century AD) in his work *The Bahir.* The Tree of Life is a diagram of Deity (or indeed any Cosmic Logos) in Manifestation shown as a hierarchical structure, and consists of ten 'lights' or centres of consciousness/intelligence termed the *Sefirot* (sing. *Sefirah* – Heb. 'Container'). The Tree of

Life is treated as a hierarchical ladder of three vertical columns or pillars.

The threefold vertical structure of the Tree of Life thus represents the essential triune make-up of the Logoi. The Theosophic model is very similar and has been defined by Djwhal Khul as 'the seven rays, regarded as the seven veiling forms of the Spirits, themselves spheroidal bands of colour rotating *longitudinally,* and forming (in connection with the seven planes) a vast interlacing network.' (Bailey 1925, p. 152)

So far as the archangelic names are concerned I intend to follow in all essentials the tabulation of the Greater Master (Fortune 1976, pp. 150-152) who related them to the Kabbalistic Tree of Life and the Sefirot. It is in essence the traditional interpretation as set out by Tyson. (Tyson 1995, pp. 752-761) For the sake of clarity I have structured my diagram (12.3) on the lines of the Theosophic

**THE PLANETARY HIERARCHY**

**THE LORDS OF LIBERATION**

Metatron, MTTRVN, מטטרון
Kether, KThR, כתר, The Crown

Tzaphkiel, TzPQIAL, צפקיאל
Binah, BINH, בינה, Intelligence

Ratziel, RTzIAL, רציאל
Chokmah, ChKMH, חכמה, Wisdom

**THE ESOTERIC ARCHANGELS OR KUMARAS**

Tzadkiel, TzDQIAL, צדקיאל
Chesed, ChSD, חסד, Love
Vishnu
**Ray 2**

Khamael, KMAL, כמאל
Geburah, GBVRH, גבורה, Strength
Brahma
**Ray 3**

Haniel, HANIAL, האניאל
Netzach, NTzCh, נצח, Firmness
Indra
*Amoghasiddhi*
AIR
**Ray 4**

Michael, MIKAL, מיכאל
**Sanat Kumara**
*Vairochana*
(FIRE)
(Rays 1-7)

**THE EXOTERIC ARCHANGELS OR KUMARAS**

Uriel, אוריאל
Hod, HVD, הוד, Splendour
Agni
*Amitabha*
FIRE
**Ray 5**

Gabriel, GBRIAL, גבריאל
Yesod, ISVD, יסוד, The Foundation
Varuna
*Akshobhya*
WATER
**Ray 6**

Raphael, RPAL, רפאל
Tiphareth, ThPARTh, תפארת, Beauty
Kshiti
EARTH
**Ray 7**

Sandalphon, SNDLPVN, סנדלפון
Malkuth, MLKVTh, מלכות, The Kingdom
*Ratnasambhava*
EARTH

12.3

Tree of Life, indicating the archangelic Name, Sefirah, Eastern equivalent and Ray number of these Lords of Flame. Something of their roles and functions is indicated below and elsewhere in this study.

As regards this particular framework of the Tree of Life, it must be made clear that no such figure has appeared amongst the geophysical crop formations, although there was one hoax. The Kabbalistic/Theosophic 'Tree' quite correctly shows this numinous system as a hierarchical paradigm with the Senior Powers at the top and the Junior Ones at the bottom. However this may not be exactly how They see Themselves or would wish us to see Them, more of a 'round-table' in fact than a 'board-table.'

## THE PLANETARY HIERARCHY (12.3)

It might be useful now to identify various groupings of the Archangelic Entities as revealed by the structure of the 'Tree of Life.'

### The Lords of Liberation

In the words of Djwhal Khul: 'Who are the Lords of Liberation, and from whence do They come? ... [They are] emanations from certain great Lives, Who are Themselves an expression of a divine Idea. ... They are three in number and one of Them is closer to the Earth and to humanity than are the other two, and it is He who can be reached by those who comprehend the nature of freedom and who desire beyond all things to be liberated.' (Bailey 1957, pp. 266-267) These three Lords comprise the uppermost Sefirot and reflect directly the upper Triad of the Earth Logos, (i.e. Rays 1-3):

Ratziel – perhaps 'The Mystery of God' (Ray 1)

Metatron – uncertain, perhaps 'Greatest' (Ray 2)

Tzaphkiel – perhaps 'The Righteousness of God' (Ray 3).

Metatron is that Seraph 'who is closer to mankind than the other two' since He represents the qualities of Love-Wisdom. These Beings are of the Order of the Seraphim and have a particular responsibility as the medium of communication between Heaven and Earth. (*Isaiah* 6:6) The Greater Master also comments: 'Ratziel ... He brought through the creative forces in early evolution. It is difficult to formulate in the human mind such beings as Metatron ... He works in the great world of Cosmic Archetypes and his influence is very rare ... for they are beyond form as we know it.' (Fortune 1976, p. 151) See also Chapter 18, Sibson: The Cosmic Laws of Thought.

### The Archangels

I turn now to the all important consideration of the Archangels of the Septenate, symbolised by the Danebury crop formation of 1997 described below. These have different names and epithets in various religious systems. The Jewish Kabbalistic system describes the Beings as the *Elohim*. In the East They are called the Raja Lords or *kumaras* (i.e. youths or princes), or buddhas. Each is a great spiritual Intelligence in its own right; They are not mere clones of each other, but reflect in their Personalities the special stresses and conditioning of their respective systems. Before looking at the component parts of the Great Council of planet Earth, we need to consider the Lord of the Council, the Archangel Michael, or *Sanat Kumara* (The Eternal Youth) and His relationship with the Spirit of our Planet, *Ibez*.

### The Earth Monad Ibez

We have considered the derivation of the name *Ibez* in Chapter 9. Djwhal Khul provides a core definition of this Great Being, the Spirit of our Planet. 'The Lord of the World, through meditation, is carrying forward processes which He instituted in His original creative meditation – back in the darkest night of the time when He decided to create this planet of ours for strictly redemptive purposes. The whole creation is the result of His directed and controlled thought – a process of sustained thinking which sweeps all the creative energies into evolutionary and cyclic activity, in conformity to the pattern which He eternally visualises.' (Bailey 1955, pp. 222-223) 'The "*Silent Watcher*", that great Entity Who is the informing life of the planet ... From the standpoint of our planetary scheme, this great Life has no greater, and He is, as far as we are concerned, a correspondence to the personal God of the Christian. He works through His representative on the physical plane, Sanat Kumara, Who is the focal point for His life and energy.' (Bailey 1922a, p. 104)

*The Archangel Michael (Sanat Kumara)*

The Archangel Michael is the guiding spirit behind this book. He 'alone ... is self-sustaining and self-sufficient, being the physical incarnation of one of the Planetary Logoi [who was formerly the Lord of the planet Venus. He is] at the head of affairs, controlling each unit and directing all evolution.' (Bailey 1922a, pp. 38-39) In this connection it is interesting that He 'took form and came to our planet 18 million years ago.' (Bailey 1925, p. 211) The date is significant. In geological terms it falls within the Miocene epoch, during which occurred the emergence of the hominid apes. One of His particular concerns therefore is to see through the physical and spiritual development of emergent humanity.

As we have already seen, the Archangel Michael, as the 'Soul' of planet Earth, is not merely the most prominent of the Septenate but is on a different level altogether. As He says of Himself, "I am in all", and thus

incorporates all Seven Rays in His person. On the Wheel of Life He stands at the hub of the Wheel as the First or Synthesising Ray. However Michael has particular affinities with Ray 5 in its aspect as the protective and refining fire of Spirit. 'He holds in control the various evil influences which might escape into the world of men.' (Fortune 1976, p. 152) In His role as guardian of mankind: 'It is solar fire which forms and likewise guards the door of initiation for the first four initiations. It is the electrical fire which forms the door of initiation for those initiations which guard the Way to the Higher Evolution.' (Bailey 1960, p. 352) Thus it is that on the Kabbalistic Tree of Life, Michael is placed in the Sefirah of *Hod* meaning 'Splendour.'

(In the Septenate, Ray 5 as such is represented by the Archangel Uriel who is known in the East as *Agni*.)

*The Six Other Archangels (Kumaras)*

The remaining six Archangels of the Great Council fall into two groups of three.

*The Three Esoteric Archangels (Kumaras)* comprise:

Ray 2. Tzadkiel – 'The Righteousness of God', whose *Sefirah* means 'Love'

Ray 3. Khamael – 'The Assembly of God', whose *Sefirah* means 'Strength'

Ray 4. Haniel – 'Firmness', also called 'the Grace of God'.

Djwhal Khul describes Them as 'withdrawn and esoteric ... their work is to us necessarily obscure ... [they] embody types of energy which as yet are not in full demonstration upon our planet.' (Bailey 1922a, p. 39) Djwhal Khul also indicates that They have a role as senior advisers: '"The Higher Three" ... still remain actively cooperating with the Lord of the World ... They do not belong to this

Solar System at all ... They act as advisers to Sanat Kumara where His initial purpose is concerned ... It is Their supreme task to see that, in the Council Chamber ... that purpose [or the Plan] is ever held steadily within the "area of preparation" ... of that Council.' (Bailey 1960, p. 267)

*The Three Exoteric Archangels* (*Kumaras*) comprise:

Ray 5. Uriel – whose *Sefirah* means 'Splendour'. Concerned with all aspects of FIRE. Equated with Agni in the East

Ray 6. Gabriel – 'The Strength of God'. Concerned with all aspects of WATER, and hence all living things on planet Earth. Equated with Varuna

Ray 7. Raphael – whose *Sefirah* means 'Beauty'. Concerned with all aspects of EARTH. Equated with Kshiti in the East.

Djwhal Khul describes them as 'the sumtotal of activity or planetary energy.' (Bailey 1922a, p. 39)

Sandalphon is something of an enigma in angelic studies. All other archangels of the Sefirot have as their epithet some quality of the Earth Logos as indicated by the last syllable *El*. The exceptions are Metatron and Sandalphon, who in rabbinic lore are said to be twin brothers. (Sisung 1996, p. 353) Tyson comments: 'Often Sandalphon is given as the angel of Malkuth [i.e. Ray 7], but Sandalphon is more properly the angel who presides over the planet Earth,' (Tyson 1995, p. 473) as opposed to *elemental* Earth. See discussion in Chapter 14 on the identification of the Five Kumaras or Buddhas of Activity, and in Chapter 24, on the House of Virgo.

In my perception, Sandalphon, although a great archangel, is not one of the Seven

Rays as such, but is effectively a composite of Ray 7, that of Earth, under the Archangel Raphael. He functions at the base of the Central Pillar below Ray 7 that is concerned with planet Earth and all that is energised by it. Sandalphon is the Lord of the Four Elements and has been described as operating at a molecular level as the Soul of the so-called inanimate world. (Fortune 1976, p. 150) The equivalent of Sandalphon in the human Monad is the *etheric body* (see Chapter 5), which is the energy structure relating to the physical body. Thus Sandalphon reflects, at the lowest level, the cosmic purposes of His great brother, Metatron, Who oversees all things that are His concern in our system, even from beyond the confines of planet Earth.

Djwhal Khul describes the origins of the Exoteric Archangels or Kumaras and their relationship with the Lord of the World: 'These Kumaras, Sanat Kumara and His three pupils, having achieved the highest initiation possible in the last great cycle, [see glossary] but having as yet (from Their standpoint) another step to take, offered Themselves to the planetary Logos ... as "focal points" for His force, so that thereby He might hasten and perfect His plans on Earth within the cycle of manifestation.' (Bailey 1925, pp. 751-752) 'There remain still with Him the three Buddhas of Activity. I would call attention to the dual significance of that name "Buddha of Activity", bearing out, as it does, the reality of the fact that Entities at Their stage of evolution are active love-wisdom and embody in Themselves the two aspects.' (Bailey 1925, p. 387) 'Sanat Kumara and His Pupils are in physical form, but have not taken dense physical bodies. They work on the vital etheric levels, and dwell in etheric bodies.' (Bailey 1925, p. 753) 'The *Buddhas of Activity* are the Triad Who stands closest to Sanat Kumara ... They are the planetary correspondences to the three Aspects of the Logoic third Aspect and are concerned with the force behind planetary manifestation.' (Bailey 1925, p. 75)

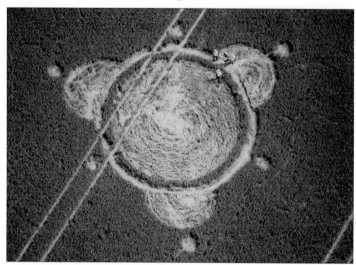

*12.4 Danebury Down, Longstock, Hampshire (OS SU33737376), 18.6.1997*

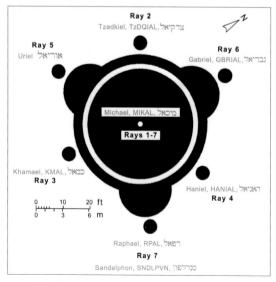

*12.5 **The Longstock 'Buddhas'***
*Archangels of the planetary hierarchy*
*Danebury Down, Longstock, 18.6.1997*

### The Longstock 'Buddhas' (12.4, 12.5)

No formation symbolises better the relationship between the Esoteric and Exoteric Archangels than the formation that appeared near Danebury Hillfort in 1997 in barley. The formation appeared to the east of Blackstake Hill, Longstock CP, Hampshire (OS SU337376) on 18.6.1997. It comprised a ringed circle (40 ft diameter) with a central, 1 ft wide, standing tuft. The central circle is defined by a ring of standing crop 2 ft wide, with an outer diameter of 42 ft. Beyond the outer, 45 ft diameter, ring are three semicircles, each with a 10 ft 9 in radius, laid out as an equilateral triangle. At the apex of each semicircle and regularly distributed between them are six 'grapeshot' satellites forming two interlocking triangles reminiscent of the Seal of Solomon. (See Burham formation of 2003.) (Chapter 10) A provisional report on this formation was published in 1997. (Green, Michael 1997, p. 6)

The inner ringed circle with the standing central tuft, effectively a *Bi* symbol, represents the Archangel Michael, Sanat Kumara, Lord of the World, surrounded by the six archangels symbolised by the 'grapeshot' circles. Three of these are depicted effectively as 'humanoid' with 'heads' on rounded 'bodies' standing well clear of the outer ring. These I would identify as the Exoteric Archangels, Kumaras or 'Buddhas of Activity.' In the case of the remaining three, the Esoteric Archangels, only their heads appear above the outer ring, their energies not yet being 'in full demonstration upon our planet.' (Bailey 1922a, p. 39) The interesting feature of this formation is that the archangels are beginning to be shown as stylised 'Beings' as opposed to abstract cosmic principles. By 1999 this approach was made even clearer with the 'buddhas' being provided with haloes.

*The Lords of Karma*

This analysis of the components of the Great Council of planet Earth must also include brief consideration of the *Lipika* (*Lipi* = writing) Lords, or the Lords of Karma. These four Beings who are concerned with the laws of Cause and Effect are effectively legal advisers originating from the councils of the Solar Logos. They are concerned with the evolution of the human kingdom, the working out of Karma at all levels of the human Monad, the care and tabulation of the *akashic* records and participation in both the Planetary and Solar councils.

'Three of Them are closely connected with Karma as it concerns one or other of the three great Rays ... while the fourth Lipika Lord synthesises the work of his three Brothers and attends to [their functioning]. On our planet, the Earth, They find Their points of contact through the three "Buddhas of Activity" [Raphael, Gabriel and Uriel] and the fourth Kumara, the Lord of the World.' (i.e. Michael) (Bailey 1925, p. 74)

Chapter 16, under the heading 'The Modena Aion', considers the role and names of the Lords of Karma further.

*Functions of the Great Council of Planet Earth*

Djwhal Khul has annotated the primary functions of the Great Council and its members:

'1. They each embody one of the six types of energy, with the Lord of the World as the synthesiser and the embodier of the perfect seventh type, our planetary type.'

[The Lords of the Council carry the burden of the Earth changes to come, for it is Their responsibility to make the adjustments in all subsequent relationships, for the cosmic interconnections require careful calibration of energies of a variety of types.]

'2. They are each distinguished by one of the six colours, with the Lord of the World showing forth the full planetary colour, [indigo] these six being subsidiary.'

[For a discussion of the colour appropriate to each Ray, see Chapter 10 under the Burham formation of 2003.]

'3. Their work is therefore concerned, not only with force distribution, but with the passing into our scheme from other planetary schemes, of Egos seeking earth experience.

4. Each of Them is in direct communication with one or other of the sacred planets.' [Logoi from other planetary systems of our solar system] (Bailey 1922a, pp. 39-40)

Djwhal Khul sums up as follows:

'The three are one, and the seven are but blended parts of one synthetic whole. They all interlace and intermingle. ... They are but the executive offices in which the business of our planet is handled, and each office is dependent upon the other offices, and all work in the closest collaboration.' (Bailey 1922b, p. 169)

# 13. THE PLANETARY HIERARCHY PART 2

This chapter concerns the planetary hierarchy depicted as crop formations. In 1999 there were a number of geophysical formations which appear to have been specifically concerned with conveying information about the personnel and organisation of the Great Council of planet Earth.

By 1999 there had been a substantial increase in the proportion of man-made formations (see Chapter 2 Part 1), with at least nine groups of hoaxers active in Wessex, and commercial profit had become a priority for many. In the vicinity of the sets of formations described below there were no fewer than *44 man-made hoaxes*. Many field workers who had meticulously recorded the formations had been put off by the hoaxers. The scientific investigators who had discovered how to distinguish the geophysical from the man-made formations in 1995 had been sidelined. Some photographers doctored their prints to remove traces of the tell-tale rings of the man-made formations. Fortunately not all photographers behaved like this, and some CCCS members such as Andrew King took photos which showed the true state of the formations. In addition, assiduous record keeping at the time by this writer, which included private flights, enabled the eight geophysical formations described below to be accurately located and assessed.

The true crop circle makers were equally aware of the difficulties that these problems posed for their human collaborators. Consequently the important Bishops Cannings formation of 6.8.1999 (13.12) was created in such a complex manner as to be utterly beyond the technical capacity of the hoaxers at the time.

In Chapter 4 I introduced the concept of Triangles of Power, as groupings of crop formations. The subject is treated fully in Chapters 19 and 20 which cover the Triangles of Power in 1990 and 1991, and here I will simply give a brief outline of the procedure for their creation.

For each Triangle of Power there is a dynamic energy centre (*Emanating Energy*) whose etheric energy is then directed to a secondary receptive point (*Evocative Force*) and then to a third point (*Magnetic Centre*). The interplay between the second and third points effectively produces a balanced energy field, whose final destination is a fourth centre, the *Distributing Centre*. Each of these energy centres is represented by a crop formation following a common theme and having related features in the design.

## THE TRIANGLES OF POWER IN WILTSHIRE IN 1999

Two major interlocking Triangles of Power (TOP for short) were identified in central Wiltshire in 1999. (13.1) They were essentially coeval and have been designated here as TOP 1999:1 and TOP 1999:2. The four stages in which these deific energies were successively grounded in the landscape (each point symbolised by a crop formation) follows in general terms the principles of the Ray system set out earlier. Each separate

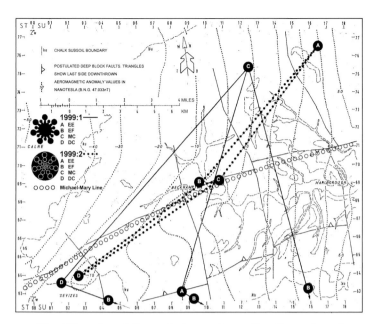

*13.1 **The 'Planetary Hierarchy'** crop formation Triangles of Power of 1999*

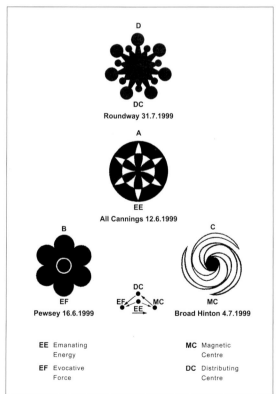

*13.2 **The Planetary Hierarchy** Wiltshire Triangle of Power 1999:1*

geophysical crop formation symbolises some important spiritual principle concerning the management of planet Earth by the Septenate, the Great Council of planet Earth, considered in the last chapter – i.e. the three esoteric archangels or kumaras, Who are not yet fully operational, and the three exoteric archangels or kumaras Who have the responsibility for the management of the planet under the Archangel Michael.

TOP 1999:1 is a classic example with the Emanating Energy centred in the middle of the pattern, which extended over several miles. As in 1990 and 1991 the principal purpose of these constructs was to convey spiritual information into the geophysical energy system of the planet using the Michael-Mary Line.

*TOP 1999:1* (13.2)

1A. *Near Cannings Cross, All Cannings CP, Wiltshire* (OS SU086631) on 12.6.1999. Wheat. (A in 13.2, and 13.3)

Emanating Energy. Overall diameter 83 ft. The formation is basically a *Bi* symbol of Deity, with a flattened ring and a standing centre. On this have been superimposed six petals springing from the centre, which are delineated by flattening segments of the centre and by leaving standing crop representing the points of the leaves in the outer ring.

This formation, like others of this series, is concerned with the number *six*, here a direct reference to the six archangels of the Great Council of planet Earth Who have the responsibility for the planet under the Archangel Michael. In this crop formation

13.3 *The six archangels of the Great Council of planet Earth, working under the Archangel Michael*
TOP 1999:1A. Near Cannings Cross, All Cannings CP, Wiltshire
(OS SU086631), 12.6.1999

13.4 *The six archangels with the Archangel Michael in the centre*
TOP 1999:1B. Pewsey White Horse, Pewsey CP, Wiltshire
(OS SU172583), 16.6.1999

13.5 *The Archangel Michael, the three esoteric archangels, and the three exoteric archangels*
TOP 1999:1C. Fiddlers Hill (near Hackpen Hill), Broad Hinton CP, Wiltshire
(OS SU125752), 4.7.1999

13.6 *The Solar Logos, the Seven Sacred Planets (the Solar Septenate) and the Seven Archangels (the Planetary Septenate)*
TOP 1999:1D. Roundway Hill, Roundway CP, Wiltshire (OS SU016636), 31.7.1999

the pattern cleverly infers that although They operate in the material world, Their origins are from God, or, to be more precise, our Earth and Solar Logoi.

1B. *Pewsey White Horse, Pewsey CP, Wiltshire* (OS SU172583) on 16.6.1999. Barley. (B in 13.2, and 13.4)

Evocative Force. Overall diameter of outer ring 108 ft. Inner circle 36 ft diameter, demarcated by a standing ring 6 ft wide. This ring is similar to those used in formation 2D (see below) which indicates that this formation is concerned with a Cosmic Logos, and in particular the Logos or Spirit of planet Earth and the Septenate which is His external

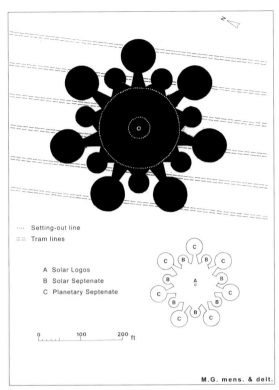

.... Setting-out line
== Tram lines

A Solar Logos
B Solar Septenate
C Planetary Septenate

0      100      200 ft

M.G. mens. & delt.

*13.7 The Solar Logos, and the Solar and Planetary Septenates*

*TOP 1999:1D at Roundway on 31.7.1999*

expression. Emerging from the outer ring are six petals representing the esoteric archangels (top three) and the exoteric archangels (bottom three).

At the centre circle representing Ray 1 (and indeed all the Rays) is the Earth Logos represented by the Archangel Michael, Soul of planet Earth.

This formation, as the Evocative Force centre, represents the physical realisation of the spiritual energy put down in formation 1A. These archangels are shown at this point of the development of TOP 1999:1 because it is their initiative and planning which determines, under the leadership of the Archangel Michael, the spiritual development of mankind.

1C. *Fiddlers Hill (near Hackpen Hill), Broad Hinton CP, Wiltshire* (OS SU125752) on 4.7.1999. Wheat. (C in 13.2, and 13.5)

Magnetic Centre. Djwhal Khul describes Magnetic Centres as 'the grounding of the Emanating Energy ... producing manifestation, quality and activity.' (Bailey 1951, pp. 460-461) Overall diameter 390 ft. 'Meticulous geophysical construction, lightly laid down in a single process, not in stages.' (Stuart Dike)

From a central circle spin clockwise three crescents, each of which in turn produces another crescent, making six in all. This vortex design is another statement about the Septenate, which from its 'solar' centre symbolising the Archangel Michael representing the Earth Logos, spring the three esoteric archangels, Who in turn give rise to the three exoteric archangels. These symbols are shown as lunar crescents representing form or manifestation. The general impression of this vortex of energy is that it constitutes a Centre of Living Motion.

1D. *Roundway Hill, Roundway CP, Wiltshire* (OS SU016636) on 31.7.1999. Wheat. (D in 13.2, 13.6 and 13.7)

Distributing Centre. This is the point on the Michael-Mary Line to which the stimulus to human understanding about the Septenate was conveyed. Both this and formation 2D, which appeared a few days later, are beautiful mandalas concerned with the wider origins of the Seven Spirits of God. In this pictogram They are shown symbolically as 'Beings' as opposed to mere sources of spiritual energy.

The distinctive feature of formation 1D, as with formation 2D, is its septenate plan-form of the inner and outer circle arrangements. Stuart Dike, who carried out a careful survey, reported the following information.

The formation consisted of seven large, and seven smaller circles, placed in sequence. Both types of circles all shared a clockwise rotation, with many displaying wonderful starburst centres, with many individual plants placed very carefully around the central point. The central flattened crop flowed into each of the smaller and larger circles, which then entwined with the rotational flow. The smaller circles placed further into the formation had an average diameter of 32 ft, whereas the larger seven circles on the outer edge of the formation had a diameter of 72 ft. All had a clockwise rotation. The central circle placed within the large expanse of flattened crop had an unusual raised outer edge of standing crop which created a circle in the centre which was 7 ft in diameter, in a clockwise rotation. The raised outer edge was about 8 in across. This distinctive feature was shared by those circles in formation 2D nearby, and is evidence that both were from the same source.

Looking in more detail at the plan of this formation (13.7), it will be noted that it is of the *Bi* design, symbolising Deity – in this case I think the Solar Logos. From the outer edge of the inner circle fan out the 'bodies' of the two rings of septenate circles. The small circles refer, I believe, to the Seven Centres of the Solar Logos, whose physical forms are the Seven Sacred Planets (see Chapter 15). The large outer circles symbolise the Septenate of our own planetary system, springing from the same solar source.

*TOP 1999:2* (13.8)

The second of the two Triangles of Power in Wiltshire in 1999 concerned with symbolism of the Septenate was very different in plan and timescale. Although the Emanating Energy arrived earlier than that of TOP 1999:1, in late May, the other three points

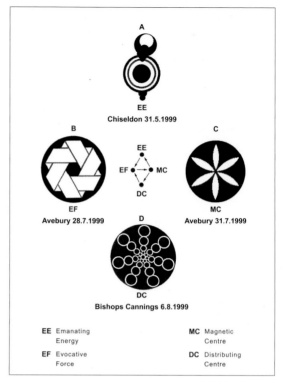

*13.8 The Planetary Hierarchy*
*Wiltshire Triangle of Power 1999:2*

appeared almost simultaneously at the end of July. The figure is also very elongated, like those of the late summer of 1991, when there was a concentration of geophysical energy to complete the figure before the end of the crop season. (See Chapter 20.)

*2A Near Barbury Castle, Burderop Down, Chiseldon CP, Wiltshire* (OS SU165767) on 31.5.1999. Barley. (A in 13.8, 13.9 and 13.13)

Emanating Energy. The appearance of this formation is bound up with the arrival of the dubious *Menorah* formation, the seven-armed candelabrum of the Jewish tradition, sited close by. Initially formation 2A was, I believe, designed to be a considered response to the appearance of the Menorah earlier the same night, but two months later it was reused as the Emanating Energy for TOP 1999:2, in part no doubt due to the *Bi* mandalic imagery

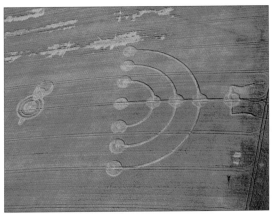

13.9 *'The Light of the World'*

TOP 1999:2A Near Barbury Castle, Burderop Down, Chiseldon CP, Wiltshire (OS SU165767) 31.5.1999

13.10 *The integrated character of the Great Council of planet Earth*

TOP 1999:2B. Beckhampton, Avebury CP, Wiltshire (OS SU097690), 28.7.1999

of the centre of the formation. It was not aligned with the Menorah formation, but appeared to point towards the Triangle of Power.

The earlier significance of formation 2A is of considerable interest. It represents a traditional type of classical oil lamp viewed from the top. The bronze prototype has typically a rimmed, sealed, circular container to hold the oil, with a small central hole in the top for filling purposes. At one end is a small projecting nozzle, at the other a lunate handle. As well as symbolising the night, this has the practical purpose of propping the suspended lamp away from the wall, so that the lighted wick in the nozzle is kept well away from the fabric of the building. The type has its origins in Roman Italy in the mid first century AD. (13.13)

There are a number of curious features about this formation. In the crop circle maker's mind there clearly was some association between the lamp and the Menorah, which would have carried lamps. As I pondered on the synchronicity of these various elements and events, the word that came into my mind

was *light*. The lamp symbol refers not to any concept, however sacred, but to a Person who emerged in the Jewish world of first century Palestine, a Person whom many have believed since to be the fulfilment of the ancient Judaic spiritual tradition. Jesus Christ of Nazareth said: "I am the light of the world. Whoever follows me will never walk in darkness but will have the light of life." (*John* 8:12) This is why I believe it is a single lamp dating to the period when the Christian church was starting its ministry.

2B. *Beckhampton, Avebury CP, Wiltshire* (OS SU097690) on 28.7.1999. Wheat. (B in 13.8, and 13.10)

Evocative Force. Formations 2B and 2C appeared close together near the Michael-Mary Line within a few days of each other, which no doubt provided the etheric stimulus to complete the Triangle of Power (with formation 2D) on 6.8.1999. Set within a circle (240-250 ft diameter) were outlined two interlaced triangles in standing crop. The central section of crop displayed an anticlockwise rotation, whereas the outer perimeter ring (19 ft 10 in wide) had a

*13.11* **The Lords of the Great Council have**
**individual responsibilities**
*TOP 1999:2C. Stone Avenue, Avebury CP*
*Wiltshire (OS SU108693), 31.7.1999*

clockwise rotation. Stuart Dike who inspected the formation reported that its execution and accuracy were quite breathtaking. The scheme has been described as a Celtic Knot, and bears some resemblance to the Buddhist *Palbheu* (endless knot), signifying harmony, although the triangles are not actually connected in the crop formation. This beautiful geophysical formation conveys in the clearest possible terms the integrated character of the Great Council as described by Djwhal Khul: 'the three are one, and the seven are but blended parts of one synthetic whole. They all interlace and intermingle.' (Bailey 1922b, p. 169)

2C. *Stone Avenue, Avebury CP, Wiltshire* (OS SU108693) on 31.7.1999. Oats. (C in 13.8, and 13.11)

Magnetic Centre. Sixfold flower-of-life (standing petals in a flat circle). Each gap between the petals was laid as a swirled (clockwise) circle with a tufted centre, merging into the next. The grain was beautifully laid:

all seed heads were aligned in parallel, and lovely Perimeter Stalks (those angled stalks of grain seen at all inner boundaries where laid stalks meet standing ones) were present in profusion (field report by Ilyes, USA National Coordinator, Crop Circle Research International).

This formation returns to the petal motif of formation 1A of TOP 1999:1. Notwithstanding the emphasis on 'collaboration', indeed 'integration' in the previous formation (2B), in terms of producing 'manifestation, quality and activity', each of the six esoteric and exoteric Lords of the Council have their own particular responsibilities – some active, some latent – as expressed here by six separate petals.

2D. *Roundway Hill, Bishops Cannings CP, Wiltshire* (OS SU026640) on 6.8.1999. Wheat. (D in 13.8, and 13.12)

Distributing Centre. The formation was destroyed by the farmer within three hours of its discovery, but not before its comprehensive recording both on the ground and from the air. This immaculate formation had four rings of seven circles delineated by standing rings. The outer ring had been laid down in a basket-weave pattern, a unique feature. The formation appeared about one kilometre east-north-east of the earlier septenate formation (1D). It was perhaps the most extraordinary formation, in terms of its physical construction, ever to have appeared. The field report by Stuart Dike stated that never before had we seen such a detailed floor construction, as we now had raised weave crop creating a basket effect. Each of the largest circles on the outside had a rotated *S* swirl with a raised centre.

The formation had a small central circle and four rings of seven circles in each ring, of increasing size. It was carefully surveyed by Andreas Müller. Diameters in metres. Central

13.12 **The four Septenates and the Etheric Web**
TOP 1999:2D. The 'Basket Weave' formation, Roundway Hill, Bishops Cannings CP, Wiltshire
(OS SU026640), 6.8.1999

circle 2.4 m. Circles in ring 4 – 1.5 m. Circles in ring 3 – 3.6 m. Circles in ring 2 – 5.9 m. Circles in ring 1 – 8 m. The standing ring around each circle ranged between 0.3 m. and 0.45 m. The overall diameter was 46.3 m. Müller noted that 'the very central circle offered a special detail … it showed exactly seven stalks still standing', which brings us back to the core message of this immensely important pair of septenate crop formations, formations 1D and 2D of the 1999 Triangles of Power.

In my seminal paper 'Who are the Crop Circle Makers?' published in the *Cereologist* in 2000 (Green, Michael 2000a, 9-13), I identified these formations as being a metaphysical statement about the hierarchical Septenates of the Cosmic Logoi. In the case of the Roundway formation of 31.7.1999 (formation 1D) it concerns only the Solar and Planetary Logoi. The ring and central circle of the setting-out lines suggests the *Bi* symbolism of the Solar Logos. The raised ring (see description above) of the innermost circle might suggest systems beyond our solar system. The Bishops Cannings formation of 6.8.1999 (formation 2D) is a much more explicit and detailed statement on the same theme. There are four Septenate levels instead of two, and there is also the significance of the 'woven web', discussed below.

Djwhal Khul when dealing with the subject of *Manas* (intelligence, the mental faculty that for humanity is an individualising principle) states: 'The originating source of manasic activity *in a solar system* is that great cosmic Entity Who embodies our solar Logos as a centre in His Body along with six other Solar Logoi Who are, in Their totality, His seven centres. [In this study I call this Entity *Archon*.] The originating source of manasic activity *in the planetary schemes* is that cosmic Entity we call the solar Logos. He is the active, directing Intelligence Who is working with definite purpose through His seven centres. The originating source of the manasic principle in a *planetary scheme* is that lesser cosmic Entity Whom we call *a planetary Logos.*' (Bailey 1925, p. 393)

*The Etheric Web of the Bishops Cannings formation*

Djwhal Khul has provided a useful definition which can be applied to the symbolism of the extraordinary crop-weave of the Bishops Cannings formation of 6.8.1999:

'The inner web of light which is called the etheric body of the planet is essentially a web … At present a pattern of squares is the major construction of the web but this is slowly changing as the divine plan works out. … The effort on Earth today (as seen by the planetary Logos) is to bring about a transformation of the web of the planet and thus slowly change the existing squares into triangles.' (Bailey 1951, p. 479)

The point being made here is that in symbolic terms 'the square represents humanity; that this is frequently spoken of as the "city which stands foursquare," [see *Revelation* 21.16] and is familiarly referred to in modern literature and discussions as the "city of man".' (Bailey 1955, p. 135) The triangle on the other hand is the archetypal symbol of Deity, as in the Spiritual

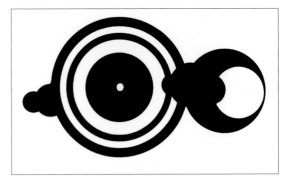

13.13 **The Solar Logos, 'the Light of the World'**

*The Chiseldon 'oil lamp' formation of 31.5.1999, replicating a bronze Roman oil lamp, c. first century AD. Lamp, Musée romain de Lausanne-Vidy*

Triad and indeed the symbol of the Sacred Fire and of the Lord of the World Himself. 'The point of the triangle is based in the courts of Heaven … and from that point two streams of power pour forth into the realm of soul and into the heart of the disciple. Thus is the Triad formed; then are the energies related unto the world of men.' (Bailey 1955, pp. 135-136) The square (the world of men) becomes two triangles and the rule of the square is ended. What then is being symbolised in the Bishops Cannings formation is the Septenate of the Earth Logos (the outer ring of seven circles) operating within the etheric, foursquare, web of mankind with the ultimate purpose of the spiritual transformation of humanity. It will be noted that in the formation the 'web' structure extends only round the outer ring of circles, thus indicating that the four successive Septenates are to be read inwards from the Septenate of the Earth Logos.

Given these interpretative markers it is now possible to 'read' the symbolism of formations 1D and 2D. As already indicated the earlier Roundway formation restricts itself to the ruling Septenates of the Earth Logos and the Solar Logos. The Bishops Cannings formation is a much clearer statement in symbolic terms, also starting with the Septenate of the Earth Logos from the outer ring of circles. The four rings of seven circles each thus represent the ruling councils of:

1. The Earth Logos – *Ibez*

2. The Solar Logos – *Bel*

3. The Logos of our local solar group – *Archon*

4. The Galactic Logos – *Aion* or 'Central Spiritual Sun.'

*The Septenate Triangles of Power*

To summarise, re-examination of this group of formations, apparently relating to the composition of the Great Council, which appeared in 1999, suggests that we are looking at two *Triangles of Power* conveying information and energy on this important subject to the Etheric Grid of the planet.

Both TOP 1999:1 and TOP 1999:2 sit squarely on the Michael-Mary Line. The whole group of formations representing two important Triangles of Power thus forms a neat isosceles triangle 3-4 miles in length, which is the fire symbol of the Archangel Michael (Sanat Kumara) – very appropriate!

# 14. THE BUDDHAS OF ACTIVITY AND THE GAIAN CORPORATE STRUCTURE

*The Buddhas of Activity are the Triad Who stands closest to Sanat Kumara, The Lord of the World. They are the planetary correspondences to the three Aspects of the the logoic third Aspect and are concerned with the force behind planetary manifestation.*

Bailey 1925, p. 75 fn. 32

## PART 1 - THE BUDDHAS OF ACTIVITY

### SUMMARY

The hands-on management of the planet is the responsibility of the Executive Council, with the Archangel Michael, (Sanat Kumara), in overall command. Under Him are the archangels or kumaras Uriel (Fire, mental power), Gabriel (Water, emotional power) and Raphael (Earth, physical power). These archangels are the three *Buddhas of Activity* quoted above. However, I believe that Haniel, (the esoteric Archangel Who is concerned with the raising of spiritual intelligence), is another of the Buddhas of Activity, as is the Archangel Sandalphon, the etheric body of planet Earth, who works under and with Raphael.

They are the embodiment of active, intelligent, loving will. 'Their functions are many and varied, and concern primarily the forces and energies of nature, and the direction of the building agencies ...' (Bailey 1922a, pp. 107-8)

They have a vast civil service of Beings at their disposal. Humanity is the special concern of the Archangel Michael Himself. Symbolism of the Five (the quintuplet crop formations) appeared in the 1980s, and that at Beacon Hill, Exton, Hampshire (1990) is considered together with other variations of the design at Nettleden, Hertfordshire, and Chilcomb, Hampshire. The formation at Bishops Cannings, Wiltshire, in 2000, introduced a humanoid, indeed buddhic, element into the design. This also applied in the most important of this group of formations, the Borstal Trimorph near Rochester, Kent in 1999. (See Part 2 of this chapter.) That beautiful mandala set out in great detail the full scope of all the planetary directorates and departments, with their management and interrelationships.

### THE EXECUTIVE COUNCIL

The Great Council has an all-important arm which directly runs the functioning of planet Earth, which might be termed its Executive Council. It consists of the *Five Kumaras*. These are the 'five Mind-born Sons of Brahma [who] are the embodiers of this manasic force [i.e. intelligent activity] on our planet.' (Bailey 1925, p. 702)

These *Five Kumaras*, or Buddhas of Activity, are five Personages each representing an essential aspect of manifestation. They include the Archangels Uriel, Gabriel and Raphael, and, I believe, the Archangel Haniel, Who is responsible for 'spiritual intelligence' and is only partly involved at present. In an earlier transmission Michael has stated that He himself is not one of the Five, although He has a close and intimate overview of Their work. Who therefore is the Fifth Member? I believe this is the Archangel Sandalphon, Who is on the same Ray (Ray 7) as Raphael and works as a unit with Him, since He is concerned with the energy systems of the planet, being its etheric body. (See Chapter 12.) Sandalphon does not appear separately in the quintuplet crop formations described below.

In the centre, managing, coordinating and synthesising the Five, is Michael (Rays 1-7). Above all He balances the energies of the Executive Council and ensures that the overriding principle of Love-Wisdom is maintained. As He has stressed (Chapter 11), all these Great Beings have an underlying unity, difficult for us to appreciate at our level.

An example of this occurs in the legend of the Middle Eastern Avatar, Zarathustra. He appears to have lived at some time between 1400 and 1200 BC amongst the Steppe pastoral peoples east of the Caspian Sea. According to Khojeste Mistree (Mistree 1982, pp. 7-9), in the *Pahlavi* account by the ninth century AD writer Zādspram, who drew on much earlier material, the story is told of Zarathustra's revelation. At the age of thirty, during the Spring festival, Zarathustra went to fetch water at dawn from the river Dāityā (probably the Oxus or a tributary) for the *Haoma* ceremony. On emerging from the water in a state of ritual purity, he was met by

*Vohu Manah* (possibly the Archangel Gabriel) in the shape of a man, fair, bright and radiant who was nine times taller than Zarathustra. The priest was taken into the presence of Ahura Mazda (the Archangel Michael) and five other radiant figures, the Holy Immortals (*Amesha Spentas*). These of course are the members of the Great Council and its Lord. (Boyce 1984, p. 75; Mistree 1982, p. 7) It is recorded that when a 'Holy Immortal' wished to communicate something He 'merged' with Ahura Mazda (Lord of Wisdom) to do so. This strange occurrence has also been recorded amongst human Monads on the emotional plane (and higher). The etheric or astral body is in a sense permeable. However a 'merging' with another person is regarded as an 'intimacy', comparable with human intercourse on this plane.

## THE BUDDHAS OF ACTIVITY AS CROP FORMATIONS

Amongst the earliest types of crop formation, as opposed to isolated circles, recorded by investigators were those which came to be termed quintuplets or quincunxes. The earliest was at Bratton, Wiltshire in July 1983. (Meaden 1991, pp. 21 ff.) Terence Meaden, a professional meteorologist, sought a scientific explanation for the design, of course not forthcoming! Indeed, for me, these strange geometrical shapes were a very early alert that we should be looking for a metaphysical, rather than a scientific, explanation.

*The Exton Quintuplet, 1990 (14.1 and 14.2)*

Of the many examples recorded in the eighties and early nineties, I have selected that found south of Beacon Hill, Exton, Hampshire (OS SU605214) on 8.6.1990, in wheat. It was carefully surveyed by John Langrish and photographed from the air by the writer. The

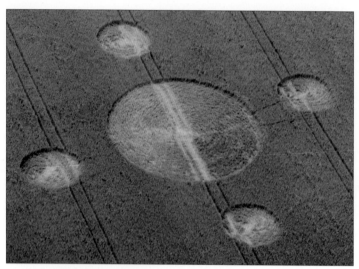

14.1 **The 'Buddhas of Activity'** *quintuplet formation at Beacon Hill, Exton, Hampshire (OS SU605214), 8.6.1990*

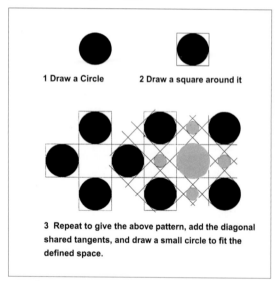

14.2 *The geometry of the Exton quintuplet formation, described by John Martineau*

diameters were: large centre circle, 83 ft; the four satellites each 30 ft.

John Martineau, the mathematician, constructed a geometrical figure in 1992 showing the principles on which the Exton formation was designed. (14.2) All geophysical formations must have been laid down on the basis of such design principles, which

constitute a study in their own right.

A single crop formation like this does not explain which *type* of five it symbolises. From the start I viewed such formations as conveying information about the Four Archangels or Kumaras with a controlling presence at the centre, i.e. Michael. Initially these formations were set out as an abstract archetype, but by the late nineties the symbolism first indicated that these were Beings, and finally buddhas, with body, head and halo – indeed the Archangel Michael and the Buddhas of Activity.

*The Nettleden formation, Hertfordshire, 1996* (14.3)

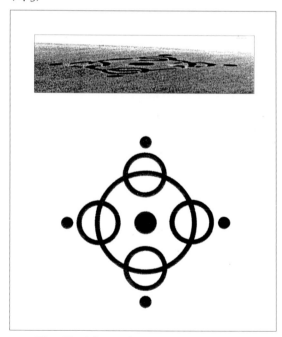

14.3 **The 'Buddhas of Activity'** *Elaborated quintuplet crop formation at Nettleden CP, Hertfordshire (OS TL027099), 3.8.1996*

The formation, which appeared at Nettleden CP, Hertfordshire (OS TL027099) on 3.8.1996, in wheat, was a development of the quintuplet design. It was carefully studied by Richard Shaw. (Shaw 1996, p. 23) The basic format was a central circle, 36 ft in diameter, with an outer ring 200 ft in diameter. This is the classic *Bi* symbol of Deity, in this case the Earth Logos. The four outer satellite rings were 69 ft in diameter, each with an

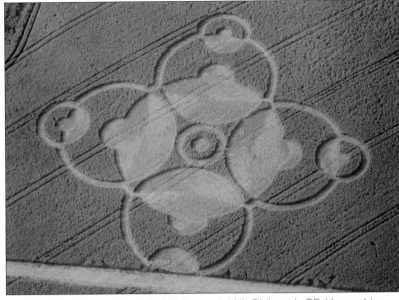

14.4 **The 'Buddhas of Activity.'** Telegraph Hill, Chilcomb CP, Hampshire (OS SU523284), 1.8.1999

outlying circle 'head' 19 ft in diameter, which symbolise the kumaras as Entities, but not yet as 'buddhas'. All crop was laid down clockwise except for the centre (23 ft in diameter) of the inner circle, where the crop was anticlockwise. This is a highly significant detail. A distinction is made between the spiritual ('unmanifest') nature of the Earth Logos, as shown in the anticlockwise lay at the centre of the central circle, and His manifest expression in the Archangel Michael (Sanat Kumara) – the outer band of the central circle being laid down clockwise as with the outer ring and the four kumara satellites. Shaw notes: 'The exact line of demarcation was almost impossible to define with any accuracy. Although the stalks were all bent sharply, as in the other circles, I found no indication that any artificial aid had been used in their construction.' The formation lay on the Michael-Mary Line, which relates it to other important formations described in this study.

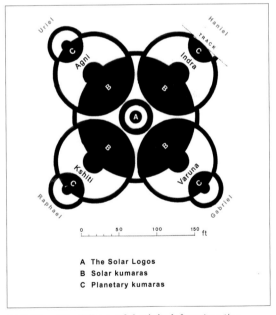

A The Solar Logos
B Solar kumaras
C Planetary kumaras

14.5 **The 'Buddhas of Activity',** forming the Solar and Planetary Executive Councils Telegraph Hill, Chilcomb, 1.8.1999

*The Chilcomb formation, Hampshire, 1999* (14.4 and 14.5)

This formation is a much more detailed exegesis of the nature of the Five Archangels or Kumaras, and it relates the planetary archangels to those of the solar system. This formation was described as appearing on Chilcomb Down, east of Winchester. Aerial photos would indicate, however, that it actually occurred on the slopes of Telegraph Hill, Chilcomb CP (OS SU523284) in wheat on or before 1.8.1999.

At the centre of the formation is a ringed circle, the *Bi* symbol of Deity, which here represents the Solar Logos. Four rings function as cartouches for the four kumaras of this Lord, which are represented in stylised form as the bowed head and shoulders of the Buddhas of Activity. Their buddhic status is indicated by the half circle forming a halo over each head. Thus as Lords of the Elements They relate to the Fohatic (*Brahmic*) energy of this solar system.

Out of the four large rings emerge four smaller buddhas which replicate in general character those features of their Solar Brothers. These, I believe, symbolise our planetary archangels or kumaras, who can be identified as such by an interesting and significant feature. I think that the lost 'head' is that of the the Archangel Haniel (*Indra*) in our planetary system. He, as we have seen, is one of the esoteric kumaras, who is conveying the buddhic energies of spiritual, intuitive intelligence, but is not as yet in full demonstration upon our planet. Hence the 'body' is in place in the crop formation, but the 'head' or controlling mind is not yet activated, or indeed present. Aerial photos by Steve Alexander show that the formation has been deliberately designed so that the track 'clips off' the head component. However, it is not absolutely symmetrically placed, so that a thin line of standing stalks still runs across the top of the shoulders. It is clear from this remnant feature that there was *no* head at

all on this buddha, although part of the halo survives to circle the figure.

The symbolic superimposition of such Beings brings out a cosmic truth demonstrated in certain other crop formations in 1999. (Green, Michael 2000a, pp. 9-13) Standing behind the kumaras of our own planetary system are the Greater Lords of the solar system, of whose energies and holistic qualities They partake. Indeed the crop circle analogy so cleverly used here is that They are effectively 'thought bubbles' of these Solar Archetypes, which are in turn 'thought bubbles' of the Brahmic aspect of the Solar Logos Himself – the 'Mind-born Sons of Brahma.'

*The Stone Pit Hill formation, Bishops Cannings, 2000* (14.6)

If the Telegraph Hill Chilcomb formation was concerned with the Exoteric Kumaras of the Solar Logos, and by extension those of the Earth Logos also, the formation that appeared at Bishops Cannings, Wiltshire, was an even more explicit statement about the latter.

It appeared in wheat to the east of the Stone Pit Hill copse beside the A361 on 25.7.2000 (OS SU033648). The formation basically consists of an elaborated central ring, 120 ft in diameter with four overlapping arcs. As with other formations depicting buddhas, each Entity is schematically indicated with rounded shoulders, a head and a halo. In the central ring is Michael shown in this way, who is controlling the Buddhas of Activity. The head of each buddha is represented by a small half-circle, 20 ft in diameter, emerging from the central ring. Three have fully formed haloes and represent, presumably, Uriel (Fire) – at the top: with Gabriel (Water) and Raphael (Earth) as an extension of the body arc of Michael. As with the Chilcomb formation, Haniel (Air) is only just beginning to emerge

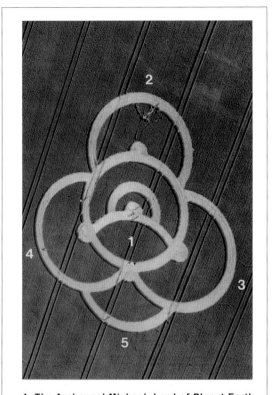

1  The Archangel Michael, Lord of Planet Earth
2  The Archangel Uriel
3  The Archangel Gabriel
4  The Archangel Raphael
5  The Archangel Haniel

14.6 *The Executive Council of Planet Earth, the Archangel Michael and the Buddhas of Activity. Stone Pit Hill, Bishops Cannings CP, Wiltshire (OS SU033648), 25.7.2000*

from the orbit of Michael indicating (as stated previously) that His influence is not as yet fully active on planet Earth. This is another formation occurring close to the Michael-Mary Line.

The kumaras are responsible as departmental managers, either individually or in collaboration with others, for all areas of planetary life. The nature of this planetary life form, Gaia, is beautifully expressed in the complex formation which appeared near Rochester in Kent on 27.7.1999. (See Part 2 of this chapter.)

# PART 2 - THE GAIAN CORPORATE STRUCTURE

## THE BORSTAL TRIMORPH, NEAR ROCHESTER, KENT, 1999 (14.7)

The circumstances of the arrival of this formation are of some interest. Geophysical crop formations are not spread indiscriminately over the countryside like confetti, but are carefully targeted at particular individuals and groups who can be relied on to take an intelligent and responsible interest, as was the case here. Chrissie Milton and Garry Peters had been asking for a crop formation in the Wouldham area all that year, and, as often happens in such circumstances, it appeared at the end of the season. Unfortunately, as with other important formations around that time, an angry farmer destroyed it before it could be properly recorded or photographed from the air.

Milton and Peters reported that the lay was beautiful, with *three* strands left standing at the centre of each circle. The nodes of the flattened crop were swollen, an indication of geophysical origin. Andrew King and Joyce Galley (Kent CCCS members) also managed to gain access and take ground photos, a general view of the adjoining hillside and a series of aerial photos after the crop had been cut. Thus, fortunately, sufficient evidence survived from these various sources (including measurements taken by Milton and Peters) for a reasonably accurate reconstruction to be attempted. I am deeply indebted to Andrew King,

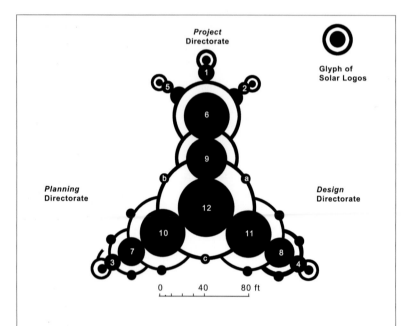

Project Directorate

Glyph of Solar Logos

Planning Directorate

Design Directorate

0    40    80 ft

### CREATIVE HIERARCHIES

**KUMARAS ('DIRECTORS')**

1 Archangel Michael (Sanat Kumara)
2 Archangel Haniel (Indra) (Air)
3 Archangel Uriel (Agni) (Fire)
4 Archangel Gabriel (Varuna) (Water)
5 Archangel Raphael (Kshiti) (Earth)

**BUDDHI ('DEPARTMENTS')**

6 *Parāśakti* ('Management')  A
7 *Kriyāśakti* ('Executive')  A
8 *Jñānaśakti* ('Design')  A/D
9 *Mantrikaśakti* ('Supervisors')  H
10 *Icchāśakti* ('Trainers')  H
11 *Kundaliniśakti* ('Craftsmen')  D
12 *Āditya* ('Workforce')  E

THE THREE FIRES
a 'Solar' - Nuclear fusion
b 'Magnetism' - Plasma energy
c 'Transmutative' - Piezo-electrical

A Angels
D Devas
H Humanity
E Elementals

M.G. after A.K. and C.M.

14.7 *The Gaian Corporate Structure*
*The Borstal Trimorph formation, Rochester, Kent
(OS TQ720623 (approx.)), reported 27.7.1999*

who generously supplied me with information concerning this spectacular formation. The site of the formation was approximately OS TQ720623. Nearby was a small ringed circle, the signature of the Solar Logos.

The formation was basically a trimorph with a large central ringed circle with three arms carrying a series of progressively smaller ringed circles spreading out to the periphery, but not regularly so. I have termed the general character of the formation as a series of 'nested buddhas', or, more correctly, buddhi, since they mostly represent unifying principles or centres of sentient intelligence rather than a great spiritually 'enlightened' individual. But even more to the point, the whole figure represents in symbolic form the Logos of this planet as a 'Transcendental Buddha' seated in the *Padmasana*, or lotus, position. (14.8) The formation was generally immaculate in construction, but a small mistake will be noted near circle 3, quickly corrected.

The buddhic type form is most clearly shown at the top, where a circle represents the body with a slightly smaller circle for the head, ringed to give the impression of a halo. This is one of five small figures at the ends of the three projections (1-5), who I believe represent the Buddhas of Activity (Sandalphon conflated with Raphael) and the Archangel Michael in charge. In the East they are termed the five transcendental buddhas (*Jinas*). According to Djwhal Khul, these great Beings, Who form the first five grades of the Twelve Creative Hierarchies, vary in their status according to the degree to which They have reached 'spiritual liberation', for They too are on a path of development. This is reflected in the symbolism of their representations in this formation. The remaining seven circles of the Creative Hierarchies, '*Department*s', Nos.

6-12, are grouped in what I have termed three '*Directorates*' corresponding to the threefold energy form of our system.

*The Project Directorate (Sixth, Ninth and Twelfth Departments)*

This directorate is presided over by the Archangel Michael as Lord of the Executive Council, Who incorporates Rays 1-7. The other two archangels especially concerned at this level are Haniel, with responsibility for ultimately bringing in the energies of spiritual intelligence for ascendant humanity and the Devic world, and Raphael, responsible for the physical aspects of life and the planet, the context in which all else takes place. As noted earlier, Raphael incorporates Sandalphon, the etheric body of the planet.

This, the premier directorate, constitutes the 'head' and 'body' of the Gaian Buddha comprising the Sixth, Ninth and Twelfth Departments, the last being common also to the other two directorates. The Sixth and Ninth Departments are concerned with the transformation or transfiguration of all beings, whether human or devic, from a physical to a spiritual state: the Ascension Process. The directorate is presided over by the three archangels or kumaras who have special responsibilities in this sphere, and are symbolically enthroned forming a crown on the aureole of the Sixth Department. As managing director, the Archangel Michael takes central place, and effectively transmutes the Love-Wisdom energy through the whole system, presiding over this department. The other two departmental heads, Haniel and Raphael, have special responsibilities for Departments Nine and Twelve respectively. Their work is as yet incomplete, and Their thrones are not (yet) assured. Consequently They are symbolically seated, with feet placed next to each other on the ground below, on

14.8 Padmasana position
Second century AD.
(Kushan) Kushan Empire
(in Gandharan Region)
(Present day Pakistan).
Walters Art Museum

14.9 Bhadrasana position
Early eighth century AD.
China. Walters Art Museum

divine impulse.' (Bailey 1925, p. 1207) Hence their epithet 'the elemental lives.' This is the realm of the fire devas operating on the physical plane, the *Agnichaitans*, whom I have termed the 'workforce' of the Gaian corporate structure in their forty-nine departmental sections.

There are three broad groups symbolised by the circles on the halo of this body of Gaia, who respond to the Three Fires of Brahma. Group *a* are concerned with the energising of the form-building devas, the function of solar or atomic activity (nuclear fusion). Group *b* deal with form-building through magnetic attraction (plasma energy), producing consciousness. Group *c* transmute energised matter (piezo-electrical effect), to produce self-consciousness in form. Yet all work as one.

The Ninth Department, *Mantrikaśakti* (= power of communication), which I have termed 'supervisors', is effectively the buddhic, spiritual, intelligence factor of the Gaian corporate structure. In its various divisions it represents the spiritual components of humanity who serve the Earth Logos. Unlike some other departments, it is both self-conscious and fully intelligent, but also has the distinguishing feature of compassion which relates it to the Second Cosmic Logos, the Christ. The epithet of these Beings is 'The Lords of Love', and they are working unremittingly to speed the Ascension Process at all levels.

It is no accident that, in this formation, the Ninth Department is symbolically placed as the 'heart centre' of the Gaian Buddha. As Djwhal Khul has been at pains to spell out,

a high throne, the 'Western' or *Bhadrasana* position. (14.9) This is suggested by the half-circle at the base of the buddha figures.

The core, quite literally, of the system is the Twelfth Department, where the Archangel Sandalphon reflects the creative energies of the Christ, the second Logos 'by whom all things were made.' I have tentatively identified this department with the ancient Vedic concept of *Āditya*, the cosmic principle of deific origins, the Mother of the Gods.

She is the sentient body of matter and energy of the Universe from which the manifestation of Deity, at all levels, draws its form. This department is concerned with the 'smallest of the small', the life or energy found at the heart of every atom. In the words of the Old Commentary: 'The devas hear the word go forth. They sacrifice themselves and out of their own substance they build the form desired. They draw life and the material from themselves, and yield themselves to the

the planetary department concerned with the human Monad has its own management structure under three Section Heads, who work closely with the Buddhas of Activity, described earlier:

Ray 1. *The Manu* (the Will Aspect)

Ray 2. *The Bodhisattva*, the Christ or World Teacher (the Love-Wisdom Aspect)

Ray 3. *The Mahachohan* or Lord of Civilisation (the Intelligence Aspect).

Each section has a number of Masters of Wisdom, Who, having achieved the Fifth Initiation, work closely with the head of their group. Below Them again are grades of initiates, disciples, probationers and 'average humanity of all degrees'. (Bailey 1922a, p. 49)

The Sixth Department, *Parāśakti* (= transcendent power) is the most senior department and it is effectively the head centre of the Gaian Buddha. If Departments Twelve and Nine operate on the energy fields of Khamael (Brahma) – Ray 3, and Tzadkiel (Vishnu) – Ray 2, the primary focus of the Sixth Department is the Archangel Michael, Who as the Earth Logos is effectively Ray 1, and incorporates all the incipient, future spirituality which is the destiny of the peoples of planet Earth. It is no coincidence that the angels of the Sixth Department are described in the Old Commentary as those who 'burned to know. They rushed into the spheres. They are the longing of the Father for the Mother. Hence do they suffer, burn and long through the sixth sphere of sense.' (Bailey 1925, p. 1197) These angels are the *Lords of Flame*, literally the 'movers and shakers' of our system who were responsible for setting up the basic energy fields when our planet came into being. They too are intimately involved in the Ascension Process, and await with impatience for the opportunities that the creation of

a new system will provide. I have described this department as 'management', since they have the responsibility for initiating and coordinating all aspects of planetary life under their senior director, the Archangel Haniel, who embodies the energies of the buddhic plane, responsible for cosmic transmutation. Neither the Ninth nor the Sixth Department carries on its halo the symbols of the Three Fires. Perhaps the buddhic energy field is supplied direct by the three archangels who stand at the head of the figure.

*The Design Directorate*

This directorate is presided over by the Archangel Gabriel (*Varuna*), whose epithet 'desire for duality' expresses two vital aspects of this sphere of activity. First, the concept of 'feeling' or desire (which is the essence of Ray 6 and has a dim reflection at a miniscule scale in the solar plexus centre of the human Monad). Second, the aspect of duality or polarisation as a vital ingredient of the creative process: those forces which produce the phenomenon we call love, sex impulse, instinct or the driving urge and motive which demonstrates later on the physical plane in activity of some kind. There is in this directorate, as in the others of this corporate structure, a clever convention symbolising a process of spiritual emergence from the centre. The threefold head of the Twelfth Buddha (9, 10 and 11) becomes the body of the buddha above it and so on until the body of the archangel of that directorate is reached: hence the epithet, the 'nested buddhas'. Only the Twelfth Department has a slightly different arrangement, as noted above.

The Eleventh Department, *Kundaliniśakti* (= energy of matter) is the province of the *Agnisuryans*, the astral plane devas, organised in seven sections. At a planetary level, these devas form the liquid aspect in the physical body of the Earth Logos, and range from great spirits who ensoul the astral plane to little Naiads precipitated in watery, physical matter. Since the animal and plant kingdoms operate at the feeling-desire level, these aspects are controlled by devas in this department. Much of the human world also functions at the astral level and connects to this sphere. The state after death (see Chapter 7), which also operates on the astral level, is also a construct of this department. At a higher level, the urge for human betterment and service to the planet by humanity itself is also a focus of activity for these angels. I have termed the Eleventh Department 'craftsmen', for its myriad devas take matter and construct the energetic forms which can be transformed (eventually) into spiritual states.

The Eighth Department, *Jñānaśakti* (= power of knowledge) operates as the head centre of the Eleventh Department, although its angels (like those of the Sixth and Seventh) are not in physical incarnation. They are called the 'Triads' for they hold in themselves the potencies of triple evolution, physical, mental and spiritual, and, consequently, are regarded as the great donors of immortality. I have designated the Eighth Department 'design', for the workings of the Devic world in this department is the very stuff of eternal life itself, the fruit of the mystic marriage of Spirit and matter.

*The Planning Directorate*

The third limb of the Gaian Buddha I have termed the 'Planning' Directorate. If the 'Project' Directorate is concerned with the spiritual implications of the Ascension Process, and the 'Design' Directorate with the emotional substructure of matter, this directorate is about intellect as a coordinating and constructive force. The directorate is presided over by the great creative Archangel Uriel (*Agni*) (3), Who carries in this system the energies of fire. His epithet, 'Light Through Knowledge', brings into focus one essential aspect of His work as one of the five Buddhas of Activity, the focus of systemic vitality intelligently applied. Like His brother Gabriel (*Varuna*) (4), He is depicted in the crop formation as being immersed in the physical creative process.

The Tenth Department, *Icchāśakti* (= power of will) is run by the *Agnishvatas*, the Solar Angels of the mental plane. These Beings are of a high spiritual order and are launched upon a most stupendous project in connection with our planetary evolution, namely the development of intellect as an essential ingredient of human (and animal) spiritual evolution. A distinction here should be made between the rational, self-conscious intellect of mankind in general, and the buddhic or intuitive intellect operating at the spiritual level characteristic in its upper reaches of the Ninth Department. In the three great departments of state, the Tenth, Eleventh and Twelfth, none is dedicated *exclusively* to any particular esoteric life form, but comprise in their myriads those Elementals and Devic Beings who construct the different types of matter at the etheric and physical levels.

Whereas the Solar Angels are mostly concerned with developing and tuning the higher centre (chakra) levels of humans, the work of the Lunar Angels is concentrated on enhancing the physical (Twelfth Department) and emotional centres (Eleventh Department). The centre of gravity of the Solar Angels is the heart centre of the human Monad, with the eventual intention of producing individuals whose very essence is 'active, intelligent love'. It is in connection with this sense of preparation that I have used the epithet 'training' for the core work of this department.

The Seventh Department, *Kriyāśakti* (= materialising ideal) is the executive arm of the Gaian corporation. If the project managers of the Sixth Department set the targets, it is the angels of the Seventh Department that ensure that the programmes of the lower departments are kept in line and on schedule. They are particularly involved in overseeing the work of the Tenth Department and promoting corporate identity. In spiritual terms, they ensure that potentiality is brought into full activity and that innate capacity demonstrates in perfect fruition. All potentiality lies in the vitalising, energising power of Uriel (*Agni*), and His ability to stimulate. 'He is life itself, and the driving force of evolution, of psychic development and of consciousness.' (Bailey 1925, p. 606)

This vitality is expressed in the formation by showing the corporate structure of Gaia as a revolving spiral form, an ethero-atomic structure of force, in which the twelve departments spiral upwards anticlockwise from *Āditya* to encompass the archangels at its pinnacle.

*Conclusion*

Andrew King has stated that the Borstal Trimorph formation is 'arguably, the most impressive formation of 1999, perhaps even any year' – an assessment with which I would agree. This is an extraordinarily important crop formation, a mandala packed full of spiritual information about the life and Intelligences of planet Earth. The ringed circle signature located near the formation is, as I have stated earlier, that of the Solar Logos (the supreme Intelligence of our system), and to my mind an indication in itself of the importance of this formation.

# 15. THE SOLAR LOGOS

*Man aims at becoming a Divine Manasputra, or perfected Son of Mind showing forth all the powers inherent in mind, and thus becoming like unto his monadic source, a Heavenly Man. [i.e. a Planetary Logos]*

*A Heavenly Man has developed Manas, and is occupied with the problem of becoming a Son of Wisdom, not inherently but in full manifestation.*

*A Solar Logos is both a Divine Manasputra and likewise a Dragon of Wisdom, and His problem concerns itself with the development of the principle of cosmic Will which will make Him what has to be called a "Lion of Cosmic Will".*

Bailey 1925, pp. 305-306

## SUMMARY

So far in this study we have looked at the teaching of the geophysical crop circle phenomenon concerning the human Monad (Chapters 5-10) and the Earth Logos (Chapters 11-14). This chapter is concerned with the Solar Logos. The chapter head quotation succinctly categorises the essential *raison d'être* of mankind, the Earth Logos and the Solar Logos. The Solar Logos has not been a central theme of the crop circle communications, which have been more about the state of humanity and its spiritual future, and the role of the Earth Logos and our own planetary system in this process. This said, there has been from the outset a series of geophysical formations clearly alluding to different aspects of the Solar Logos as a formative force behind and controlling our planetary system. Others like the Roundway/ Bishops Cannings Triangles of Power of 1999 (see Chapter 13) refer to the Solar Logos as part of the numinous structure of Beings overshadowing our system.

## THE KARMIC DESTINY OF THE SOLAR LOGOS

This is a huge and complex subject, and there are certain initial postulates which must again be emphasised, before examining the crop formations.

*The Solar Logos* is the physical and psychic manifestation of the Solar Monad, Who is the Spiritual Being of the solar system. What is visible to us is only the raw physicality of a system whose expression at higher etheric levels constitutes a structure of spiritual life and activity. This is the 'Light behind the Light' as it is sometimes expressed.

The Solar Logos as an expression of the Solar Monad is not merely another major spiritual Entity in our part of the Cosmos, but *the* spiritual power. Although sometimes described as 'the God of our system', He is not God, THE ONE, but, as One of the Divine Sparks emanating from the Central Spiritual Fire, He partakes of the Divine nature. (Fortune 1976, p. 59) He contains 'within Himself, as the atoms of His body of manifestation, all groups of every kind, from the involuntary group-soul to the egoic groups on the mental plane. He has (for the animating centres of His body) the seven major groups or the seven Heavenly Men [i.e. the planets] who ray forth their influence to all parts of the logoic sphere, and who embody within Themselves all lesser lives, the lesser groups, human and deva units, cells, atoms and molecules.' (Bailey 1925, pp. 255-256) In short: 'He is the sumtotal of all manifestation, from the lowest and densest physical atom up to the most radiant and cosmic ethereal Dhyan Chohan.' (Bailey 1925, p. 256)

Djwhal Khul has categorised three types of solar energy:

1. *Monadic.* Dynamic energy – an electrical impulse creating pure fire and producing light

2. *Egoic.* Magnetic energy – a radiatory impulse creating solar fire and producing heat

3. *Personal.* Individual energy – a rotary impulse creating fire by friction and producing moisture or concretion. (See Bailey 1925, p. 1047.)

*Solar Development.* The Solar Logos of our system is on a path of development, like all Beings in the Cosmos. Indeed the development and growth of any one Being is dependent on the simultaneous growth of all the elements of His make-up. Time is the key factor in this process, indeed it was created for this very purpose. The primary achievement of the Solar Logos has been the development of the synthetic Ray or Energy of Love-Wisdom 'for verily and indeed "God is Love." This Ray is the indigo Ray [see Chapter 10] and is the blending Ray. It is the one which will, at the end of the greater cycle, absorb the others in the achievement of synthetic perfection. It

is the manifestation of the second aspect of Logoic life. It is this aspect, that of the Form-Builder, that makes this solar system of ours the most concrete of the three major systems. The Love or Wisdom aspect demonstrates through the building of the form, for "God is Love," and in that God of Love we "live and move and have our being," and will to the end of aeonian manifestation.' (Bailey 1922a, p. 3)

## THE SOLAR LOGOS AS BEL

*Bel* appears to be an ancient Indo-Aryan word with a wide geographical distribution meaning 'beautiful' or 'shining'. It appears in this form in Middle English; in Old French as *bel* (m) and *bele* (f); in Latin as *bellus* (m) and *bella* (f).

The god-name *Belatucadros*, the 'Fair Shining One', is known from dedications and shrines from northern Britain in the Roman period. The same cognate identity is to be found in the Deity *Belenus* occurring in the same area. According to the late Dr Anne Ross, *Belenus* is one of the oldest Celtic gods, traces of whose cult are discernible from northern Italy, through Gaul to the British Isles. (Ross 1967, p. 376) The name means 'shining' and has survived as the greatest of the pastoral festivals of the Celtic year – *Beltane* (or *Beltene*) (May Day Eve), celebrated by the lighting of fires on the hilltops. Proinsias MacCana says that the second element of the word Beltene, 'tene', is the word for 'fire', and the first, 'bel', probably means 'shining, brilliant'. (MacCana 1970, p. 32) In Gaulish votive inscriptions, *Belenus* is linked with Apollo, thereby establishing His solar character. A charming legend of the prehistoric sanctuary at Callanish tells how, at the summer solstice, when the cuckoo sings, a 'Being of Light' passes from the rising sun down the stone avenue. The old islander who described this numinous experience used an

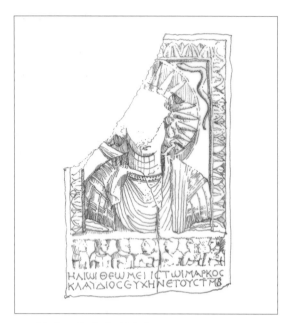

*15.1 Votive Relief of Helios
C. second century AD. National Museum of
Damascus, Syria*

ancient Gaelic term for this 'Being' which has the meaning of the 'Shining One'.

A classical relief of the Sun god *Helios*, 20 in by 14 in, from Syria (Damascus Museum Acc. C7939), c. second century AD, shows a bust framed in an ovolo border, with a snake at the top right. (15.1) The full frontal, curly-haired head has been deliberately defaced, probably by Christians. It has a solar radiate halo with a lunar crescent at its base. The figure is dressed in senior military uniform as would befit an emperor. Indeed, at the end of the third century AD, the emperor Aurelian revived the cult of solar monotheism as a means of unifying the Empire under himself as Avatar of the Unconquered Sun God. Above the dedicatory inscription on the bottom of the relief are what appear to be winged busts of the Seven Archangels, three facing to the right and four to the left.

## THE SOLAR LOGOS AS 'THE GRAND MAN OF THE HEAVENS'

*The Litchfield crop formation, 1990 (15.2, 15.3)*

This was the earliest of the Logoi formations representing the Solar Logos, dated 8.6.1990, or possibly a little earlier. The site lay on the slopes of Lower Woodcott Down just west of the A34 trunk road, north of Litchfield, Hampshire (OS SU461550) in barley.

*15.2 Lower Woodcott Down, Litchfield, Hampshire (OS SU461550), 8.6.1990*

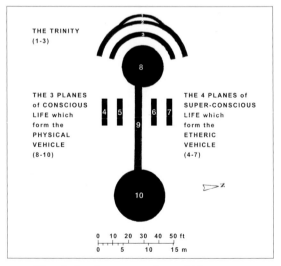

*15.3 **The Solar Logos as Grand Man of the Heavens**, and His Ten Planes of Manifestation. Litchfield, 8.6.1990*

The stylistic convention adopted for all these schematic humanoid-type figures is the dumb-bell, two circles linked by a column. The upper circle was laid down clockwise, 28 ft in diameter; the lower circle, also clockwise, was 35 ft in diameter; the connecting corridor was 5 ft wide, but not centrally placed. The four boxes were 4 ft by 18 ft and spaced between 7 ft and 8 ft apart. The distinctive haloes over the 'head' formed three half rings, 4 ft wide, of which the first and second were melded together. The overall length of the formation was 138 ft 6 in.

The identification as the Solar Logos is clear from the halo type, which is one of the earliest symbols to appear in Europe. The half-circle glyph occurs in many fourth and third millennium passage tombs in Western Europe, and in particular in the initiation basin from Knowth, Ireland (see also Chapter 4), which has the characteristic three-ringed head and the solar rays. (15.4)

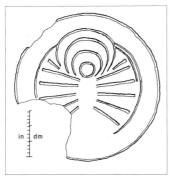

15.4 Petroglyph of the Solar Logos, showing the haloes. Bowl interior of the stone initiation basin from the north recess, east tomb of the Knowth Passage Grave, County Meath, Ireland, c. 3100 BC

Here the Solar Logos is symbolically depicted as a schematic humanoid, perhaps, in the words of Djwhal Khul, 'to express the gradual development in time and space of the inherent capacity [for apotheosis] of a human being, of a Heavenly Man [a planetary Logos] and of the Grand Man of the Heavens.' (a Solar Logos) (Bailey 1925, p. 234) This latter term is the one I am also using here to describe the Ten Planes of Manifestation of the Solar Logos. 'He manifests through the Sun and the seven sacred planets, each of whom embodies one of His seven principles, just as He in His totality embodies one of the principles of a greater cosmic Entity.' (Archon) (Bailey *loc. cit.*)

There are *Ten Planes of Manifestation* of the Solar Logos. (15.3) The lower seven equate very roughly to the functions of the Seven Rays of our Earth Logos (Chapter 10), but not entirely so since they represent a corresponding but higher function. They may be briefly tabulated as follows:

*The Trinity (Nos. 1-3)*

1. The Father (Spirit)

2. The Son (Life)

3. The Mother (Form).

The Trinity reflects the constitution of a 'Second Cosmic Logos, Spirit-Matter, Life, the Spirit of the Universe.' (Bailey 1925, p. 3) The Ten Sefirot of the Kabbalistic Tree of Life (see Chapter 12) also reflect the Planes of the Solar Logos as the 'God' of our system. At a planetary level I have linked the Trinity, when considering the archangelic influences, to the three Beings Ratziel, Metatron and Tzaphkiel, who embody emanations or aspects of the solar Trinity in our planetary system. There is a curious detail in connection with the triple halo of the Litchfield formation. The upper two arcs are conjoined to emphasise the close identity of the Father (1) and the Son (2). As Jesus Christ stated during His ministry on Earth: "The Father and I are one." (*John* 10:30) This detail alone is enough to identify the Christ as the Second Figure of the Solar Trinity.

*The Planes of Super-Conscious Life 4–7*

These four planes of super-conscious life or four central vibrations are the *'four cosmic ethers, and therefore form the body of objectivity of a Heavenly Man in exactly the same sense as the four physical ethers of the solar system form the etheric body of a man.'* (Bailey 1925, p. 325) They are:

4. *Ether 1.* Atomic. First plane of manifestation – Ādi. 'The Sea of Fire'

5. *Ether 2.* Sub-atomic. Monadic plane of spirit – *Anupadraka*

6. *Ether 3.* Super-etheric. Plane of the Divine Monad – *Atmic*

7. *Ether 4.* Super-gaseous. The intuitional plane – *Buddhic.*

*The Planes of Conscious Life 8–10*

'The three planes of conscious and self-conscious life ... form the dense physical vehicle ... of the Grand Man of the Heavens.' (Bailey 1925, p. 916) They are:

8. *Cosmic gaseous.* Physical mental

9. *Cosmic liquid.* Physical astral

10. *Cosmic dense.* Physical dense.

## THE SOLAR LOGOS AS A DIVINE MANASPUTRA

*The Etchilhampton crop formation, 1990 (15.5, 15.6)*

This was the second of the Logoi formations concerned with the Solar Logos. It appeared on the north slopes below Etchilhampton Hill, Stert CP, Wiltshire (OS SU033604) in wheat. It had all the

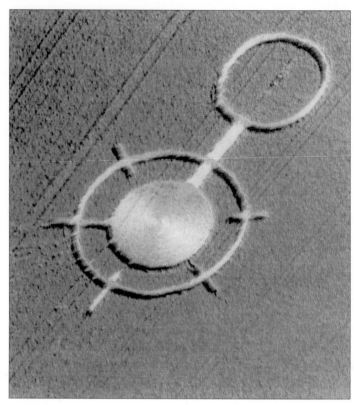

15.5 Etchilhampton Hill, Stert, Wiltshire (OS SU033604) 29.7.1990

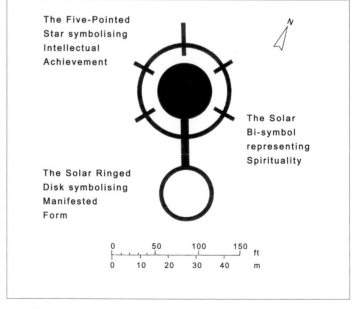

15.6 *The Solar Logos as a Divine Manasputra (Son of Mind)* Etchilhampton Hill, 29.7.1990

hallmarks of a genuine geophysical formation. It appeared on 29.7.1990 and was examined by Colin Andrews and Pat Delgado, but not surveyed. The drawing (that reproduced here was by Wolfgang Schindler) is based on aerial photos. Andrews reported that 'The link spurs [i.e. the 'solar rays'] striking out from the outer ring were flattened in an outward direction, while the opposing spurs were flattened inwards. The two rings and large circles were spiralled. This was a very heavily flattened formation where not a single plant was left standing.' (Delgado and Andrews 1990, p. 66) There was also an extraordinary electromagnetic occurrence. 'An electrostatic detection device revealed an unusual fluctuation in one part of the flattened crop. ... That evening after we had all left for home, Mike Carrie, a director of Cloud 9 ... decided to walk into the circle ... While standing in the area of the single ring, he ... was greeted by a loud noise around his head. ... He later told us that from his technical experience he recognised how powerful the energy must have been that was responsible. ... "Nothing could be seen, but whatever caused it was right around my head, just inches away".' (Delgado and Andrews, *loc. cit.*)

This single formation (in terms of what was later to appear) was part of a 'logoic group' in 1990 that stressed that planet Earth and other formations in our solar system were 'Cosmic Entities'. In beautiful symbolic terms the *Bi* symbol of Deity of the upper part of the formation represents the spiritual aspect of the Solar Logos, while the linked lower ring indicates the physical form. The 'solar rays' of course are the identifying feature and enabled it to be identified as a 'Solar Entity' at the time by even non-expert observers.

But why were there five rays? One explanation is that they refer to the governing body of the Solar Logos. Djwhal Khul describes these Solar Beings as the *Five Creative Hierarchies*. (Bailey 1925, pp. 1196-1203) This interpretation is strengthened by the added prominence given to the 'top ray', the Lord of the Council, the Solar Logos Himself. 'The first great Hierarchy is emanated from the Heart of the central Spiritual Sun. It is the Son of God Himself, the First Born in a cosmic sense, even as the Christ was the "Eldest in a vast family of brothers" and the "first flower on the human plant".' (Bailey 1925, p. 1196)

But this is not the only significance of the number five in connection with the Solar Logos. Under the cosmic Ray system, Ray 5 is associated quite simply with 'intelligence' or *Manas* (see chapter head), and I think that this is its significance here. Djwhal Khul speaks of '*Mental Energy* ... purely mental thought forms, animated by self-engendered fire, or by the *fifth principle*, [my italics] and therefore part of the sphere, or system of control, of the Monad.' (here Solar Monad) (Bailey 1925, p. 47) We therefore return in this elegant and simple crop formation to the concept of the Solar Logos as a Divine Manasputra or Son of Mind revealed as a *Monadic Flame Divine*.

## THE SOLAR LOGOS AS A DRAGON OF WISDOM

*The East Grinstead crop formation, 1993* (15.7, 15.8)

One of the surprises on taking up this subject again after a lapse of twenty years was the discovery of the ramifications of the dragon connection. Although I was aware of this back in 1990 (Noyes 1990, p. 166), I did not specifically relate it to our own Solar Logos.

*15.7 Imberhorne Farm, East Grinstead, West Sussex (OS TQ367382), 10.8.1993*
*With thanks to the Emmett family*

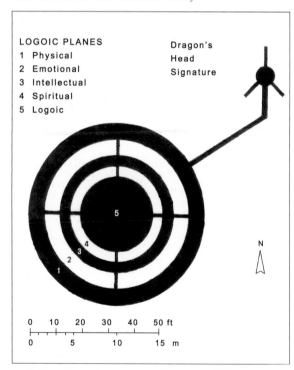

LOGOIC PLANES
1 Physical
2 Emotional
3 Intellectual
4 Spiritual
5 Logoic

Dragon's
Head
Signature

5
4
3
2
1

N

0   10   20   30   40   50 ft

0      5        10      15  m

*15.8 **The Solar Logos as a Dragon of Wisdom***
*Imberhorne Farm, East Grinstead, 10.8.1993*

However there is a connection, which I have explored in terms of the crop formations of the Alton Barnes Triangles of Power of 1990. (Chapter 19)

The strange formation which appeared at East Grinstead in 1993 lay well away from the Sussex crop circle localities of that time, and may perhaps have related to a particular crop circle investigator, namely Marcus Allen, who, together with Terry Morrison, carried out a careful survey of the formation after the harvest. It lay near a historic farmstead, 'Gullege', on land farmed by Imberhorne Farm, between East Grinstead and Crawley Down, West Sussex (OS TQ367382), and appeared in wheat on 10.8.1993, approximately. The farmer discovered it by accident when harvesting, and the photograph was taken from the top of the harvester. The formation was reported in the *East Grinstead Courier* of 20.8.1993, which drew the attention of local crop circle investigators.

This interesting mandala does not belong to the 'logoic group' of formations described earlier, but marks the beginning of a new theme which was to develop year by year in the mid nineties, namely teaching about the apotheosis of the human Monad. Its striking feature is of course the extension or neck terminated by a dragon's head. In 1990 I drew attention to prehistoric petroglyphs which used similar symbolism relating to the Cosmic Dragon (Green, Michael, 1990, p. 166), but in this context I believe it constitutes an unusual signature of the Solar Logos in terms of His function as a Dragon of Wisdom.

*The quality of Love-Wisdom*

The special feature of the cosmic Dragon of Wisdom revolves round that dual aspect of Love-Wisdom, so frequently quoted in this study. Love in isolation, a kind feeling about something or somebody, unless intelligently acted upon, degenerates into mere useless sentiment. Knowledge or intelligence (*Manas*) in isolation can end in selfish, negative activity. The Cosmos, even our own system, is full of clever entities who have seriously gone to the bad. Wisdom, that is knowledge spiritually applied, (i.e. buddhic energy), combined with love expressed as kindness, is the great formative power of the Cosmos as directed by God. Jesus Christ said to His followers: 'be wise as serpents and innocent as doves' (*Matthew* 10:16), again expressing this dual quality. The dove in Jewish tradition is characterised by amativeness. (Smith, W. 1875, p. 209)

The special cosmic quality of Love-Wisdom, it might be argued, is a unique product of our solar system, its testing ground being planet Earth under the Archangel Michael. Djwhal Khul speaks obliquely of the origins in our system of this great dual quality, which He describes as a 'mystery.' 'This is hidden in the karma of the solar Logos, and ... His relationship to another solar Logos [evidently Sirius]. ... This is the true "Secret of the Dragon," and it was the dragon-influence or the "serpent energy" which caused the influx of manasic or mind energy into the solar system. Entangled closely with the karma of these two cosmic Entities, [our Solar Logos and that of Sirius] was that of the lesser cosmic Entity Who is the Life of our planet, the planetary Logos. [i.e. Ibez] It was this triple karma which brought in the "serpent religion"

and the "Serpents or Dragons of Wisdom" in Lemurian days.' (Bailey 1925, pp. 1203-1204) See also Chapter 19 on the dragon connection.

The double-ringed circle which is the primary feature of the East Grinstead formation makes a subtle allusion to these various concepts, but in its totality relates to the special contribution of the Love-Wisdom aspect of the Solar Logos to mankind, namely the apotheosis of the individual human Monad.

The metaphysical symbolism of this process as spelt out in the geophysical crop formations has used three primary types of mandala: *linear*, as in the Baverstock formation of 1991, *ringed*, as in the extraordinary Cowdown formation of 1995 at Andover, and as a *cosmic wheel*. The wheel symbolism is dealt with in Chapter 22. The first two mandalas of 'initiation' are discussed in Chapter 8. The East Grinstead formation is an initial statement about both the 'ring' and 'wheel' type of symbolism of the human Ascension Process.

At one level of interpretation its central circle and two flattened rings may be regarded as a simple statement of the triune nature of the Solar Logos (the three Rays of Aspect) and the 'spokes of the wheel' as the four Rays of Attribute. If that represents the exoteric 'meaning' of the formation, the esoteric message is much more subtle.

The four rings round the central circle (including those of the standing crop) constitute form, which with the circle make five in all. Each ring, starting from the outside, is narrower than the preceding one by about one foot, an ingenious feature which I am sure is quite deliberate. If it were not for the Cowdown formation in 1995 (Chapter 8), which brilliantly describes in symbolic terms the process involved, it would be difficult to understand what is being alluded to. Each ring is a developmental stage of the human

Ascension Process, whose climax on completing the 'round' is marked by an initiation or transference into the next ring, plane or 'mode of being'. A summary description of each ring from the outside inwards is:

1. Physical
2. Emotional
3. Mental (intellectual)
4. Spiritual or buddhic.

When the central circle is reached after the four initiations (see Chapter 9), the human Monad as a Master of Wisdom makes contact with the Solar Logos and begins his greater spiritual journey.

15.9 *Martinsell Hill, Clench, Pewsey CP, Wiltshire (OS SU173639), 11.8.2000*

## THE SOLAR LOGOS AS A FIVE-POINTED STAR

*The Clench crop formation, 2000 (15.9, 15.10)*

No formation brings together more elegantly the teaching about the Ten Planes of Manifestation with that of the Love-Wisdom aspects of the Solar Logos as the formation which appeared near Clench, Wiltshire in 2000: one of the last great geophysical mandalas to occur in Wiltshire. It arrived on 11.8.2000 in wheat on the north slopes of Martinsell Hill, Pewsey CP, Wiltshire (OS SU173639). The immaculate spiralled clockwise swirl of the circles indicates that this was a genuine geophysical formation. The overall diameter recorded by Lucy Pringle was 180 ft. The double-ringed circle at the centre indicates that we are dealing with the Solar Logos. Springing from the inner ring, which in such formations symbolises Ray 2 or 'Life', are streams of energy which form an outer 'penumbra' of ten circles – the Ten Planes of Manifestation. Each circle is the same size,

0 10 20 30 40 50 ft
0 5 10 15 m

THE TRIUNE NATURE OF THE SOLAR LOGOS
1 Spirit 2 Life 3 Form

THE FIVE PETALS as a symbol of the mergence of Buddhi and Manas (LOVE - WISDOM)

THE TEN PLANES OF MANIFESTATION as an expression of the Trinity, the 4 planes of Superconscious Life and the 3 planes of Conscious Life

15.10 *The Solar Logos as a Five Pointed Star Martinsell Hill, Clench, 11.8.2000*

(about 50 ft in diameter) suggesting that in terms of manifestation each 'plane' is of equal importance.

This important formation highlights some of the most significant aspects of the Solar Logos. We start with the ten outer petals, the number *ten* itself. Djwhal Khul categorically states that this number represents 'the totality of manifestation or the Whole [representing] the ten (10) of perfect manifestation, or the perfect MAN.' (Bailey 1925, p. 4) *Ten* is both a symbol and a statement 'of the *arupa* universe [where the] formless [*arupa*] lives are those which are functioning in and through the etheric body of the Logos.' (Bailey 1925, p. 616) The essential organisation of these subjective lives or the Intelligent Consciousness within the forms (see Bailey 1925, p. 827) falls into the following ten categories:

1. Logos 1 – Will or Power

2. Logos 2 – Love-Wisdom

3. Logos 3 – Active Intelligence overshadowing Matter, organising itself under the following heads:

4. Will or Power (Ray 1)

5. Love-Wisdom (Ray 2)

6. Active Intelligence (Ray 3)

7. Harmony, Beauty and Art (Ray 4)

8. Knowledge or Science (Ray 5)

9. Abstract Idealism and Devotion (Ray 6)

10. Organisation (Ray 7).

The essential make-up of the Solar Logos is the same as that of His creation, the Earth Logos, and the human Monad itself. Truly we are made in the image of God. (*Genesis* 1:26)

At a physical level the centres (chakras) of the Solar Logos are represented by the planetary systems of the solar system, each of which constitutes a great Archangelic Being. According to Djwhal Khul the Planetary Lords can be categorised as 'Sacred' or 'Non-sacred' according to Their level of initiation (see Bailey 1951, p. 513) as follows:

| Ray | Sacred Planets | Sign | Energy |
|---|---|---|---|
| 1. | Vulcan: said to be within the orbit of Mercury (Bailey 1925, p. 206) | | |
| 2. | Jupiter | | |
| 3. | Saturn | Pisces | Intelligent substance |
| 4. | Mercury | Aries | Unity through effort |
| 5. | Venus | Taurus | Light through knowledge |
| 6. | Neptune | Gemini | Desire for duality |
| 7. | Uranus | Cancer | Mass Life |
| | *Non-sacred Planets* | | |
| 1. | Pluto – dwarf planet (Rees, M. 2009, p. 204) | | |
| 3. | Planet Earth | | |
| 6. | Mars | | |

Djwhal Khul however identifies 12 planets, two of which (both Non-sacred), are un-named by him, but might perhaps be equated with the dwarf planets *Eris* and *Ceres*. (Rees, M. 2009, p. 205) The distinction between the Sacred and the Non-sacred planets is that the Logos of a Sacred Planet has taken five cosmic initiations, whereas in the case of a

Non-sacred planet the Logos has taken only three. (Bailey 1951, p. 504) So far as this study is concerned, the Seven Sacred Planets and the three Non-sacred Planets may be considered to constitute the Ten Petals of the Clench crop formation, each of which, it will be noted, is paired with another petal.

Amongst the heterogeneous material that Djwhal Khul gathered together for his study on Esoteric Astrology are references to the Twelve Creative Hierarchies, which he assembled in tabular form. (Bailey 1951, pp. 34-35) This material had been 'derived from various sources', and he was diffident about the accuracy of some of it: 'much ... may seem obscure and ... erroneous.' He classifies these Hierarchies into two categories of which four 'have reached liberation and are focussed upon the Cosmic Astral Plane.' I believe that these four have taken the Five Initiations and represent certain Sacred Planets, namely those on Rays 3-6 (Saturn, Mercury, Venus and Neptune). The Logos of Uranus on Ray 7 'exists on the highest etheric level' and will join the other four hierarchies when the sixth Creative Hierarchy (planet Earth) has measured up to cosmic opportunity and is itself nearing liberation. Our Logos is particularly 'active on the intellectual plane'. The remaining Seven Creative Hierarchies or 'States of Being' are those of our own Earth Logos dealt with earlier. The Hierarchies of Rays 1 and 2 (Vulcan and Jupiter respectively of the Seven Sacred Planets) are not mentioned in Djwhal Khul's tabulation and have presumably passed out of our system altogether.

The beauty and subtlety of the Clench crop formation, however, lies in the quinquefoil pattern that emerges as standing crop from the interplay of the elements of the flattened wheat. This is not merely the five-pointed star of *Mahat* (the transcendent principle of intellect) cosmic force, but the five lotus leaves described by Djwhal Khul as evocative of the 'love petals' of the cosmic lotus where 'the energy of the knowledge petals and the energy of the love petals are now so actively fused and blended ...' (Bailey 1953, p. 517) that the jewel of the solar lotus, i.e. the essential nature of the Solar Logos, is now clearly visible.

## THE SOLAR LOGOS YANTRA

*The Barbury Castle formation, 1991* (15.11, 15.12)

One of the most important crop formations to have occurred at any time was that which appeared north of Barbury Castle, Wiltshire, on the night of 16/17.7.1991 in a wheatfield (OS SU152769). In spiritual terms the formation should strictly be described as a *yantra* or sacred geometrical diagram.

The formation was surveyed by John Langrish and an account of its physical characteristics, including lights and sound phenomena, was published by George Wingfield. (Wingfield 1991, pp. 27-29) It was John Michell, however, who first recognised its metaphysical importance and described it as a 'world of symbolism ... some of it already apparent and some still awaiting recognition.' (Michell 1991, pp. 24-25) Michell's perception was endorsed by his friend and colleague the late John Haddington who drew attention to the alchemical and kabbalistic dimensions of the formation in *Global Link-Up* No. 49 of October/November 1991. This was referred to in Brian Grist's scholarly paper of later in 1991: 'Alchemy and Chaos at Barbury Castle' (Grist 1991), which brought all this material together, including a studied assessment of the claims that it was hoaxed, which he dismissed. This writer also surveyed the Barbury Castle formation in July 1991, and with his wife Christine experienced its extraordinary paranormal capacity for spiritual communication and healing, and in a paper in 2000 discussed its importance in terms of teaching about the spiritual Ascension Process for mankind. (Green, Michael, 2000b, p. 11) In its landscape context in 1991, the formation also functioned as a Distributing Centre of the major Triangle of Power in Wiltshire that year. (See Chapter 20)

As Grist demonstrated, the three-in-one triangle, the apex of which carried a central circle, is related to the *Solomanic pentacle*. It was used by Pythagoreans and subsequent occultists, including alchemists, for casting spells. Detailed diagrams survive from the fifteenth century, but I suspect that something like this mandala has been known and used since the pre-Christian, Hellenistic period in the Near East, particularly at the ancient library at Alexandria. I think that such a diagram was essentially 'revealed knowledge' rather than a clever geometrical theorem dreamed up by a Babylonian, Greek or Renaissance mathematician.

First, which of the multifarious Cosmic Beings does this symbol represent? Cosmogenesis follows much the same pattern whether it is The One, a universe, a galaxy, a solar system or a planet. As will be explained, this formation can be confidently regarded as a symbol of our own Solar Logos.

The formation can be divided into three basic elements which represent a two dimensional view of an essentially three or more dimensional construct. The first and critical point is that it is a diagram of the First, Second and Third Cosmic Logoi, i.e. Deity in Manifestation.

The central circle or sphere, as it might have been envisaged, is the *Primum Mobile* or First Cosmic Logos at the Centre of All.

*15.11 Barbury Castle, Wroughton CP (OS SU152769), 17.7.1991*

Surrounding it are two rings, vibrations as it were from the centre, the Second and Third Cosmic Logoi representing the principles of Life and Form (see discussion above). They comprise, together with the central circle (Spirit), the threefold undivided Trinity ('*Deus est Trinus et unus et omnia in omnibus*').

The Trinity is reflected in the second element of the design, the triangle, or if considered as a geometric solid, the tetrahetral figure. The advantage of a two dimensional image is that the angles or quoins look like *rays* emitted from the central circle, piercing the third element of the design, the three circular motifs which are such a striking

*15.12(a) Barbury Castle, Aerial Photograph*

feature. Each of the three deific rays issuing from the *Primum Mobile* of the formation touches a symbol on one of the points of the triangle. *Figura 1* (15.12) of Cornelius Petraeus' *Sylva philosophorum* of seventeenth century date (Bibliotheek der Rijksuniversiteit, Leiden, *Cod. Voss. chem.* q. 61, F. 1, pp. 4-12) clearly identifies the elements of Deity depicted in similar positions on a similar figure as *Pater*, *Filius* and *Spiritus Sanctus* in the traditional Christian format. The drawing is, perhaps, in the light of those times, the best guide to their interpretation. The difficulty over the Holy Spirit as the Third Person of the Trinity arises from a problem which has afflicted the Peoples of the Book (Judaism, Christianity and Islam) who have not been able to recognise the feminine aspect of Deity.

Form or matter and its creation have from time immemorial of mankind been considered 'feminine'. But even in this context this is not strictly accurate, since in the heavenly realms sex and sexuality in human terms are not a factor. 'For when they rise from the dead, they neither marry nor are given in marriage, but are like angels in heaven.' (*Mark* 12:25)

So whence is the Holy Spirit poured out 'upon all flesh'? (*Acts* 2:17) One could describe this as the living essence of Deity which permeates all matter throughout the Cosmos, conveying in different degrees life, intelligence and love. Djwhal Khul expresses it thus: 'From the Christian standpoint, the greater Builders [i.e. Devas] are the Holy Spirit, or force overshadowing and fecundating matter ...' (Bailey 1925, p. 617)

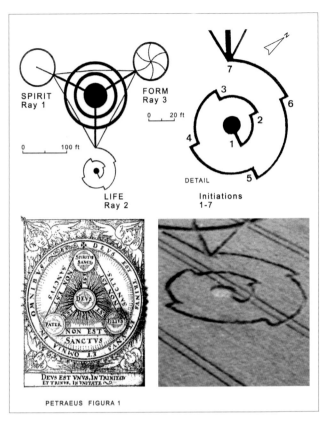

SPIRIT
Ray 1

FORM
Ray 3

0    20 ft

0    100 ft

LIFE
Ray 2

DETAIL

Initiations
1-7

PETRAEUS FIGURA 1

*15.12(b) **The Solar Logos Yantra***
*Barbury Castle, 17.7.1991*

Two centuries ago Iolo Morganwg expressed it beautifully:

'Question. What material did God use in the formation of the world, namely, the heaven and the earth, and other things known and conceived?

Answer. The manred, [Old Welsh = flowing particles] that is, the smallest of all the small, so that a smaller could not be, which flowed in one sea through all the Ceugant [Old Welsh = the Circle of Infinitude] – God being its life, and pervading each atom, and God moving in it, and changing the condition of the manred, without undergoing a change in Himself.' (Williams, J. 1862, pp. 262-263)

*The western symbol* of the Barbury Castle formation, the circle with a line running through to the centre, is the *Mahadiva* yantra (Maha = great: diva = God). To regard it merely as a sexual symbol (the male principle penetrating the female nexus) is rather too simplistic in cosmic terms. Better, I believe, to view the elements of the symbol as the great creative ray of light (Ray 1) issuing from the First Cosmic Logos to produce all the constructs of manifestation. It is the 'Father' or 'Spirit' aspect of the tripartite Deity.

*The northern symbol* is a sixfold structure having the appearance of a wheel or toroid. It appears in the ancient world as an Indo-Aryan solar glyph. It equates with the 'Holy Spirit/Mother' or 'Form' aspect of Ray 3 concerned with the material and spiritual evolution of our system, and relates to the Law of Love. (See Chapter 18.) It concerns activity with ordered love for its impulse. The convergence of these two aspects, wisdom and love, as represented on the western and northern Barbury Castle elements, creates the conditions which enable humanity and the devic creations to develop spiritually – i.e. the Ascension Process.

*The eastern symbol* is the most curious of the three, and consists of a ratcheted spiral turning anticlockwise from a small central circle, which I identify as the 'Son' aspect of planet Earth, its Logos and life forms. There are six ratchets with the seventh leading off the system to the Ray or path going to the Solar Logos. I am confident that this is an inspired diagram of the Ascension Process of spiritual initiations, primarily of mankind, but also of the animal and Devic world. The brilliance of this mandala is that it conveys with maximum economy the concept of expansions of consciousness with ever widening arcs of growth, ever raising the individual (and thus corporately the Earth Logos Himself) to apotheosis in the Solar

Logos. The initiatory process is considered in detail in Chapters 8 and 9.

At this point Iolo Morganwg, who in the teaching of Celtic mysticism describes the *Great Turning* as *Abred*, an archaic Welsh word which means essentially 'transmigration', must have the last word on this process.

'T[eacher]. Why is it requisite to traverse Abred?

D[isciple]. Because where there is a beginning there must needs be an increase and an improvement. And in order to magnify man in respect of vital goodness, and to improve and prepare him for Gwynvyd [the place of purity or heaven] God arranged it so.' (Williams, J. 1862, p. 249)

... humans 'are removed gradually to a higher degree, where they receive an accumulation of life and goodness, and thus they progress from grade to grade, nearer and nearer to the extremity of life and goodness.' (Williams, J. 1862, p. 211)

'D[isciple]. I came, having traversed about from state to state, as God brought me through dissolutions and deaths, until I was born a man by the gift of God and His goodness.

T[eacher]. Who conducted that migration?

D[isciple]. The Son of God, that is, the Son of man.' (Williams, J. 1862, p. 245)

Which brings us to the identity of the whole of this third symbol. It is of course, the Second Ray of Life, the Christ energy, the Second Person of the Solar Logos.

The Solar Logos is the controlling Entity of this solar system, whose centres comprise certain planetary Beings as already indicated. He in turn forms part of a greater cosmic Entity, and indeed it is on this principle of morphic resonance, as Rupert Sheldrake terms it, that the Cosmos is constructed. As the oft quoted saying of the Ancient Wisdom has it: 'What is below is like that which is above; and what is above is like that which is below: to accomplish the miracle of the one thing.' (Tyson, p. 711) To reiterate, first, the Solar Logos is, like all Beings throughout the Cosmos, on a path of spiritual development, and in this sense is an Imperfect God. Second, His primary characteristic is 'unconditional love', reflecting the nature of the centre of a greater Being, which He occupies as the 'Grand Man of the Heavens.' This greater Being, whom I term 'Archon', is discussed in the next chapter.

# 16. THE GALACTIC LOGOI AND BEYOND

*... perdifficilis ... et perobscura quaestio est de natura deorum*
*(The question of the nature of the gods is ... most difficult and obscure.)*

Cicero
*De Natura Deorum I, i*

## SUMMARY

This chapter is concerned with the great Entities who form systems beyond that of the solar system, up to the One, the Only God. *Archon* refers to an Entity whose centres (chakras) are Solar Entities moving together in the Orion Arm of our Milky Way galaxy. The galaxy itself is another great Entity, *Aion*. Our galaxy itself forms part of the local group of galaxies, *An*, of whom the three Rays of Aspect are the Triangulum galaxy (Ray 1), the Andromeda galaxy (Ray 2), and our own Milky Way galaxy (Ray 3). Beyond this again are the seven elements of the *Virgo Supercluster*, and still greater groupings.

We examine two carvings from the ancient Roman world representing Aion: a relief in the Modena Museum, Italy, which has been described as 'the ultimate in Mystery Iconography', and a named portrait of Aion from the Zoilos frieze in the Roman city of Aphrodisias in Turkey.

## COSMIC LOGOI

*Archon* is the ancient Greek term for ruler (ἄρχων). The term appears in the Gnostic teachings of the ancient world with reference to a class of spiritual Beings who are the creators of the physical matter of the Cosmos, and hence, by extension, of planet Earth itself. As archons are concerned with 'form' as opposed (in their terms) to 'spirit', Gnostics defined them as inherently evil. (See Walker 1983, p. 38.) This is not a view I personally hold, since I regard every element of the Cosmos as working under the rule of God. I have used the term Archon to refer to our *local solar group*, a stupendous group of solar Entities which are moving and linked together with our own solar system, and represent the other centres of Archon. Djwhal Khul reverentially refers to this great Entity as 'The ONE ABOUT WHOM NAUGHT MAY BE SAID' (Bailey 1925, p. 520), in the sense that His Life and Being are beyond our comprehension. Our Solar Logos is the physical centre of Archon.

Although initially reluctant to talk much about Archon, over the course of time Djwhal Khul dropped sufficient hints for an understanding to be formed of this Being's centres in terms of solar systems. It may be briefly tabulated thus: with their approximate distances in light years (LY) from the Sun:

Ray 1. MERAK in *Ursa Major* (the Great Bear). 80 LY

Ray 2. SIRIUS in *Canis Majoris* (the Great Dog). 8.6 LY

181

Ray 3. ALCYONE in *Taurus* (the Bull) – one of the Pleiades. 403 LY

Ray 4. ALDEBARAN in *Taurus* (the Bull). 67 LY

Ray 5. THUBAN in *Draco* (the Dragon). 303 LY

Ray 6. BETELGEUSE in *Orion* (the Hunter). 498 LY

Ray 7. THE SOLAR SYSTEM.

[Distances from www.stelladatabase.com (Ed.)]

*16.1 The Milky Way Galaxy, showing 'Archon' and 'Aion'*

The Archon group of solar systems travel together in the Orion Arm of our Milky Way galaxy. (16.1) Djwhal Khul makes frequent reference to the numinous qualities of the Great Bear Constellation, the Pleiades Cluster and the Sun Sirius. (Bailey 1925, p. 1058) These three can be considered as connected with the Rays of Aspect of Archon. The Sun Sirius, the brightest star in the sky and only 8.6 light years from the Sun, is probably the epicentre of the Archon group of solar systems.

Archon forms part of *Aion*, the Milky Way galaxy itself, still a very small unit indeed of the whole. The Milky Way galaxy with its spiral arms traces a flattened disk, over 150,000 light years across and populated by older stars, some of whom date back to the birth of the galaxy 13.8 billion years ago. Our galaxy contains more than 100 billion stars, which makes planet Earth, indeed the Archon group itself, barely more than a molecule in terms of its physical relationship to the galaxy. Its spiritual relationship, however, may be on a different scale altogether.

Following the principles of morphic resonance, the vast physical structure of Aion in turn forms part of a greater Being, or to be more precise in this case, a centre of another Entity whom I term *An*. (This is the name of the ultimate Deity of the Celtic world where the word in Old Welsh *Ân* has the connotation of the great primary principle, and is found in such compound words as *Annwyn*, the other-world existence.)

An is what is known in astronomy as the *local group of galaxies*. (16.2) At least forty five galaxies are known in the local group, which is a discrete identifiable unit about 9.8 million or more light years in diameter. The galactic Entities there are at all stages of development, with perhaps only the mature, spiral galaxies actually forming the main spiritual centres. I am sure that the Seven Ray System operates here, and one might make a shrewd guess that perhaps the Three Rays of Aspect are represented by:

Ray 1. The *Triangulum* galaxy 'Floculent spiral' in the Aries constellation. The third largest member of the local group.

Ray 2. The *Andromeda* galaxy in the Pisces constellation. This is the largest member of the local group and is moving towards our own Milky Way galaxy with which it will begin to merge in around 4.5 billion years.

Ray 3. The *Milky Way* galaxy, the second largest in the local group.

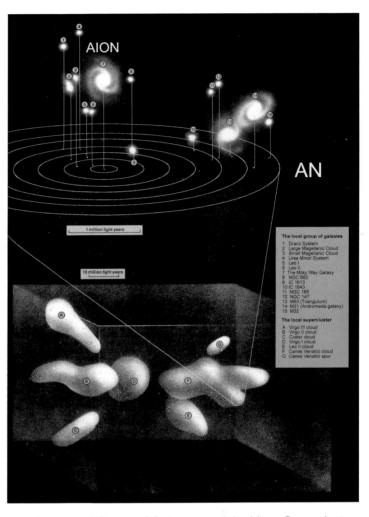

16.2 *The Local Group of Galaxies and the Virgo Supercluster, showing 'Aion' and 'An'*

I believe it would be entirely speculative to try to identify the galaxies which form the four Rays of Attribute of An, since their distinctive criteria may be very different from those in our own system.

Again following the principles of morphic resonance, the local group of galaxies forms part of the *Virgo Supercluster*, a curious organic-looking cluster structure of, yes, *seven* distinct elements, in all about 100 million light years in length. This in turn forms part of

the *Laniakea Supercluster*, which undoubtedly forms part of still greater groupings in ours the twelfth and most physical of the universes. The other universes which form the centres of the One, the Only God, are coterminous with ours and operate at higher vibrational levels. The lower universes still function to a degree at some level of physicality, and the echo or shadow of their existence is represented in our own universe by the omnipresent so-called 'dark matter', or 'dark energy' whose nature in scientific terms is still speculative. (Rees, M. 2009, p. 27)

The Thunderbolt    The Cosmic Egg

'North' Karmic Angel: Purity

'East' Karmic Angel: Love

The Rod of Power

The Zodiac Signs

Mithraic Inscription

Deific Snake of Initiation

'West' Karmic Angel: Service

'South' Karmic Angel: Dedication

The Twelve Houses of the Zodiac

*16.3 Relief of Aion, depicting the Galactic Ascension Process*
*Mid second century AD. Museo Estense, Modena, Italy*

## THE MODENA AION (16.3) AND THE ZOILOS AION (16.4)

*Hermetic Iconography.* Returning now to our own Milky Way galaxy and Aion, there are two ancient Roman images that convey His character and attributes. The first is a stone plaque believed to be of mid second century AD date at the Galleria Estense at Modena, Italy, which, judging by the partly-erased inscription of a woman's name and the title *Felix Pater* (Auspicious Father), may have come from a Mithraic temple in the vicinity.

Joscelyn Godwin in a perceptive study says of this piece that its 'multiple ramifications and the profundity of its symbolism ... may be regarded as the ultimate in Mystery iconography.' (Godwin 1981, p. 170)

The anthropoid winged Deity emerges from the flames of the Cosmic Egg. (See Chapter 4.) The solar rays and lunar crescent behind His head, balanced by the cloven hooves for feet, indicate that He is a great Cosmic Entity passing through the state of physical manifestation as part of the spiritual Ascension Process. The Modena figure is synchronistic in the sense that it brings together attributes of many Mediterranean and Near Eastern deities featured in the Hermetic mysteries. There is, however, no clear attribution on the relief itself to identify this Being. Scholars have suggested various identities (Godwin 1981, p. 170), but I believe that the internal evidence points to one in particular, Aion, since the Lord of our Galaxy must necessarily reflect all the attributes of His creation operating within the constraints of *time*, the constant of our system, symbolised here by the circle of the Zodiac which is the spiritual *cursus vitae* for humanity and other life systems of our galaxy. It will be noted that *Aries*, the House that marks the beginning of the Ascension Process, is depicted at the top of the Zodiac, with the *Little Turning* proceeding House by House clockwise; and the *Great Turning*, likewise, proceeding anticlockwise. (See Chapters 22-24.)

Aion carries two great symbols of power. In His right hand He grips the vajra or thunderbolt. (See Chapter 20.) At one level this symbolises 'the highest aspect of divinity ... called electric fire.' (Bailey 1927, p. 350) Its twofold aspect is reflected in the qualities of the bodhisattva *Vajrapani* (the Holder of the Vajra) who inter alia embodies the qualities of wisdom and compassion (love). (McArthur

2004, p. 57) The left hand of Aion carries a great staff, which I believe to be the Rod of Power, or Sceptre of Initiation, which vests its holder with the ability to focus and transfer power. Such transforming power is absolutely critical for all initiates on the threshold of a new spiritual plane of activity. (See Chapters 19 and 20.)

The naked figure of Aion is wreathed around by a serpent whose head appears above the figure resting on the cosmic egg. This etheric snake, or *daimon*, appears in association with other Hermetic images, said to be of Aion, which are lion-headed and occur at Mithraic shrines across the Roman world. The writer's encounter with a leonine humanoid *Paschat* in 1994 (channelled by Paul Bura) is related in Chapter 1. I believe that similar encounters in Mithraic contexts may account for this iconography. Returning to the snake – what is its symbolic significance?

That brilliant classical scholar, Jane Harrison, recognised in a relief of a snake from Piraeus inscribed to Zeus Meilichios (Διὶ Μειλιχίῳ), and dating to the fourth century BC, that 'Zeus, father of gods and men, is figured by his worshippers as a snake.' (Harrison J.E. 1962, p. 18) Indeed she suggests that in the ancient Greek world the supreme Deity, in this case Zeus, was revealed as having a serpentine form before being given the anthropoid Olympian image. The Hermetic vision of the priest Nechepso at Alexandria c. 150 BC also envisaged the Creator as a serpent. As discussed in Chapter 15 in the case of the Solar Logos, there is clearly a 'dragon connection'. The original physical forms of some of these great Cosmic Beings were obviously not necessarily humanoid.

Turning to the imagery of the coils round the figure, the Archangel Michael has given us a clue when He uses the term 'freedom' in relation to the passage of the initiatory procedure. In a very real sense those great Cosmic Beings, by submitting to the full incarnatory process, have voluntarily 'bound' Themselves. In the imagery of the constricting serpent of the One God, each experience of spiritual growth of its multiform make-up in terms of initiations releases 'one coil', so to speak, of the serpent. In this instance, if I am correct, we are dealing with the Milky Way galactic Being, Aion, Who on the evidence of the Modena figure has accomplished three Cosmic Initiations, with four yet to come (the four coils). I do not know the nature of these great Cosmic Initiations (Sirian Initiations as they are termed in our system) of which those of our own planet, instituted by the Earth Logos, are but pale reflections. (See Chapters 8 and 9.) Two things, however, can be asserted. First, the spiritual growth of any Cosmic Being depends on the corresponding spiritual growth of the myriad entities of its make-up. When they achieve a certain critical mass, then an initiatory stage has been reached. Second, the seven great Cosmic Initiations (there are subsidiary tests and levels of achievement) are the great archetypes, in their general character, of our own miniscule system.

On the Modena Aion, the masks of ram, lion and goat on the figure's torso refer to the Zodiac signs of Aries, Leo and Capricorn respectively since they mark the critical points at which the human Monad (and probably other monadic life forms in the Galaxy) achieves incarnation, individuation and apotheosis.

In the four corners of the plaque are four male busts facing inwards. They do not represent the four winds since their faces are in repose. They have a much more significant, spiritual, meaning. They represent 'the four levels of the etheric body of both God and man, viewing them from what we call the energy or physical angle ... These four etheric levels, or these four grades of vital substance constitute what is called the "true form" of all material objects or phenomena, and they are responsive to the *four higher types of spiritual energy* [my italics] which we usually call divine.' (Bailey 1934, p. 550)

Djwhal Khul quotes in this connection from some:

'wonderful words from an ancient writing in the Masters' Archives. It is said to date back to early Atlantean times. The material on which the writing is found is so old and frail that all that the Masters themselves can touch and see is a precipitation made from it, the original being kept at Shamballa. It runs thus, with certain deletions, which it is wiser not to insert: [I have also edited it slightly, author.]

"At the four corners of the square, the four angelic [Beings] are seen ... Four words they utter forth ... From out the North a word is chanted forth which means ... *be pure*.

From out the South the word peals out: *I dedicate*.

From out the East, bringing a light divine, the word comes swinging round the square: *Love all*.

From out the West, answer is thrown back: *I serve.*"' (Bailey 1934, p. 547)

'... in the thoughts of purity, dedication, love and service, are summed up the nature and the destiny of man [and not only mankind], and it should be remembered that they do not stand for so-called spiritual qualities, but for potent occult forces, dynamic in their incentive and creative in their result.' (Bailey 1934, p. 548)

This extraordinary transmission, which could refer precisely to the sort of image conveyed by the Modena relief, can now be shown to explain the meaning of this quartet of busts. It also clarifies a pattern of cosmic governance which has become evident as this study progressed.

Every Cosmic Being is advised and controlled by a group of four Celestial Entities brought in from the system above of which it forms part. Ultimately this arrangement derives from the One, but the particular character of this intervention will have been determined by the Controlling Entity of this the Twelfth Universe. Our Earth Logos, Ibez, has four Lords of Karma advising the Great Council of planet Earth who 'are literally planetary mediators, representing our Planetary Logos and all that concerns Him in the greater scheme of which He is but a part.' (Bailey 1922a, p. 41)

'The names of the Lords of Karma signify, symbolically and from the angle of their inner meaning, Relationship, Enlightenment, Pain and Return.' (Bailey 1957, p. 116) The Solar Logos Bel, and the Archon group of solar systems, have a similar arrangement of Karmic overview, although we know no details. Likewise Aion, which makes the angelic Beings, described in the Atlantean script mentioned above, so interesting. There are of course Karmic Lords operating at galactic level, but originating from the local group of galaxies Being, An. Their attributive 'names' are a direct reflection of the qualities of those at our Solar and Planetary levels, but operating at a much higher spiritual level.

| *Galactic* | Purity | *Planetary* | Pain |
|---|---|---|---|
| | Dedication | | Enlightenment |
| | Love | | Relationship |
| | Service | | Return |

These great Beings operate at every level as a quaternary since They are dealing with 'basic combinations of matter.' (Bailey 1925, p. 153)

I share Joscelyn Godwin's concern about the unevenness of Mithraic material as a whole and whether it was part of an invented religion rather than a revealed one. (Godwin 1981, p. 99) However, the Modena Aion is unique amongst Mithraica and shows so many levels of spiritual, intuitive understanding that it must be the product of revealed wisdom, almost certainly visionary.

The best portrait of Aion in my opinion (and identified by name as such) is the first century BC bas relief carving from the so-called Zoilos frieze from a monument in the Roman city of Aphrodisias in south-west Turkey. (Erim 1986, p. 138) Aion is shown as an old man, seated and hooded in a reflective pose, the very archetype of the 'Silent Watcher.' (16.4)

*16.4 Aion from the Zoilos Frieze Aphrodisias, Turkey. First century BC*

# 17. SIBSON: THE GEOPHYSICS OF THE CROP FORMATIONS

*The Formulas 'express a past, indicate a revelation, and ground the thinking aspirant in the world of meaning because it is in that world that he must learn to work and live ...'.*

Bailey 1955, p. 320

## SUMMARY

In this chapter and the next we examine a set of crop formations which appeared at Sibson, Cambridgeshire, between 1990 and 2001. This chapter develops the theme, begun in Chapter 2 Part 3, of the way genuine geophysical formations are created; the next chapter addresses the *meaning* of the Sibson formations.

Jim Lyons has kindly contributed Notes on three of the Sibson formations studied, and on geophysical effects of earth energies.

## THE SIBSON SITE

There was a general awareness amongst crop formation investigators that the Sibson site was a particularly suitable test area for scientific investigation. To the best of my knowledge, of the 15 formations occurring between 1990 and 2001, none were man-made. Furthermore, they appeared in a discrete area, which provided a rare opportunity to examine geotectonic and related aspects in relation to their creation. This was accompanied by marked parapsychological activity which cannot entirely be accounted for by natural geomorphic phenomena.

## THE CROP FORMATIONS: BASIC DETAILS (17.1-17.4)

My first plan (17.1) shows all the formations, coloured individually so that they can easily be distinguished, as some overlapped or overlaid another. The next three illustrations (17.2-17.4) show individual formations in more detail. Formations A and B are lettered rather than numbered, as in my interpretation they are not part of the main sequence – see the next chapter. Measurements give the outer diameters to the nearest foot except where specified.

Formation A. OS TL095964. Field 16/1. July 1990, probably 9.7.1990. Reportedly a plain circle. Not inspected.

Formation B. OS TL094968. Fields 3 & 18/3. Probably 20.7.1990. Wheat. Glyph. Circles 12 ft 4 in and 14 ft. Curved path, broken after cutting through and scorching hawthorn hedge (crop & grass verge unaffected).

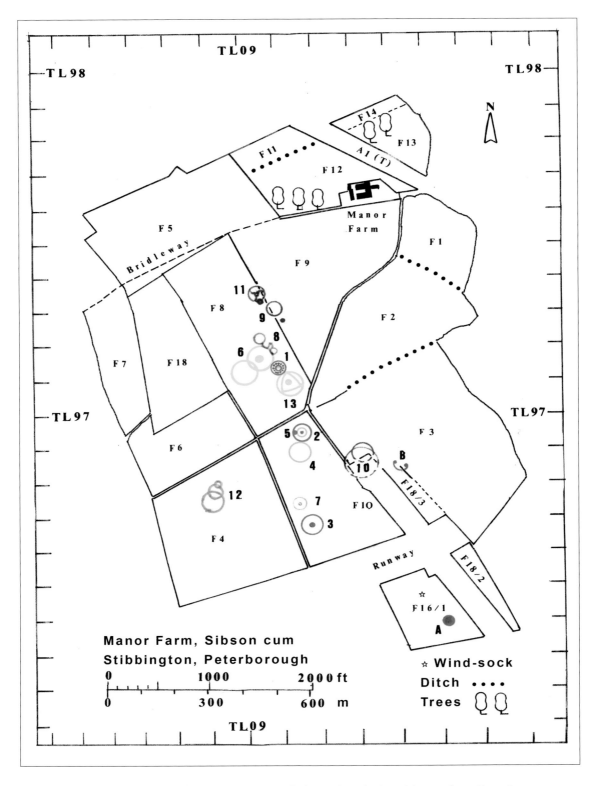

17.1 The Sibson crop formations 1990 to 2000. Coloured to distinguish one from the other

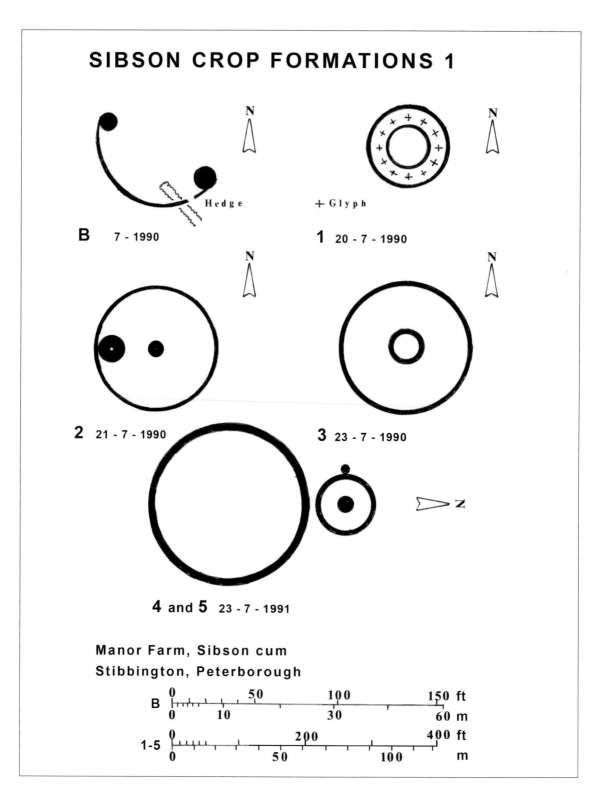

# SIBSON CROP FORMATIONS 1

N

Hedge

+ Glyph

**B** 7 - 1990

**1** 20 - 7 - 1990

N

N

**2** 21 - 7 - 1990

**3** 23 - 7 - 1990

Z

**4** and **5** 23 - 7 - 1991

Manor Farm, Sibson cum
Stibbington, Peterborough

| | 0 | | 50 | | 100 | | 150 | ft |
|---|---|---|---|---|---|---|---|---|
| B | 0 | 10 | | | 30 | | | 60 m |

| | 0 | | | 200 | | | 400 | ft |
|---|---|---|---|---|---|---|---|---|
| 1-5 | 0 | | 50 | | | 100 | | m |

17.2

# SIBSON CROP FORMATIONS 2

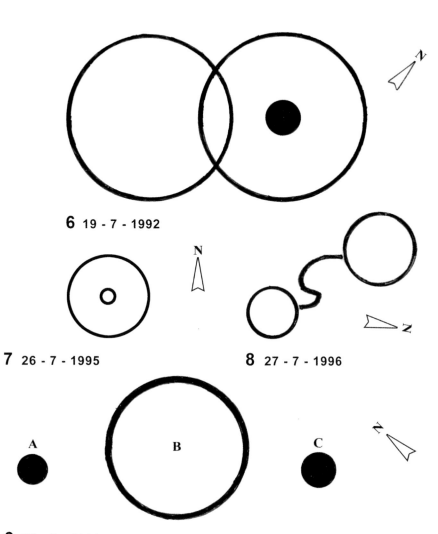

**6** 19 - 7 - 1992

**7** 26 - 7 - 1995

**8** 27 - 7 - 1996

**9** 28 - 7 - 1998

Manor Farm, Sibson cum
Stibbington, Peterborough

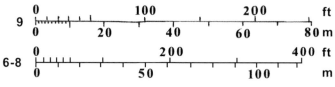

*17.3*

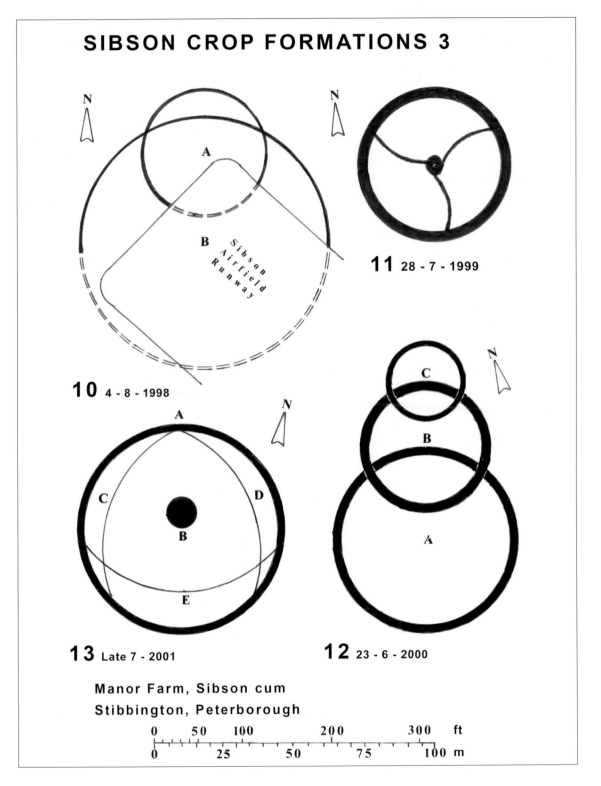

## SIBSON CROP FORMATIONS 3

**11** 28 - 7 - 1999

**10** 4 - 8 - 1998

Sibson Airfield Runway

A

B

**13** Late 7 - 2001

A

C

B

D

E

**12** 23 - 6 - 2000

C

B

A

Manor Farm, Sibson cum
Stibbington, Peterborough

0    50    100         200         300    ft
0        25         50        75       100  m

17.4

Formation 1. OS TL090971. Field 8. 20.7.1990. Wheat.
Inner ring 59 ft. Outer ring 118 ft. Not examined on ground. Air photos show faint traces of 12 features, possibly glyphs, symmetrically placed between the rings.

Formation 2. OS TL091969. Field 10. 21.7.1990. Wheat.
Central circle (clockwise (cw) spiralled flattened crop) 25 ft. Ring (cw) 190 ft. Inner tangential circle (cw) 40 ft with standing centre.

Formation 3. OS TL091967. Field 10. Probably 23.7.1990. Wheat.
Inner ring 51 ft. Outer ring 210 ft.

John Michell (Michell 1990, p. 5) wrote that formations 1, 2 and 3 were first spotted by Peterborough Parachute Centre parachutists on 25.7.1990. My information, however, would suggest the dates above.

Formation 4. OS TL091969. Field 10. 23.7.1991. Wheat.
Ring (cw) 236 ft. Ring width 9 ft.

Formation 5. OS TL091969. Field 10. 23.7.1991. Wheat.
Central circle (cw) 25 ft. Ring (cw) 94 ft. Outer tangential circle (anticlockwise (acw)) 15 ft. The formation was located over formation 2 of 1990.

Formation 6. OS TL090971. Field 8. 18/19.7.1992. Wheat.
Intersecting rings forming a *vesica piscis* (fish bladder symbol). One ring with a central circle. South ring (acw) 250 ft. North ring (cw) 250 ft. North central circle (acw) 55 ft.

Formation 7. OS TL091967. Field 10. 26.7.1995. Barley.
Central ring (acw) 23 ft. Outer ring (cw) 120 ft.

Formation 8. OS TL090972. Field 8. 27.7.1996. Wheat.
North ring (acw) 110 ft. South ring (acw) 81 ft. Connecting glyph 95 ft long.

Formation 9. OS TL090973. Field 9. 28.7.1998. Wheat.
Central ring (cw) 133 ft. North circle (cw) 25 ft.
South circle (acw) 32 ft. See Note 1.

Formation 10. OS TL093968. Field 3 & airfield runway. 3/4.8.1998.
North circle (acw) 144 ft. South circle (cw) 282 ft. See Note 1.

Formation 11. OS TL090973. Field 8. 28.7.1999. Wheat.
Inner ovoid circle 20 ft (cw). Outer ring 163 ft (cw). Three curved radial spokes, 22 ft radii. The formation had complex telluric energy fields. See Note 1.

Formation 12. OS TL089967. Field 4. 23.6.2000. Wheat.

Three intersecting rings forming a double *vesica piscis*. South ring 205 ft (acw). Middle ring 143 ft (cw). North ring 89 ft (acw). Mathematical properties based on the Kelvin Wedge theory (on the wake of ships). (See Jim Lyons' red annotations in illustration 18.15 in the next chapter.)

Formation 13. OS TL091971. Field 8. Late 7.2001. Wheat.
Symbol or monogram. Ring with inner circle and three internal arcs. Inner circle 38 ft (acw). Outer ring 236 ft (acw). 3 arcs 146 ft radii (acw).

## AUTHENTICATION

The Sibson formations were bounded by the A1 trunk road to the east and the B671 road to the west, but not overlooked by either road. The Nene Valley railway lies in a deep cutting and tunnel to the north. To the south is the Sibson Airfield. The fields in which the formations appeared were overlooked by the farmer's house at Manor Farm and the conning-tower of the airfield from which there was 24 hour surveillance. It is inherently unlikely, although not impossible, for hoaxing to have taken place without being observed from either place.

No scientific tests were made of the five formations of 1990. However, examination on the ground by Paul Gregan of the Peterborough Evening Telegraph and his photographer resulted in their commenting that 'they were far beyond the capacity of any normal hoaxer. The flattened corn stalks had not been trampled, they looked more like they had been carefully plaited together.'

It is also recorded that at formation B, where the curved path of the glyph cut through a hawthorn hedge, the hedge was scorched although no damage was done to the crop or the grass verge of the field.

In 1991 extensive crop sampling tests were carried out on features of formation 5 by Montague Keen, then Scientific Officer for the Centre for Crop Circle Studies (CCCS). His report (K003/SIBS/791) mentions that the 'stems were intact, apart from the basal bending.' There were positive results from the UK's National Institute of Agricultural Botany (NIAB) at Cambridge, who examined plant samples, and reported that disease was not a factor in the bending of the stems, and that the circle stems were found to be crushed about mid-height, a mysterious feature attributed by Keen to the 'flattening force'. Keen, who was the first person to enter the formation, noted that there was 'a total absence of any visible approach to, or sign of disruption at, the centre of the untouched circular area around which the broad ring was described.'

In 1992 formation 6 showed no evidence of breakage or snapping of the stems (except at the base where bent).

In 1995 soil samples from formation 7 were collected by the late Christine Saltmarshe and sent to the ADAS (Agricultural Development and Advisory Service) laboratory at Wolverhampton for Nitrate-N readings from inside the formation and a control outside. Jim Lyons commented on the results of these tests: 'the central value exceeded the control by over 350%. Other circumstances relating to the creation of this formation led to a strong conviction that this was geophysically created. The dowsing pattern was also classic.' In 1995 all the formations were dowsed by Jim Lyons & Michael Newark – both seed and on the ground – and produced positive results.

In 1996 seed dowsing for aura tests were carried out on formation 8. Lyons' comments on the results: 'aura tests indicated genuineness of the formation although the energy levels were not dramatically high.'

Jim Lyons' Note 1 below covers dowsing and other observations made about formations 9 and 10, of 1998. Newark also reported positive dowsing results from these formations.

Farmers' mobile phones cut out when harvesting formation 9.

Formation 11, of 1999, is also covered in Note 1.

Formation 12, of 2000, caused my tape recorder to break.

Formation 13, of 2001, gave us some problems, for, although some found it acceptable as a geophysical event, others did not like it. Thanks to a careful survey, it was possible to plot the formation accurately. If this had been hoaxed, I would have expected the setting-out points of the arcs to be in the flattened crop along the perimeter of the outer circle. However, this was not the case. The setting-out points were in the standing crop and there is no evidence from the aerial photo that this had been disturbed. (See illustration 18.16 in the next chapter.)

Aerial photos of the formations show none of the ring structure associated with man-made ones manufactured using rollers or boards. The formations at Sibson may, on the basis of these various results, be regarded as geophysical with some degree of confidence.

## GEOPHYSICAL FEATURES (17.5 AND 17.6)

My physical geography plan (17.5) includes heights above sea level, a stream, the spring line and some wells. The geophysical plan (17.6) highlights the geology of the area and the aeromagnetic anomaly values. The geological structure of the area is marked by basal igneous activity, particularly that of the *Lower Palaeozoic shales* associated with the Caledonian deformation. The granodiorites of this system, which run as a belt north-west to south-east beneath the site, have saturated densities around 2700 kg m³, approximating

to grain densities. This band of deep basaltic activity is shown in the aeromagnetic anomaly survey (OS sheet 52°N-02°W, 1980), which indicates a complex pattern of local magnetic 'highs' and 'lows' associated with plutonic activity. Sibson lies in a trough between two such 'highs', each about 4 miles distant.

The OS map shows a falling series of anomaly values in nanotesla running from south-east to north-west, almost at right angles to the aquifer flow. It may be significant that the dominant reading of the area is zero, the same as that in the Beckhampton (Wiltshire) area of crop formation activity.

When the Sibson crop formations are plotted in relation to the solid and drift geology of the Nene valley, they are found to be concentrated on an outcrop of the *Blisworth Clay*. This Great Oolite Clay is part of the Midlands Jurassic sequence. Structurally it is uniformly argillaceous with an exceptionally plastic consistency making it effectively impermeable.

Overlying the Blisworth Clay to the south, in the area of the Sibson aerodrome, is a layer of *Cornbrash*, a hard, detrital, shelly limestone. At its basal levels (as here) it forms a brown, marly limestone, very ferruginous. This level is generally permeable.

Underlying the Blisworth Clay belt is the *Blisworth Limestone* (Great Oolite Limestone) which emerges as a level running north-west to south-east. The limestone at the top weathers to a calcareous permeable loam.

At the top of the site there is also evidence for *periglacial features,* the result of the area being subjected to the cold climatic environment induced by the glacial ice cover of the last Ice Age (Devensian Glaciation). Extremes of cold caused contractions in the ground and resulted

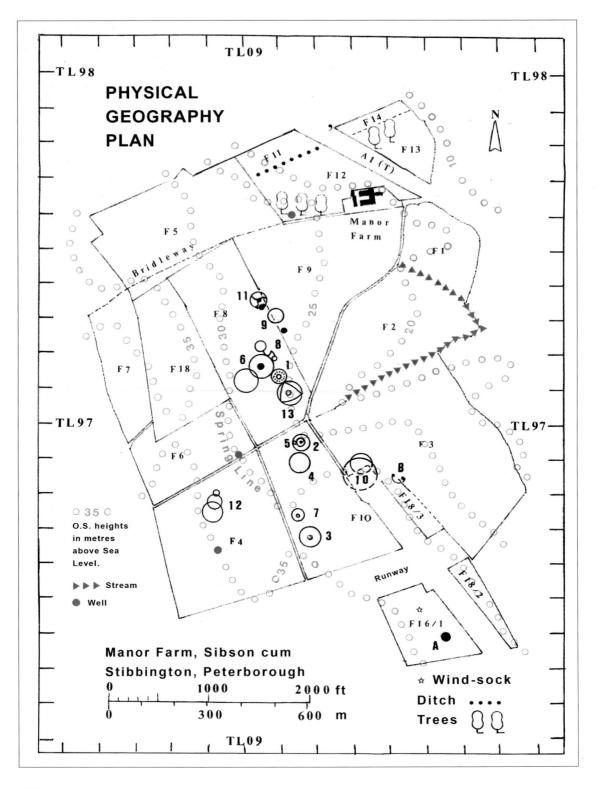

# PHYSICAL GEOGRAPHY PLAN

Manor Farm, Sibson cum Stibbington, Peterborough

O.S. heights in metres above Sea Level.

Stream
Well

Wind-sock
Ditch
Trees

17.5

in cracks and splits developing. During their formation they were constantly infilled with wind-blown debris and their own collapsed sides. Aerial photos of the Sibson site show these periglacial features in the area of the Cornbrash as a system of linear, rectilinear, and even polygonal crop marks. No doubt they originally covered the entire area, but fluvial action when the Nene Valley was formed in the Flandrian (Post Glacial) phase, c.10,000 BC, washed out the lower levels of this activity. Such buried channels would have the same effect as field drains draining off the subsoil water. It is noticeable that the crop formations are generally careful to avoid such areas, which would disrupt an even aquifer flow.

## GEOHYDRAULIC (17.6)

As the contours indicate, the ground gently falls away from south-west to north-east about 32 ft (10 m) over a distance of about 2600 ft (800 m), producing an interesting aquifer effect. Rainwater falling on the Cornbrash at the top of the slope would percolate through to the Blisworth Clay, which would function as an aquiclude. The resulting spring line along the interface of the Cornbrash and the Blisworth Clay is marked by a series of wells. In wet weather the subsoil water can be heard running downhill in field 18. The subsoil water passes through the ferruginous loam overlying the Blisworth Clay, and on reaching the Blisworth Limestone boundary, it is absorbed within the deeper sequences and forms the ground water of the Nene Valley.

## GEODETIC (17.7)

This is the key process by which the diffuse energy fields from the plutonic basal levels are directed, concentrated and manipulated to make the crop formations. Unfortunately the study of geodetics as a rational discipline is not generally accepted by the scientific community largely because the process operates at subtle energy levels, and is thus believed to be instrumentally unquantifiable. Although the concept that the planet is surrounded by a structured electromagnetic field is one that has been known for a long time, there is not, at the time of writing, an agreed terminology or indeed understanding of how exactly the process works. In postulating an operational scheme at Sibson, therefore, I have drawn on my own practical experience in this field and have provided anodyne terms largely agreed in discussion with Jim Lyons. The geodetic plan has been drawn up on the basis of map dowsing corroborated by field work. Although the general picture is, I believe, accurate, the details are only approximate, since in some cases the precise location of the crop formations (and thus their relation to the energy grid) is uncertain.

The focal point of the process at Sibson is an *energy centre* lying below formation 13 (OS TL091971). The energy centre is one of the innumerable global 'acupuncture points', many of them associated with prehistoric and later sacred sites. They operate as 'connectors' between various subtle energy levels and also as 'attractors' for the electromagnetic fields and currents. It is my perception that the energy centre is presided over by an Intelligence controlling the crop formation process, as discussed below.

The energy centre operates as a cross-over point for two major *energy lines*. These are, by analogy, the arteries for an associated grid of smaller energy lines, or capillaries, which convey subtle energy currents to any

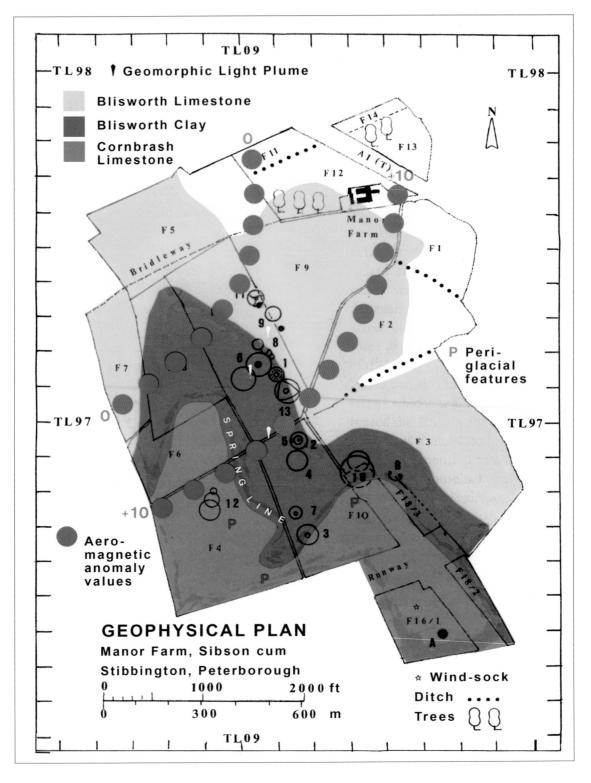

**GEOPHYSICAL PLAN**

Manor Farm, Sibson cum
Stibbington, Peterborough

*17.6*

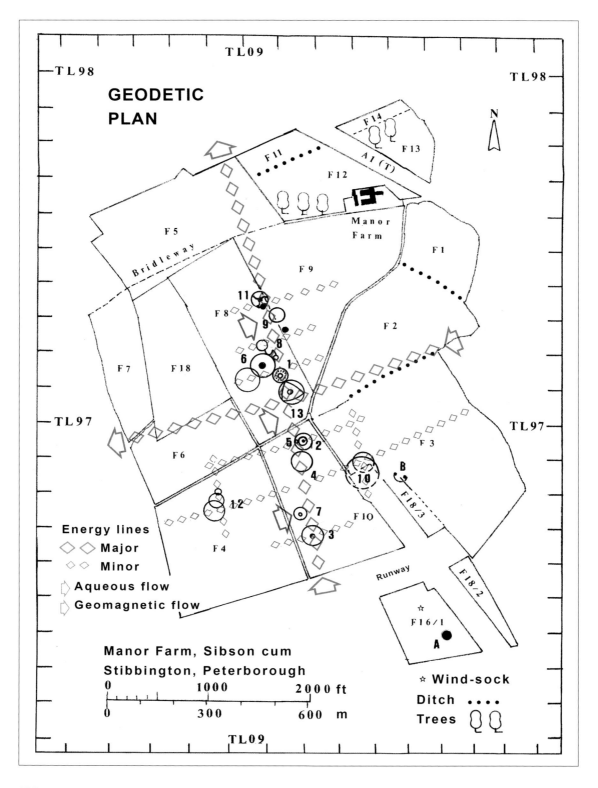

*17.7*

designated part of the site. The analogy is with the meridian system of acupuncture. These energy lines are effectively the telluric network identified by Hartmann and Curry, and on this site the operational grid between 150 ft and 200 ft square or oblong. No attempt has been made to identify the directional flow of the telluric energy or the precise width of the lines since these vary according to seasonal and other factors.

## CREATION OF THE CROP FORMATIONS

It is probable that most crop formations are formed in direct association with the centres or lines of the energy grid, and that when a crop circle is created, a strong magneto-gravity field floods through the telluric grid from the centre, infusing the space within and around the site of the formation.

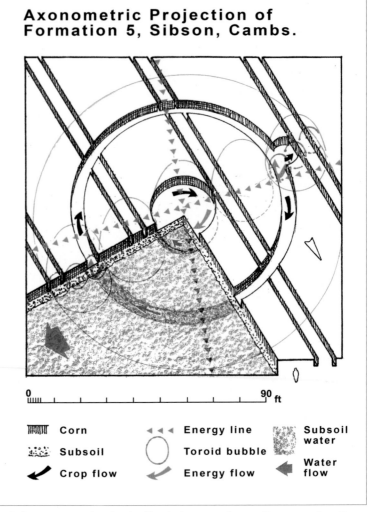

**Axonometric Projection of Formation 5, Sibson, Cambs.**

0 _____ 90 ft

| | Corn | ◄◄◄ | Energy line | | Subsoil water |
| | Subsoil | ◯ | Toroid bubble | | |
| ⬋ | Crop flow | ⬋ | Energy flow | ◄ | Water flow |

*17.8 Some geophysical effects in crop formation construction*

At Sibson the subsoil and its junction with the impervious Blisworth Clay then comes into play. It is where the ferruginous subsoil meets the clay that the pattern matrix of the crop formations is probably formed in water, with the resultant electromagnetic fields inducing air currents which produce the formation at about ground level. This level where subsoil and impervious clay meet is the median plane of the formations, which, as shown by Jim Lyons' models, (Lyons J. (1998a) 'Bubbles and Knots' in *The Circular*

# 31, May 1998, p. 4ff. and Lyons J. (1998b) 'Silbury Torus Formation' in *The Circular* # 32, September 1998, p. 17), extend both above and below ground level.

Illustration 17.8 shows this theory in action as an axonometric projection of formation 5. Below the crop there is the subsoil with water below it, and the three-dimensional toroid energy bubbles, in red, creating patterns in the corn.

For more on the geophysical effects of earth energies see Jim Lyons' Note 1 to this chapter.

## GEOMORPHIC LIGHTS (17.6)

Balls of light and light plumes were observed both on and off the site; in the latter case they appeared sometimes to be related to the arrival of crop formations.

### 15/16.7.1992

**8.00 am.** 'Smoky misty cloud spiralling in area of field 8. Shaped like a bullet head about 20 ft high. Disappeared in seconds.' Observed by farmer, D. Hope. Appearance of formation 6, 19.7.1992. Ball of light photographed by Beth Davis in central area of formation 6, late July 1992. (See illustration 18.7 in the next chapter.)

### 26.7.1993

Crop watch by Christine Saltmarshe in car at track junction (OS TL091970).

**03.00 am.** Flash in sky over top of site lasting about 30 seconds, then another flash.

**03.01 am.** Narrow column of misty light, 10 ft wide spiralling anticlockwise with several subsidiary centres forming high plume positioned itself by the side of car for 3 or 4 minutes, then moved to front of car and disappeared.

**04.00 am.** Saltmarshe leaves car and walks down track about 70 yards to OS TL091969. Light plume reappears, about 6 ft high and stands beside Saltmarshe for several minutes: reportedly feminine energy, beneficent, but purposeful. Had inner radiance, not exactly a mist but more like a heat haze with crystal sheen.

Saltmarshe's presence on site seemed to interrupt the formation creation. No formation appeared in 1993 or 1994, nor again in 1997 when there was another crop watch.

### 26/27.7.1995

At home of Saltmarshe at Alconbury Weston, Cambridgeshire, about 13-14 miles from Sibson: 'Looked out of daughter's bedroom window in early hours and was aware of swirling golden light in garden.' Formation 7 appeared soon afterwards.

### 14.11.1997

After the abortive crop watch, Saltmarshe reported another event at Alconbury Weston, four months after the usual crop formation date: 'Went into my daughter's bedroom at about 6.30 am. I could see light flickering on the other side of the curtain and pulled the curtains back. There was the same swirling mist as previously.'

### 4.8.1998

Saltmarshe reports that the same light phenomenon appeared in the early hours in the garden of her home in Alconbury Weston, 'towards the sky.' Formation 10 appeared on 3 or 4 August.

### 16.11.1998

The swirling mist appeared again in the garden of the Saltmarshe home at about 6.45 am low on the ground. It dissipated after a few minutes.

These parapsychological experiences in connection with crop formation appearance are extraordinarily interesting. The plumes of light may, or may not, be a natural geomorphic occurrence, but their regular appearance at Saltmarshe's home some miles away is something else. I have an overwhelming impression that an Entity (see further on) had appropriated a natural light phenomenon and was using it to communicate with us. The November appearance of the light phenomenon in 1997 and 1998 should be noted.

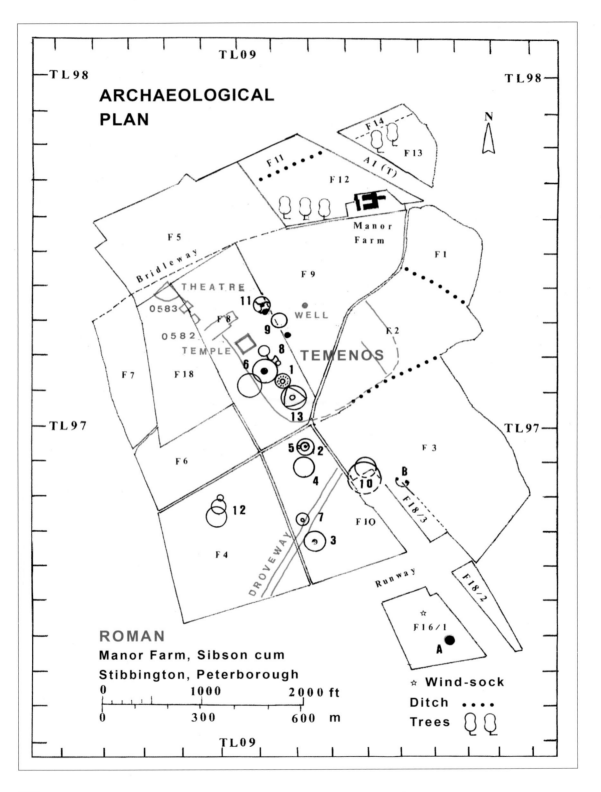

**ARCHAEOLOGICAL PLAN**

TL 98     TL 09     TL 98

N

F 14

F 13

F 11

F 12

A 1 (T)

Manor Farm

F 5

Bridleway

F 9

F 1

THEATRE

0583

F 8

11

9

WELL

F 2

0582

TEMPLE

8

TEMENOS

6

1

F 7

F 18

13

TL 97     TL 97

F 6

5 2

4

F 3

10

B

F 18/3

12

7

F 10

3

F 4

DROVEWAY

Runway

F 18/2

F 16/1

A

**ROMAN**

Manor Farm, Sibson cum
Stibbington, Peterborough

0    1000    2000 ft

0    300    600 m

☆ Wind-sock

Ditch ....

Trees

*17.9*

## ARCHAEOLOGY (17.9 AND 17.10)

In 1844, when the Nene Valley railway line was built, three mutilated statues, all of Barnack stone, were uncovered. The statues represented Hercules, the torso of Apollo and a life-size figure of Minerva. The exact location of these finds is uncertain, but is said to have been in the area of Wansford station (OS TL090978). This material had clearly been re-deposited from a temple or shrine, possibly with the intention of reusing it to erect a pottery kiln or other building. The find site was about a quarter of a mile from the nearest crop formation, and although identification of the site of the original shrine must necessarily be speculative, there are archaeological indications that it may have been further south in the centre of the crop formation area.

*17.10 Statue of Minerva*
*Second century AD, found at Sibson*

Aerial photos appear to indicate a large stone-walled enclosure (*temenos*) in the area of fields 8 and 9, of which the west wall and south west corner are visible, together with part of the east wall. Outside the enclosure to the west there is a small kite-shaped enclosure reminiscent of the simpler forms of the Gallo-Roman, Celtic theatre types associated with shrines. There are no visible features in the centre of the temenos, except a large pit or well (OS TL092975). However an aerial photo (August 1998) of formations 9 and 10 also shows the rectangular structure of a Romano-Celtic temple about 25 ft wide west of formation 9, within the temenos.

The late Jocelyn Toynbee described the second century Minerva from Sibson (17.10)

as the most remarkable from Britain, even though missing her helmeted head: 'In her vanished right hand the goddess held what appears to have been either a sceptre, with a rounded terminal, or a spear reversed, with the butt-end uppermost. ... The end and a small portion of the shaft are visible against the right shoulder. The right hand (now missing) when found held an owl and the spear shaft. The left hand rests on the rim of a circular shield with a round external boss; and the shield in its turn rested on the mouth of a long-necked vase, of which only the pear-shaped body, standing on a small pedestal beside Minerva's left foot, now survives. Up the body of this vessel (and once, presumably, around the neck) writhes a snake, the head and neck of which appear in low relief on the lower part of the outside of the shield.' (Toynbee 1964, p. 78)

This slightly unusual Deity in a Romano-British context is provided with attributes which are highly revealing of her role and function. The reversed spear indicates that she is not a tutelary war goddess, like the tribal Deity Brigantia, who is also represented as Minerva. Rather it emphasises her beneficent role as Goddess of Wisdom. The water pot indicates a Deity presiding over a *nymphaeum*. In this case, the upright pot with the long neck indicates that the nymphaeum is centred round a sacred well. The snake imagery is also highly significant. In general terms, the snake is the symbol of something sacred. It stands for the *Genius Loci*, the guardian spirit of a place.

The Deity worshipped here, therefore, is not the Olympian Athene/Minerva, but a tutelary nymph *(genius* or *daimon)* who has the attributes of the Wisdom of Minerva, but is immediately responsible for this sacred area, with a holy well perhaps as its focal centre.

## THE INTELLIGENCE FACTOR

There is a tacit agreement among most students of the geophysical crop formation phenomenon that, whatever the geodetic and geophysical factors at work, an 'Intelligence' must be involved in the design of the formations. There is absolutely no agreement on what or who this Intelligence might be. It is my perception that here we are dealing with, in the broadest sense, 'an Intelligence of the natural world of this planet'. I am not concerned with its precise identity, although there are plenty of archaeological and metaphysical clues. The important point is that the 'Intelligence' not only has the responsibility for organising the design, but also of transforming a diffuse plutonic surge operating at subtle energy levels into a concentrated physical electromagnetic field capable of flattening the crop.

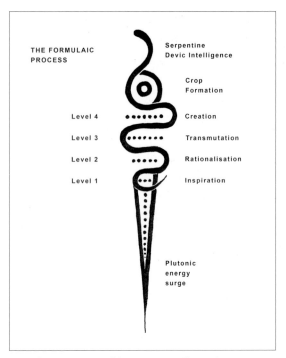

*17.11 Symbol on a Mycenaean Oinochoe 1350-1300 BC*

It has been recognised for thousands of years that this creative process has a fourfold structure known as *The Formulas*. The scheme encompasses not only making crop formations but is indeed the structure of the creative process throughout the Cosmos. To illustrate this I have reproduced a symbol or diagram taken from a Cypriot *oinochoe* (wine jug) of Mycenaean date (1350-1300 BC), which admirably brings out all the salient features. (17.11)

The central figure is a writhing serpent, the Devic Intelligence, which encompasses the four levels of the formulaic process from the plutonic energy surge to the creation of the crop formation. This serpent, which is both an Intelligence and the Subtle Energy itself, is precisely the same serpent which writhes up the water pot of the Sibson Minerva statue. This vessel, symbolising the sacred well of the nymphaeum, is the spiritual centre of the phenomenon at Sibson. The serpent is also represented in formation 8 there.

*Level 1. Inspiration.* This carries the concept of the visualised ideas, the dynamic purpose of the Divine Thinker. The Thinker in this context is the Presiding Intelligence of this planet. In Kabbalistic terms this sphere is termed Atziluth, the World of Emanation directly in contact with the Divine. It is highly significant that this level on the oinochoe is represented by three dots, symbolising the Trinity, or threefold energy pattern of manifested Deity.

*Level 2. Rationalisation.* A primal desire is transformed into an intellectualised concept or design. This is the operation of *Manas* (intelligence) as part of the creative process. In Kabbalism this is the sphere of Beriah, the World of Creation. It is symbolised by five dots, the sacred numeral for Intelligence.

*Level 3. Transmutation.* The idea is now conceived as a structured intelligent concept but remains to be realised in physical form. Level 3 is concerned with establishing at subtle energy level the design matrix of the crop formations, which is carried out by vitalising the geohydraulic constituents at subsoil level. The Kabbalistic term for this process is Yetzirah, the World of Formation, the design level of the creative process. The seven dots of this level represent the sevenfold nature of Deity in manifestation, both latent and concrete.

*Level 4. Creation.* This is the sphere of the implementation of the design. The formative process in crop circles is achieved through subtle energy fields operating through vortex bifurcations, the magnetic shell structures of counter-flowing magnetic field lines and the winding energy fields of the torus knot, as postulated by Jim Lyons. In Kabbalism this is termed Assiah, the World of Making (form).

## CONCLUSION: A GEOPHYSICAL MODEL

I have felt it necessary to review a number of disparate matters in connection with the Sibson crop formations since they all appear closely interrelated. The model that I am tentatively suggesting is a sequential process, under the control of a local non-human Intelligence, operating at subtle-energy levels, but capable of physical expression.

1. The process starts as an energy surge at deep geological basal levels, possibly sparked by some such cyclic cosmic activity as solar flares. The electromagnetic energy fields are directed up through an energy centre (position related to a Roman sacred site at Sibson) to the telluric energy network on the surface. It is possible that at Sibson, as in Wessex, the process is assisted by a deep geological fault system.

2. At surface level the electromagnetic energy field is spread through the telluric system to a suitable aquifer locality, namely the Blisworth Clay aquiclude, where the magnetic field is coupled with the gravitational field.

3. Here there is an interaction with a chemically charged ionised sheet of water gently flowing through the subsoil, over the impermeable clay. The water provides the medium for the design matrix of the formation, operating at the median level of the resultant 'energy bubble.'

4. The projected energy field is then constructed in accordance with the principles of vortex bifurcation and the winding energy of torus knots. A key factor is the necessary recognition that we are dealing with a local, non-human Intelligence, which has the responsibility for designing and constructing the formation. In this process the contribution of water as a conscious design element is paramount.

# NOTE 1

*Part 1 – Key Points of a Study of Sibson Formations 9 and 10*

1.  The alignment of formations [at Sibson] over the years at around 10 deg. west of North is indicative of a set of consistent pattern–forming conditions.

2.  The (relative) simplicity of the formations is indicative of a limited set of criteria used in their creation.

3.  The asymmetric nature of the 1998 Sibson formation [formation 9, illustration 17.12], with its side circles, correlated with the underlying energy line positioning which was also offset.

4.  The dowsable spiders–web patterns within the side circles followed a slightly unusual pattern in that there were just two radial lines per circle, diametrically opposed to form a circle diameter. These aligned with the main energy lines outside the formation.

5.  The distribution of energy within each of the side circles followed the now classic marquee roof shape.

6.  The retained energy in the seed heads gave rise to an aura measurement which relative to that from seeds measured at the centre of the circle fell to one half its value at exactly half the radius of the circle.

7.  Tests on crop samples from the centre

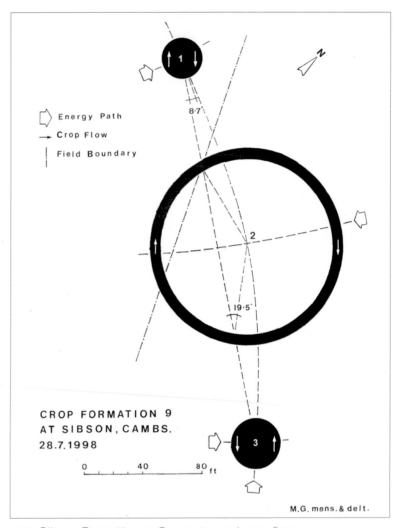

Energy Path
Crop Flow
Field Boundary

CROP FORMATION 9
AT SIBSON, CAMBS.
28.7.1998

0        40        80 ft

M.G. mens. & delt.

*17.12 Sibson Formation 9. Geometry and crop flow*

annulus and side circles showed significant variations in nitrogen/nitrate levels (in parts per million) compared with control samples.

8.  An analysis of the geometry of the formation clearly indicated the tell-tale 19.5 deg. angle which reveals the underlying tetrahedral geometry involved in the process of pattern creation.

9.  A study of the formation's underground water flows revealed by dowsing shows how the streams 'frame' the pattern. Of

particular significance, however, was the fact that only one blind spring was associated with the pattern. Often, 4 or 5 can be involved in very complex shapes. The solitary spring was located right at the centre of a side circle.

10. A study of the local geological features of the area revealed no chalk bed which usually retains many vertical flowing springs. This phenomenon is believed to be responsible for the simple features of the formation.

11. ... Sibson formation [10], occurring several days after the first [9], still retained the basic lineage in terms of its location along a north/south oriented line. It too demonstrated its tetrahedral geometry origins having again a 19.5 deg. angle associated with the linking of the two circles.

12. Although the seed heads were not tested in the laboratory for nitrogen/nitrate changes, dowsing the aura of the samples indicated levels of density of retained subtle energy comparable with Sibson [9].

Jim Lyons, 18.11.1998

*Part 2 – Sibson Formation 11 – Visit Report 01/08/99*
[Illustration 17.13]

## GENERAL

The formation which occurred around the 27th July around the time of the full moon was in the same style as ones dating from previous years. The pattern closely resembled one of the 'legs' of the Barbury Castle formation, namely an annulus with three curved radial arcs emanating from a central circle. The crop flow of both this circle and the outer annulus was swept clockwise. Flow along the radial arcs was outward.

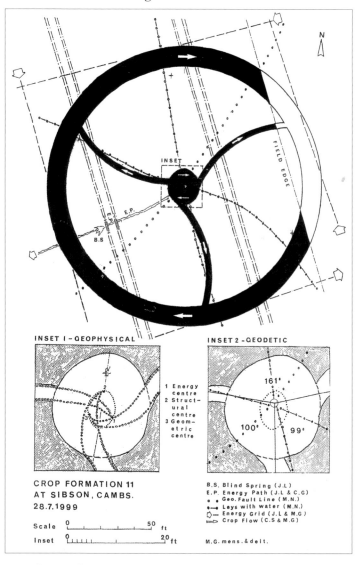

*17.13 Sibson Formation 11. Geometry, geophysical and geodetic aspects*

## GEOMETRY AND DOWSING

The main directional energy lines governing the formation were orientated NS-EW and were exactly tangential to the formation. They 'drove on the left' which dictated the clockwise crop lay. The eastern end of the formation had already been harvested but this was no impairment to detecting the pattern of the formation in the ground. What was of interest was the widening of the annulus width as it both flowed into and out of the harvested section. The excess width of crop lay amounted to about 1 ft. Indications were that the formation came down after harvesting had taken place. The central circle of around 21 ft diameter had a central section of around 5 ft in diameter as defined by dowsing its ring that contained a typical crude spiralled form of crop flow. Outside this region in the remainder of the circle, the crop lay was tangentially laid down in a neat fashion. There were no other dowsable rings within this inner circle. However, two diametrically opposed radials were present which were aligned in angular fashion closely with the centres of two of the spiral arms.

The angular exit locations of the spiral arms from the central circle were overall asymmetric. However, in fact the two northerly arms were aligned symmetrically about North and subtended an angle at the centre of the formation of close to 160 deg. This can be surmised to be 180-19.471 deg. indicating the underlying tetrahedral geometry of the formation. The third southerly located arm ran almost tangentially from the central circle, this subtending an angle at the centre of the circle relative to the NW spiral arm of around 110 deg. (90+19.471 deg.?). Again this is indicative of the tetrahedral nature of the geometry The radial crop flow overlaid that within the annulus indicating that the circular flow went down first followed by that in the arms.

The formation exhibited other unique characteristics. Firstly, the source of underground water in the form of a blind spring was visible as initially a small patch of 'lodged' crop. This then took a westerly path as a narrow wavy line visible in the crop, emerging into the annulus. The crop however, was beneath that within the annulus and hence was laid first. This narrow line continued out of the formation to join up with the next tram line. A second feature was the laying of crop within two of the tram lines traversing the formation. This occurred mostly at the right hand edge of the tram lines when facing north but extended a considerable way both north and south outside the formation. There were places in the field where this flow turned around to join up into a closed path. The Energy stored in the crop at the southerly end of this crop flow was highly energised.

Generally the crop was significantly energised with seed heads from the centre circle displaying an aura which extended almost to the edge of the formation. Samples were collected from a number of locations and will be tested for nitrogen/nitrate variations.

## CONCLUSIONS

The formation was typical of the Sibson formations over the years. It displayed its simple geometric and underground water properties. New clues involving water sources and energy line flow were identified. Overall the formation was pleasing, well executed and a perfect example of a simple geophysical formation.

Jim Lyons, 3.8.1999

## NOTE 2

*Geophysical Effects of Earth Energies*

The key to the origin and formation of Crop Circles is so called Earth Energies. That the energies of place affect humans and other living matter has been known for millennia. The problem is knowing exactly how these energies, which display remarkably subtle effects at times, are related to existing accepted scientific understanding. From studies now being carried out by the British Society of Dowsers (BSD), it is being realised that the energy is at least a combined effect of Nature's two long range forces, the earth's magnetic and gravitational fields. Despite centuries of study the formal link between these two forces is not yet understood. However, there are circumstances where the two become inextricably bound and this is in the presence of an environment where free electrons exist. Those electrons gyrate around the earth's magnetic field lines because of the Lorentz force and at the same time, because of their mass, are affected by anisotropies in both the gravitational and magnetic fields. The result is essentially gravity or internal waves which are widespread in meteorology with the magnetic field pressure acting as the restoring force on any displacement. An analysis of this situation shows that the energy density balance between the two forces gives rise to a characteristic length which turns out to be a well known measurement in earth mysteries, namely the megalithic yard – 2.72 ft.

Coupled gravity and magnetic waves have been well studied in oceanic environments where they affect large scale weather patterns. The coupling between the forces is by means of the conducting ocean currents. The resulting waves propagate vertically and generally form cones of energy rising over the sea surface. It is believed that this effect gives rise to the well known patterns seen on calm seas by mariners over the centuries. They are circular in form with radii of often several hundred metres. The wave pattern structure, as best can be assessed from descriptions, are not unlike crop circle patterns. Coupled magneto-gravity waves over land are virtually unstudied by the main scientific community, not being recognised as having any significant properties. The reason is that the coupling between the forces is not so obvious. However, work in the BSD has shown the importance of underground streams which generate free electrons at all times. These streams are now known to be a vital factor in the shape of Crop Circles and generally bound the outer edge of the patterns. Work to date has shown that there is usually one blind spring associated with a formation, being located at the centre of one circular source in the pattern. Blind springs are vertical movements of water and it is these that give rise to the vertical magneto-gravity waves with their anisotropic conical vertically orientated motion. It turns out that the particle motion within the conical wave fronts is predominately circular in the vertical plane which when viewed around the cone manifests itself as a toroid.

It is now known that these waves interact with living matter in very particular ways. The process is one of electro-chemistry. It appears that the main detection mechanism for subtle energies in humans is the glands, in particular the pineal gland. Although the wavelength of the magneto-gravity waves is generally at least metres because the motion interaction of the waves is vorticular, it turns out that the shape of the gland is important for their detection. In the pineal gland, as its name implies, it is pine or egg shaped. Nature uses this technique widely to 'capture' the cosmic energies to evolve life. All birds and many mammals rely on the laying of eggs. The resonant nature of the shape means that the egg's contents respond to ambient fields. In the pineal gland, it is to be expected that there will be release of hormones when in sufficiently strong fields. This year, we have undertaken hormone testing which showed the release of oestrogen, progesterone and other relevant hormones. Because objects such as batteries have free electrons in their electrolyte, they are very susceptible to ambient fields. In essence, they cannot function as batteries in the presence of these fields because their basic current flow mechanism (from linear to gyratory flow) is disrupted. Once outside the fields, they revert to their standard functioning. The same basic argument goes for the effects of energies on soil and crops though here the short lived ambient microwave field is the cause of more permanent disruption in the basic nitrate balance in the cell structure. More detailed biological study is needed here to establish the exact process.

Thus the general geophysical forces due to magnetic and gravitational effects, when related to specific earth points involving energy line intersection, are now known to influence energy flow in well defined ways. They cause significant effects on all living matter because of their disruption of the normal cell processes and the overall result is the creation of crop patterns which are strongly correlated with the basic molecular structure of the substance which offers the linking mechanism, namely water.

Jim Lyons, 11.12.1998

# 18. SIBSON: THE COSMIC LAWS OF THOUGHT

*Laws are only the unalterable conditions brought about by the activity, the orientation and the emanated decisive thoughts of the One in Whom we live and move and have our being ...*

Bailey 1955, p. 62

Having considered the geophysical background of the Sibson crop circle phenomenon, and the metaphysical source of the Entities involved, we reach the critical issue of the meaning of this series of formations. I have concluded that we are looking, despite their simplified format, at some of the most profound of the crop formations considered in this study – which symbolise what Djwhal Khul terms 'The Laws of Thought.'

The manifest Cosmos through the Twelve Universes, and every system therein down to the minutest, is ordered by the rule of law, the 'unalterable conditions' of the chapter head above. This body of teaching must be regarded as the most important that we have received in this medium of communication. We start this momentous subject with a statement by Djwhal Khul:

'There are three great Laws, that we might term the fundamental laws of the cosmos ... and seven ... we might consider secondary laws, though, from the standpoint of humanity, they appear as major ones.' (Bailey 1925, p. 567)

In my initial study (Green, Michael 2005, pp. 79-90) I followed Djwhal Khul's classification but had great difficulty equating the subsidiary (Solar) Laws in the prescribed sequence. I have since come to realise that the Seven Solar Laws are not, primarily, those shown in the Sibson series of formations, which are in fact subsidiary *Cosmic* Laws, although there is some overlap. In my revised interpretation the complete Sibson series between 1990 and 2001 should now be tabulated as follows. (18.1, 18.2)

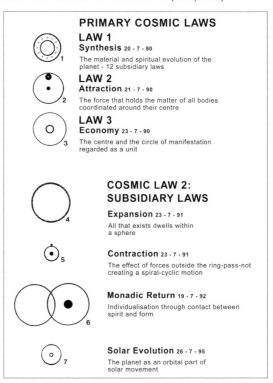

**PRIMARY COSMIC LAWS**

**LAW 1**
**Synthesis** 20 - 7 - 90
The material and spiritual evolution of the planet - 12 subsidiary laws

**LAW 2**
**Attraction** 21 - 7 - 90
The force that holds the matter of all bodies coordinated around their centre

**LAW 3**
**Economy** 23 - 7 - 90
The centre and the circle of manifestation regarded as a unit

**COSMIC LAW 2: SUBSIDIARY LAWS**

**Expansion** 23 - 7 - 91
All that exists dwells within a sphere

**Contraction** 23 - 7 - 91
The effect of forces outside the ring-pass-not creating a spiral-cyclic motion

**Monadic Return** 19 - 7 - 92
Individualisation through contact between spirit and form

**Solar Evolution** 26 - 7 - 95
The planet as an orbital part of solar movement

*18.1 The Sibson, Cambridgeshire, Crop Formations 1990 to 2001, representing the Cosmic Laws of Thought. Formations 1-7*

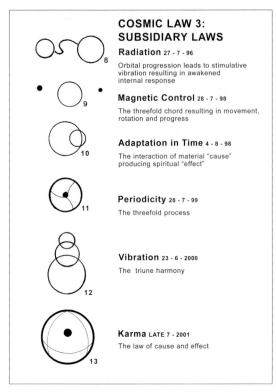

**COSMIC LAW 3:
SUBSIDIARY LAWS**

**Radiation** 27 - 7 - 96
Orbital progression leads to stimulative
vibration resulting in awakened
internal response

**Magnetic Control** 28 - 7 - 98
The threefold chord resulting in movement,
rotation and progress

**Adaptation in Time** 4 - 8 - 98
The interaction of material "cause"
producing spiritual "effect"

**Periodicity** 28 - 7 - 99
The threefold process

**Vibration** 23 - 6 - 2000
The triune harmony

**Karma** LATE 7 - 2001
The law of cause and effect

*18.2 The Sibson, Cambridgeshire, Crop
Formations 1990 to 2001, representing the
Cosmic Laws of Thought. Formations 8-13*

## PRELIMINARY FORMATIONS

*Formation A.* A plain circle used as a
'pointer' or 'marker' to draw
attention to this locality
for the benefit of local crop
researchers, in this case George
Wingfield, members of whose
family lived nearby (18.3)

*Formation B.* The *Varuna* signature (no
photograph, see illustration
17.2, in previous chapter, and
also below)

## THE PRIMARY COSMIC LAWS (18.1)

*Formation 1.* The Law of SYNTHESIS
(18.4) The formation
was distinguished by the
appearance of the twelve

separate glyphs, symbolising
the *Twelve Laws of Thought.*

*Formation 2.* The Law of ATTRACTION
(18.4)

*Formation 3.* The Law of ECONOMY
(18.4, 18.5)
The three great Cosmic Laws,
reflecting the energies of
the Three Rays of Aspect,
appeared with formation B,
the signature glyph of Varuna
(the Archangel Gabriel), all
in 1990, the first year of the
series.

## THE SUBSIDIARY COSMIC LAWS (18.1, 18.2)

*Subsidiary laws of Law 2 (the Law of Attraction)*

*Formation 4.* The law of EXPANSION
(18.6)

*Formation 5.* The law of CONTRACTION
(18.6) Formations 4 and 5
occurred together as a unit,
indicating the linked theme of
these two Laws.

*Formation 6.* The Law of MONADIC
RETURN (18.7)

*Formation 7.* The Law of SOLAR
EVOLUTION (18.8)

*Subsidiary laws of Law 3 (the Law of Economy)*

*Formation 8.* The Law of RADIATION
(18.9)

*Formation 9.* The Law of MAGNETIC
CONTROL (18.10)

*Formation 10.* The Law of ADAPTATION
IN TIME (18.10, 18.11)

*Formation 11.* The Law of PERIODICITY
(18.12, 18.13)

*Formation 12.* The Law of VIBRATION
(18.14, 18.15)

## THE LAW OF KARMA

*Formation 13.* Symbol of *the Lords of Liberation* (18.16)

## THE SERIES SUMMARISED

There are thus a 'pointer' (formation A), a signature (formation B) and Twelve Cosmic Laws of Thought (formations 1-12). They reflect the Twelve Universes or centres of GOD, *the One Boundless and Immutable Principle.* The Twelve Laws in turn may be broken down into the Primal Triad of *the First Cosmic Logos* (formations 1-3), then the Nine Subsidiary Laws pertaining to *the Second Cosmic Logos* (formations 4-7) and *the Third Cosmic Logos* (formations 8-12) respectively. The Law of Karma is symbolised by formation 13, the last of the series.

*The Nine Subsidiary Laws,* all of which are aspects of the Rays of Attribute, have a special significance of their own, since they control the spiritual development of the human Monad. In the words of Djwhal Khul they may be considered to be the 'nine signs which carry a man from the stage of imprisonment in form to the freedom of the kingdom of God, from the state of embryonic consciousness to the full flower of divine knowledge, from the condition of human awareness to the conscious wisdom of the initiated disciple.' (Bailey 1951, p. 320)

Looking at the Nine Laws in a slightly different perspective, the four subsidiary Laws of the Second Cosmic Logos (Laws 4-7) concern the development of cosmic structure, and their fourfold type reflects the principle of developing form or matter. The five subsidiary Laws of the Third Cosmic Logos reflect the activity of the five Mind-born Sons of Brahma in this and all other systems in developing and balancing these principles at both the macrocosmic and microcosmic levels.

The Tibetan Master, Djwhal Khul, and the Greater Master, have in their communications described the Laws of Thought in some detail, and in this study I have made reference to their views where appropriate. Here I am primarily concerned to tabulate the essential features as they relate to the crop formations at Sibson between 1990 and 2001.

## SYMBOLS OF THE COSMIC LAWS

### LAW 1

*The Law of Synthesis* Sibson formation 1 (18.1, 18.4)

'It is the law that demonstrates the fact that all things – abstract and concrete – exist as one.' (Bailey 1925, p. 567) From Djwhal Khul's description it is evident that existing as one is the principal motive, indeed *raison d'être* of all Cosmic Beings, including Aion, the Logos of our galaxy, the central Spiritual Sun of our system. 'It is the sumtotal, the centre and the periphery, and the circle of manifestation regarded as a unit.' (Bailey 1925, pp. 567-568) This crop formation reflects with utmost simplicity this great cosmogenic principle by the use of that most ancient of symbols, the *Bi* symbol, which in its open centre expresses the numinous state of the First Logos of Spirit and in the open outer band the manifested state of Form of the Second Logos.

This earliest of the cosmic symbols at Sibson had a feature which indicated the special nature of this group of formations. It had twelve glyphs arranged within the open outer band denoting Form. Although unable to identify these symbols, their number and location suggested to this writer that what was to follow would be concerned with that momentous theme, the Cosmic Laws of Thought. The appearance of these glyphs in the outer band is a reminder that the Laws of Thought have their primary application in the

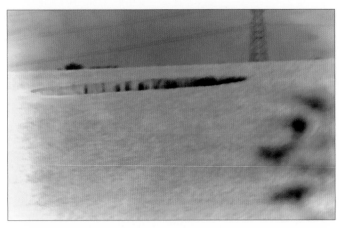

18.3 Sibson Formation A, 9.7.1990
*Reportedly a plain circle*

18.4 The three huge Sibson formations of 1990
*The Primary Cosmic Laws of Thought*
*Right: Formation 1, 20.7.90*
*Centre: Formation 2, 21.7.1990*
*Left: Formation 3, 23.7.1990. Outer ring 210 ft wide*

The loss of this information, which would have provided important clues to the interpretation of the Twelve Cosmic Laws, was highly regrettable, a view which was also apparently shared by the geophysical crop circle makers who put down a similar, perhaps identical, formation some 60 miles distant, south of Birmingham, near Hopwood (OS SP026768) on 9.8.1996, for the benefit of the CCCS West Midland crop circle investigators, who had also been working on the Sibson site. The formation was another *Bi* symbol, 113 ft in diameter (as against 118 ft in the case of Sibson formation 1). The central ring had what appeared to be 'hieroglyphic type letters looking like some sort of script' (personal communication of August 1996 from Michael Newark, of the West Midland Group). Alas they were never recorded due to an uncooperative farmer who refused entry to *bona fide* investigators, and the symbols were trashed by unauthorised sightseers.

It is possible, indeed highly likely, that the Hopwood glyphs were similar to that used in Sibson formation 8 (see below) which appeared to have been derived from the archaic *Gupta* script, partly because their flowing characters make them easy to construct in a crop formation, but also as a security measure since their interpretation would be unintelligible to the non-specialist.

LAW 2

*The Law of Attraction* Sibson formation 2 (18.1, 18.4)

At a mundane level this is a gravitational

world of matter, where the use of *form* is the catalyst for *spiritual* growth.

Unfortunately the formation was recorded only on (rather poor) aerial photos and never inspected on the ground. The twelve glyphs were evidently quite simple, probably the initial (in whatever ancient script) representing the abbreviation of a word (i.e. notaricon cryptography).

*18.5 Sibson Formation 3, 23.7.1990. The Law of Economy. Inner ring 51 ft wide, outer ring 201 ft wide*

law that 'holds the matter of all physical plane bodies, and that of the subtle bodies coordinated around their microcosmic centre.' (Bailey 1925, p. 568) 'In the case of *rotary* motion ... the impulse emanates from within the ring-pass-not [Djwhal Khul defines this as 'the periphery of the sphere of influence of any central life force.' (Bailey 1925, p. 41)] and is produced by the impact of the positive charge upon the negative charges. This is true of all atoms, cosmic, solar, individual, chemical and so forth. When, however, the effect of the rotation of the atom is so strong that it begins to affect other atoms outside its individual ring-pass-not, another influence begins to make itself felt, which draws together, or dissipates, those contacting coalescing atoms. Thus forms are built under the impulse of aggregated forces of some one kind, and these forms in turn produce effects

on other cohering atomic forms, until the rhythm is built up, and a vibration instigated which is a continuation of the rotary motion of the individual atoms, and the modification produced on them by their group activity. This causes progression and simultaneous rotation. The movement forward is modified considerably by the internal atomic activity, and this it is which causes the motion we call spiral cyclic. It demonstrates in all forms as a tendency to repeat, owing to the backward pull of the rotating atoms, and yet is offset by the strong progressive impulse of the form activity.' (Bailey 1925, pp. 1039-40)

At a spiritual level also this gravitational law thus 'holds that matter of all physical plane bodies is coordinated around their microcosmic centres' in the sense that every unit of the Cosmos is programmed to find full expression and development by symbolically moving to the outer limits of manifestation, and is equally driven to return to the centre (God) carrying the fruits of its experience for assimilation and further development. The process is symbolised in crop formation 2 by having the *Bi* disc of Deity with a small circle (actually a tiny version of the *Bi* disc) lying just within the periphery of the outer ring. This beautifully and economically expresses the fact that the Monad (of any system) having achieved apotheosis at the outer limits of experience (and thus symbolised by the *Bi* disc), is ready to return to Him Who sent him forth. Strictly speaking this process is expressed in the subsidiary law of *Monadic Return* (see formation 6).

18.6 Sibson Formations 4, left, and 5, right, both of 23 7.1991. The Laws of Expansion and Contraction respectively

This spiral-cyclic activity, which is distinctive of all forms, is expressed in four subsidiary laws connected with Cosmic Law 2: the laws of *Expansion, Contraction, Monadic Return,* and *Solar Evolution.* These four laws dealing with different aspects of monadic development in form might refer to a universe, a galaxy, a solar system, a planetary system, or even the human Monad in principle.

Cosmic Laws 1, 2 and 3 appeared first, in that order, and they were followed by the Subsidiary Laws, also in date order.

## COSMIC LAW 2: SUBSIDIARY LAWS

*The Law of Expansion* Sibson formation 4 (18.1, 18.6)

'This law of a gradual evolutionary expansion of the consciousness indwelling every form is the cause of the spheroidal form of every life in the entire solar system ... all that is in existence dwells within a sphere ... It requires the two types of force – rotary and spiral-cyclic, to produce this.' (Bailey 1925, pp. 1040-1041) 'All is done under the Law of Expansion, by the method of spiralling progression, cyclic

growth, rotary repetition, and the summation of each greater spiral is the expansion of the consciousness into that of the sphere which enclosed the lesser ovoid, and the escape of the life imprisoned in the sphere. It is merged in its greater whole.' (Bailey 1925, p. 1044) At Sibson this law was symbolised by a large simple ringed circle.

The outer limits of the sphere of Logoidal or Monadic consciousness are marked by the ring-pass-not. The ring-pass-not thus *contains* all developing life for the purposes of spiritual evolution. But it also *excludes* (see Law 5). As the Greater Master puts it: 'For without limitation – finiteness – there can be no manifestation, and without death or the discarding of the outworn, there can be no progress' (Fortune 1976, p. 43), which brings us to Law 5.

*The Law of Contraction* Sibson formation 5 (18.1, 18.6)

This law does not appear under this heading in the classification by Djwhal Khul, but relates to *the Law of the Attraction of Outer Space* described by the Greater Master. (Fortune 1976, pp. 126-128)

The characteristic feature of Sibson formation 5, which appeared with formation 4 in 1991, is that beyond and touching the ring-pass-not of the *Bi* symbol of Deity lies a small circle, symbolising a unit of consciousness.

'Now it is ever the aim of "will" to function unconditioned, just as it is ever the tendency of "form" to condition the unmanifest. ... The will to live of the Logos, then, expresses itself through succeeding phases of form until the densest phase is reached. It can no further project the conditioning vehicle of its manifestation, and it strives to free itself from the bondage of form and continue onwards – to employ a metaphor of space – towards those areas of ether which have not been circumscribed and conditioned by the primal Logoidal Will.' (Fortune 1976, p. 126) 'When a unit of consciousness that has not fulfilled the law escapes, it is an unconditioned will ... it is the temptation to escape from the laws that have built us up and to exercise the powers gained under these laws without the equivalent responsibility ... this is the mystery of evil (positive evil), personified as devil.' (Fortune 1976, pp. 127-8)

The ring-pass-not thus *contains* for the purposes of spiritual evolution, but it also excludes all that which would not be contained and has forced itself beyond the sphere of influence of the Logos into the ring-chaos of the universe. Here may be seen reflected against the outer edge of that great abyss, the ring-pass-not, 'all those moulds which are marred in the making – all those evolutionary concepts that fail in their realisation – all misplaced forces and souls [i.e. Personalities] that have failed in their task, being rejected by their Individualities [i.e. Spirits] – all that in fact which it is desired to reject from the Logoidal consciousness.' (Fortune 1976, p. 127)

Here the Personality, looking outwards from within the sphere of Logoidal consciousness, sees 'the reflected images of all falsified hopes and abortive attempts at manifestation ... and it is tempted to continue forward ... into ... where there is no law, and men are as gods.' (Fortune 1976, p. 127) But the human Monad (and indeed every Monad) 'having attained the summit of its powers, it has to reject the temptation of the desire-image reflected from Outer Space, and retrace its steps in humility back to the source of its life; winning the

realisation that freedom is attained not by escape from limitations and conditions but by adjusting the balance to a perfect equilibrium. ... The Temptation of the Nadir comes to all in the course of evolution.' (Fortune 1976, p. 127)

*The Law of Monadic Return* Sibson formation 6 (18.1, 18.7)

'There is the impulse which drives every atom [or cosmic unit] to self-determination, and this is the secret ... of individualisation. ... There is the impulse which forces the individual atom towards group determination and is the secret of ... "Initiation", or the process of passing out of the human or self-determined individualised Life into the higher kingdom ... There is finally the impulse which forces the planetary groups, the sum total of all atoms and forms, to a conscious realisation of the nature of the all-enclosing group, the solar atom.

The Monad [Spirit] ... forms his ring-pass-not [and all direct contact ceases. Meanwhile] 'the inherent life of the atomic matter thus constituted produces [development] through long aeons ... energised by the Life of the Monad [and modified by the life of the Indwelling Logos.] This it is which has produced graded concretion, and brought animal-man to the stage where the upward pull of the Monad itself began to be felt. At the same time, the Monad on its own plane began to respond to the self-engendered energy of the lower form, the two rhythms contacted, individualisation occurred and the pilgrim manifested in his true nature. Then – as far as concerns the Monad [whether human, planetary or solar], progressive life forward begins. *It is truly cyclic, repetitive and spiralling.* [my italics]

*18.7 Sibson Formation 6, 19.7.1992. The Law of Monadic Return. Ground shots below*

*The Tutelary Spirit of Sibson in the form of a 'light ball' with a misty surround*

*The Vesica Piscis of the formation, where the 250 ft wide rings intersect*

Thus the cycles run until the higher rhythm … is so dominant that the influence of the form is negated and leads to its eventual discarding. Simultaneously with this, the highest rhythm of all makes itself felt, leading to increased activity upon the highest planes, and producing in time a negation of the sheath life of the Ego.' (Personality and Soul) (Bailey 1925, pp. 1048-1049)

In the words of the *Chandogya Upanishad*: 'Where there is creation there is progress. Where there is no creation there is no progress: know the nature of creation. Where there is joy there is creation. Where there is no joy there is no creation: know the nature of joy. Where there is the Infinite there is joy. There is no joy in the finite.' (Mascaró 1973, p. 18)

Sibson formation 6 expresses these sublime truths by two equally sized overlapping circles, forming in the centre the elongated 'fish bladder' or *vesica piscis* symbol. One of these circles, consisting of an open ring, symbolises 'form or manifestation'. The other circle is the familiar *Bi* symbol representing Deity but perhaps in this context conveys the concept of *Spirit* with the small central circle representing the Monad.

The key feature is of course the vesica piscis symbol at the centre. This numinous centre was 'highly-charged' in etheric terms, and was the place where I and Beth Davis encountered, in July 1992, the Tutelary Spirit of Sibson, in the form of a 'light ball' with a misty surround. (See photos by Beth Davis, 18.7.) It is perhaps significant that this psychic occurrence took place close to the Roman temple.

This formation can be viewed as referring to each of the spiritual states symbolised by the Law of Monadic Return. It reflects the need for Spirit (the Monad of whatever type) to interact with form to experience all the pleasures and pains of manifested life as part of spiritual growth, and then to relinquish the physical state and return to the Spiritual Centre for de-briefing and another cycle of activity.

I cannot emphasise too strongly the importance to the human Monad of the *Cosmic Law of Attraction* and the three subsidiary Laws of Thought which define its working. The *Law of Expansion* is concerned with the *structure* of spiritual development; the *Law of Contraction* deals with the *role of manifestation* as part of the cosmogenic process; while the *Law of Monadic Return* lays down the all-important process of *spiritual development* through the cycle of return to the Godhead. This majestic cosmic procedure really is 'the meaning of life and everything' which the American Erik Beckjord so desperately wanted to know the truth about in 1994 (see Chapter 1), as indeed have so many other thoughtful people down the centuries.

At Sibson, formation 2 (the Law of Attraction) and formation 5 (the Law of Contraction) symmetrically overlaid each other in the years 1990 and 1991 respectively, perhaps to emphasise the significance of their spiritual connection. Formation 7 (the fourth subsidiary law of the Cosmic Law of Attraction), concerned with Solar Evolution, brings together the three preceding subsidiary laws to show the functioning of the Cosmic Logoi expressed as the familiar *Bi* symbol. It is significant that the central circle is shown as a ring, similar to formation 3 (the Cosmic Law of Economy). Now the Earth Logos of our system is the Seventh Ray (that concerned with physical manifestation) of our Solar Logos. The plain ring is specifically concerned with form, and thus I believe that this particular type of *Bi* symbol refers explicitly to our own Earth Logos.

*18.8 Sibson Formation 7, 26.7.1995*
*The Law of Solar Evolution*

*The Law of Solar Evolution* Sibson formation 7 (18.1, 18.8)

This law 'is the sum-total of all the lesser activities.' This summary statement might be considered to define the relationship of the planetary atom and the solar atom:

'The planetary atom has, as all else in nature, three main activities:

First. It rotates upon its own axis. ... Second, [it] revolves orbitally around its solar centre. This is its expression of rotary-spiral-cyclic action ... The third activity ... carries it through space along with the entire solar system, and ... embodies its "drift" or inclination towards the systemic orbit in the heavens.' (Bailey 1925, pp. 1054-1057)

Likewise: 'the solar atom must be considered as pursuing analogous lines of activity and as paralleling on a vast scale the evolution of the planetary atom.

The entire solar sphere, [including eight recognised planets, over 140 moons and countless small bodies such as comets and asteroids] the logoic ring-pass-not, rotates upon its axis, and thus all that is included within the sphere is carried in a circular manner through the Heavens.' (Bailey 1925, p. 1057) This great cycle takes approximately one hundred thousand years to complete.

'Like the planetary atom, the solar atom not only rotates on its axis, but spirals in a cyclic fashion through the Heavens ... It deals with the revolution of our Sun around a central point and with its relation to the three constellations ... The Great Bear, The Pleiades and The Sun Sirius. These three groups of solar bodies are of paramount influence where the spiral cyclic activity of our system is concerned. ... [They] are related to the logoic Spiritual Triad, *atma-buddhi-manas*, and their influence is dominant in connection with solar incarnation, with solar evolution, and with solar progress.' (Bailey 1925, pp. 1058-1059)

The 'central point' and the 'three constellations' named here refer to the local solar group of which our Sun forms part, namely *Archon*, discussed in Chapter 16.

The seven solar bodies of Archon travel together as a group, along the Orion Arm Spiral of our Galaxy, about their own centre of gravity, which is likely to be Sirius. However, the Archon solar group also spirals in a cyclic fashion around the galactic plane of Aion. This disc also carries a photon field esoterically known as the *photon belt* which Archon and consequently planet Earth is due to re-enter again circa AD 2015. [Michael Green's last draft of this chapter was in 2014, (Ed.)] The psycho-dynamic energies of this galactic field have massively affected the human Monad in the past. The last time in the mid ninth millennium BC it brought about the advent of agriculture and the first planetary civilisations. This time, as Joeb (channelled by Paul Bura) remarked to me, there will be 'great global change involving a transformation of mankind's awareness' and a 'massive spiritual upheaval' ... 'which will start in earnest about 2012-14, although it will not come into full effect until some decades later.'

'Further, it must be added that the third type of motion to which our system is subjected, that of progress onward, is the result of the united activity of the seven constellations (our solar system forming one of the seven) which form the seven centres of the cosmic Logos. [i.e. Archon] This united activity produces a uniform and steady *push* ... toward a point in the heavens unknown as yet to even the planetary Logoi.' (Bailey 1925, p. 1059)

I believe that Djwhal Khul has picked up on a truth that covers more than mere physical movement of these great cosmic systems, for he goes on to say: 'so all moves forward to some unfathomable and magnificent consummation which will only in part begin to be visioned by us when our consciousness has expanded beyond the cosmic physical ... and the cosmic astral [plane] until it can "conceive and think" upon the cosmic mental plane.' [This] 'is the consciousness and knowledge of a solar Logos.' (Bailey 1925, p. 1060) St Paul, putting a gloss on the Old Testament text of *Isaiah* 64:4 expresses something of the same mystery:

''What no eye has seen, nor ear heard, nor the human heart conceived, what God has prepared for those who love Him.' – these things God has revealed to us through the Spirit; for the Spirit searches everything, even the depths of God.' (*1 Corinthians* 2:9-10)

Djwhal Khul points to the tens of millions of suns and constellations which are the physical manifestation of as many millions of intelligent existences, and to the fact that all these intelligent cosmic, solar and planetary Logoi are constituted of living sentient bodies – indeed the development of the celestial Logoi entirely depends on the independent, spiritual development of their component Entities achieving a certain 'critical mass'. Hence the 'constitutional drive' expressed by Djwhal Khul as a 'steady push' of all those Elements ready for spiritual development. Interestingly he noted that only one-seventh of the possible cosmic appearances are incarnating. The rest are 'waiting their turn to manifest, and holding back from incarnation until ... suitable and better conditions may eventuate.' (Bailey 1925, p. 1059)

For those Cosmic Entities, of whatever grade, however, Who are incarnating and are firmly on the spiritual path, the same *cursus vitae* lies ahead through the spiritual planes as it does on a miniscule scale for the human Monad. In the greater spheres of spiritual life such progression will take these Cosmic Entities 'onward and upward' through the higher Universes of Logoic life that represent the centres of the One and Only God. It should be remembered that this Universe is the Twelfth, the most physical. Planetary, solar, galactic and larger cosmic Logoic groups and all other Entities have defined physical lives, though They may last for aeons of time in our terms, but eventually They too, after reaching physical maturity, die in this, the Twelfth Universe and are transformed into more developed spiritual Beings that 'progress onward' as Djwhal Khul expresses it.

*Love-Wisdom*

As might be expected with a great Cosmic Law, the Law of Attraction, that is concerned with the deific processes of the Second Ray, this is essentially about the stupendous creative process, indeed cosmogenesis, affecting every unit of the Cosmos. It remains now to examine briefly the essential motivation at Monadic level that lies behind this sublime process, which, as has been so often mentioned in this study, is the nexus of *Love-Wisdom*.

Djwhal Khul covers this immutable principle of Deity under several different Laws according to its activity on three spiritual levels. 'On the second plane [i.e. the level of Spirit] we have the Law of Cohesion – love. On the second plane of the manifesting Triad [i.e. the level of Soul] the Law of Magnetic Control – love. Again lower down on the second plane of the Personality, the Law of Love.' (Bailey 1925, p. 583, fn. 82) The Sibson formations concerned with the Cosmic Laws of Thought and the Subsidiary Laws appear to deal specifically with the *Law of Magnetic Control*, considered below under formation 9.

We have seen (formation 2) how every unit of the Cosmos is programmed to find full expression and development by moving to the outer limits of manifestation, and is equally driven to return to the Deific Centre carrying the fruits of experience for assimilation and further development.

As the Greater Master puts it: 'Evolution [by those on the Spiritual Path] is accomplished through the withdrawal of the perfected Life [having reached the limits of manifestation] from the forms which separate, the synthesis of the principles which the forms were designed to express ... and the realisation of the ideals by the Logoidal Consciousness.' (Fortune 1976, p. 133)

As we began to read in Chapter 9:

'It will be seen then that the essence of evolution is unification; and the manifestation of the unifactory principle upon the planes of manifestation is Love. Whether that love be intellectual sympathy on the plane of the concrete mind, or physical unity upon the plane of matter, *Love in all its aspects is the symbol of the Logos as One*. [my italics] Whoso loves, however dim may be his concept of Love, is manifesting a unification, and unification is the goal of Evolution. God is One. Love makes one – therefore it is truly said "God is Love". Whosoever expresses Love, brings Spirit, which is One, into manifestation. To be separate is to be dead. Therefore choose Love and live.' (Fortune 1976, p. 133)

These profound principles are an expression of Ray 2 of Deity, that embodiment of Love-Wisdom.

## LAW 3

*The Law of Economy* Sibson formation 3 (18.1, 18.4, 18.5)

This: 'is the law which adjusts all that concerns the material and spiritual evolution of the Cosmos to the best possible advantage and with the least expenditure of force. It makes perfect each atom of time, and each eternal period, and carries all onward, and upward, and *through*, with the least possible effort, with the proper adjustment of equilibrium, and with the necessary rate of rhythm.' (Bailey 1925, p. 568) At our level it is concerned with the material and spiritual evolution of our planet and ourselves. It reflects the Activity Aspect of Ray 3 of Deity.

The Greater Master expands these ideas under the heading of the Law of Limitation:

'Limitation is the first law of manifestation, therefore it is the first law of power. ... In order to bring any energy into manifestation it is necessary to provide it with a form or vehicle ... For the Logos to manifest It has to circumscribe Itself [so that the Energy can work to full effect, for] to involve a force without directing it is to disperse it. It is only by a knowledge and utilisation of the Law of Limitation that power can be conserved.' (Fortune 1976, p. 112)

To bring the practical applications of this Law down to the level of the human Monad:

'When it is desired to put through an enterprise, first proceed to think the matter out in all details, clearly outlining the end it is desired to achieve. Next consider the means whereby that end may be achieved. [Then] proceed to eliminate all desire for anything unconnected with that aim.' (Fortune 1976, p. 112) In other words exercise the faculties or forethought, concentration and discrimination. 'What is below is like that which is above; and what is above is like that which is below: to accomplish the miracle of the one thing.' (Tyson 1995, p. 711) For thus are achieved the deific processes of creation through all cosmic systems down to that humble entity, the human Monad. This is why the First and Greatest of all the Cosmic Laws reflects the energies of the First Ray of Spirit operating through the Second and Third Rays.

Sibson formation 3 reflected with utmost simplicity this great cosmogenic principle, once again by the use of the *Bi* symbol.

## COSMIC LAW 3: SUBSIDIARY LAWS

*18.9 Sibson Formation 8, 27.7.1996. The Law of Radiation*

*The Law of Radiation* Sibson formation 8 (18.2, 18.9)

'*Radiation is the outer effect produced by all forms in all kingdoms when their internal activity has reached such a stage of vibrationary activity that the confining walls of the form no longer form a prison, but permit of the escape of the subjective essence.*' (Bailey 1925, p. 1060)

The divine activity covered by this law has a number of practical applications which might be summarily expressed as follows:

'The atom in a form revolves upon its own axis, follows its revolution, and lives its own internal life. This concerns its primary awareness. As time progresses it becomes magnetically aware of the attractive nature of [its surroundings], and becomes conscious of the form which surrounds it.' (Bailey 1925, p. 1064) Later it becomes aware 'that it also follows an orbit around a greater centre of force within a greater form ... which impels it to move within certain specific cycles. ... Finally, the attractive pull of the greater centre becomes so powerful that the positive life within the atom ... feels the force of the central energy, ... this ... penetrates through the ring-pass-not, evokes no response from ... the electronic or negative lives within the atomic periphery, but does evoke a response from the essential, positive nucleus of the atom [which is of the same nature]. Through this process ... every atom in turn becomes an electron.' (Bailey 1925, pp. 1064-1065)

Thus 'the atomic cycle is completed, the dense form is dispelled, the true form is dissipated, and the central life escapes to find its greater magnetic focal point.' (Bailey 1925, p. 1065) 'As a planetary [or other] scheme nears its consummation it becomes "radioactive," and through radiation transfers its essence to another "absorbent planet," or planets ... Its essence, or true Life, is absorbed by a receiving constellation [or body] and its outer "case" returns to its original unorganised condition.' (Bailey 1925, p. 1062)

In Sibson formation 8 the whirling path which connects the two rings is at one level symbolic of the 'lightning-strike' of radiation, but it is also, I believe, a glyph of notaricon type as mentioned above. It is similar to certain simple letter-forms in the ancient Gupta script (Gaur 1992, p. 220), but it may also possibly be a cursive form of the hieratic language of *Senzar* (see Chapter 3), where it would be the notaricon for Sirius (which was in ascendant at the time of the appearance of the formation). In this context, it is a reference to the love or attraction principle being the primary synthesising factor at work.

To sum up: orbital progression leads to stimulative vibration, an awakened internal response and ultimately transmutation.

*The Law of Magnetic Control* Sibson formation 9 (18.2, 18.10, and 17.12 in the previous chapter)

This law dealing with the principle of love 'holds sway paramountly on the buddhic plane, and in the development of the control of this law lies hid the control of the personality by the Monad [i.e. Spirit] via the egoic body.' (Bailey 1925, p. 569)

'Through this law, the force of evolution drives the Ego [i.e. Soul] to progress through the cycle of reincarnation back to union with his kind. Through separation he finds himself, and then – driven by the indwelling buddhic or Christ principle [of Love-Wisdom] transcends himself, and finds himself again in all selves. ... The lower is always controlled from above, and the effect the buddhic levels have on the three lower [i.e. the physical, emotional and mental bodies] is paramount ... It is the Law of Love in the three worlds, that holds all together, and that draws all upward ...' (Bailey 1925, pp. 583-4)

This law is another difficult concept to convey in symbolic linear terms. However, Sibson formation 9 may indeed show the

*18.10 Right. Sibson Formation 9, 28.7.1998. The Law of Magnetic Control*

*Left. Sibson Formation 10, 4.8.1998. The Law of Adaptation in Time*

Sibson
Airfield
Runway

N

⬭ Energy Path
→ Crop Flow

0    50    100         200 ft

M.G. mens. & delt.

*18.11 Sibson Formation 10. The Law of Adaptation in Time*

truth of this principle by having a small circle (symbolising the Ego or Soul) travelling along the line of the energy path through the ring (symbolising the Personality in reincarnation/ manifestation) and emerging on the other side as a circle again, but on a different alignment, see the diagram at illustration 17.12.

*The Law of Adaptation in Time* Sibson formation 10 (18.2, 18.10, 18.11)

In dealing with spiritual fire as a controlling factor of the Ascension Process of the human Monad, Djwhal Khul states: 'active heat or *prana*; this animates all, and is the driving force of the evolving form. ... This fire is the basic vibration of the little system in which the monad or human spirit is the logos, and it holds the personality or lower material man in objective manifestation thus permitting the spiritual unit to contact the plane of densest matter. It has its correspondence in the ray of intelligent activity [i.e. Ray 3] and is controlled by the Law of Economy [see formation 3 above], in one of its subdivisions, the Law of Adaptation in Time.' (Bailey 1925, pp. 45-6)

The principles by which the Third Logos (i.e. Ray 3) operates in the case of the human Monad are succinctly summed up by Djwhal Khul as follows:

'a. His *goal* is the perfect blending of spirit and matter.

b. His *function* is the manipulation of ... matter, so as to make it fit, or equal to the demands and needs of the Spirit.

c. His *mode of action* is rotary or, by the revolution of matter, to increase activity and thereby make the material more pliable.

All these three concepts are governed by the Law of Economy, which is the Law of Adaptation in Time and Space, or the line of least resistance. This line of least resistance

is that which is sought for and followed on the matter side of existence.' (Bailey 1925, pp. 142-3)

There is much that is obscure about this Law as described by Djwhal Khul. It has features, however, that may relate it to the *Law of Impaction* as set out by the Greater Master. He describes it thus: 'Impaction may be defined as the act of bringing a force of a subtler plane through to a denser plane upon the involutionary arc [which is] the act of advancing a force in evolution by developing it upon the "form" aspect. ... the stream of evolving life issuing from the Logos has to descend into matter in order to be organised; and having developed "form" by its confinement in matter, it uses that form as a mould; or more strictly speaking, a framework ... and when the framework of the dense is withdrawn, the subtle maintains the form it assumed because the system of stresses then developed has become a habit.' (Fortune 1976, p. 124)

If I understand this process correctly, it implies that to develop further, the Spirit, having reached a certain stage of development in a given state of form, needs to withdraw and abandon it for further development elsewhere. This process as it affects the human Monad is described earlier in this study, where the physical and etheric bodies, once abandoned by the Spirit, eventually disintegrate.

This again is a difficult concept to convey as a mandalic symbol, but I believe is expressed, quite simply, in Sibson formation 10. This appeared on the northern edge of the local airfield and was, I thought at the time, an accident, since half the formation was under the runway. This is clearly seen in the diagram at illustration 18.11. However, I was wrong, since it appears to have been done deliberately.

This law is concerned with the dynamics of Spirit entering form, and then, having achieved a level of development, ultimately shedding the physical sheaths and carrying away the lessons it has learnt in that state to a new physical structure for further spiritual growth. What better way to express this than by having the new spiritual form emerging from the broken and partially destroyed ring of manifestation under the airstrip?

*The Law of Periodicity* Sibson formation 11 (18.2, 18.12, 18.13)

In one of His great 'Introductory Postulates on Cosmic Fire' Djwhal Khul introduces this law as follows: 'There is a basic law called the Law of Periodicity. This law governs all manifestation, whether it is the manifestation of a Solar Logos through the medium of a solar system, or the manifestation of a human being through the medium of a form. This law controls likewise in all the kingdoms of nature.' (Bailey 1925, pp. 5-6)

All the subsidiary laws of Law 3 are concerned in one way or another with the spiritual Ascension Process of all Monads, and in particular with the role of physical form and intelligence (*Manas*) in this procedure. Periodicity is, as the Oxford English Dictionary has it 'the quality or character of being periodic or regularly recurrent.' As a metaphorical symbol, therefore, the image is essentially cyclic, of which there are three recurring components:

'a. The activity which produces *involution*, or the submergence in matter of Life or Spirit.' [The Latin verb *involvo* from which the word involution is derived has the sense of 'to envelop' or 'to cover'. This is

18.12 Sibson Formation 11, 28.7.1999.
The Law of Periodicity

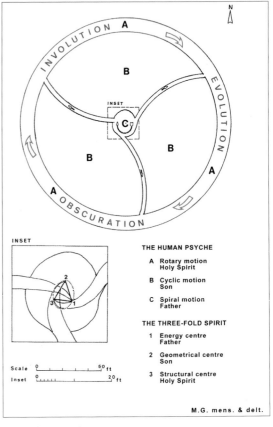

18.13 Sibson Formation 11.
The Law of Periodicity

the meaning of the expression used here by Djwhal Khul, where the Spirit is enveloped by Matter so that the former may develop. It does *not* express the secondary English meaning of retrograde development.]

b. The activity which produces the equilibrium of these two forces, matter and Spirit, or manifestation, or the processes of *evolution*.

c. The activity which withdraws the central energy from out of the responsive form and produces obscuration.' (Bailey 1925, p. 1029)

*Obscuration* of course does not refer to the condition of the Spirit, which continues its course onward and upward. However, it is true of the processes which affect the form aspect in the next phases of this great cycle. The abandoned form has to pass through the stages of dissolution so that its essential atomic structure may be returned to the Cosmos for recycling and reuse in another form or structure. Thus is the great cycle expressed with the maximum economy and efficiency as set out in Laws 10 and 11.

The process in the case of a small unit of consciousness such as the human Monad is relatively quick, but in the case of larger cosmic entities, not to mention the psychic detritus which has moved beyond the ring-pass-not of any system, it may have to await the passing of an entire *manvantara* (see glossary) before the operation is completed.

It is the role of the First Logos (Ray 1) to both create and destroy that which is created so that the creation process may continue. Djwhal Khul expresses it thus: 'The purpose of the First Ray, and its main work, is to produce cessation and the death of all forms in all kingdoms in nature and on all planes. The energy of this ray Lord brings about the death of an ant or of a solar system, of an organisation, a religion or a government, of a race type or of a planet. His will or purpose works out through the law of periodicity.' (Bailey 1936, p. 65)

The Greater Master describes the process as the *Second Death*: 'Life, having evolved beyond the capacity of lowly forms to give it expression, builds itself into higher forms. ... It is only by the abandonment of the simpler form that life can enter the more complex ... the consciousness which is of the higher life sees the birth of a new manifestation and rejoices, for it sees the fuller expression of its potentialities.' (Fortune 1976, p. 119) '*The Law of Periodicity is the effect produced by the amalgamation of these two types of force with a third.* The two types of force or energy are the activity of the first Aspect, [i.e. Ray 1, the Father aspect] and the energy of the second aspect. [i.e. Ray 2, the Son aspect conditioned by Love-Wisdom] ... When this blended dual force is brought in touch with the rotary activity of matter itself, we have ... the Ego [expressing Ray 3, Holy Spirit or Mother aspect], for instance, which is rotary-spiral-cyclic. [Eventually this process] results in the stimulation ... the periodical emergence of form, and in the steady, though slow, progress towards a goal.' (Bailey 1925, pp. 1033-4)

Sibson formation 11 expresses these principles admirably, in simple symbolic form. The formation was subject to careful surveys and examination by Michael Newark, Jim Lyons, and the writer. See the drawing 18.13.

The basic form, the *Bi* symbol for Deity, has at its centre the threefold structure of the Trinity, from which emerge the three curved arms indicating their *cyclic* movement caused by the rotary motion of the outer ring. The three recurrent phases of activity or progressive development are each indicated on the plan – *Involution* followed by *Evolution* and then *Obscuration* (for the form aspect only). In terms of the Spirit this must be regarded as the *spiral* movement of the central spiritual Ascension Process.

*The Law of Vibration* Sibson formation 12 (18.2, 18.14, 18.15)

This law deals 'with the key note or measure of the matter of each plane. By knowledge of this law the material of any plane in its seven divisions can be controlled.' (Bailey 1925, p. 219) Speaking of the effects of vivifying the centres at initiations of the human Monad, Djwhal Khul states: 'A gradual grasp of the law of vibration as an aspect of the basic law of building, the law of attraction, is brought about, and the initiate learns consciously to build, to manipulate thought matter [*Manas*] for the perfecting of the plans of the Logos, to work in mental essence, and to apply the law on mental levels, and thereby affect the physical plane.' (Bailey 1922a, p. 140) Djwhal Khul has much to say on the outworking of this law, to which the reader is referred.

Again, these concepts are difficult to convey as a symbol. Djwhal Khul uses the analogy of harmonics to describe the gradual ascent of the human Monad, and the need of the Personality to achieve a vibration reciprocal to the Ego (i.e. Soul) so that unimpeded access can be made to the 'Spiritual Triad' or the 'true threefold Ego' itself. He says:

'When I use the term "reciprocal vibration" ... I mean the adaptation of the Personality or Lower Self, to the Ego, or Higher Self, the dominating of the Personality ray by the ray of the Ego and the combining of their tones. ... eventually you will have the basic note of matter, the major third of the aligned Personality, the dominant fifth of the Ego,

*18.14 Sibson Formation 12, 23.6.2000. The Law of Vibration. Largest ring 205 ft wide*

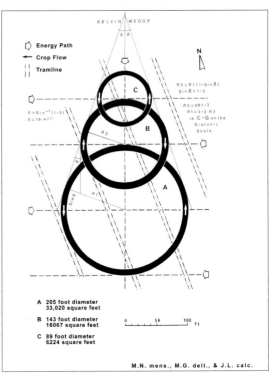

*18.15 Sibson Formation 12. The Law of Vibration*

followed by the full chord of the Monad or Spirit ... During our various incarnations we strike and ring the changes on all the intervening notes, and sometimes our lives are major and sometimes minor ... In due time, each note fits into its chord, the chord of the Spirit; each chord forms part of a phrase, the phrase or group to which the chord belongs; and the phrase goes to the completion of one seventh of the whole. The entire seven sections, then, complete the sonata of this solar system, – a part of the threefold masterpiece of the Logos or God, the Master Musician.' (Bailey 1922b, p. 4)

At a cosmic level the greater Entities, whom we have examined in Chapter 16, also have their harmonic components, giving rise to the expression "the harmony of the spheres", first used by that Master of Wisdom, the Greek Pythagoras in the sixth century BC. He, having ascertained that the pitch of notes depends on the rapidity of vibrations, and also that the planets move at different rates of motion, concluded that the planets must make sounds in their motion according to their different rates; and that, as all things in nature are harmoniously made, the different sounds must harmonize.

Sibson formation 12, again of an immensely simple type, consists of three overlapping rings. A drawing with some of the geometrical detail is at illustration 18.15. As Jim Lyons has demonstrated, it includes a harmonic C-G on the diatonic scale. When I tried to record the tonal structure in terms of actual sound in the formation at the time, the equipment completely malfunctioned and the tape was twisted into a tight ball. I was never able to use the tape recorder again. A

similar geophysical formation occurred at Marlborough, Wiltshire, on 3.7.2003. Indeed most of the Cosmic Law symbols occurred in the Wiltshire/Hampshire area between 1990 and 2003 as crop formations, but not as a coherent sequence as at Sibson.

## THE LAW OF KARMA
## SIBSON FORMATION 13 (18.2, 18.16)

The *Law of Karma*, which is listed by Djwhal Khul amongst the Cosmic and Solar Laws, is included by me at the end of this series. The Law of Karma in metaphysical terms is 'the law of cause and effect, or ethical causation ... It is the power that controls all things, the

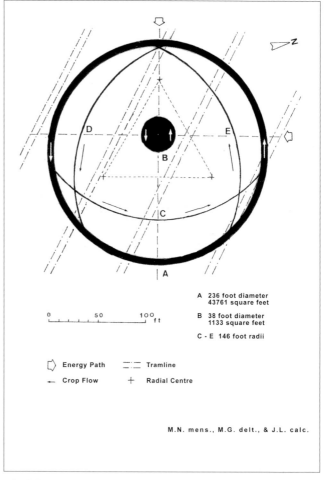

A  236 foot diameter
43761 square feet

B  38 foot diameter
1133 square feet

C - E  146 foot radii

0    50    100 ft

Energy Path    Tramline
Crop Flow    + Radial Centre

M.N. mens., M.G. delt., & J.L. calc.

*18.16 Sibson Formation 13. The Law of Karma*

resultant of moral action ...' (Bailey 1922a, p. 219) It is particularly concerned with Ray 1, the Will aspect of Deity. It is the synthetic law of the system of Sirius (Ray 2 of Archon – see Chapter 16) and predicates the effect the Sirian System has on our solar system, essentially that of the great cosmic principle of Love-Wisdom.

The Law of Karma thus has its origins outside our system and operates to ensure that the due processes of development in the Cosmos are observed. There are four *Lipika Lords* (Recording Angels) who advise the Earth Logos on these matters. My feeling is that this law is not, strictly speaking, covered in the Sibson series of crop circle symbols, but has been replaced by a symbol of a related and transforming function.

Sibson formation 13, in its rather rushed and untidy construction, appears to be almost an afterthought, although apparently part of the main sequence. Illustration 18.16 sets out its geometry. At first sight the formation appears to represent, in diagrammatic form, a three-dimensional picture of the planet viewed as a globe of manifestation with a spiritual centre. However, it is my perception that the apparent northing and easting grid lines also represent the overlapping arcs of three great Agencies whose centres form an equilateral triangle around the spiritual centre of the planet, and whose influence effectively overshadows, indeed encompasses, the Earth. These Beings are termed, in the Ancient Wisdom, the three Lords of Liberation. Indeed both the Lords of Karma and the Lords of Liberation have one aspect in common; both represent an input of spiritual power from outside our planetary system. To use a Christian expression, if the Lords of Karma represent cosmic 'law', the Lords of Liberation demonstrate cosmic 'grace' in action.

'The note They strike and the quality They emanate reaches out and makes an impact upon the most developed of the sons of men found at any particular time upon the Earth. These then proceed to make the sensed idea their own and to familiarise the thinkers of their time with the formulated concept. In this way great motivating, divine purposes become controlling factors in human progress.' (Bailey 1957, p. 266) For an identification of these Lords and a general discussion see Chapter 12.

Djwhal Khul does not make it clear from where these great angels originate. He states that 'They issue forth via that highest spiritual centre *wherein the Will of God* is held ...' (Bailey 1957, p. 269) 'God' I think in this context would be the Solar Logos of our system. This would suggest to me that They are messengers or Avatars from the Three Rays of Aspect of that great Cosmic Being, Archon, of whom our solar system constitutes one centre.

Whether or not the sacred geometry of this formation, given its metaphysical parameters, can be established is unclear. However, the above quotation from Djwhal Khul does mention 'The note They strike ...' if this is not just a metaphor in this context. Nevertheless the fact that the Crop Circle Makers may be drawing our attention to this important matter again at this time in the World's history does appear to be significant.

## CONCLUSION

So what does it all mean, and what practical applications might result from a systematic study of the Sibson and similar formations?

There is clearly room for discussion about the identification of any symbol and its relationship with a particular law – even within my terms of reference. But to do so here would unreasonably extend this chapter. I consider that the Sibson paradigm is more than just a set of mandalas for our edification. I believe that the formations may constitute analogues encoding important information for humanity. At first sight this may seem difficult since most of the laws appear to be abstract formulae, not necessarily susceptible to mathematical analysis.

One possible approach is their relationship to the creative nature of vibration and harmonics. As Djwhal Khul puts it 'all that exists is based on sound or on the Word.' (Bailey 1922b, p. 51) The 'Word' in this instance represents articulated ideas, and of course is the basis of the ancient mantric tradition. The science of harmonics properly applied affects every aspect of human psychology and physiology – and indeed not merely mankind. We have been aware of this for some time, and the mathematical analysis of formation 12 shows how the application of sacred geometry and consequent mathematical formulae and musical notation might be applied. This now needs to be considered for all the other laws where applicable. Clearly this type of information (about which Djwhal Khul was so reticent all those years ago for fear of its misuse) has now in the context of the crop circle phenomenon been provided in greater detail over a wider sphere of subjects – but obviously still with certain built-in safeguards. The advanced thinkers of humanity need to know the principles behind such weighty concepts and their possible application in such areas as medicine and agriculture for example.

We are really only at the beginning of formulating an intellectual, indeed spiritual, rationale of this material. Beyond this lies the transmutation of these formulative ideas into practical spheres of activity – which, if I am right, will involve many other specialists beyond the immediate circle of the crop circle community.

What I have set out here is a theoretical interpretation based on both my own belief systems and a not inconsiderable experience of other 'states of reality'. Some may not feel comfortable with the nomenclature and terms of reference I have used, but it is the best I have to hand – perhaps some of the best that is to be found anywhere in this age. But I am aware that it is only a facet of the truth, which every great culture has expressed in different ways in terms of its own religious experience.

The geophysical crop circle phenomenon is utterly mysterious, but serious investigators have had the amazing experience that if one is prepared to take it seriously as an intellectual and spiritual paradigm, the Crop Circle Makers will come more than half-way to meet us in terms of an understanding of what is being conveyed.

One final thought as we leave the ten year series of the Sibson group of formations. Careful examination of their overall pattern in the landscape shows a marked isosclean geometrical form, indeed mandala, of a seated figure in the *Padmasana* or lotus position. At the northern, head end, are formations concerned with the spiritual and intellectual aspects, whereas at the broad southern end are concentrated symbols concerned with the physical or form aspects. As we have seen in earlier chapters such humanoid buddhic figures have appeared elsewhere as crop formations, and here I believe we have another depicted – a Cosmic Lord of our system – to remind us that we are not dealing with arid formulations in the *Cosmic Laws of Thought*, but the living aspects of a Deific Being. In short, They accommodate themselves to our own intellectual limitations, which is perhaps the best we can reasonably hope for at this time.

# 19. TRIANGLES OF POWER: INTRODUCTION AND THE TRIANGLES OF POWER IN 1990

*The "moments in time and the events in space which lead to those episodes in the life of the soul wherein force becomes energy and energy becomes life"*

Bailey 1951, p. 462

The late twentieth century can now be seen, with hindsight, as a remarkable but transient episode in the history of the crop circle phenomenon in England. 1990 and 1991 were particularly significant. For although a few important formations were to appear in the next decade or so, never again would the genuine geophysical phenomenon be so active in the fields of Wessex.

*The state of research in 1990/1991*

The crop circle community was fortunate in those two golden years to have an exceptionally large number of skilled investigators, surveyors and aerial photographers to record the phenomenon. This writer was amongst them, but like all the others, he had then little idea what was happening, let alone what it all meant in metaphysical terms.

The crop circle caravan swept on, and only those with a really good personal archive can now re-examine the evidence in detail. It was necessary to establish exactly when, where and in what context formations appeared, and the crucial significance of their intermeshing symbolism. The result presented here for the first time is truly extraordinary, a window into the minds and purposes of the Light Workers who constructed the geophysical formations, and their adversaries, the Forces of Darkness.

## THE SCIENCE OF TRIANGLES

Even in 1991 this writer recognised that the primary purpose of the formations in Wessex at that time was concerned with the occult 'Science of Triangles.' I quote from what I wrote then:

'*Archon* [but see below], through its various centres, is in the process of laying down an energy matrix in southern England. The purpose of this energy-field, which is using the geodetic etheric structure of the planet, is to raise the level of consciousness of humankind [and it might also be added those of the Devic world and certain intelligent animals]. … The geodetic grid, familiar to dowsers, has an analogy at the microcosmic level with the acupuncture points and meridians of the human body…

The mechanics of laying down the energy-matrix is based on a relatively simple system of electromagnetism, using what is known occultly as the 'triangle of power' principle. ... *Archon* ... is putting down a carefully-ordered system of triangles marked at the apexes by major crop formations. The sides of these triangles are two or three miles in length, and the overall structure acts as a great coil or battery and combined transformer, which is effectively plugged into the geodetic grid of the planet. The triangular base or distributing centre at ground level is the lowest point of a process which brings the emanating energy ... to a receptive force centre which synthesises the responsive point of negative energy [rather like a modern electrical appliance]. The resulting energy is then passed through a secondary triangle at ground level.'(Green, Michael 1991, p. 139)

In 1991 I believed that this whole process was directly organised by Archon, that great Cosmic Being, of whom our solar system is a centre. (Chapter 16) Although I believe that the process has His cognisance, it was mainly organised by our Solar and Planetary Logoi. Certainly it is usually their signatures which appear with the 1990 and 1991 formations.

I clearly recognised then the principles on which the process was organised, but not exactly how this was registered in physical terms as crop formations in the landscape. The symbols were as yet obscure and their complex interplay not yet understood.

*Dangers in the Science of Triangles*

Were we meant to understand what the 1990-91 cosmic game-plan was hoping to achieve? I believe the answer is yes, but interpreting the symbols does require more than usual specialist esoteric knowledge. Given that the mystery of the Science of Triangles is capable of human understanding, why has it taken so

long – over 20 years, for us to understand the processes?

Part of the answer is that nearly all concerned with crop circle studies were and are highly resistant to the idea that the phenomenon might be a spiritual communication from what might be generically termed 'God.'

Djwhal Khul was well aware of the importance, and perhaps the dangers, of the science of triangles, described as 'vast, abstruse and complicated.' (Bailey 1951, p. 462) Indeed it represents the principles of a process which starts as a spiritual 'intention' and ends as a physical 'manifestation' in whatever sphere is intended. It represents, effectively, the deific creative process in which ' "moments in time and the events in space ... lead to those episodes in the life of the soul wherein force becomes energy, and energy becomes life." Such a momentous event or crisis is now taking place in the life of humanity today.' (Bailey, *loc. cit.*) Such a transmission is equally applicable to the creative processes of a solar system, a planet, a nation, an individual, or even a centre in the human body. Hence also the dangers of these processes in the wrong hands, whether hoaxers or unprincipled occult activists.

**THE FORCES OF DARKNESS**

It has been a shock, re-examining this subject now, to discover how pervasive and active the Forces of Darkness were in 1990 and 1991. The re-examination was made possible by the advances made in the middle 1990s in detecting man-made formations.

Certain hoaxers always claimed that they were aware of a 'higher power' when creating their designs and choosing their locations. Some even invoked such a 'presence' before beginning work. (Green, Michael 2002, p. 22)

It is both their and our misfortune that the 'higher power' that they were channelling, or were 'over-shadowed' by, was demonic. It is extraordinary how certain formations, from their construction clearly man-made, embody, in their esoteric symbolism, knowledge way beyond the capacities of the hoaxers involved, and also how they managed to place formations in localities exactly calculated to do maximum damage to the activities of the Light Workers of the genuine phenomenon.

## THE GEOPHYSICAL CONNECTION

In 1990 and 1991 the crop circle community watched, uncomprehendingly, a great battle fought out between the Light Workers and the Forces of Darkness for the control of the Michael-Mary Energy Line in the area of Silbury Hill.

This locality is a major nexus of particular geophysical features and the Michael-Mary Line. This line, which connects energy centres of our living planetary eco-system, is of critical importance for understanding what was being attempted by the Light Workers. It is crossed in the area of Silbury Hill by an ancient geological discontinuity known as the Variscan fold-belt. This appears to have been formed some 280 million years ago by a collision between two tectonic plates. This fault-line with a former subduction zone to the south passes through Beckhampton towards Trowbridge to the west. The deep block faults in the Newbury area rise to the surface at Warminster and are associated with heightened aeromagnetic values. (For a general discussion of the geophysical phenomena see Smith, D.G., ed. (1982) *The Cambridge Encyclopedia of Earth Sciences*, p. 232.) These electromagnetic fields appear to be generated by deep, basal, plutonic activity. Its importance in the context of the 1990/1991

phenomenon lies in these fields providing a medium giving access to the planetary core as well as diffusion through the etheric meridian system of the Earth.

## THE MECHANISM OF THE TRIANGLES OF POWER

Into this complex geophysical nexus the Light Workers attempted to plant a series of energy fields for the benefit of certain planetary life forms. The only evidence now of this momentous activity is in the records of the crop formations made at the time. What were the forces involved; where did they originate; and above all, what were the ethero-physical processes involved to achieve these effects?

Back in 1991 the writer thought (see above) that only triangular bases, which I called '*distributing centres*' were showing up as physical formations. This worked well enough for the three Alton Barnes 'dragon' formations in 1990 (see below), but clearly was not applicable for the 1991 formations. I now use the term '*Distributing Centre*' for the *fourth* point in the groups of formations, as described below. Only by plotting every formation over those two years in the Wessex area and constructing a detailed time-line flowchart was it possible to work out the complex etheric planning of the Triangles of Power.

If we had but realised, a guidance template was actually provided at the time at Houndean Bottom, near Lewes, East Sussex in late July 1990. (19.1) Unlike any other formation in Sussex before or since, it was signed by the Earth Logos. (Wolfgang Schindler picture archive, 1995) This formation (described in Thomas 1996, p. 28), depicted the complete process of the creation of the Triangles of Power as we might, indeed should, have expected to find them in the landscape.

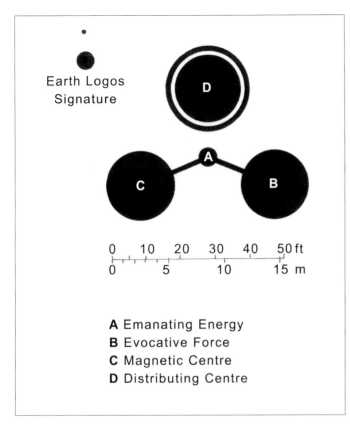

Earth Logos
Signature

0  10  20  30  40  50 ft
0      5      10      15 m

**A** Emanating Energy
**B** Evocative Force
**C** Magnetic Centre
**D** Distributing Centre

*19.1 Prototype Triangle of Power. Houndean Bottom Lewes, East Sussex (OS TQ392096), 22.7.1990*

There are a number of stages in the process of conveying the raw energy fields from their deific source. This type of energy is too powerful to be assimilated directly by physical forms. The process might be viewed as the workings of a cosmic 'gear box'. Djwhal Khul sets out the mechanisms. (See Bailey 1951, pp. 459 ff.) He postulates a process which has a dynamic energy centre (*Emanating Energy*), in the Houndean formation represented by the small central circle, 'A' in 19.1. The requisite energy field is directed to a secondary, receptive area (*Evocative Force*). At Houndean this process is shown as a pathway leading to a circle, 'B'. The energy field is then passed to a responsive point of negative energy (*Magnetic Centre*), 'C'. The relationship between the Evocative

Force and the Magnetic Centre is, in the words of Djwhal Khul, a 'source of violent interplay between the two points of the base line.' (Bailey 1951, p. 460) This is symbolised in the Houndean formation by their being linked by paths to the Emanating Energy source, 'A', which in the triangular relationship balances the subsequent force. The final stage is the creation of a fourth element, the *Distributing Centre*, at Houndean a ringed circle, 'D', which will produce physical manifestation, quality and activity.

The energy matrix which circulates this force is illustrated by Alice Bailey, (Bailey 1951, p. 460) and is essentially a combination of the two esoteric ternaries forming a quaternary or diamond shape. The energy field thus circulates round a figure of eight. However, in the Houndean formation there is an interesting variation to the geometrical figure, although the circulation principle remains the same. The apex of the first triangle is reversed so that it lies in the centre of the second triangle. This is of great mystical, indeed spiritual, significance, indicating that the *Primum Mobile* (The One, Boundless, Immutable Principle: The One Absolute Reality), lies at the centre of All, not on the periphery. The most important of all the 1990/1991 Triangles of Power was number 3 of 1991 (see next chapter). It exactly replicates the Houndean formation (without the paths), but on an enormous scale.

The terms 'energy field' 'Evocative Force' etc are not merely figures of speech. Strong electromagnetic fields were experienced by various observers, including me, in different contexts, and were noted at the time. This was so even at the small formation at Houndean where the energy field was particularly felt by those standing where the conditioned energy passed into the ringed circle or Distributing Centre. They experienced a jolt of energy, like electricity, go up the back of their legs. (Thomas, *loc. cit.*)

## UNRAVELLING THE CODE OF THE TRIANGLES

First came the realisation that the complete process in linear form from spiritual inception to physical expression was set out in the landscape, with each force or energy appropriately symbolised as a crop formation. Second, it became evident that the assemblage of these symbols was far more complex than originally thought. Third, the process in creating each energy field was not instantaneous, but staggered over a period of 10 days or more. The later triangle groups in 1991 were more quickly put down than the ones at the beginning of the season, largely because they were reusing some of the energy points. The staggered appearance of formations has been enormously important for interpreting the source and meaning of the symbols.

Let us summarise the process:

A: The energy fields are initially inspired by a positive, qualified, out-going ray energy or Emanating Energy.

B: This in turn is conditioned by a qualified secondary energy or Evocative Force.

C: The resulting force is grounded by the earthing effect of the Magnetic Centre, producing:

D: A physical effect in the Distributing Centre.

In Djwhal Khul's words, the process 'depicts the interplay of [a being's] monadic life, soul energy and personality force, as these three focus on the physical plane, producing manifestation and appearance.' (Bailey 1951, p. 461)

In this great creative act, these three forces represent progressively the deific Rays of Aspect in action. Ray 1 embodies 'the dynamic idea of God' at stage A. Ray 2 is concerned with 'the first formulations of the plan upon which the form must be constructed,' imbuing the end result with the qualities of Love and Wisdom at stage B. Ray 3 'materialises the idea and purpose of God the Father, under the guidance of God the Son' at stage C. (Quotations from Bailey 1936, p. 159) The final stage D represents the Rays of Attribute, which in 1990 and 1991 were symbols of the threefold reflection of the Rays of Aspect, and this brings into physical form the purposes of God. The two great formations of 1990 and 1991 (the Beckhampton formation of 25.7.1990 and the Barbury Castle formation of 17.7.1991) reflect in their triplicity the creative energies of each of the cosmic powers concerned.

The Triangles of Power of the Forces of Darkness, who operate on the threefold basis of the Emanating Energy, the Evocative Force and the Distributing Centre, the classic *Triple Hecate* matrix, have only three points. They lack a Magnetic Centre, which is the input of Ray 3 energies. The reason for this lies in the past history of the cosmic rebellion of Evil in our system, which cannot be entered into here.

## SIGNATURES, SYMBOLS AND CIPHERS

Many formations have signature symbols. These are primarily the large and small circle of the Earth Logos, the small and large ringed circle of our Solar Logos and the small and large double-ringed circle of our local solar group, namely Archon.

Many of the formations of 1991 are distinctive symbols of the three Rays of Aspect, and may now with some confidence be attributed to the Office concerned. To use another analogy they represent the Coat of Arms of that particular cosmic department. The four Rays of Attribute also have their symbols, which for the most part are the personal signatures of the Beings holding office.

Lastly there are the various symbols of intelligent marine life forms which appeared at the end of the 1991 season. These are probably the glyphs of the deva or angel supervising each class of marine animal.

Needless to add, the Forces of Darkness were quickly onto the significance of these signatures, and the hoaxers provided a whole series of bogus glyphs attached to their creations in both 1990 and 1991, in particular the Earth Logos signature for the 1990 formations.

To sum up, we have four types of ideograms indicating the origin of stakeholders of the Triangles of Power:

1. Signature symbols of the Earth, Solar and local solar group Logoi

2. Symbols of the Departments of the Rays of Aspect and Attribute

3. Personal glyphs of holders of these Offices of State

4. Glyphs of deva Intelligences of certain intelligent planetary life forms (other than humanity).

## NAMING AND NUMBERING THE TRIANGLES OF POWER

For identification purposes I have abbreviated 'Triangle of Power' as 'TOP', and to distinguish man-made Triangles of Power from geophysical ones, I have *lettered* the man-made triangles, with the individual formations numbered e.g. TOP A1, TOP A2 etc., whilst the geophysical triangles are *numbered*, with their individual formations lettered, e.g. TOP 1A, TOP 1B. The exception is my treatment of the 1990 Hampshire Triangles of Power, where, because of the numerous overlaps between triangles, I have numbered all the triangles and the formations themselves sequentially.

## THE TRIANGLES OF POWER IN WILTSHIRE IN 1990 (19.2)

To the best of my knowledge Triangles of Power as a crop circle phenomenon did not appear in England before 1990. I believe that there were five groups of formations of this type that summer in Wiltshire: three were made by hoaxers – TOP A1-3 (broken red line on my map), TOP B1-3 (solid orange line), and TOP C1-3 (not on my map); two were created by the Light Workers – TOP 1A-D (green line) and TOP 2A-D (blue line).

The Forces of Darkness got off to an early start with two Triangles of Power TOP A and TOP B in the Bishops Cannings area, together with a third, TOP C, some distance away at Upton Scudamore, all in Wiltshire. All three were placed on or near the Michael-Mary Line, with the intention of conveying a negative energy field into the system to block positive work by the Light Workers. The three operations appeared sequentially over a period of two months. It is extremely unlikely that the human hoaxers were consciously aware that they were putting down Triangles of Power patterns, but only felt unconsciously driven to make formations on certain dates and at particular places.

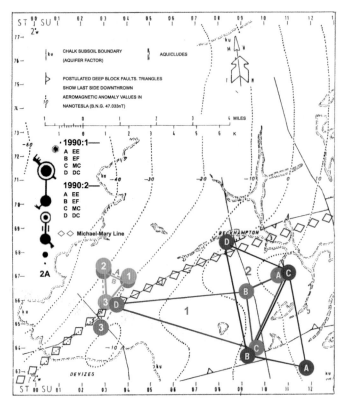

*19.2 The Wiltshire Triangles of Power of 1990*

same night by being overlaid by a geophysical constellation pattern of *Centaurus* with the *Crux* constellation positioned in the centre of the man-made formation, as described in Chapter 4. (4.9)

*TOP 1990:B (19.2)*

The reaction of the Forces of Darkness to the neutralising of their Stone Pit Hill formation was to produce another formation (B3) acting as a Distributing Centre half a mile to the north, centrally placed on the Michael-Mary Line. This occurred on 1.6.1990. The same Emanating Energy and Evocative Force positions as in TOP A appear to have been retained.

The new formation was:

B3. *Morgan's Hill* (OS SU030659) on 1.6.1990

Distributing Centre. Four-ringed circle with four satellites on the second ring forming a quincunx similar to TOP A2. The ring structure of the circle clearly indicated its man-made origin. Nearby was a fake Earth Logos signature. This formation was neutralised by the geophysical quincunx of TOP 1D, described below.

*TOP 1990:C*

This was the third attempt by the Forces of Darkness to tamper with the Michael-Mary Line in Wiltshire in 1990. The location was some 18 miles to the south-west of the Bishops Cannings area. Fortunately this group of formations was discovered and surveyed by the Terence Meaden team early in July. Typical of operations by the Forces of Darkness, the three formations were closely spaced within half a mile of each other. These man-made formations

*TOP 1990:A* (19.2)

This was a small group of formations forming an isosceles triangle one and a half miles in length in Bishops Cannings CP, Wiltshire.

A1. *Baltic Farm* (OS SU643669) on 3.5.1990

Emanating Energy. Ringed circle with a fake Earth Logos signature.

A2. *Morgan's Hill* (OS SU032664) on 13.5.1990

Evocative Force. Triple-ringed circle with four satellites on the central ring forming a quincunx. The exact position of this formation is uncertain.

A3. *Stone Pit Hill* (OS SU030650) on 19.5.1990

Distributing Centre. Four-ringed circle (fourth ring added later) with a fake Earth Logos signature. This formation had its negative energies neutralised the

238

were all signed with a fake signature of the Earth Logos. All three are recorded as appearing on the same night (2.7.1990), although this is difficult to believe in the light of the amount of work involved.

C1. *Norridge Common* (OS ST859470) on 2.7.1990

Emanating Energy. Four-ringed circle with four satellites on the second ring forming a quincunx. Fake Earth Logos signature in adjoining field.

C2. *Norridge Common* (OS ST863469) on 2.7.1990

Evocative Force. Linear triplet with large, three-ringed, central circle. Fake Earth Logos signature adjoining it.

C3. *Upton Scudamore* (OS ST866472) on 2.7.1990

Distributing Centre. Three-ringed circle with four satellites on the second ring forming a quincunx. Fake Earth Logos signature adjacent.

This formation had its negative energies neutralised the same night by being overlaid by a geophysical constellation pattern of *Boötes* as described in Chapter 4. (4.10, 4.11)

*TOP 1990:1* (19.2 and 19.3)

The next move by the Light Workers in the Bishops Cannings area was to neutralise the negative energy field created by TOP B, before the major Triangle of Power of the season, TOP 2, could be put down later in July. TOP 1 of 1990 (like TOP 1 of 1991) was early in its season and the symbols were small and mainly registered the

respective points of the triangles. However there were some significant features.

1A. *East Kennet Village (near)* (OS SU112673) on 6.7.1990 (my estimate)

Emanating Energy. Small double-ringed circle (overall diameter 24 ft 4 in) and small circle (diameter 4 ft 6 in). Dimensions from Stanley Morcom's survey. (Morcom 1991, p. 13)

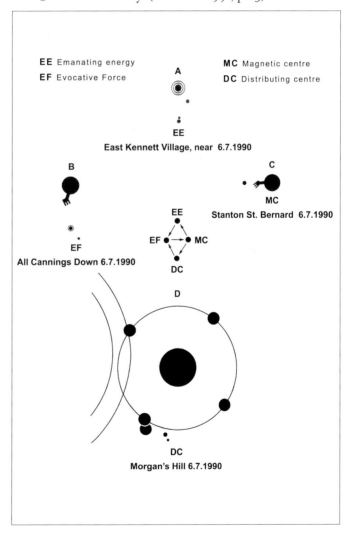

*19.3 Wiltshire Triangle of Power 1990:1*
*Formation D is shown overlapping and neutralising formation TOP B3 of 1.7.1990, the outer rings of which are on the left.*

This was about 112 ft north-west of formation TOP 2C, which lay about half a mile west of East Kennet village. It could have been mistaken for the signature symbol of TOP 2C, were it not for the fact that it had an even smaller signature symbol, of the Earth Logos, about 25 ft in length. In addition, from an aerial photograph taken by George Wingfield on 27.7.1990, the date formation TOP 2C was discovered, (Green, Michael 1990, p. 153) we see formation TOP 2C and its signature clear-cut, whereas formation 1A is very indistinct and overgrown. I believe that formation 1A occurred on 6.7.1990, the same day as the other formations of TOP 1.

There is another factor which links formation TOP 2C with TOP 1, which is very strange indeed, and is connected with the symbol chosen for formations 1B and 1C.

In TOP 1 both the Evocative Force and the Magnetic Centre used the symbol of a circle with a three-talonned claw attachment reaching for a 'ball'. For the spiritual significance of this mystical symbol see 'The Jewel of the Law' in Chapter 10.

1B. *All Cannings Down*, (OS SU093658) on 6.7.1990 (my estimate). (19.4)

Evocative Force. A circle with a three-talonned claw attachment reaching for a ball, which is itself ringed, with a small circle beside it indicating that it is doubling as the signature of the Solar Logos. The claw points towards formation 1C,

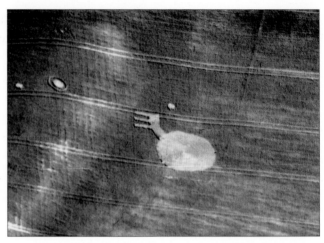

19.4 TOP 1990:1B. All Cannings Down, All Cannings (OS SU093658), 6.7.1990

19.5 TOP 1990:1C. Stanton St Bernard CP (OS SU094639), 6.7.1990

19.6 TOP 1990:1D. Morgan's Hill (OS SU030659) 6.7.1990, showing it neutralising TOP B3 of 1.7.1990

whose claw in turn is swinging round towards formation 1D.

1C. *Stanton St Bernard CP* (OS SU094639) on 6.7.1990 (my estimate). (19.5)

Magnetic Centre. Again a circle with a three-talonned claw. It appeared below the west slope of Milk Hill. This was not noticed until overflying took place in connection with the Alton Barnes Formation TOP 2A, but I believe it appeared with the rest of the formations of TOP 1, on or slightly before 6.7.1990.

1D. *Morgan's Hill* (OS SU030659) on 6.7.1990. (19.6)

Distributing Centre. A ringed circle with four satellites on the ring forming a quincunx (circle 62 ft diameter; ring 210 ft diameter; satellites 20 ft diameter each).

1D was planted to neutralise the negative energies of TOP B3. The ring of 1D, with one of the satellites, clips the outer ring of formation TOP B3. I believe the satellite concerned represents the Archangel Uriel (Agni). The fake Earth Logos signature provided by the hoaxers for B3 had its large, 20 ft diameter, circle neutralised by another satellite of 1D representing, I think, the Archangel Raphael (Kshiti). The smaller signature circle of TOP B3 was then reused to form the larger circle of a geophysical signature of the Earth Logos (circles 6 ft and 4 ft diameter respectively).

As we will see, the Distributing Centre, as the planetary receptor, is always signed by the Earth Logos, so

formation 1D must represent this function. The use of the quincunx here refers to the functions of the Third Ray of Aspect (central circle) concerned with all aspects of physical manifestation, represented by the four linked outlying circles, or four Rays of Attribute. For the metaphysical significance of the quincunx see Chapter 4. The Forces of Darkness had evidently attacked all these functions with its own formation, necessitating a counterbalancing response.

*TOP 1990:2* (19.2 and 19.7)

The major exercise of the season was the Dragon Triangle of Power which appeared

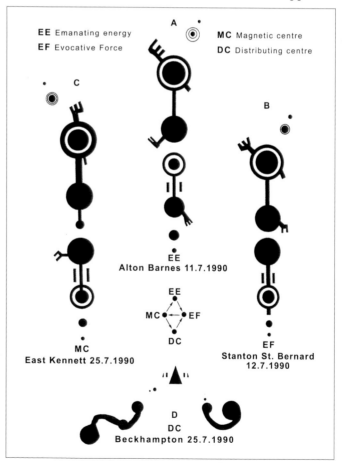

*19.7 The 'Dragon' formations*
*Wiltshire Triangle of Power 1990:2*

around Alton Barnes. The sequence was as follows:

2A. *Alton Barnes* (OS SU117631) on 11.7.1990
  Emanating Energy. (19.8)

2B. *Stanton St Bernard* (OS SU093636) on 12.7.1990
  Evocative Force. (19.9)

2C. *East Kennet* (OS SU112673) on 25.7.1990
  Magnetic Centre. (19.10)

2D. *Beckhampton* (OS SU083684) on 25.7.1990
  Distributing Centre. (19.11 and 19.12)

Stanley Morcom records 2C as arriving on the night of 26/27 July (Morcom 1991, p. 9), but it is hardly likely to have arrived after formation D. The probability is that it came down on the same night. TOP 2 forms a trapezoidal geometrical figure.

19.9 TOP 1990:2B. Stanton St Bernard (OS SU093636), 12.7.1990

19.10 TOP 1990:2C. East Kennet (OS SU112673), 25.7.1990

The appearance of the Alton Barnes formation 2A on 11.7.1990 brought the phenomenon to the notice of the international media and the British public. It was to be, almost literally, a 'nine day wonder', because on 25 July a blatant hoax at nearby Bratton very publicly caught out two prominent crop circle experts. The media and British public

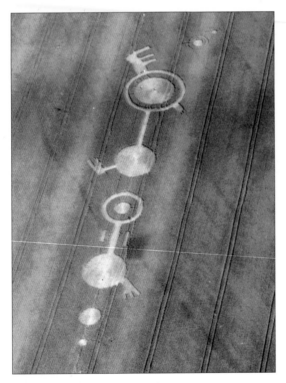

19.8 TOP 1990:2A. Alton Barnes (OS SU117631), 11.7.1990

*19.11 TOP 1990:2D. Beckhampton (OS SU083684), 25.7.1990*

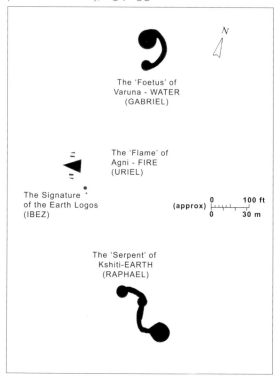

*19.12 TOP 1990:2D, Beckhampton, 25.7.1990*
*The Distributing Centre*

switched off, and never really connected again with the phenomenon. (Wingfield 1990, pp. 8-10)

In 1990 nothing like the dragon formations of TOP 2 had ever been seen, and a detailed re-examination of their symbolism and significance is overdue. Every element of their construction had a specific symbolic meaning which needs to be appreciated in interpreting the whole.

*Components of TOP 2*

The signatures of these formations are those of the Earth Logos, the Solar Logos, and Archon.

Each of the pictograms 2A, 2B and 2C comprises two elements (apart from the signature), symbolising two distinct aspects, which might be broadly categorised as the Spirit/Soul and the Personality. Each Entity is a dumb-bell having a spiritual/intellectual unit (ringed circle) and form (plain circle), connected by a path. Each lower Entity has a box on either side of the path. Each upper Entity carries across the ringed circle a Rod of Power, each with a slightly different terminal symbolising the status or type of gift on offer by that Entity.

Given that these pictograms originate with these Cosmic Beings, I believe that the two supreme gifts that are being offered and brought to the solar system are Love and Wisdom (*wise-compassion*), the qualities particularly associated with Ray 2, to be identified here by the Entity formations with two boxes. Each upper 'Entity' formation carrying the Rod of Power would thus be the Initiating Power, Ray 1. Pictogram 2A has the Ray 2 Entity with the intellectual/spiritual component (ringed circle) uppermost and therefore represents the Emanating Energy. The other two pictograms (2B and 2C) have the Ray 2 Entity reversed indicating the importance of the physical component as the energy passes through the Evocative Force (2B) and Magnetic Centre (2C).

## THE DRAGON CONNECTION

The striking feature of these three pictograms is that they are schematic representations of *dragons*, complete with eye (the signature), body (Entity formations), clawed limbs, and tail (3 diminishing circles). What then is the significance of this symbolism?

The disturbing and inescapable implication is that the Solar Logos, amongst others, is indeed a dragon, at least in the sense that His Spirit originated in all likelihood in another centre of Archon; a centre where the primary life form is reptilian, indeed dragon-like. The centre in question is the star system Thuban in the constellation of Draco ('the Dragon').

This extraordinary revelation, spelt out here, may explain why humanity has for thousands of years been preoccupied with the idea that the great force of nature was a dragon. It may also explain why the predominant life forms on this planet for nearly 200 million years were the dinosaurs, perhaps intended to evolve into an intelligent humanoid form if cosmic arrangements had worked out differently.

Djwhal Khul nowhere directly relates the Solar Logos to a dragon, but makes a number of hints that this is indeed the case. Nowhere is this clearer than in his section on the 'Path of Earth Service' for human spiritual initiates, of which this is an abstract:

'The adepts who stay upon this Path are distinguished by a dual attribute ... They are animated by *wise-compassion*. ... The adepts ... are called esoterically the "beneficent dragons" and the energy with which they work and the stream of living force upon which they are found emanates from the constellation of the Dragon ... The "beneficent dragons" are distinguished by their "luminosity" ... When the adept enters through the "luminous door" he has before him four ... esoteric IDENTIFICATIONS, [i.e. initiations] ... These four identifications are connected with the fourfold lotus of the Solar Logos, or with His twelve-petalled heart centre. ... These four Identifications ... are each preceded by three lesser identifications, ... corresponding to the twelve-petalled lotus. ... The form through which the adept must work in order to demonstrate his control of the energy concerned may not here be given. It may only be stated that luminosity is gained upon the battle ground *through a fight with a dragon*. [my italics] The following summation may be found suggestive:

EARTH SERVICE

Attributes ... Wise Compassion

Source ... Constellation of the Dragon

Method ... Twelve cosmic Identifications

Hierarchy ... The sixth

Symbol ... A green dragon issuing from the centre of a blazing sun.

Behind the sun and overtopping it can be seen two pillars on either side of a closed door.

Quality gained ... Luminosity.'

(Bailey 1925, pp. 1245-47)

The choice of the Sixth Hierarchy here is highly significant. This is the realm of the Archangel Gabriel (*Varuna*) (*Poseidon* in the Greek world), Ray 6 of the Great Council of planet Earth. 'These sixth and seventh Hierarchies ... provide the substance forms of the three worlds ... [and] deal with the working out in the physical vehicle of all divine purposes.' (Bailey 1951, p. 49) The sixth Hierarchy is responsible for the liquid and gaseous input of the planet; and is literally 'the life of forms of all the etheric bodies of every tangible object.' (Bailey 1951, p. 50) Hence it was Gabriel (*Varuna*) who was given priority in conveying the energy fields in 1990 and 1991.

Further illumination on the dragon aspect is provided in Djwhal Khul's discussion of certain cosmic relationships:

'The relation of the fifth Hierarchy [that concerned with the exercise of intelligence or mind-matter] to a certain constellation has also a bearing upon this mystery. This is hidden in the karma [in this context, 'destiny'] of the solar Logos, and concerns His relationship to another Solar Logos, and the interplay of force between Them in [this cosmic age].

This is the true "secret of the Dragon" and it was the dragon-influence or "serpent energy" which caused the influx of manasic or mind energy into the solar system.' (Bailey 1951, p. 45)

The other Solar Logos is Sirius, and this reference by Djwhal Khul touches on one of the most beautiful mysteries of our system: the relationship between our Solar Logos, 'Bel' and the 'Lady' of Sirius:

'... sevenfold brooding Mother, the silver constellation, whose voice is as a tinkling bell, and whose feet pass lightly o'er the radiant path between our worlds and hers.' (Bailey 1925, p. 1258)

For true spiritual transformation to the heavenly realms two qualities only are required: Love and Wisdom or Love-Wisdom. For the exercise of Wisdom, intelligence (*Manas*) is a necessary component, and it is that the Logos of Sirius has contributed to the solar system. However, intelligence is not enough on its own, it needs the deific transformation into Wisdom, which might be defined as 'knowledge transformed by love'. It has regrettably been one of the triumphs of the Forces of Darkness of this Age to separate intelligence and knowledge from their higher qualities of love, which will cause great trouble for mankind in the near future.

'Entangled closely with the karma of these two cosmic Entities, was that of the lesser cosmic Entity Who is the Life of our planet, the planetary Logos. It was this triple karma [in past civilisations] which brought in the "serpent religion" and the "Serpents or Dragons of Wisdom," ... It had to do with solar or planetary Kundalini, or Serpent fire. A hint lies in the fact that the constellation of the Dragon has the same relation to the ONE [Archon] greater than our Logos as the centre at the base of the spine has to a human being. It causes stimulation, and vitalisation and a consequent co-ordination of the manifesting fires.' (Bailey 1951, pp. 45-46)

*The Dragon Rods of Power*

With the cosmic dragon connection in mind, it is time to examine the Rods or Sceptres of Power carried by each of the three crop circle dragons.

Each rod has as its terminal a three-pronged instrument reflecting the three Rays of Aspect of the Logos, but each symbolises something different. Formation 2A, the Emanating Energy of Ray 1 of the Solar Logos, carries a key, of the ancient slide-key variety. There is here a clear reference to the keys of the solstitial gates, listed below, which were later symbolised in the *Yantra* which appeared as a crop formation of uncertain origin at Windmill Hill (OS SU098709) on 16.7.1999. (19.13)

1. The gate of the southern quarter leads to the Way of the Ancestors (*pitr-yāna*), the route of reincarnation which all living forms are obliged to follow, with the intention eventually of passing beyond the Circle of Necessity. The silver key opens the gate of Cancer, the way of reincarnation.

2. The gate of the eastern quarter leads to the priestly, solar way, described above as the 'luminous door' of Earth Service.

3. The gate of the northern quarter leads to the Way of the Gods (*deva-yāna*), the route which releases humanity from the incarnation round of birth and death. This is the golden key of Capricorn, destined for use by those of mankind who achieve spiritual life.

4. The gate of the western quarter leads to the Royal Way, the route of the Devic world, the Way of Varuna, the Lord of the Waters.

In one sense the Solar Logos carries all the keys, but, if my insight is correct that Triangle of Power 2 relates to all life forms on this planet, then perhaps the key carried by formation 2A opens the gate to the Royal Way of Varuna or the Archangel Gabriel. The formation has the 'double-ringed circle' signature of Archon.

*Formation 2B*, the Evocative Force of Ray 2 of the Solar Logos, continues the theme of the Archangel Gabriel (*Varuna*), since it carries the Trident of Poseidon whose energising power of *water* is critical to the survival of all life forms of the planet. Varuna was to play an important role in the Wessex formations of 1991 also. The formation has the single-ringed circle signature of the Solar Logos.

*Formation 2C*, the Magnetic Centre of Ray 3 of the Solar Logos, has a rod surmounted by an outstretched dragon's claw. The double-ringed circle signature of Archon has been moved over to this side so that it doubles as a ball. It is significant that formations 1B and 1C of the first Triangle of Power in 1990 also combined the claw and ball motif – see above.

The Dragons of Wisdom are 'the "Benign Uniters" and "the Producers of the Atonement." Esoterically, They are the "Saviours of the Race" and from Them emanates that principle which – in conjunction with the highest aspect – lifts the lower aspect up to Heaven.' (Bailey 1951, p. 46) This great esoteric truth was symbolised in a later formation occurring in mid July 1994 at Hackpen Hill, Berwick Bassett, in which a dragon's arm made up of six circles holds a seventh circle in its talonned claw. (10.6, 10.7) As well as symbolising the Jewel of the Law (see Chapter 10) it is highly significant that the circle clasped by the claw is the fourth largest in size i.e. it represents also the qualities of Ray 4, or that of the Archangel Haniel (Indra) of our system. These energies concern buddhic or spiritual wisdom, as yet only partially in evidence amongst humankind. In other words this quality of life, equally applicable to the Devic world as to the human, is offered as a gift from the Solar Logos: it cannot be gained by the application of the intellect alone. The Hackpen Hill formation was signed with the circle and satellite of the Earth Logos.

*Formation 2D.* (19.11 and 19.12), the final element of the second Triangle of Power is the Distributing Centre which appeared at Beckhampton on 25.7.90 (New Moon), thirteen days after the arrival of formations 2A and 2B. This time lapse appears to represent the usual creative span of the Triangles of Power, as became evident in 1991. As in the case of the Barbury Castle formation of that year, the Beckhampton Distributing Centre had three highly significant components.

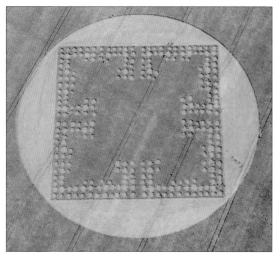

*19.13 The 'Kalachakra Palace' formation of Windmill Hill, Avebury CP, Wiltshire (OS SU098709), 16.7.1999*

Note that the formation is signed by the Earth Logos (large and small circle beside the triangle symbol for the Archangel Uriel (Agni)), not the Solar Logos. This is important. It indicates that the formation as a whole is a symbol of a planetary *receptor* point of energy rather than a Solar or higher *infuser* agency. To use another analogy, it is a socket rather than a plug. The situation of the formation is also significant. It is placed three and a half miles north-north-east of formation 2C, on the Michael-Mary Line, which was the scene of activity in early July 1990 when a quincunx of the Forces of Darkness was neutralised by formation TOP 1D.

The three symbols within this formation were identified by the writer in 2000. (Green, Michael 2000a, p. 13) They are the personal glyphs of the three Lords of Attribute on the Great Council of planet Earth Who are directly concerned with physical manifestation.

To recap, these Lords of Attribute are:

The Archangel Uriel (*Agni*) – Ray 5, Lord of Fire, concerned with intellectual development,

and symbolised by a triangle or 'House of fire'. He operates on the Second Cosmic Plane (two small triangles) and the five units of this glyph indicate His hierarchical position on Ray 5.

The Archangel Gabriel (*Varuna*) – Ray 6, Lord of Water, is concerned with all plant and animal life. The symbol of Varuna represents (amongst other things) a foetus.

The Archangel Raphael (*Kshiti*) – Ray 7, Lord of Earth, concerned with the geophysical structural form of the planet, and symbolised by a snake.

The disposition of these glyphs is a flattened isosceles triangle, which was notable on inspection by investigators for possessing an immense electromagnetic field which damaged electronic equipment and caused visionary experiences (notably to Ralph Noyes).

At whom was this symbolic imagery aimed? In 1990 I thought it must be for the Spiritual Ascension Processes of humanity. I believe that this was too narrow a definition. The Cosmic sources, the symbolism of the formations and the nature of the 'Receptor Agents' as defined above (Distributing Centres) suggests that a wider group was intended, namely life forms as a whole on this planet. This great body of life and intelligence operating on the etheric planes of course includes those Spirits concerned with the welfare of humanity. However, the Devic world as a whole needs to be prepared for the necessary traumas that will transform this planet in the near future.

## THE TRIANGLES OF POWER IN HAMPSHIRE IN 1990 (19.14)

The Wiltshire formations, although the most important of their kind, were not the only Triangles of Power in southern England in 1990. They covered a large area, whereas the small, discrete group close to Chilcomb,

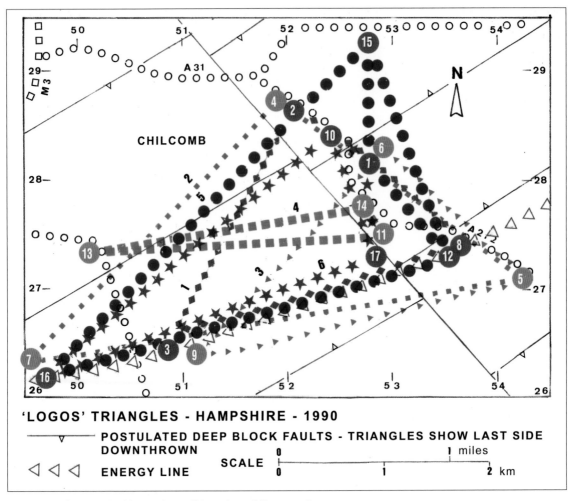

'LOGOS' TRIANGLES - HAMPSHIRE - 1990

⎯⎯▽⎯⎯ POSTULATED DEEP BLOCK FAULTS - TRIANGLES SHOW LAST SIDE
DOWNTHROWN

◁ ◁ ◁ ENERGY LINE

SCALE

0 ——————————— 1 miles
0 ———————— 1 ———————— 2 km

*19.14 The Chilcomb, Hampshire, Triangles of Power of 1990*

south-east of Winchester, was only about two square miles in area, into which were packed some 17 formations and six Triangles of Power. In what follows I must express my gratitude to the late Richard Andrews, former member of the CCCS Council, dowser, and an outstanding and scrupulous fieldworker. This was countryside he knew and loved well, and before his untimely death in 1999, he took the trouble to go over the crop circle scene there with me, drawing my notice to formations which I should otherwise have missed.

*Geomorphic structure.* Geologically, Chilcomb lies in a basin of the Cretaceous chalk deposits where the Middle and Lower Chalk are exposed (Melbourn Rock). As in Wiltshire, there are deep block faults which belong to the Mere system of the Wessex basin. Unknown even to Richard Andrews at the time, there is a major energy line between Fawley Down and Longwood Warren. An appreciation of the existence of this energy line (which links with others, such as the Michael-Mary Line, to make up the geomorphic energy body of planet Earth) is critical for an understanding of what occurred in this locality between May and August in 1990.

*The 1990 Chilcomb, Hampshire, crop formations* (19.14)

The formations are listed below in order of their appearance (or discovery), with one exception (No. 9). Each has its exact location indicated. On my map and in the list below the genuine, geophysical formations and triangles are shown in green or blue, and those of the Forces of Darkness in red.

 1. 18.5.1990. *The Punchbowl, Itchen Valley CP* (OS SU528281)

 2. 23.5.1990. *Velpins Bank Plantation, Chilcomb CP* (OS SU520286)

 3. 25.5.1990. *Morestead Down, Owslebury CP* (OS SU508264)

 4. 28.5.1990. *Velpins Bank Plantation, Chilcomb CP* (OS SU519287)

 5. 29.5.1990. *Longwood Estate, Itchen Valley CP* (OS SU542271)

 6. 30.5.1990. *The Punchbowl, Itchen Valley CP* (OS SU528283)

 7. 2.6.1990. *Hazeley Down, Twyford CP* (OS SU495263)

 8. 6.6.1990. *Middle Warren, Longwood Estate, Itchen Valley CP* (OS SU536274)

 9. 25?.5.1990 *Fawley Down, Owslebury CP* (OS SU511264)

 10. 16.6.1990. *Telegraph Hill, Chilcomb CP* (OS SU524284)

 11. 19.6.1990. *Longwood Estate, Owslebury CP* (OS SU529275)

 12. 28.6.1990. *Longwood Estate, Itchen Valley CP* (OS SU535272)

 13. 30.6.1990. *Twyford Down, Twyford CP* (OS SU501273)

● 14. 3.7.1990. *Fawley Down, Owslebury CP* (OS SU526277)

● 15. 6.7.1990. *Chilcomb Down, Itchen Valley CP* (OS SU527293)

● 16. 3.8.1990. *Hazeley Down, Twyford CP* (OS SU497262) (Illustrations 4.6 and 4.7)

● 17. 11.8.1990. *Longwood Estate, Owslebury CP* (OS SU528272)

Several formations form part of more than one Triangle of Power (TOP), so for reference I have listed all six Hampshire 1990 Triangles below, with the numbers of the formations listed above forming the various elements – the Emanating Energy (EE), Evocative Force (EF), Magnetic Centre (MC) and Distributing Centre (DC).

TOP 1.   1. EE (18.5.1990)

2. EF (23.5.1990)

8 MC (6 (or 4?).6.1990)

Note apparent anomaly over date of actual, physical appearance.

3. DC (25.5.1990)

TOP 2.   5. EE (29. 5.1990)

4. EF (28.5.1990)

7. DC (2.6.1990)

TOP 3.   5. EE (29.5.1990)

6. EF (30.5.1990)

9. DC (25.5.1990)

TOP 4.   11. EE (19.6.1990)

14. EF (3.7.1990)

13. DC (30.6.1990)

TOP 5.   1. EE (18.5.1990)

12. EF (28.6.1990)

15. MC (6.7.1990)

16. DC (3.8.1990)

TOP 6.   1. EE (18.5.1990)

10. EF (16.6.1990)

17. MC (11.8.1990)

16. DC (3.8.1990)

Of these formations exactly half were man-made. Two of the 'negative' formations (4 and 9) are very strange indeed and may not be *entirely* man-made. As I have indicated earlier, the negative formations made by human hoaxers can be the products of over-shadowing by a dark and sinister agency (non-human) acting through them. The dates of discovery were supplied by Richard Andrews, usually on the basis of information from the farmer. But I suspect that in some cases the date given is later than when they were said to have appeared, and perhaps reflects the date when they were first *noticed*. Unlike Wiltshire, the area was not regularly over-flown on a daily basis by CCCS fliers.

The battle between the Light Workers and the Forces of Darkness for control of the energy line was, as in Wiltshire, the distinctive feature of the interplay between the six Triangles of Power that I have identified in the Chilcomb area during the summer of 1990.

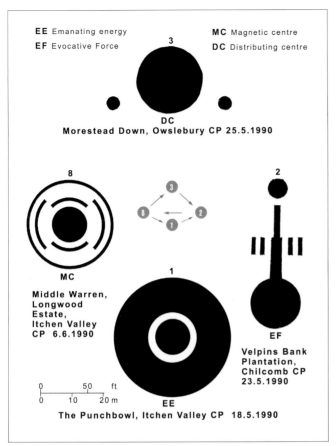

EE Emanating energy
EF Evocative Force
MC Magnetic centre
DC Distributing centre

**3**

**DC**
**Morestead Down, Owslebury CP 25.5.1990**

**8**

**2**

**MC**
Middle Warren,
Longwood
Estate,
Itchen Valley
CP 6.6.1990

**1**

**EF**
Velpins Bank
Plantation,
Chilcomb CP
23.5.1990

0    50    ft
0    10    20 m
**EE**
**The Punchbowl, Itchen Valley CP 18.5.1990**

*19.15 Hampshire Triangle of Power 1990:1*

*Hampshire TOP 1990:1* (19.15)

The series started with a ringed circle (formation 1) of geophysical origin on 18.5.1990. It symbolised, appropriately as a *Bi* symbol, the source of the Emanating Energy for the three Light Worker Triangles of Power TOP 1, TOP 5 and TOP 6. Almost at once the Forces of Darkness mounted a counter-attack with what became the 'Gaia' figure (formation 2) on 23.5.1990. This was originally a pan handle formation, which I believe was transformed into a Gaia figure as a function of the Evocative Force of TOP 1 by the Light Workers. It was an expression of the *leitmotif* of the series, i.e. the sacredness of form as an expression of Deity, in particular the archetypal

feminine principle. This in turn was balanced by the Magnetic Centre reported on 6.6.1990 as formation 8. This was a symbol of the Five, the four Rays of Attribute and their originator, Ray 3, the feminine energy of our Earth Logos. The point of contact with the energy line, symbolised initially by a large single circle on Morestead Down, appeared on 25.5.1990 and acted as the Distributing Centre (formation 3).

This is another, apparently simple, formation with a complicated history. Initially, the plain circle, 72 ft in diameter and swirled clockwise, appeared on its own. A few days later it was joined by two small circles, symmetrically disposed about it, (also clockwise and 14 ft in diameter), on 30.5.1990. They were situated on the side facing the direction of the incoming energy of the Evocative Force (formation 2) and Magnetic Centre (formation 8). Six weeks later, and almost certainly associated with TOP 5, two medium sized circles appeared on 7.7.1990. They were 35 ft in diameter and swirled anticlockwise. They were situated close to formation 3 and were, like the others, of geophysical origin and straddled the energy line. As I understand it, each pair of circles was a 'source of violent interplay between the two points' (Bailey 1951, p. 460) and acted both as a *protective force field* and a *purifying agent* for the energy line. The complicated sequencing of events at formation 3 can be worked out from the annotated survey by John Langrish on 9.7.1990 and a series of aerial photos.

*Hampshire TOP 1990:2*

This was concerned with neutralising the energies of TOP 1. The Emanating Energy

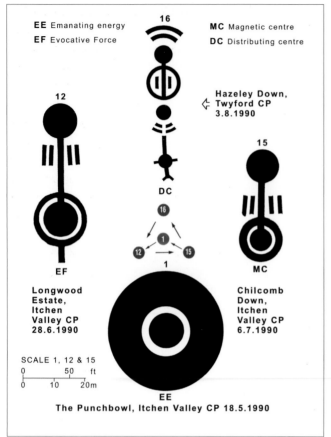

EE Emanating energy
EF Evocative Force

MC Magnetic centre
DC Distributing centre

16

12

Hazeley Down,
Twyford CP
3.8.1990

DC

16

15

1

12    15

1

EF

Longwood
Estate,
Itchen
Valley CP
28.6.1990

MC

Chilcomb
Down,
Itchen
Valley CP
6.7.1990

SCALE 1, 12 & 15
0        50   ft
0    10   20m

EE

The Punchbowl, Itchen Valley CP 18.5.1990

*19.16 Hampshire Triangle of Power 1990:5*

was a triple ringer, made with a plank, at Longwood Estate (formation 5). The two adjacent circles, also hoaxed, indicated the direction of the two other points of this Triangle of Power (the triangles of the Forces of Darkness lack a Magnetic Centre, as noted above). The second point of TOP 2 (formation 4) was put down to replace formation 2, over which they had lost control. It was an extraordinary formation, if that is the right word. It was a very small, irregular dumb-bell situated close to formation 2 in an adjoining field. I do not think it was exclusively man-made. The Distributing Centre of this Triangle of Power was formation 7, a travesty of the later Logoi formations in the area. It was

situated close to but not on the energy line, which passes to the south. It was not easily attributable to any particular hoaxers. Again, a non-human source is possible. Pat Delgado reported that it had a negative, depressive feel about it. (Delgado and Andrews 1990, p. 35)

*Hampshire TOP 1990:3*

This was another group of formations by the Forces of Darkness, but this time accurately placing the Distributing Centre (formation 9) on the energy line. It shared the Emanating Energy of TOP 2 (formation 5). The Evocative Force, formation 6, appeared close to formation 1 in the Punchbowl. Its radial appearance indicated the use of planks in its construction, also used for the strange little formation at Fawley Down which was the Distributing Centre (formation 9). It is significant that the Distributing Centres of TOP 1 and TOP 3 appeared on the same date (25.5.1990) and in the same vicinity.

*Hampshire TOP 1990:4*

The primary purpose of this, the last Triangle of Power of the Forces of Darkness, appears to have been to block the connecting energy lines of TOP 6, the most important of the geophysical series.

Formation 11, a ringed circle, was the Emanating Energy of TOP 4. Like formation 5, this was supplied with two smaller (man-made) formations. All appear to have been made with planks. However, this was not the end of the matter. Two much larger geophysical circles were placed nearer the single-ringer. They appear to be an attempt to neutralise the negative energies of TOP 4 so that TOP 6 could be completed. The Evocative

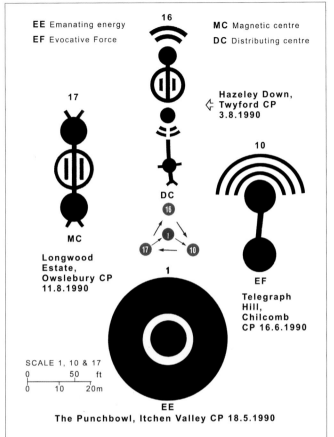

EE Emanating energy
EF Evocative Force

MC Magnetic centre
DC Distributing centre

16

17

Hazeley Down,
⇐ Twyford CP
3.8.1990

10

DC

16

MC

17 ← 10

Longwood
Estate,
Owslebury CP
11.8.1990

1

EF

Telegraph
Hill,
Chilcomb
CP 16.6.1990

SCALE 1, 10 & 17
0          50      ft
0      10    20m

EE
The Punchbowl, Itchen Valley CP 18.5.1990

*19.17 Hampshire Triangle of Power 1990:6*

Force of TOP 4, formation 14, was another ringed circle, but no details are available. The Distributing Centre was formation 13, a poorly made haloed dumb-bell with two boxes. It was reported to have arrived on 30.6.1990.

*Hampshire TOP 1990:5 (19.16)*

Having shaken off or neutralised the negative input of TOP 2-4, the Light Workers produced two important Triangles of Power concerned with cosmogenesis or 'Coming into Being'. TOP 5 is the largest of all this type and is an absolutely classical example of its kind, following the template provided at Houndean Bottom. Its height was 3 miles. The Emanating Energy was formation 1, already described. The Evocative Force and

Magnetic Centre were fine geophysical Logoi formations, male (formation 12) and female (formation 15). Each formation was of a dumb-bell shape with four boxes. The lower part of the body was ringed, making it effectively a *Bi* symbol – Deity expressing itself in form. The masculinity of formation 12 is expressed as the male member attached to the bottom of the pictogram. The Distributing Centre (formation 16) is a marvellous diagram of cosmogenesis and is described in detail in Chapter 4, (4.6, 4.7). The group as a whole must be considered as an expression of the sacredness of sex, particularly as a human function.

*Hampshire TOP 1990:6 (19.17)*

If TOP 5 refers to the 'mechanics' of cosmogenesis, TOP 6, the last of the 1990 series, is concerned with the cosmic principle of cosmogenesis, indeed the hallowed nature of all God's creation, particularly so far as humanity is concerned. TOP 6 shared the same points and symbols for the Emanating Energy and Distributing Centre as TOP 5 (formations 1 and 16 respectively). Formation 1, the ringed circle, which is the site of the initial Emanating Energy, is a type of *Bi* symbol which has 'matter' symbolised both at the numinous centre of Deity, but also as His creation shown as a broad encompassing ring. Then the Evocative Force, formation 10, is shown as an Entity whose triple half-rings indicate that this Being is made up of the Trinity of Spirit, Soul and Personality. As we have seen, creation is the product of deific thought, inspiration and power at many levels of the Cosmos, whose intelligent functionaries might be termed 'Logoi',

'Emanations' or, more poetically, 'Sons of God' in Hebrew. The Magnetic Centre (formation 17) is also of great interest. It appeared much later than formation 10, indeed it was the last formation to appear that summer at Chilcomb, arriving on 11.8.1990, after the negative energies of TOP 4 had been cleared. Formation 17 is a simplified version of the great mandala, formation 16, and emphasises the 'divinity' of all aspects of cosmogenesis. Formation 17 tempers and adjusts the raw energy in the crop circle scene. The threefold aspect of Deity is symbolised in the ringed centre of Spirit. Springing from the centre are two creative aspects of Deity symbolised as circles. They might be defined as the Soul (Ray 2), the creative function of Deity ('All things came into being through Him' – *John* 1:3) whose nature is Love-Wisdom, and Form itself (Ray 3). Both circles are rayed indicating their deific nature.

Creation is one of the glories of God, and is celebrated in that beautiful passage in the Book of Job in the Old Testament, 'I [GOD] laid the foundation of the Earth ... when the morning stars sang together and all the heavenly beings shouted for joy.' (*Job* 38:7)

# 20. THE TRIANGLES OF POWER IN 1991

*Remember that when we talk and think in symbols, we are placing something between ourselves and reality – something protective, interpretative and significant, but something nevertheless veiling and hiding.*

Bailey 1960, p. 178

The growing level of interest in the crop circle phenomenon as a result of the appearance of the Alton Barnes dragons in 1990, together with a fully mobilised Centre for Crop Circle Studies (CCCS, founded 1990) ensured that recording mechanisms were fully in place by 1991. It was very necessary, for an unprecedented number of entirely different types of formations appeared, using more complex arrangements and new symbolic glyphs, between early June and late August in Wessex. All were signed with glyphs associated with the Earth Logos and His hierarchy.

## THE PLANNING PROCESS

The season's developments can now be broadly divided into six main phases, each organised differently, with specific targets in mind.

1. Two major Triangles of Power (TOP A and B) were put down by the Forces of Darkness in June 1991 to damage the Michael-Mary Line, and to delay the programme of the Light Workers, as in 1990.

2. This was countered by a geophysical Triangle of Power placed nearby (TOP 1 A(ii)-D). The main group (TOP 2-8) did not effectively begin until this neutralising process was complete: a waste of a month

of possible crop circle activity, which was no doubt the intention of the Forces of Darkness.

3. The three Triangles of Power TOP 2-4 brought a new type of structure to the process. They had different symbols at the apexes reflecting different types of energy and the Planetary Lords behind them. These appear to be Triangles of Power reflecting the special concerns of three Lords of Attribute, the Archangels Haniel, Uriel and Gabriel, Who are particularly active at this time in connection with the needs of humanity.

The Archangel Haniel (*Indra*) (TOP 2) is concerned with the spiritual development of humanity and His emergence will, in time, usher in true spirituality for the bulk of the race.

The Archangel Uriel (*Agni*) (TOP 3) is concerned with intellectual development.

The Archangel Gabriel (*Varuna*) (TOP 4) is concerned, in this context, with the emotional aspect of humanity, which at present is perhaps the highest state to which it can as a whole aspire.

Each of these qualities of the Lords of Attribute is reflected in the threefold structure of the Barbury Castle formation, see Chapter 15 and illustrations 15.11 and 15.12, which was to function as the Distributing Centre for all the Triangles of Power for the rest of the season. The reuse of this Distributing Centre, the uncertainty of some dates, and also the reuse of formation TOP 2B by TOP 3, makes working out the sequence and timespans of TOP 2-4 particularly difficult. However, the likelihood is that TOP 2 took fifteen days, TOP 3 seven days and TOP 4 five days. The progressive shortening reflected a realisation that time was running out in terms of the growing season of the crops.

4. The next stage, which to some extent was co-terminus with TOP 2 and 3, was master-minded by the Archangel Gabriel as the Emanating Energy (TOP 4A). Four Triangles of Power, TOP 5-8, were put down in late July and early August. They appear to have been concerned with intelligent marine animals, which as a class seem to be a life form at greatest risk in ecological terms at this time. The symbol of the Evocative Force and Magnetic Centre in each case was shown as a particular animal (not easily distinguished, but dolphins and some species of whale seem to be indicated).

5. By mid August harvesting was taking place and the Triangles of Power operation had clearly run out of time. It would appear that one further group of animals was started, with the Little Bedwyn turtle of 19.8.1991, but never completed.

6. Almost the last formation of the series in 1991 was the Serpentine formation at Highclose Farm, Hungerford CP Hampshire on 18.8.1991. This was not part of a Triangle of Power, but constituted a symbolic statement summing up the purpose of this type of phenomenon in 1990 and 1991.

The proliferation of Triangles of Power as a crop circle phenomenon was never again so great as in 1990 and 1991, probably as a result of the growing pervasive influence of the Forces of Darkness, evidenced by increasing hoaxing from then onwards. However, see Chapters 5 and 13 for Triangles of Power in 1994 and 1999.

## MAN-MADE WILTSHIRE TRIANGLES IN 1991

There were two groups of man-made formations (based on the evidence for their construction) included here, both early in the 1991 season and apparently linked.

*TOP 1991:A*

The sequence appears to be as follows:

A1. *Avebury Trusloe* (OS SU079700) on 9.6.1991

   Emanating Energy. Linear formation with three linked circles. Two small lateral circles.

A2. *Lockeridge* (OS SU137663) on 21.6.1991

   Evocative Force. 'Rod of Power' but lacking lateral circles.

A3. *Roundway Hill* (OS SU027646) on 25.6.1991

   Distributing Centre. Linear formation with three linked circles.

The designs of the formations are of considerable interest and indicate heavy 'overshadowing' of the human hoaxers by demonic entities. In particular there is the use of certain spiritual symbols, unknown at a conscious level to the hoaxers, but part of the occult vocabulary. In two cases here they occurred before their general use in geophysical formations during the 1991 season. The first was formation A1, which was unfinished by the hoaxers (the ring of the middle circle was not completed). This formation had two small lateral circles which is the trademark of the Emanating Energy formations of TOP 2 to 8. The second was formation A2, a classic 'Rod of Power' (see below). The linear triple circle Distributing Centre (formation A3) was, needless to add, put down close to the Michael-Mary Line, its arrival timed to coincide with the new moon.

*TOP 1991:B*

B1. *Yatesbury Airfield* (OS SU065705) on 24.6.1991

Emanating Energy. Linear Gaia formation.

B2. *Lurkely Hill* (OS SU125667) on 24(?).6.1991 (Surveyed 29.6.1991)

Evocative Force. Linear 'haloed' Gaia formation.

B3. *Roundway Hill*. See TOP A above

Distributing Centre, reused.

The apparent reason for slightly moving the positions of A1 and A2 to B1 and B2 was a countermeasure by the Forces of Light. The man-made A1 at Avebury Trusloe, the Emanating Energy that initiated the series on Sunday 9.6.1991, had been quickly followed by a geophysical crop formation, 1A(ii), which appeared in the same field, probably on the night of Friday 13/14.6.1991. I believe that its purpose was to block the energy from formation A1.

## THE RESPONSE OF THE LIGHT WORKERS TO TOP A AND B

TOP 1, a geophysical neutralising Triangle of Power, with its fourfold structure, was the response by the Light Workers to the negative energy placed by the Forces of Darkness along the Michael-Mary Line. It was, perhaps appropriately, that of the Earth Logos, as reflected in the symbols used.

However, TOP 1 had a troubled beginning due to a false start with 1A(i). (20.3) This Gaia-type formation was reported at Firs Farm, Beckhampton (OS SU083677) on 6.6.1991, and was evidently intended to be part of the Gaian dumb-bell series. In general appearance and size it was similar to 1B at Alton Barnes. For maximum effect it had been sited directly on the Michael-Mary Line. However, careful examination of the extant aerial photos, particularly that by Busty Taylor (Taylor, B. 1992, p. 4) shows that its larger circle had been subsequently surrounded by a broad, man-made ring about 15 ft wide. The push-marks using a board are particularly clear on the aerial photo. That it had been added to the geophysical formation is evident, because the two stages do not completely synchronise, with a small crescent-shaped gap appearing between the two on one side. This man-made accretion by the Forces of Darkness appears to have completely neutralised this formation as an element of the geophysical Triangle of Power. Consequently a replacement had to be made – 1A(ii) – two miles to the north a week later.

*TOP 1991:1* (20.1 (map), 20.2 – plan with all man-made accretions removed)

1A(ii). *Avebury Trusloe* (OS SU076700) on 13/14.6.1991. (20.4)

Emanating Energy. 'Logos' design: 'body' circle 49 ft 9 in diameter, 'head' circle 30 ft diameter. Overall length 162 ft 8 in. Two angled side boxes 42 ft 4 in by 3 ft, with boxes at head end. The formation has analogies with the Hampshire 1990 formation 12 (see Chapter 19), which also had angled boxes. It was subsequently damaged by hoaxers who added 3 'spurs' to the small circle. A notable feature of this formation was its healing properties, experienced by a friend and his wife.

The writer and his wife also experienced its properties. On the evening of Saturday 15.6.1991 we were driving eastwards through a heavy rainstorm along the Cherhill Road, the A4. Opposite Knoll Down (about a third of a mile away from formation 1A(ii)) we passed through a distinct electromagnetic force-field which made our skin tingle. It must have been about 50 yards wide. This was almost certainly the energy field emanating from 1A(ii), which had appeared the previous night, and was projecting an electromagnetic field towards the site of 1B, which was to appear as a crop formation on 5.7.1991.

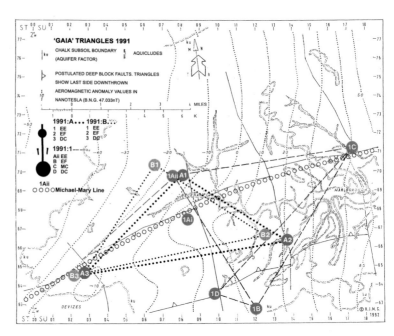

20.1 The 'Gaia' crop formation Triangles of Power of 1991. East Kennet area of Wiltshire

1B. *East Field, Alton Barnes* (OS SU117630) on 5.7.1991. (20.5)

Evocative Force. A simple Gaia design; 'head' circle 18 ft 9 in diameter, 'body' circle 60 ft 6 in diameter, overall length 99 ft. Earth Logos signature about 60 ft to the northeast. Small spur added to 'head' circle by hoaxers.

1C. *Rough Down, Ogbourne Maizey* (OS SU174711) on 11.7.1991. (20.6)

Magnetic Centre. A 'pan-handle' formation which was perhaps intended to symbolise the classical *Luna* with her mirror (Green, Michael 1990, pp. 141-142), or the Earth Goddess, whose planetary energies would be involved

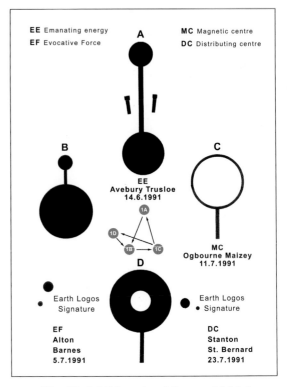

20.2 *The 'Gaia' Triangle of Power* 1991:1 East Kennet area, Wiltshire

1A(i) Beckhampton
(SU083677) - 6.6.1991
1 and 2 - geophysical
3 - man-made

1    2    3

*20.3 TOP 1991:1A(i). Beckhampton
(OS SU083677), 6.6.1991*

*20.4 TOP 1991:1A(ii). Avebury Trusloe
(OS SU076700), 14.6.1991*

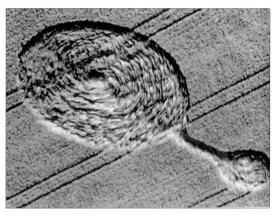

*20.5 TOP 1991:1B. Alton Barnes
(OS SU117630), 5.7.1991*

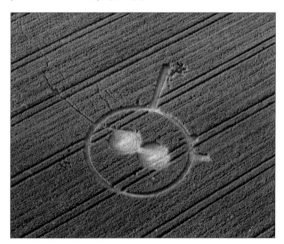

*20.6 TOP 1991:1C. Ogbourne Maizey
(OS SU174711), 11.7.1991*

*20.7 TOP 1991:1D. Stanton St Bernard
(OS SU098637), 23.7.1991*

by the Magnetic Centre. Ring 60 ft 6 in in diameter, 3 ft wide, spur 11 ft long and 4 ft wide. The formation is orientated so that the spur points towards TOP 1D. There does not appear to have been an Earth Logos signature. The formation was extensively damaged by hoaxers who added additional spurs and two circles in the centre, giving the formation the nickname of 'two eggs in a frying pan.' Gill Wookey of the Dains Riding Centre

(Marlborough) reported that horses at Maisey Farm immediately adjacent were very restless the night that 1C appeared.

1D. *Milk Hill, Stanton St Bernard* (OS SU098637) on 23.7.1991. (20.7)

Distributing Centre. Another 'pan-handle' formation. The circle has a broad ring with standing centre, a *Bi* symbol of Deity. Ring c. 60 ft diameter, 25 ft wide. Spur 40 ft long, 5 ft wide. Earth Logos signature about 10 ft to west of main formation. Spur points in direction of 1C.

20.8 The 'Logos' crop formation Triangles of Power of 1991 East Kennet area of Wiltshire

## TRIANGLES OF POWER STIMULATING HUMANITY, TOP 2, 3 AND 4 (20.8, 20.18 (MAPS))

Once measures had been put in hand to counteract the activities of the Forces of Darkness, three important Triangles of Power next appeared in the Kennet area of Wiltshire. To my mind, TOP 2 and 3 relate exclusively to humanity. TOP 2 is concerned with human beings on the spiritual path (those who are part of the Ascension Process, see Chapters 8 and 9). TOP 3 relates to a larger group, those whose mental faculties are developing and consequently are on the Wheel of Incarnation, see Chapter 23. TOP 4 is concerned not only with humanity, but also with developed animals and birds whose emotional capacities are being developed. Those who fall into this category, which includes the generality of mankind, are in the early stages of the Wheel of Incarnation. The archangels responsible for overseeing TOP 2, 3 and 4 are respectively Haniel, Uriel and Gabriel.

*Symbols of Power*

Four new types of symbol appeared with TOP 2 and 3. Of these the Distributing Centre at *Barbury Castle*, which appeared on 17.7.1991 and relates to all the 1991 Triangles of Power 2-8, is one of the most important crop formations of all time. It is a communication from our Solar Logos, the author of this series generally, discussed in detail in Chapter 15. Each of the stages of the creative process has a different type of symbol at the points of the triangles, reflecting on a lower scale the energy of the three Rays of Aspect: Will or Power; Love-Wisdom; Active Intelligence. Their combined output is of course at the Distributing Centre, which in its trimorphic design is also a symbolic statement of the function of the Lords of Aspect.

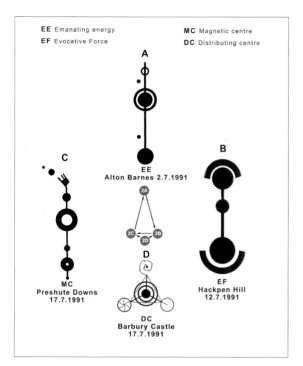

*20.9 **The Stimulation of Spiritual Humanity*** *Wiltshire Triangle of Power 1991:2*

*20.10 **The Rod of Power of Haniel*** *TOP 1991:2A. Alton Barnes (OS SU115629) 2.7.1991*

*TOP 1991:2* (20.9)

2A   *East Field, Alton Barnes, Alton CP* (OS SU115629) on 2.7.1991. (20.10)

Emanating Energy. 'Rod of Power' symbol of Haniel.

2B.   *Hackpen Hill, Broad Hinton CP* (OS SU127751) on 12.7.1991. (20.11)

Evocative Force. 'Thunderbolt' symbol. Animal disturbance in the vicinity at 4.00 am.

2C.   *Preshute Down, Broad Hinton CP* (OS SU145747) on 17.7.1991. (20.12)

Magnetic Centre. 'Hand of Atonement' symbol. Earth Logos signature.

2D.   *Barbury Castle, Wroughton CP* (OS SU152769) on 17.7.1991. (20.13)

Distributing Centre. The 'Solar Trimorph' symbol. 'Lights and other phenomena.'

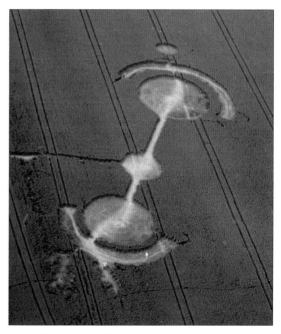

*20.11 **Thunderbolt*** *TOP 1991: 2B. Hackpen Hill (OS SU127751) 12.7.1991*

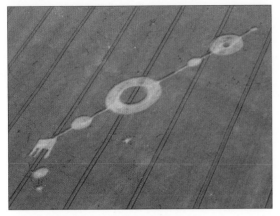

*20.12 **The Hand of Atonement***
*TOP 1991:2C. Preshute Down*
*(OS SU145747), 17.7.1991*

*20.13 TOP 1991:2D-8D. Barbury Castle*
*(OS SU152768), 17.7.1991*

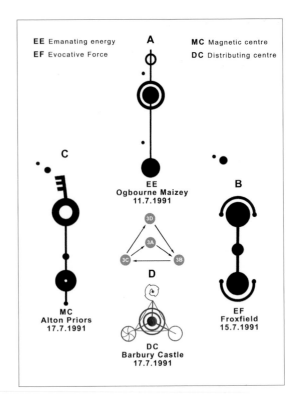

*20.14 **The Stimulation of Intelligent Mankind***
*Wiltshire Triangle of Power 1991:3*

*TOP 1991:3* (20.14)

3A. *Rough Down (Maisey Farm), Ogbourne Maizey, Ogbourne St Andrew CP*
(OS SU178708) on 11.7.1991. (20.15)

Emanating Energy. 'Rod of Power' symbol of Uriel.

3B. *Rudge Farm, Froxfield CP*
(OS SU287683). Reported 20.8.1991, but appeared much earlier. (20.16)

Evocative Force. 'Thunderbolt' symbol. Earth Logos signature.

3C. *Tawsmead, Alton Priors, Alton CP*
(OS SU115620) on 17.7.1991 (probably, although first surveyed 19.7.1991). (20.17)

Magnetic Centre. 'The Golden Key of Capricorn' symbol. Earth Logos signature.

3D. *Barbury Castle.* See TOP 2D above

Distributing Centre, reused.

*TOP 1991:4* (20.18, 20.19)

4A. *Norridge Common, Upton Scudamore CP*
(OS ST861471) on 21.7.1991. (20.20, 20.21)

Emanating Energy. 'Trident Rod of Power' symbol of Gabriel.

4B. *Hackpen Hill.* See TOP 2B above
Evocative Force, reused.

4C. *Manor Farm, East Kennet CP* (OS SU111676) on 26.7.1991. (20.22)

Magnetic Centre. 'The Silver Key of Cancer' symbol. Earth Logos signature.

4D. *Barbury Castle.* See TOP 2D above Distributing Centre, reused.

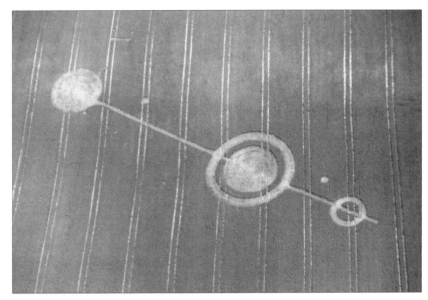

20.15 **The Rod of Power of Uriel**
*TOP 1991:3A. Ogbourne Maizey (OS SU178708), 11.7.1991*

## THE COSMIC SYMBOLS

*The Rods of Power* – 2A to 8A (20.10, 20.15, 20.20)

Ray 1, at stage A, the Emanating Energy of each Triangle of Power, embodies 'the dynamic idea of God' and is appropriately symbolised by the Rod of the Great Initiator. This type of formation is a symbol of the 'Rods of Power' or sceptres used by the greater Logoi. They are symbols of 'office' and are primarily used for initiatory purposes. (Bailey 1922a, pp. 126 ff.) They invest Occult Initiators with the ability to focus and transfer power. All three have a similar basic form: the central staff has a ball-foot terminal (circle), a central hand grip (ringed circle or circle), and a terminal ring or prong at the head with a central divider. These three main features, of course, also symbolise the Logoic make-up of any Being: *Spirit* (at the head) Ray 1; *Soul*, central element – Ray 2; and *Personality*, ball foot – Ray 3.

20.16 **Thunderbolt**
*TOP 1991:3B. Froxfield (OS SU287683), 15.7.1991*

*20.17 **The Golden Key of Capricorn**
TOP 1991:3C. Alton Priors (OS SU115620), 17.7.1991*

This type of Rod of Power is very ancient with origins, literally, off-planet. Early human civilisations used similar sceptres, and the earliest known group of such objects from the Judean Desert Treasure found in 1961 (late Chalcolithic period, second half of the fourth millennium BC) have sceptre fittings with the same ball-feet, handgrips and terminals. (The Metropolitan Museum of Art 1986, pp. 72ff.)

Each formation has two small lateral circles on the left-hand side. One circle lies close to the head of the formation, the other to the base. These double circles indicate that the formations have a similar function, namely that they are the point of Emanating Energy for their respective Triangles of Power. Second, the circles lie on the left-hand side of the formations, and thus indicate that they relate to aspects of manifestation. Third, their location in

the formations indicates that one circle symbolises a focus of energy associated with the Evocative Force, and that the second circle is a focus of energy associated with the Magnetic Centre. None of these Rods of Power has a signature, since the design of the formation is a signature in itself.

*The Rod of Power of Haniel –* TOP 2A (20.10)

Strictly speaking, I believe that Entity that the Rod of Power of 2A refers to is the Solar Logos, since it is His responsibility to induct humanity through the spiritual initiatory process. It will be noted that the central pathway or 'rod' runs unimpeded throughout the length of the sceptre, thus symbolically raising the Initiate from the lowest to the highest levels. As noted above, Haniel is the archangel concerned with the spiritual development of mankind.

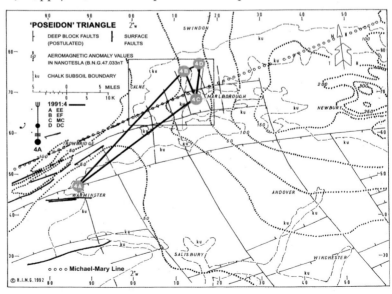

*20.18 The 'Poseidon' crop formation Triangle of Power of 1991 East Kennet area of Wiltshire*

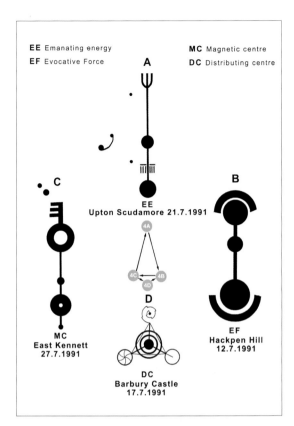

EE Emanating energy
EF Evocative Force
MC Magnetic centre
DC Distributing centre

A

EE
Upton Scudamore 21.7.1991

C

4A

4C 4B
4D

D

MC
East Kennett
27.7.1991

DC
Barbury Castle
17.7.1991

B

EF
Hackpen Hill
12.7.1991

*20.19 **The Stimulation of Astral Beings**
Wiltshire Triangle of Power 1991:4*

### The Rod of Power of Uriel – TOP 3A (20.15)

I believe that the Entity this symbolises is perhaps the Earth Logos. There is a deliberate break in the central circle since the emphasis for the generality of mankind before they can reach the spiritual initiations is for 'the awakening of the life to intelligent work on the mental plane.' (Bailey 1922a, p. 127) Uriel is the archangel concerned with mankind's mental development. I believe that the terminal ring at the head of 3A represents the cage which holds the so-called 'Flaming Diamond' used by Sanat Kumara, the Archangel Michael, the One Initiator and Lord of the World. The diamond is charged with pure electrical force from Sirius, the source of intelligence (*Manas*). (See Chapter 19 and below.)

*20.20 **The Trident – the Rod of Power of Gabriel or Poseidon***
*TOP 1991:4A. Upton Scudamore
(OS ST861471), 21.7.1991*

### The Rod of Power of Gabriel – TOP 4A-8A (20.20, 20.21)

This Rod of Power is used as the Emanating Energy for one Triangle of Power concerned with humanity, and four concerned with cetaceans.

This crop formation is especially important in bringing together various symbolic elements indicating its metaphysical identity and function, which enabled me to decipher it. Apart from the features it shares with formations 2A and 3A, it has special features. Its signature (20.21 A), represents, inter alia, a living foetus in the womb for whom a watery environment is essential. And it is angled in relation to the main formation as if water was being poured out of a dish. Springing from the head of the main formation is the trident of Poseidon, the Greek God of the waters.

The complex arrangement of eight boxes either side of the middle of the formation indicates the status and function of the great Being depicted. There are two horizontal boxes,

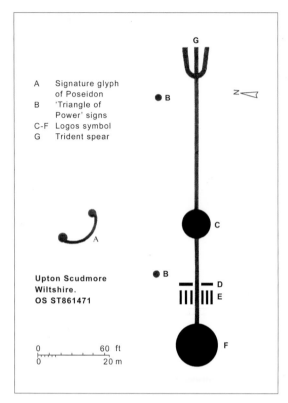

A Signature glyph of Poseidon
B 'Triangle of Power' signs
C-F Logos symbol
G Trident spear

Upton Scudmore
Wiltshire.
OS ST861471

0          60 ft
0      20 m

*20.21 The Trident of Gabriel or Poseidon depicted in the Upton Scudamore formation of 21.7.1991*

indicating to my mind that the Being operates at the Second Planetary Centre, which is the Centre where the love of God is manifest: this is the operating field of the Seven Lords (archangels) who run our planet. The six vertical boxes indicate the Ray or function of the archangel in question. The Lord of the Sixth Ray is the Archangel Gabriel (*Varuna*), and also the Greek God *Poseidon*, concerned with all aspects of water, and hence all living things on planet Earth, and in particular their emotional development.

*The Thunderbolt* – TOP 2B, 3B and 4B (20.11, 20.16)

This type of formation clearly represents the Eastern *vajra* or thunderbolt symbol, which we first met in Chapter 16. The vajra symbol is here clearly intended as a type of Ray 2, the Lord whose essential quality is Love-Wisdom. The symbols of the crop formation are arranged along a central path (as in the case of the Rod of Power) with a near-central handgrip knob (circle). In the traditional vajra the terminals are open cages, probably each intended to contain a diamond charged with electrical force (see the 'Flaming Diamond' of the Rod of Power, above). It is the energy interplay between the two diamonds that constitutes the magnetic power of this emblem. The crop circle features that depict these terminals are subtly different, since they are represented by haloed circles. The halo in crop circle symbolic shorthand indicates a Supreme Being, or in other words the structure of the formations suggests that we are looking at the psychic interplay between two great powers who are also individualised. And indeed in esoteric, spiritual terms this is precisely what we have. Ray 2 symbolises the interplay of energies between Ray 1's spiritual *desire* for expression in matter and Ray 3's *intelligent* reciprocal response. Where desire is transformed into *love* and intelligence is transmuted into *wisdom*, the two essential qualities of cosmic transfiguration are encapsulated in Ray 2, symbolised by the balanced form of the vajra symbol.

The vajra symbol is very ancient, originally believed to have been the symbol of the Vedic god Indra, who in esoteric terms encapsulates the numinous properties of spiritual (buddhic) wisdom (the Archangel Haniel in Christian terms). At a more mundane level the thunderbolt is obviously an appropriate symbol for Indra as Lord of Air presiding over the activities of the heavens. This type of symbol with such important transcendent properties is hardly likely to have been dreamed up by a clever priest. It is spiritually

*20.22 **The Silver Key of Cancer***
*TOP 1991:4C. East Kennet (OS SU11676)*
*26.7.1991*

inspired, probably at a visionary level, through some such discipline as *Raja Yoga*. In its developed form the *Vajrayana* system appears as a Tantric or esoteric system of Himalayan and northern *Mahayana* Buddhism.

At a more esoteric level, the comments by Djwhal Khul in his commentary on the Yoga Sutras of Patanjali (possibly dating to the late second millennium BC) are revealing:

'Two words are used by translators to convey this idea of compact cohering force *i.e.* the diamond, and the thunderbolt [which conveys] the idea of electrical force. All that we can know of God or of man is the quality of his energy as it demonstrates in force and activity, hence ... the highest aspect of divinity is called electric fire.' (Bailey 1927, pp. 349-350)

However, as with the crop formation depictions of the Rods of Power, the symbolic

representation of the vajra has its origins off-planet in the numinous realms. So where does the idea for this symbol come from? Amongst my field notes when I measured up formation 2B in 1991 I have a scribbled reference that the vajra is somehow connected to a double sun system. This was perceptive because I believe it relates to the binary system of Sirius, which is Ray 2 of the Being I call *Archon*, of whom our solar system is a centre.

Sirius A is a main-sequence star with a white dwarf companion which orbits it every 50 years. It is a spectral type A star twice the mass of our Sun and 23 times as luminous. These binary stellar properties at a physical level reflect the metaphysical property of Love-Wisdom which is a spiritual quality of Archon. The electromagnetic field between these two suns must be colossal, and the resulting energy matrix might well have been considered a suitable symbolic type of a system held taut between two polarities.

*The Hand of Atonement* – TOP 2C (20.12)

This enigmatic crop formation is also linear in form, and is superficially similar to formations 3C and 4C. Like them it appears to have two components. The top element in 2C is a claw-hand reaching out to a signature of the Earth Logos, with a circle on the pathway connecting it to a ring. (In the case of 3C and 4C this terminal is of key type directly attached to the ring.) At the other end of the formation is a Gaia-type pictogram centred around a ring-form reminiscent of the *Bi* disc of Deity, or perhaps in this context the spiritual component of the Earth Logos, whose signature appears on all three formations. These particular formations then are extraordinarily important since they point to the spiritual purpose of this numinous contact with humanity from God. In the case of TOP 2 it is Deity reaching out to mankind on planet Earth, offering eternal life to those on the spiritual path. (The hand or claw is symbolic of the triune nature of God described earlier in this study.) Hence my categorisation of this formation as the *Hand of Atonement* rather than the *Hand of God*, which was its nickname amongst the crop circle community at the time.

*The Keys to the Celestial Gates* – TOP 3C and 4C (20.17, 20.22)

TOP 3C, I believe, symbolises something different since we have a key rather than a hand. The significance of the solstitial gates, and the appropriate keys to open them, are discussed in the previous chapter. I believe that the thrust of TOP 3 concerns the heightening of the powers of *intelligence* for the generality of mankind, which in turn leads to the gate of the 'Way of the Gods' (*deva yāna*). The crop formation symbolises the 'golden key' to the Gate of Capricorn destined for use by those of mankind who are prepared to start the process of spiritual life. This gate leads beyond the Dharmic Wheel or Circle of Necessity (to release into spiritual life from the ceaseless round of birth and death).

TOP 4C is another key, the silver key which opens the gate of Cancer, the way of reincarnation. This gate on the metaphorical

southern quarter of the Kalachakra Mandala leads to the route of reincarnation which all living forms have to follow, with the intention eventually of passing beyond the Circle of Necessity. This includes the majority of mankind at present.

*The Solar Trimorph* – (TOP 2D, 3D, 4D, 5D, 6D, 7D and 8D) (20.13)

This *yantra* (sacred geometrical design) was discussed in Chapter 15 as a symbol of the Solar Logos. The three distinctive symbols on the apexes were considered in terms of the three Rays of Aspect, or the Trinity in Christian parlance. Here they are considered in terms of the three great spiritual stages which concern not only humanity but also the higher animals of the natural world.

*The western symbol*, I believe, characterises those on the final stages of the spiritual path – 'advanced Souls' as they are sometimes termed, who have a *direct path* in terms of achieving apotheosis. This is symbolised by the line stretching to the centre of the circle. TOP 2D

*The eastern symbol*, a ratcheted spiral, represents a much larger percentage of humanity who is passing through the middle stages of the initiatory process. In particular the mental processes are being developed, since the quality of *Manas* is an essential component of the spiritual life. TOP 3D

*The northern symbol*. This is a sixfold flower pattern since 'six is the number of the great work of the period of manifestation.' (Bailey 1951, p. 128) It includes a large proportion of humanity operating primarily at the emotional level. It also includes the higher animals of the natural world who function at this level too. TOP 4D, and also TOP 5-8D

## TRIANGLES OF POWER STIMULATING CETACEANS, TOP 5-8

The four remaining 1991 groups were evidently concerned with sea mammals. Cetaceans generally are under global threat of extinction due to climate change and overfishing. The Emanating Energy and the Distributing Centre of TOP 5 to 8 were the same as those of TOP 4, but the Evocative Force and Magnetic Centre took on the images of four different sea creatures. Which precise cetaceans they represent is necessarily somewhat speculative, with the exception of the first to appear (in TOP 5), which is almost certainly the Common Dolphin (*Delphinus delphis*). The others, in order of appearance, may represent the Porpoise (*Phocoena phocoena*), the Sperm Whale (*Physeter catodon*) and the Bottlenose Whale (*Hyperoodon ampullatus*). All four types of cetaceans have the waters of the British Isles as part of their habitat.

*TOP 1991:5 (20.23, 20.24)*

5A. *Norridge Common, Upton Scudamore.* See TOP 4A above
Emanating Energy, reused.

5B. *West Woods, Lockeridge, West Overton CP* (OS SU136661) on 30.7.1991. (20.25)
Evocative Force. 'Dolphin' formation. Earth Logos signature.

5C. *Firs Farm, Beckhampton, Avebury CP* (OS SU087680) on 3.8.1991. (20.26)
Magnetic Centre. 'Dolphin' formation. Earth Logos signature.

5D. *Barbury Castle.* See TOP 2D above
Distributing Centre, reused.

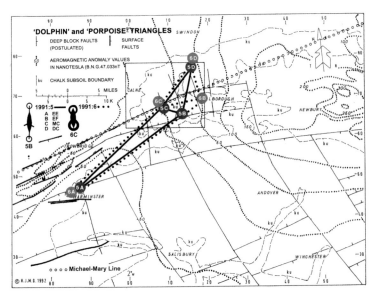

20.23 The 'Dolphin' and 'Porpoise' crop formation Triangles of Power of 1991. East Kennet area of Wiltshire

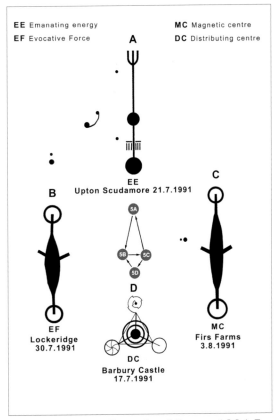

20.24 'Dolphin' Triangle of Power 1991:5

*20.25 'Dolphin' TOP 1991:5B. Lockeridge (OS SU136661), 30.7.1991*

*20.26 'Dolphin' TOP 1991:5C. Firs Farm Beckhampton (OS SU087680), 3.8.1991*

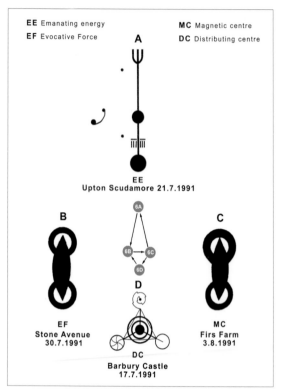

**EE** Emanating energy  **MC** Magnetic centre
**EF** Evocative Force  **DC** Distributing centre

A

EE
Upton Scudamore 21.7.1991

B  6A  C

6B  6C

6D

D

EF
Stone Avenue
30.7.1991

MC
Firs Farm
3.8.1991

DC
Barbury Castle
17.7.1991

*20.27 Wiltshire 'Porpoise' Triangle of Power 1991:6*

*20.28 'Porpoise' TOP 1991:6B. Stone Avenue (OS SU108695), 30.7.1991*

*TOP 1991:6 (20.23 (map), 20.27)*

6A. *Norridge Common, Upton Scudamore.* See TOP 4A above
Emanating Energy, reused.

6B. *Stone Avenue, West Kennet, Avebury CP* (OS SU108695) on 30.7.1991. (20.28)
Evocative Force. 'Porpoise' formation. Earth Logos signature. This signature appears to have included a half moon glyph, the first and only time this occurred. This may be the symbol of another planet, possibly Neptune, whose astrological sign is the trident.

6C. *Firs Farm, Beckhampton. Avebury CP* (OS SU082679) on 3.8.1991. (20.29)
Magnetic Centre. 'Porpoise' formation. Earth Logos signature.

6D. *Barbury Castle.* See TOP 2D above
Distributing Centre, reused.

*TOP 1991:7* (20.30 (map), 20.31)

7A. *Norridge Common, Upton Scudamore.* See TOP 4A above Emanating Energy, reused.

7B. *Waden Hill, West Kennet, Avebury CP* (OS SU108688) on 3.8.1991. (20.32) Evocative Force. 'Sperm Whale' formation.

7C. *Firs Farm, Beckhampton, Avebury CP* (OS SU081679) on 10.8.1991. (20.33) Magnetic Centre. 'Sperm Whale' formation.

7D. *Barbury Castle.* See TOP 2D above Distributing Centre, reused.

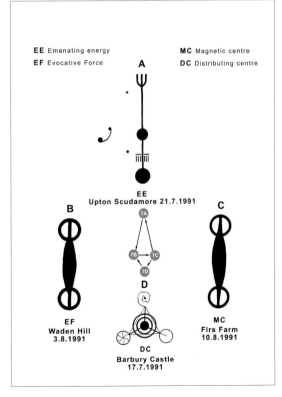

20.30 *The 'Whale' crop formation Triangles of Power of 1991 East Kennet area of Wiltshire*

20.29 *'Porpoise' TOP 1991:6C. Firs Farm Beckhampton (OS SU082679), 3.8.1991*

20.31 *'Sperm Whale' Triangle of Power 1991:7*

*20.32 '**Sperm Whale**' TOP 1991: 7B. Waden Hill (OS SU108688), 3.8.1991*

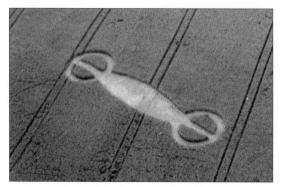

*20.33 '**Sperm Whale**' TOP 1991:7C. Beckhampton (OS SU081679), 10.8.1991*

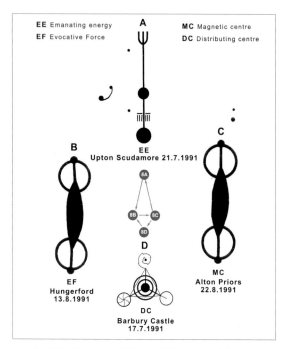

*20.34 '**Bottlenose Whale**' Triangle of Power 1991:8*

*20.35 '**Bottlenose Whale**' TOP 1991:8B Hungerford (OS SU308677), 13.8.1991*

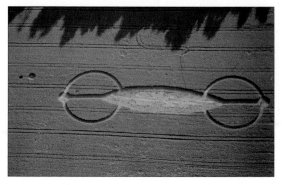

*20.36 '**Bottlenose Whale**' TOP 1991:8C. Alton Priors (OS SU128621), 22.8.1991*

*TOP 1991:8* (20.30, 20.34)

8A  *Norridge Common, Upton Scudamore.* See TOP 4A above

Emanating Energy, reused.

8B.  *Froxfield,    Hungerford    CP* (OS SU308677) on 13.8.1991. (20.35)

Evocative Force. 'Bottlenose Whale' formation.

8C.  *Wilcot, Alton Priors CP* (OS SU128621) on 22.8.1991. (20.36)

Magnetic Centre. 'Bottlenose Whale' formation. Earth Logos signature.

8D.  *Barbury Castle.* See TOP 2D above

Distributing Centre, reused.

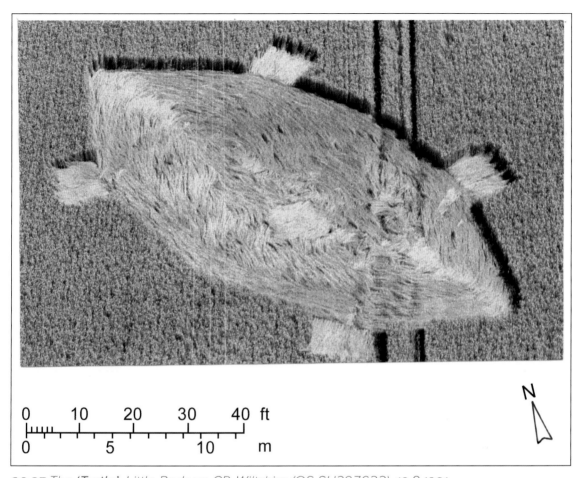

0  10  20  30  40  ft

0       5        10     m

N

*20.37 The 'Turtle'. Little Bedwyn CP, Wiltshire (OS SU297622), 19.8.1991*

## THE TURTLE CROP FORMATION (20.37)

One of the last crop formations to appear in the area in 1991 represented, I believe, a turtle, and was recognised as such by investigators at the time. No record survives of its exact location, but dowsing would suggest that it was found in Little Bedwyn CP, Wiltshire, almost exactly one mile south of Froxfield, its nominal find spot – OS SU297662. It appears to have arrived on 19.8.1991.

The excellent aerial photo by David Parker shows that the pointed oval body had a head at the south end, and that the four short, club-shaped legs were clawed. The geophysical crop patterning of the back would suggest that some attempt was made to represent the scutes or plates of the carapace shell. It is difficult to identify the crop formation turtle with any particular species, but the *Chelonia* Order generally is considered to be 'critically endangered.'

The formation occurred under a local overhead power line and unusual crop damage appeared around the power poles on either side suggesting some local electromagnetic effect may have occurred when the circle event happened. The formation was about 90 ft long and 40 ft wide.

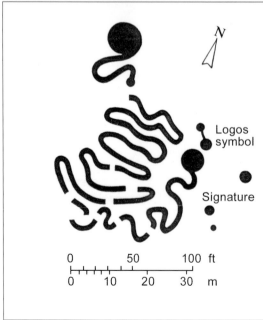

*20.38 Serpentine crop formation Highclose Farm, Hungerford CP, Hampshire (OS SU315686), 18.8.1991*

The formation may have been part of the Triangles of Power series, possibly the Evocative Force of a group which included the 'Trident Rod of Power' and the 'Solar Trimorph' as the Emanating Energy and Distributing Centre respectively. Unfortunately no corresponding turtle forming a Magnetic Centre was recorded. Time had run out, and at this late stage in the season the crop was being cut. I think it likely that the intention was to include other species of animals in following years as occurred with other thematic subjects in different parts of the country. The activities of hoaxers in the area from 1992 onwards may have put a closure on such a project.

## THE SERPENTINE CROP FORMATION (20.38)

This formation – almost the last to appear in Southern England in 1991 – was identified at the time as a snake. It appeared at Highclose Farm, Hungerford CP, Hampshire (OS SU315686) on 18.8.1991. It is not, strictly speaking, part of the Triangles of Power series, but represents to my mind a summary of the essential purpose of the TOP phenomenon, perhaps even a statement about a key aspect of the crop circle phenomenon as a whole. David Parker's photo brings out the strong geophysical quality of the formation. 'The pathways had strong dowsable energy counterflows. Some of them have no connection with the tramlines, making a hoax impossible,' as a crop circle investigator commented at the time.

A number of important elements make up this formation:

1. A straightforward Earth Logos signature on the south-east side.

2. A small Logos symbol on the east side consisting of a dumb-bell with a linked larger and smaller circle. This, I believe,

indicates that we are dealing not so much with a Cosmic Principle (although it is that, as we will see) but with an Entity.

3. This Entity has the overall shape of a squatting figure with a crop circle head about 20 ft in diameter, a fragmented snake-like body and a tail terminated by a 20 ft diameter circle. It is the serpentine body that identifies this Entity as: 'that ancient serpent, who is called the Devil and Satan, the deceiver of the whole world.' (*Revelation* 12:9)

But it is more than that, for it is a phenomenon which faces every person on the planet at personal level. In occult terms Djwhal Khul terms it the *Dweller on the Threshold*, which is the sum total of human negativity both at a corporate and a personal level. 'The selfishness, the sordid motives, the prompt response to evil impulses for which the human race has been distinguished has brought about a condition of affairs unparalleled in the system. A gigantic thought form hovers over the entire human family, built by men everywhere during the ages, energised by the insane desires and evil inclinations of all that is worst in man's nature, and kept alive by the promptings of his lower desires. *This thought form has to be broken up* [my italics] and dissipated by man himself during the latter part of this round before the conclusion of the cycle ...' (Bailey 1925, p. 948)

At a personal, human, level it results in the worst aspects of the Personality brought face to face with the Spirit and Soul of the human Monad – the *Angel* – versus the *Dweller*. Djwhal Khul identifies three areas of conflict in particular:

'1. Upon the physical plane ... the dense and the etheric forces.' ... [Perhaps symbolised by the circle at the end of the tail of the formation. These are faced] upon the *Path of Purification*.

2. Upon the astral plane ... the pairs of opposites [(emotions). Perhaps symbolised by the small circle below the head feature. These are faced] upon the *Path of Discipleship*.

3. Upon the mental plane the Angel of the Presence and the Dweller on the Threshold are brought face to face. [This is symbolised by the large 'head' circle and a separate circle some 25 ft in diameter which was found 150 ft north of the formation and on alignment with it. This happens] upon the *Path of Initiation*.' (Bailey 1951, pp. 54-55)

This profound formation is thus a mandala summarising the negative forces facing humanity in particular in the shape of the *Dweller on the Threshold* – a process which is in full operation at this time. It is no accident that the body of the *Dweller* is broken up in the crop formation into 10 compartments, for ten symbolises the limit of 'relative perfection'. (Bailey 1925, p. 827)

## THE RODS OF POWER

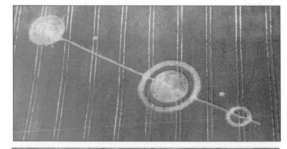

## THE THUNDERBOLTS

## THE KEYS

# 21. SYMBOL AND ARCHETYPE

*Do not suddenly break the branch, or*
*Hope to find*
*The white hart behind the white well.*
*Glance aside, not for lance, do not spell*
*Old enchantments. Let them sleep.*
*'Gently dip, but not too deep'.*
*Lift your eyes*
*Where the roads dip and where the roads rise*
*Seek only there*
*Where the grey light meets the green air*
*The hermit's chapel, the pilgrim's prayer.*

T.S. Eliot
*'Usk' (1936), in Collected Poems, 1909-1935*

We started this study of my experiences in connection with the crop circle phenomenon with magic and mystery, indeed 'the wilder shores' of mysticism and eschatological thought. To what end has all this led us?

T.S. Eliot in his *alter ego* as a leading publisher in the twentieth century would have been familiar with Arthurian legend and may have come across that Elizabethan play 'The Old Wives Tale' where Zantippa goes to the Well of Life and is spoken to by the head therein: "Gently dip but not too deep, for fear you make the golden beard to weep …". That brilliant Celtic scholar, the late Dr Anne Ross, identified the legend to which this play makes reference, namely that of the Scandinavian god of Wisdom, Mimir, whose decapitated head was preserved by Odin in a well, where it was capable of speech and prophesy. (Ross 1967, pp. 109-110)

In this study I have dipped into many such wells, in metaphorical terms, and various golden heads have spoken, to greater or lesser effect! Although ultimately we must return, like T.S. Eliot, to wider spiritual horizons, nevertheless these other esoteric excursions have not been without value, since they have provided a broader base for this spiritual study than in any of today's more conventional systems of religious belief.

## ASTROLOGY

Now we turn to what Djwhal Khul considered the greatest of the metaphysical systems of spiritual thought, *astrology*: 'the purest presentation of occult truth in the world at this time, because it is the science which deals with those conditioning and governing energies and forces which play through and upon the whole field of space and all that is found within that field.' (Bailey 1951, p. 5)

However we start with an immediate and serious problem. Ever since the beginning of the Western Enlightenment in the seventeenth century, astronomers and scientists have dismissed the notion that the movement of our Sun and Planets against the background of random groups of celestial bodies ('the Constellations') can in any way affect human life and destiny. Notwithstanding that many sections of human society, particularly in the East, consider that astrology is the art of judging the occult influences of the stars upon human affairs, and thus of critical importance in their lives; most educated, rational people in the West regard the subject as an illusion, indeed as frankly risible.

If however we start with the premiss that "space is an entity", and that it is 'with the life of this entity and with the forces and energies, the impulses and the rhythms, the cycles and the times and seasons' (Bailey 1951, p. 7) of its living components with which we are concerned; then what Djwhal Khul describes as esoteric, *scientific* astrology and the principles that lie behind it are truly relevant to humanity. We start with the concept that the heavenly bodies and their groupings in the Cosmos represent the conglomeration of the basic, raw, physical elements of Entities that at other levels of existence (explored elsewhere in this study) have life, intelligence and purpose. It is that divine purpose for humanity that forms the basis of what might be termed sacred astrology, which is the subject of this chapter and those that follow.

## BEROSUS

Marcus Vitruvius Pollio, a clever Roman architect and engineer, scoured the libraries of first century Rome for material for his monumental study on the building sciences. His purview, particularly in relation to the orientation of buildings and what might be loosely termed geomantic studies, also included astronomy and astrology. In Book IX of his *Ten Books of Architecture* he states:

'The rest which relates to astrology, and the effects produced upon human life by the twelve signs, the five planets, the sun and the moon, must be left to the discussions of the Chaldeans, whose profession it is to cast nativities, and by means of the configurations of the stars to explain the past and the future. The talent, the ingenuity, and reputation of those who come from the country of the Chaldeans, is manifest from the discoveries they have left us in writing. Berosus was the first of them. He settled in the island and state of Cos, and there established a school. Afterwards came Antipater and Achinapolus, which latter not only gave rules for predicting a man's fate by a knowledge of the time of his birth, but even by that of the moment wherein he was conceived. In respect of natural philosophy Thales the Milesian, Anaxagoras of Clazomenæ, Pythagoras the Samian, Xenophanes of Colophon, Democritus the Abderite, have published systems which explain the mode in which Nature is regulated, and how every effect is produced. Eudoxus, Endæmon, Callippus, Melo, Philip, Hipparchus, Aratus, and others, following in the steps of the preceding, found, by the use of instruments, the rising and setting of the stars and the changes of the seasons, and left treatises thereon for the use of posterity. Their learning will be admired by mankind, because, added to the above, they appear as if by divine inspiration to have foretold the weather at particular seasons of the year. For a knowledge of these matters reference must therefore be made to their labours and investigation.' (Gwilt 1826, pp. 282-283)

Modern astrologers would like one to believe that their subject in its present construct is of immense age, stretching back to the beginning of recorded history. It is not so. The earliest reference to the twelve signs of the Zodiac (that is to say the Houses), as opposed to definitions of the constellation patterns, dates only to 410 BC. This is on the earliest surviving horoscope 'for the son of Shuma-usar, son of Shuma-iddina, descendant of Deke, who was born 'when the Moon was below the Horn of the Scorpion, Jupiter in the Fish, Venus in the Bull, Saturn in the Crab, Mars in the Twins. Mercury, which had set ... was ... invisible.'' (Parker D. and J. 1983, p. 23)

Slightly later, c.400 BC, there is a reference to Babylonian astrology in the Hippocratic medical work *On Diets*. In the centuries before the birth of Christ, 'astrology appealed to various sections of Greek society, among them not only philosophers and scientists, but such men as Hippocrates, the physician and 'father of medicine', who taught astrology to his students so that they could discover the 'critical days' in an illness. He is said to have remarked that any man who does not understand astrology is a fool.' (Parker D. and J. 1983, pp. 36-37) The medical connection is significant. Kos (or Cos) was the leading medical centre of the East Greek world centred around the shrine of Asklepios, and the focus of a substantial pilgrimage trade, both patients and practitioners. A major study of current medical practice *The Hippocratic Treatise* was compiled at Kos between 430 and 330 BC. Such studies were given a major fillip in 331 BC with the founding of the Library at Alexandria, which was to become the focus of scientific research in the classical world for the next thousand years.

Who was Berosus? He is traditionally described as being a bilingual priest of Baal (i.e. a Hellenist) from the Seleucid kingdom who wrote a history of Babylonia c. 290 BC. (Boardman, Griffin and Murray 1986, pp. 201 and 845) It is likely that he was one of the many clever Hellenes in the late third century BC who trawled the ancient civilizations of Egypt and Mesopotamia looking for easily assimilated, esoteric knowledge. By and large they were not very successful. The subtle Egyptian priest was as likely to treat the Greek neophyte with the same suave evasions as the present day Oxbridge don hands out to eager American PhD students! As Plato recounts in Timaeus, the old priest of Sais said to the Greek philosopher Solon, (c. 600-560 BC) "... you Greeks are always children ... for you possess no truly antique tradition, no notion hoary with time ..." Berosus was evidently luckier or smarter than most. Having assembled the elements of his new system he set up business at Kos where he could be assured of a steady turn-over of curious students, who would spread his ideas throughout the Greek-speaking world. The special features of his system, which has made it such a profitable business for generations of astrologers, relied on a restructuring of certain ancient mandalic principles in relation to the developing study of astronomy.

## CHALDEAN ASTROLOGY

What might be termed Chaldean astrology has been traced back at least to the second millennium BC in the form of what is termed 'Omen literature', relating particularly to national and royal interests. The collective propositions of *Enūma Anu Enlil* (Barton 1994, p. 12) of early second millennium BC date, is an example of such formulations: 'when the Moon occults with Jupiter, that year a king will die ... when Jupiter goes out from behind the moon, there will be hostility in the land.' Accurate and tabulated observations were not made until the mid seventh century BC (Barton 1994, p. 14) and here they relate particularly to the movements of the planets and the moon, and eclipses of the sun.

*21.1 Symbols of Cosmic Deities on a stele of the Assyrian King Assurnasirpal II (reigned 883-859 BC) from Nimrud*

1994, 13) Likewise glyphs of the solar, lunar and stellar deities also appear, and were particularly used on stelai set up as boundary stones commemorating royal proclamations. A stele of the Assyrian king Assurnasirpal II, who reigned 883-859 BC (21.1) shows symbols of *Aššur* (helmet); *Šamaš*, the Sun God (winged solar disc); *Sin*, the Moon God

*21.2 Symbols of Cosmic Deities on a boundary stone of King Nazi-maruttaš of Babylon (reigned 1307–1282 BC)*

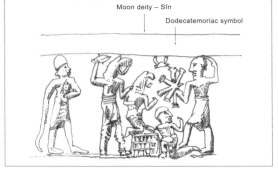

*21.3 Dodecatemoriac symbol on grey haematite cylinder seal of the Old Babylonian period (c. 1950-1651 BC) from Nērebtum*

In the construction of the ephemerides (i.e. the computed places of a heavenly body for every day of a given period) for calculation of the lunar calendar, the names of constellations, especially along the ecliptic, are given. The Zodiac, however, as we understand it, does not appear.

This is not to say that the symbols and nomenclature did not exist. By about 700 BC in the *Mul-Apin* text, a list of seventeen constellations contained names of ten of the twelve now known as Zodiacal signs. (Barton (crescent); *Adad*, the storm God (thunderbolt); and *Ištar*, Goddess of Sex and Warfare (on a stellar disc). (Black and Green 1992, p. 31) A boundary stone or *kudurru* of Nazi-maruttaš king of Babylon c. 1307–1282 BC (21.2) has not only these glyphs but also a scorpion, then a symbol of the goddess *Ishara* (now identified as the Zodiac sign of Scorpio) and a lamp, a symbol of the god *Nusku*. (Black and Green 1992, p. 145) There may even have been the beginning of a dodecatemoriac, mandalic system in Mesopotamia since a seal of the Old Babylonian period (21.3) shows such a symbol as a wheel structure behind a 'crescent-shaped' god, possibly *Sin*, identifying the lunar 'mansions' standing in the moon's path. (Black and Green 1992, p. 20)

An actual Zodiac list appears on a clay tablet of probably fifth century BC date and from Babylon. (BM 77824) It equates the twelve months of the year with the constellation Houses of the Zodiac. It has also added certain significant constellations which appear in the relevant months, such as the Pleiades (May), Orion (June) and Pegasus (March), which do not form part of the later Zodiacal canon. (Finkel and Seymour 2008, p. 194) In addition to the information included on the tablet, I have included in the approximate and simplified tabulation below the Babylonian names of the Zodiac Houses together with the Hellenistic or classical names when the systems merged to provide a definitive classification around 400 BC. (Whitfield 2001, pp. 19 and 22)

| Month | Babylonian Constellation c. 700 BC | Babylonian Name c. 700 BC | Babylonian Constellation c. 400 BC | Classical Zodiac | Classical Name |
|---|---|---|---|---|---|
| April | Luhunga | The Hired Man | Luhunga | Aries | The Ram |
| May | Mul/Guanna | The Mane/The Bull of Anu | Mul | Pleiades/Taurus | The Bull |
| June | Mastabbagal-gal | The Great Twins | Mas | Gemini | The Twins |
| July | Allul | Meaning not known | Kusu | Cancer | The Crab |
| August | Urgula | The Lion | Ura | Leo | The Lion |
| September | Absin | The Furrow | Absin | Virgo | The Maiden |
| October | Zibanitum | The Scales | Zibanitu | Libra | The Balance |
| November | Girtab | The Scorpion | Girtab | Scorpio | The Scorpion |
| December | Pabilsag | The Archer | Pa | Sagittarius | The Archer |
| January | Suhurmas | The Goatfish | Suhur | Capricornus | The Sea Goat |
| February | Gula | The Great Star or Giant | Gu | Aquarius | The Water-man |
| March | Zibbati | The Tails | Zib | Pisces | The Fisher |

## THE ZODIAC COMPILATION TABLETS (21.4, 21.5)

Possibly the earliest graphic representations of the Signs of the Zodiac (as opposed to symbols of the Mesopotamian deities) that have survived are shown on fragments known as the Zodiac Compilation Tablets. (Finkel and Seymour 2008, pp. 195-6) They consist of the top half of one tablet (1), at the time of writing at the Staatliche Museen zu Berlin; and two fragments of another tablet (2), the top half also in the Berlin museum, and the bottom half in the Louvre Museum, Paris. The tablets are conventionally dated to the third to second century BC reign of an Antiochus (c. 281-164 BC). However the pictorial register may refer to an auspicious occasion, such as the capture of Babylon in 312 BC by Seleucus, effectively marking the foundation of the Seleucid dynasty. The fragments of these tablets are recorded to have been found in Uruk (Warka), and I believe came from the temple C complex of the Eanna temple (Uruk IV).

Tablet 1 has on one side 'part of a circle divided into twelve sections, of which 6, 7, 8 and 9 survive, which are combined with Pisces, Aries, Taurus and Gemini.' (Finkel and Seymour *loc. cit.*) Evidently the Zodiac by this stage was in its Hellenistic format. On the other side of the tablet is an illustrated zone with long cuneiform 'omen' prognostications above and below it with similar compilations on the reverse side. This upper zone was probably matched by a similar illustrated panel on the reverse, lower part of the tablet (now missing) as was the case of tablet 2. Each panel illustrates the astronomical state of a section of the night sky along the line of the Ecliptic on a particular occasion, including the planetary positions and the moon phase. Tablet 2 has two adjoining panels and covers two only of the Houses of the Zodiac, Leo and Virgo. It is likely therefore that the complete set of the Zodiac Compilation Tablets amounted to some six tablets in all, of which only two survive in part covering three Houses. The Zodiac Houses along the Ecliptic are shown in reverse, i.e. looking from space towards planet Earth, which suggests that the series was copied from the outside of an astrological globe. The first globes of this type that have survived belong to the Roman period, of which the best known is the 'Farnese Atlas': a statue of Atlas carrying an astrological globe dating to the first century BC. (Whitfield 2001, p. 27)

*Tablet 1, Ecliptic Zone of Taurus (21.4)*

There are three elements in this register, which taken from left to right comprise:

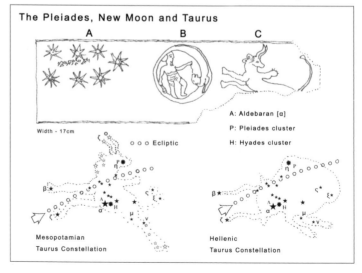

*21.4 Zodiac Compilation Tablet 1, pictorial register*
*The Eanna Temple, Uruk. Third to second century BC*

A. Seven stars arranged as two lines of three with the seventh star placed between the rows at the far end. A cuneiform inscription reading *Mas-tab-ba-gal-gal-la* (or similar) indicating in this case the *Pleiades*, is located between the rows of stars.

These stars, which also appear as seven dots in other contexts, are of considerable interest. 'The symbol of seven dots ... is first known in unequivocal form in Mitannian glyptic art, [from about 1500 BC onwards] and became common in the Neo-Assyrian and Neo-Babylonian Periods. ... the dots are normally shown simply in two rows of three, with the seventh dot placed between the rows at the far end. From ... Middle Assyrian times ... the seven dots appear as a symbol in close association with other clearly astral symbols ... In Assyrian, Babylonian and later art, they were regarded as a representation of the Pleiades.' (Black and Green 1992, p. 162) They were sometimes shown as stars (as here) rather than dots.

During the millennia from about 3500 BC onwards there must have been clever, psychic priests watching the stars on the Ziggurats or 'temple towers' of Mesopotamia who were not only studying the heavens, but were also communicating with the Intelligences of this and other worlds. Zarathustra on the banks of the Oxus River some 1500 miles to the east was also contacted at this time by the seven Holy Immortals, the Amesha Spentas. (Chapter 14) Only thus could the Babylonian priests have known of the 'Seven and Seven', whose nature and functions are described in detail in Chapters 12 and 15.

The primary Seven, represented by dots, are the Seven Archangels presided over by the Archangel Michael, Lord of planet Earth, the seventh dot placed between the rows, at the end. The significance of their being distinguished by dots rather than stars is that They belong to our planetary system. Above the Seven of planet Earth are the Seven Sacred Planets of our solar system discussed in Chapter 15, which are centres (chakras) of the Solar Logos. Two of these are shown on tablet 2, namely Jupiter (Marduk) and Mercury (Nabu). Of the other Sacred Planets the Babylonian name for Saturn was Ninurta and that for Venus Ishtar.

There are other septenary stellar groupings beyond our system, the next being that which comprises the energy centres of Archon (see Chapter 16) of whom the Mesopotamian astrologers were already aware. They are symbolised here by the Seven Stars of the Pleiades (whose star Alcyone is in itself the Third Ray of this group). Furthermore the Seven Lords who comprise the Council of Archon can also be identified as discrete Babylonian star systems:

| Ray | Star System | Babylonian Name | Meaning |
|-----|-------------|-----------------|---------|
| 1 | Merak | Akanna | The Lord of Heaven |
| 2 | Sirius | Du-shisha | The Director |
| 3 | Alcyone | Temenu | Foundation Stone |
| 4 | Aldebaran | Dil-gan | Messenger of Light |
| 5 | Thuban | Tir-an-na | Life of Heaven |
| 6 | Betelgeuse | Gula | Great Healing Goddess |
| 7 | The Solar System | Šamaš | Light of the Sun |

These epithets and honorific titles of the members of the Septead of Archon appear to be entirely appropriate, given the nature of the Beings concerned.

B. A lunar disc showing the *New Moon*. The bearded Deity (left) holding a club in his right hand and a lion-serpent on a leash in his left hand is presumably Nanna-Suen (Sîn), the moon god, whose animal was a lion-dragon. (Black and Green 1992, p. 135)

C. A bull prancing to the left but looking to the right. In the context of the Pleiades it must represent *Taurus*, but has some interesting features, not helped by missing its lower rear half through a break in the tablet. The animal itself is the humped Asiatic species, but its main interest is that it does not represent the conventional, Hellenic head and shoulders with the tips of the horns marked by Taurus *Beta* (El Nath) or Taurus *Zeta*, neither of which are described as horns in Babylonia but as the furthest extremity of Taurus as Shur-narkapti-sha-iltanu ('the star of the Bull towards the north') and Shur-narkapti-sha-shūtū ('the star

of the Bull towards the south') respectively. The picture on the tablet would suggest that these stars represent the termination of the front legs, with the Hyades marking the front of the body, and that Aldebaran (Taurus Alpha), is not the 'Eye of Taurus' as established in the Hellenistic Zodiac, but Ku, I-ku or I-ku-u 'the Leading Star of Stars marking the heart of Taurus.' Its ancient Akkadian name, Dil-oaw, 'The Messenger of Light', perhaps reflected the importance of Aldebaran certainly as the focus of and possibly representing the entire Zodiac House of Taurus. (Hinckley Allen 1963, p. 383) If the horns are transposed for the front legs of Taurus then, conjecturally, Taurus *Mu* and *Nu*, together with Taurus *Sigma* and *Xi*, represent the legs and tail respectively. The Pleiades then fall into place as the head of the Bull with Alcyone (Taurus *Eta*) as the eye of Taurus.

If this identification is correct, then the tips of the horns would be represented by Perseus *Zeta* and *Omicron*. The present, rather unsatisfactory, representation of the head and shoulders only of Taurus, instituted during the Hellenistic period, was no doubt contrived so that Aldebaran would become the Eye of the Bull. A view in the classical world that also viewed Taurus as a complete figure is echoed by the writer Hyginus who localised the Pleiades as part of the body of Taurus. (Hinckley Allen 1963, p. 392)

*Tablet 2, Ecliptic Zones of Leo and Virgo* (21.5)

There are two pictorial registers on opposite sides of this tablet which fit together to provide a continuous ecliptic

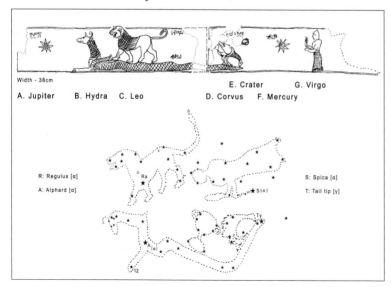

Width - 38cm

A. Jupiter    B. Hydra    C. Leo          D. Corvus    F. Mercury
                                   E. Crater    G. Virgo

R: Regulus [α]          Ra          S: Spica [α]
A: Alphard [α]                      T: Tail tip [γ]

*21.5 Zodiac Compilation Tablet 2, pictorial registers*
*The Eanna Temple, Uruk. Third to second century BC*

zone. Taken from left to right the following astrological elements are identifiable:

A. An eight-pointed star with a cuneiform inscription reading MARDUK (or similar) to its left identifies it as the planet *Jupiter*.

B. *Hydra, the Water-snake* or dragon, identified as such by a cuneiform inscription above the body. On this tablet it is shown as a composite animal with the head, neck, winged shoulders and forelimbs of the great Babylonian dragon, Tiāmat, meaning 'the sea' (Black and Green 1992, p. 177), and the body of a scaled serpent. This archetypal creative force is shown on 'a uranographic stone from the Euphrates, of 1200 B.C., "identified with the source of the fountains of the great deep." (Hinckley Allen 1963, p. 248) Star 12 may have represented the forepaw of the celestial Tiāmat.

As a constellation it stretches from its head (6 stars) south of Cancer and just north of the celestial equator to its tail in the southern hemisphere between Libra and Centaurus. Its ancient length was perhaps slightly shorter than the present constellation, with its termination perhaps represented by Hydra Gamma. This may have been the Akkadian star En-Te-Na-Mas-Luv or En-Te-Na-Mas-Mur, the Assyrian Etsen-tsiri, 'the Tail-tip.' (Hinckley Allen 1963, p. 248) On the second register the Tail-tip is shown as being pecked by the celestial raven or crow, *Corvus* (D). The star *Alphard* (Hydra Alpha) is derived from Al fard al shūja = 'The solitary One in the Serpent.' It has also been variously described by medieval astronomers as the serpent's backbone, neck and heart.

C. *Leo, the Winged Lion*, perhaps the most important House of the Zodiac, associated with the Sun. In tablet 2 he stands on the back of Hydra and is identified by a cuneiform inscription near its tail with the meaning of Arū (or similar), a lion. (Hinckley Allen 1963, p. 253) This distinctive constellation system had already been identified more or less in its Hellenistic form by the Babylonian period, and represents a crouching lion just north of the celestial Equator. The Babylonian artist who drew the lion on the clay tablet originally made it too long, and had to rub out and redraw the hind quarters and tail. The star Leo Alpha (Regulus) was the Akkadian Amil-gal-ur, 'King of the Celestial Sphere.'

D. *Corvus, the Raven (or Crow)*. The bird is clearly shown on the tablet as pecking the end of the tail of Hydra. 'Nor is the reason for the association of Corvus with Hydra evident, although there is a Euphratean myth ... making it one of the monster ravens of the brood of Tiāmat that Hydra represented; and upon a tablet appears a title that may be for Corvus as the **Great Storm Bird** or **Bird of the Desert**, to which Tiāmat gave sustenance, just as Aratos [early third century BC] described [the bird] pecking the folds of Hydra.' (Hinckley Allen 1963, p. 181) This small constellation is one of the original 48 constellations of the Ancient Greeks and in legend was the sacred bird of the god Apollo, and was also associated with *Crater* (the cup) (E). There is a damaged cuneiform inscription above the bird.

E. *Crater, the Cup*. This small representation of a two-handled cup on its side has the base facing upwards. There is a short cuneiform inscription above it. It may be associated with the *Mixing Bowl* in the Euphratean myth of Istar-Kirke. (Hinckley Allen 1963, p. 183) *Crater Alpha* has from antiquity been identified with the base of the cup, as in the Latin designation for it, *Fundus Vasis*.

F. An eight-pointed star with a cuneiform inscription reading Nabu (or similar) to its left identifies it as the planet *Mercury*.

G. *Virgo, the Virgin.* This is the last identifiable stellar feature in this register, but there may have been more since the end of the tablet has been damaged. There appears to be part of a cuneiform inscription to the right of the figure. The woman represented stands holding a barley (or wheat) stalk in both hands, which is to be identified with *Alpha Virginis* which in Babylonian times represented the whole constellation.

In Mesopotamia the woman may have personified Nanaya, the wife of Bel or Marduk, the patronal god of the city of Babylon. (Black and Green 1992, p. 128) She wears the peaked, horned cap as a mark of her divinity and in her long flounced skirt reflects the characteristics of a *lama* (Akkadian *lamassu*), a beneficent, anonymous female Deity. Her holding a barley or wheat stalk may identify her also with the goddess Šala of the Hurrian peoples of northern Mesopotamia, indicating that she was an agricultural Deity linked with the constellation then called the Furrow (now Virgo), whose brightest star, in modern terminology, is *Spika* or 'ear of grain'. (See Black and Green 1992, p. 173.)

Thus the stages can now be traced by which a numinous, agricultural emblem, 'the ear of grain', is first identified with a particular star *Spika*. By extension the constellation round *Spika* is next identified with a Mesopotamian agricultural goddess, Šala, who holds the ear of grain. Finally by the second century BC, the centre of attention has shifted from the barley stalk to the woman herself, who has become Virgo the Maiden.

Particular attention has been given to these drawings on these two surviving Zodiac Compilation Tablets, not merely because these are the earliest graphic representations of the Houses of the Ecliptic and their associated constellations, but because they illustrate a major stage of the shift around 200 BC to the Hellenistic Zodiac as formulated by some such person as Berosus – a system which has survived in all essentials to the present day.

Two aspects stand out even from the limited material covered in these tablets. The names of constellations or months with agricultural connotations tend to be replaced under Hellenistic influence by reference to legendary subjects. Secondly, the earlier importance of a particular, notable star in a section of the Ecliptic is transferred to the shadowy, projected outline of an animal or subject in a surrounding constellation cluster of stars. One of the earliest representations of a celestial map of Ptolemaic date is that copied during the Umayyad period as a ceiling fresco. It occurs in a domed room of a bathhouse at the fortified palace of Qusayr Amra in Jordan, built in the eighth century, sometime between 723 and 743 AD, by Walid Ibn Yazid, the future Umayyad caliph Walid II. Most of the Hellenistic constellations are represented, although now in a damaged condition.

### EGYPTIAN ASTROLOGY

The state of the art in Egypt was probably less helpful to Berosus, except in one respect. In its origins the system was aimed at predicting the rising of Sothis, the Dog Star, and the beginning of the all-important inundation. It was therefore primarily an astronomical system, and the main Egyptian contribution was to devise a more or less accurate calendar of twelve months of thirty days each; plus five or six (in a leap year) epagomenal days. The Egyptians also systematised a daily equinoctial system of twelve daylight and twelve night hours, which under the Hellenistic and Egyptian systems were hours of equal length. The other distinctive feature of this system was the use of decans, thirty six constellations identified from their heliacal (i.e. the last hour before sunrise) rising. (Lamy 1981, pp. 74-5)

In her study of ancient astronomy, Solange de Mailly Nesle states:

'It is difficult, in any respect, to speak of true astrology among the Egyptians, except insofar as astrology may have been accessible solely to the initiated, royalty, and the priesthood, and may have thus far eluded rediscovery in our era. (De Mailly Nesle 1981, p. 28)

'I am inclined toward the latter viewpoint: astrological practices definitely existed in Egypt, but astrology was of a mystical nature, beyond the secular sphere, and its lore was only revealed to the initiated, who were seeking a means of salvation and ultimate freedom for the soul. This was an esoteric form of knowledge, instead of being an esoteric science, as it later became among the Greeks. Pythagoras must have been aware of this occult knowledge, which set the stage for dissemination of Chaldean astrology.' (De Mailly Nesle 1981, p. 28, fn. 1)

*21.6 Zodiac ceiling relief, Osiris Shrine, Temple of Hathor, Dendera, Egypt, c. 50 BC*

Berosus brought together the calendrical features of the Egyptian system, the symbolism of the Chaldean astrologers and the Pythagorean numerology of the Greeks to construct a truly elegant astrological model. None of this would have been possible however without the accurate observational material which had been collected in the temple libraries of Mesopotamia, which provided the bedrock of his system. By subtly counterpoising a fixed structure of the heavens against the movements of the wandering stars (including the sun) a brilliant, flexible system of prognostication was devised suitable for any event or person, anywhere. The ancient world immediately fell on these ideas which were taken up, developed and adapted to the local systems. Nowhere is this better demonstrated than the Zodiac on the ceiling of the chapel dedicated to the rebirth of Osiris at the Egyptian temple of Hathor at Dendera. (Cauville 1997, pp. 7-38) (21.6) The temple and the Zodiac date to the mid first century BC. The Zodiac comprises the circumpolar stars ("the stars which never set"), whose identification goes back to the third millennium BC, and the twelve zodiacal constellations or houses. The southern constellation includes Sirius (the dog-star identified with Isis) and Orion (Osiris). The thirty six decans process round the border of the figure and the four cardinal points are symbolically marked by four goddesses. This great mandala, now in the Louvre, is of extraordinary importance, and represents one of the last great statements of the cosmic mysteries of Ancient Egypt. It brings together the primary constellations (both in the northern and southern hemispheres), the Houses of the Zodiac, a basic statement about the movements of the planets, and the movement of 'time' in terms of the progression of the decans. However, this is still not the Zodiac exactly as the concept developed in Mesopotamia and ancient Greece.

The Zodiac was a stimulus to other new belief systems of this period, notably Mithraism, which emerged in the third century BC in Cilicia and was one of the most potent religions of the Roman Empire until suppressed by organised Christianity

(Cumont 1956, p. 188 *et seq.*) The Zodiac was taken up because it worked as a rational structure. And it worked, and works, because behind it lies a metaphysical reality, as al-Ghazali rightly observed:

'The visible world was made to correspond to the world invisible, and there is nothing in this world but is a symbol of something in that other world.'

Abu Hamid Muhammad al-Ghazali
(AD 1058-1111)

Berosus astutely made this reality the mandalic core of his system, possibly intuitively, but perhaps more likely he took it from esoteric teaching of the Magi priests of Persian Zoroastrianism. This teaching in turn was based on an ancient Indo-Aryan system of spiritual transformation, the Great Turning, which is the subject of this study. This profound structure of the ultimate realities of existence has nothing to do with the casting of horoscopes for paying customers, to which conventional astrology has long been traduced, but is a living tradition setting out the means of apotheosis for mankind. Indeed the very name *Zodiac* is a clue to the origins of the system, since it is derived from the Ancient Greek *zōidiakòs kýklos,* meaning 'cycle or circle of little animals' – the wheel of animals. '*Zōē*' means 'life' in general and since the signs are not exclusively of animal forms, the more appropriate identification would appear to be the Wheel of Life.

# 22. THE GREAT TURNING

*"Amid the whirling forces, I stand confused. I know them not, for, during all my past, they swept me up and down the land wherein I moved, blinded and unaware. From place to place and point to point, they drove me up and down the land and nowhere was there rest.*

*I know them now and here I stand and will not move until I know the Law which governs all this movement up and down the land. I may revolve and turning face the many different ways; I face some wide horizons and yet today I stand.*

*I will determine for myself the way to go. Then onward I will move. I will not travel up and down the land nor turn in space. But onward I will move."*

*From the 'Old Commentary'*

Bailey 1951, p. 20

## THE WHEEL OF LIFE

The Wheel of Life, the Great Turning, is a peculiarly Indo-Aryan concept with origins that can be traced to central Asia during the E pi-Palaeolithic period. It was carried eastwards across the Bering Straits before the landbridge was broken, and became the medicine wheel of the North American Indian. It was taken southwards into the Indian sub-continent and became a feature of Vedic and later, Hindu belief. The mandalic pattern survived amongst older, shamanistic, groups such as the animist traditions of Tibet and Mongolia. By following the linguistic patterns across western Asia and Europe, the wheel symbol can be traced through the Zoroastrian systems and is implicit in the Sufi concept of Tasawwuf, more generally known as Tarīqah or the spiritual path in Islam.

'A spiritual path is one through which man is able to transcend his own human limitations and approach the Divine. Therefore, the path itself cannot be man-made ... Anyone who accepts the reality of the spiritual life must accept the fact that the spiritual way must contain within itself a grace which is not man-made, that it must ultimately be a path which God has ordained and placed before man to follow.' (Nasr, Seyyed Hossein 2000, p. 123)

Which brings us back to the Wheel of Life, or Zodiac, where astrology's 'contemplative and symbolic side conforms closely to the basic spirit of Islam, which is to realise that all multiplicity comes from Unity and to seek to integrate the particular in the Universal.' (Nasr, Seyyed Hossein 1978, p. 165)

The Wheel of Life can be traced in symbol and esoteric teaching across the Celtic cultures of Central and Western Europe. Although greatly divided in both space and time, there is a surprising homogeneity in their religious beliefs so that, say, Irish symbols can be directly illuminated by the Vedas of India. This cultural retentiveness has been noted by Alwyn and Brinley Rees in the ancient social structures of Celtic Britain (Rees, A. and B. 1961, p. 187 for example), but its relevance in terms of belief systems has been largely overlooked in the narrow specialisms of Celtic scholarship.

The fact of Indo-Aryan cultural expansionism and diffusion can hardly be gainsaid in the light of the explicit linguistic evidence. Its cultural mechanism however is still a matter of considerable debate, especially in terms of coordinating the archaeological and linguistic evidence. Colin Renfrew makes a case for postulating the arrival of those peoples, who were to develop the Celtic cultural characteristics in Western Europe, before 4000 BC, bringing with them the genesis of pastoralism and agriculture. (Renfrew 1987, p. 245)

However a critical assessment by J. P. Mallory would posit a more uncertain archaeological-linguistic correlation, and associates Indo-Aryan peoples with the 'Corded Ware' cultures of Western Europe arriving in the third millennium BC. (Mallory 1989, p. 244)

The view that 'Celtic' culture originally spread from Western Europe, more particularly Iberia, has more recently been promulgated by Barry Cunliffe and John T. Koch. A multi-disciplinary study involving various authorities in archaeology, genetics, language and literature has been brought together under the title *Celtic from the West*. (Cunliffe and Koch 2010)

Renfrew's suggested time-scale would agree well with the symbolic evidence from the Boyne valley passage tombs of c. 3200 BC (carbon 14 evidence) (O'Kelly 1982, p. 12) where the earliest glyphs of the Wheel of Life occur. Indeed the oral mythology of the arrival of these peoples is almost certainly reflected in that extraordinary Irish survival, the *Lebor Gabàla Érenn* (The Book of the Conquest of Ireland), even though distorted by the hour-glass of Celtic Christianity. (O'Rahilly 1984, p. 90 et seq.)

Corporately the esoteric belief systems of the Indo-Aryan peoples constitute one of the premier strands of the Ancient Wisdom, which was introduced in Chapter 4. The oral traditions and secretive nature of their belief systems are major problems for those attempting to unlock the gates of their mysteries.

For example, Caesar, writing c. 52-51 BC, says about the Druids: 'they learn by heart a great number of verses', but it would appear that nothing was transmitted in written form. Certainly nothing has survived, which is regrettable since according to Caesar it included 'many things, concerning the stars and their motion, the extent of the world and of our earth, and the "nature of things" (*natura rerem*), and the limitless power and majesty of the immortal gods.' Above all, the immortality of the Soul and its rebirth; all matters considered in some detail in this study. (Chadwick 1966, pp. 44 and 52)

Despite the valiant attempts of various Celtic scholars to construct a viable religious structure from references in classical writers and early medieval transcriptions, only the faintest echoes of ancient folk beliefs survive, and nothing of the body of teaching that made the Druids one of the premier mystery schools of the Indo-Aryan tradition. Likewise the dogged scholarship of modern archaeologists has assembled the flotsam and jetsam of Celtic material culture in abundance, but the results give little clue to the metaphysics behind the relics, since obsessive secrecy reduced even the most sublime symbols to little more than the briefest notation or aide-mémoire. The stark presentation of the four or eight-spoked 'solar' wheel, which is the primary Celtic mandala of the Great Turning, should be compared with the rich symbolism, for instance, on Tibetan mandalas, expressing the same concepts.

The very intensity of archaeological research, which has yielded for the first time an adequate body of dated material and sites, makes it possible now to employ a truly diagnostic approach to the subject. Old problems such as the nature of the Indo-Aryan migrations can now be tackled afresh from the archaeological as well as the linguistic angle. But archaeological expertise, even the most far-ranging multi-disciplinary variety, is not enough when considering the beliefs of an ancient people. Joscelyn Godwin identified the problem in his study of classical mystery religions: 'Too long have we learnt about ancient religion from unbelieving academics or Christian chauvinists, divorcing it on the one hand from life and on the other from faith.' (Godwin 1981, p. 7) To regard the mythology and religious relics of former cultures merely as ethnological curiosities to be explained away in terms of contemporary concerns with ecology, technology, economics and social organisation is to close the door on the most profound motivations and experiences of ancient man. To understand the mind of the shaman and the tribal peoples passing through the rites of passage, it is necessary for the researcher to enter into their world, to travel into other levels of reality, to partake in their rites and to meet their gods.

The elucidation of the Great Turning therefore represents a radically new interpretation of Indo-Aryan symbolism and its place within the wider context of prehistoric metaphysics.

The Wheel of Life is a mandala of spiritual transformation round which mankind, both individually and corporately, must pass to achieve theophany. It is not the only ancient symbolic paradigm however. There were in the prehistoric world of north-west Europe three basic symbolic mandalas which illustrated the evolving path of the Soul, the Wheel of Life, the Tree of Life, and the Trojan Maze.

The Tree of Life is a statement in *organic* terms of the spiritual growth of man through various levels. One of its most developed and sublime expressions is the Ladder of Jacob used in Kabbalistic teaching today. It is not covered here, and the reader is referred to the leading authority in this field, Z'ev Ben Shimon Halevi (Warren Kenton) whose principal work is perhaps *Tree of Life: an Introduction to the Cabala* (1976, London: Rider).

We will return to the Wheel of Life after consideration of the Trojan Maze.

## THE TROJAN MAZE

### *The ancient name*

This, the oldest type of maze representation, is sometimes described as *Cretan* or *Trojan*. Nigel Pennick discusses the origins of both names in detail. (Pennick 1990, pp. 21 ff.) An ancient Greek coin of Knossos, Crete, shows this maze on the reverse referring to the classical Labyrinth and its association with the legendary King Minos of c. 1600 BC and the Minotaur monster. The name *Truia* (Troy) occurs associated with this maze on the Etruscan Tragliatella wine jug (seventh century BC), evidently referring to the *Lusus Trojae* (Game of Troy) where the maze was the ground layout for complex cavalry manoeuvres. (Pennick 1990, p. 59) The name *Troy* is also cognate with North European,

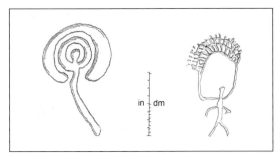

*22.1 Petroglyphs of the Sacred Cloak of Gaia. West Horton, Northumberland (left) and Alta, Finnmark (right)*

Old German and Celtic words meaning 'turn', referring to the twists and turns of the maze layout.

The Maze is, in a sense, an organic approach to developing spiritual consciousness. In my Introduction, I recounted how, under what was I believe its ancient name, *the Great Turning*, it came to be the title of this book. As a prehistoric petroglyph it is without doubt both the oldest and perhaps the most profound of the symbols concerning the apotheosis of mankind. Its ancient name in the Celtic world of the British Isles was perhaps Sidi or the *Round of Incarnations* in Old Welsh. Another term may have been Y Cantrefi or the *States of Being*.

### The sacred image

The Maze symbol is built up round an image of the planetary Earth Goddess, Gaia, Who was experienced by my late friend Paul Bura as *Ayesha* (Aesu). The image is of the goddess whose body and outstretched arms are opened wide to form a *cross*, with Her inner and outer garments flung outwards forming a penumbra round Her body and head. This type of representation, perhaps originally based on the flares of the *Aurora Borealis* or Northern Lights in the northern skies, has appeared on other petroglyphs from Alta, Finnmark on the tip of Norway within the Arctic Circle. A stick figure (22.1, right) shows this penumbra as a

cloak, tied beneath the chin, and thrown over the figure's head. Professor Helskog dated it to the earlier fourth millennium BC. (Helskog 1988) More recent research by Magne Gjerde suggests up to a thousand years earlier. Once the general type is identified, it can be seen that there are many examples of such petroglyphs in Northern Britain. That from West Horton, Northumberland, (22.1, left) clearly shows the inner and outer garments of Gaia, although not yet delineated as a maze symbol. Each layer of clothing, like the turnings of the maze, represents a human stage of development, expansion of consciousness or initiation, as discussed in Chapter 8.

### The Quadrants of the Fixed Cross. (22.2)

In Theosophical terms the initiations can be summarised here as aspects or quadrants of the 'Fixed Cross' as Djwhal Khul terms it. (Bailey 1960, p. 693)

A. The process of the First Initiation. The Personality coordination of the *physical* (circuit 1), the *emotional* (circuit 2) and *mental* faculties (circuit 3): spiritual conception.

B. The Soul begins to dominate the Personality during a period of *nascent spiritual growth* (circuit 4), representing the processes of the Second Initiation.

C. The combined Soul and Personality proceed through a process of *aspiration* (circuit 5), *learning* (circuit 6), and *enlightened service* (circuit 7), all aspects of the Third Initiation.

D. The movement to the centre (8) is symbolic of the *renunciation* of incarnational ties as the individual becomes firmly linked to the Higher Spiritual aspect of its psyche. This constitutes the Fourth Initiation. The Fifth to Seventh Initiations in our system do not require physical reincarnations.

## THE CELTIC MAZE (22.2)

In Celtic terms the journey through the maze can be described as follows.

*The Little Turning (circuits 1-3)*

From *Annwn* (the abyss) representing non-human consciousness the individual enters the labyrinth for the first group of circuits which take one in a process of devolutionary spirals to the outer limit of the planetary ring-pass-not. This process is called in the ancient Druidic-Bardic system *Abred* – the cycle of numerous incarnations, described by the Stone-King we met in the Introduction as the 'the Little Turning'.

*The Great Turning (circuits 4-8)*

In this great cycle the individual begins with circuit 4 the processes of spiritual evolution or the return to the centre – you might term the whole process as one of apotheosis or *Gwynvyd* (the circle of purity/felicity) as it was known. The last brief movement at the climax where 'earth-peace' is achieved (Stone-King) is called *Ceugant* (the Presence of Deity) in the Celtic system. As the Stone-King states, the Great Turning lies *within* the Little Turning.

What is so interesting in this mandala is that spiritual 'ascension' is not shown as a steady progression of the human Monad from the outer to the inner planes of Deity but as a journey from the inner core of the Earth Logos, representing Deity, to find its fullest human expression on the outer rim of the figure when the mental faculties are at their maximum capacity (the Little Turning). Only then does the human Monad return 'in humility' through various spiritual stages to the inner planes of the Earth Logos.

The shaman of the prehistoric world with the tribal children around him would have chanted the various stages as he pointed

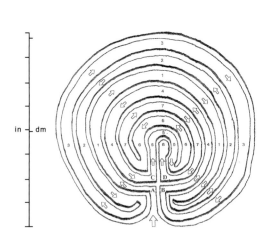

| THEOSOPHICAL SPIRITUAL ASCENSION PROCESS | CELTIC 'STATES OF BEING' – Y CANTREFI |
|---|---|
| THE QUADRANTS OF THE FIXED CROSS | Y CAER – 'THE SPIRITUAL PLANES' |
| A Personality individuation | |
| B Nascent sprituality | |
| C Spiritual growth | |
| D Spiritual service | |
| THE LITTLE TURNING | ABRED – THE LITTLE TURNING |
| 1 Physical development | 1 Sidi – The Round of Incarnations |
| 2 Emotional development | 2 Pedryvan – The Fourfold Man |
| 3 Mental development | 3 Vediwid – The Perfected Man |
| THE GREAT TURNING | GWYNVYDD – THE GREAT TURNING |
| 4 Nascent spiritual growth | 4 Rigor – The Door to Eternal Life |
| 5 Spiritual aspiration | 5 Wydr – The Spiritual Identity |
| 6 Spiritual learning | 6 Vandwy – The Summation of Ascension |
| 7 Enlightened service | 7 Ochren – The Edge of Eternity |
| 8 APOTHEOSIS | 8 CEUGANT – APOTHEOSIS |
| | Nwyvre – The Achievement of the Love-Wisdom of Earth Peace |

*22.2 Human Spiritual Development symbolised by the circuits of the Maze petroglyph, Rocky Valley, Tintagel, Cornwall (OS SU073894)*

to each circuit. I believe the terms he may have used were probably similar to the ancient Welsh (Celtic) terms which saw each stage as a stronghold (*Caer*) which had to be stormed. I have provided the Old Welsh terms, with their meaning, for these strongholds. They fit extraordinarily well in spiritual terms and should be compared with the classification set out in Chapters 8 and 9 of this study.

The Trojan or Celtic Maze, this wonderful mandala, is sublime in its simplicity and appropriateness as a guideline for humanity, even today. All spiritual systems of the Ancient Wisdom cover the same basic concepts and development, even though the terms and visual imagery differ from culture to culture, and age to age.

## THE QUATERNARY (FOUR-SPOKED) WHEEL

As we have seen, the oldest of prehistoric mandalas, the Maze, has at its core a fourfold division, which Djwhal Khul terms 'the quadrants of the Fixed Cross.'

This ancient quadripartite symbol first came to my attention back in 1976 when I was directing archaeological excavation at

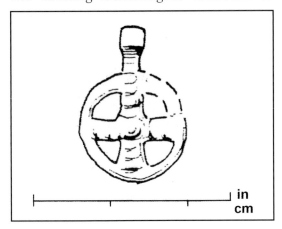

*22.3 The Quaternary Wheel Pewter wheel amulet from Durovigutum (Roman Godmanchester), c. AD 150*

*Durovigutum*, Roman Godmanchester. I personally found a cast pewter amulet in a rubbish pit in the northern cemetery of the Roman town. It is a very simple pendant design consisting of a wheel with four ribbed spokes. (22.3) Associated material from the deposit would date it to the early-mid second century AD. (Green H.J.M. 1986, p. 40) It represents the end of a long tradition in the Celtic provinces as a totem of numinous power, and rightly so too. Dr Miranda Green has traced the history of the spoked wheel in prehistoric Europe as a symbol of the Sun god (Green, Miranda 1989, pp. 164 ff.), but it is of course much more than that, for the Wheel of Life emphasises the *cyclical* nature of spiritual development. Like the wheel itself its envisioning appears to relate to the movement of the steppe nomads in their wagons across the western world. The symbol is universal in the Indo-Aryan world, and the wheel itself is found in wetland areas (such as Switzerland and Slovenia) and as ceramic models of wheeled vehicles from the fourth millennium BC graves at Budakalàsz and Szigetszentmàrton in Hungary. (Scarre 2005, p. 411) It appears in British contexts during the Wessex-Middle-Rhine phase of the Beaker culture early in the second millennium BC.

*The Wheel of Life crop formations – 1989-1997*

As befits one of the great Indo-Aryan mandalas, the geophysical crop circle makers had somewhat to say about the four-spoked wheel. This took the form of a series of such symbols put down between 1989 and 1997 highlighting different aspects.

This group of formations, stretching across central England, can be seen to form a classic Triangle of Power – the largest ever to have been put down and over the longest period of time. (22.4) The longest side measures 145 miles. Each formation was carefully placed to

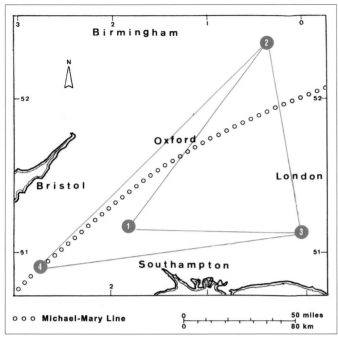

*22.4 The Quaternary Wheel Triangle of Power Wheel crop formations, Southern England, 1989 to 1997*

diameter, had a 5 ft wide outer band and a 9 ft 10 in diameter centre which air photos clearly show had initially a Swastika pattern in relief. Recorded by Colin Andrews and Pat Delgado: air photos by Busty Taylor.

Overall the design is that of the *Bi* symbol of Deity. Its notable feature, characteristic of all Swastika symbols, is the concept of *movement*, in this case clockwise on the outer ring and anticlockwise in the centre. Thus the symbolism of the Swastika and the Cross within a circle may be considered in their ancient, spiritual context as virtually synonymous – the former with its bent arms having the refinement of indicating movement,

be noticed by and accessible to some of the best crop circle investigators around at the time, with aerial photo coverage by leading photographers.

Noting the overall *Bi* design of these wheels it is clear that this mandala is concerned with Deity, and more particularly, the Solar Logos.

The stages of development of Triangles of Power are set out in Chapter 19.

1. *The Swastika* (22.5)
*Parsonage Down, Winterbourne Stoke CP, Wiltshire* (OS SU067406) on 5.8.1989
Emanating Energy

The 62 ft 3 in diameter circle was divided into four quadrants with plants combed out at right angles from the four partings. A 9 ft 10 in wide ring, around the circumference, was put down first before the quadripartite design. A central circular feature, 16 ft in

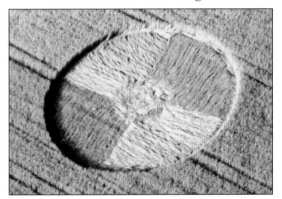

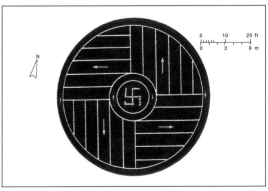

*22.5 **The Swastika**. Winterbourne Stoke, Wiltshire (OS SU067406), 5.8.1989*

whose significance will become apparent below.

2. *The Templars' Cross* (22.6)
   *Belton's Hill, Spaldwick CP, Cambridgeshire*
   (OS TL127736) on 27.7.1991
   Evocative Force

The central 83 ft diameter circle had a central standing tuft. A ring of 195 ft diameter, 10 ft wide, broken into sections attached to the ends of 10 ft wide radial spokes. Surveyed by Beth Davis.

The clockwise movement round the periphery of the formation is thus broken up into eight stages representing perhaps alternating movement and stasis (see paragraphs on the Woodhouse Crag petroglyph below).

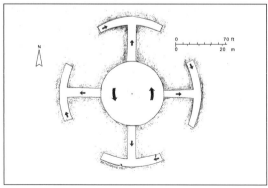

*22.6 **The Templars' Cross***
*Belton's Hill, Spaldwick, Cambridgeshire*
*(OS TL127736), 27.7.1991*

3. *The Dragon* (22.7)
   *'Gullege', Imberhorne Farm, East Grinstead,*
   *West Sussex* (OS TQ367382) on 10.8.1993
   Magnetic Centre

This formation was discussed in Chapter 15, on the Solar Logos. The 'body' of the formation is a straightforward wheel design nearly 70 ft in diameter. The overall concept, with a central circle, 28 ft in diameter, is again the *Bi* symbol of Deity. The circle and

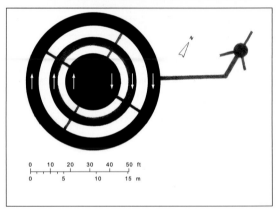

*22.7 **The Dragon***
*Imberhorne Farm, East Grinstead, West*
*Sussex (OS TQ367382), 10.8.1993. With*
*thanks to the Emmett family*

the four outer rings symbolise the successive stages of the human Monad's development – physical, emotional, mental, spiritual and Logoic – which have to be experienced to achieve apotheosis. The dragon's head appendage, I believe, identifies this process with the Solar Logos, under whose *aegis* the entire procedure has to be achieved by stages on the Wheel of Life.

4. *The Wheel of Life* (22.8)
   *Globelands, Haselbury Plucknett CP, Somerset* (OS ST471116) on 17.7.1997
   Distributing Centre

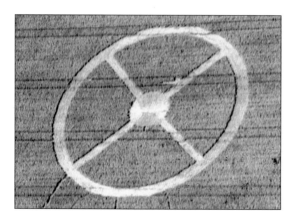

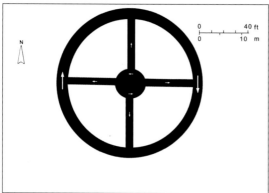

*22.8 **The Wheel of Life***
*Globelands, Haselbury Plucknett, Somerset (OS ST471116), 17.7.1997*

Central circle, 25 ft diameter; ring, 120 ft diameter, 10 ft wide; cruciform paths, 7 ft wide. Recorded by David Kingston: aerial photo by Lucy Pringle.

This simple geophysical formation completes the series begun 8 years previously in 1989. It is sited directly on the Michael-Mary Line and is the Distributing Centre of the series. But what precisely is it 'distributing'? And what indeed was the purpose of installing such a large Triangle of Power over such a long period

of time, when most of these phenomena were put down in a single season in a small area of the countryside?

The main reason, I believe, was to avoid the attention of the Forces of Darkness, who were sharp to notice crop formations of potential spiritual importance, and damage them if they could. On the other hand, all four were sited in localities which had the attention of experienced investigators, not necessarily those of the Centre for Crop Circle Studies.

As formations reflecting the symbolism of the various points of the Triangles of Power, each is concerned with some special aspect.

1. *The Swastika* – Emanating Energy, Ray 1

   As the Ray 1 source of this series, this formation is in a sense a summary of the total process. The clockwise direction of the crop in the outer band speaks of the Little Turning, whereas the design of the crop-quartering and the inner Swastika (anticlockwise) indicate that the Great Turning is alluded to.

2. *The Templar's Cross* – Evocative Force. Ray 2

   This formation brings through the essential qualities of Love-Wisdom by emphasising the aspect of spiritual growth – i.e. 'becoming' as opposed to 'being'. (See Chapters 23 and 24.) It may be significant that this mandala resembles the insignia of the Order of Templars – a militant, medieval order of chivalry, notable for their bravery and religious piety.

3. *The Dragon* – Magnetic Centre. Ray 3

   This formation, in particular, emphasises the physicality, indeed 'grounding' of this energy field. The perceived influence of this formation, as discussed in Chapter 15 (The Solar Logos as a Dragon of Wisdom), is that the ring structure of the main circle refers to the Logoic make-up as an agent for spiritual growth – since it includes every aspect of its physical make-up.

4. *The Wheel of Life* – Distributing Centre. Rays 1-3

This brings together all the aspects referred to in the previous three formations as a simple four-spoked wheel. It includes allusions to both the Little Turning (outer ring – clockwise), and the Great Turning (inner circle – anticlockwise) in the same way as the Swastika formation.

This group of formations forming a Triangle of Power must be regarded as the most important of its type in connection with the spiritual development of humanity. It sets out in mandalic form, as has been done for thousands of years in ancient Indo-European cultures, the processes through which mankind has to pass to achieve apotheosis, or what Djwhal Khul terms 'Spiritual Unfoldment.' (Bailey 1951, p. 58)

*The Swastika petroglyphs* (22.9)

An ancient Swastika symbol found as a petroglyph at Woodhouse Crag, Ilkley Moor, West Yorkshire, appears to carry the same metaphysical information as this group of crop formations. It may date to the earlier part of the third millennium BC. A strikingly

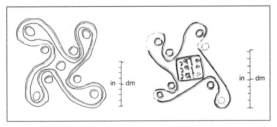

*22.9 Swastika Petroglyphs*
*Left – Woodhouse Crag, Ilkley Moor, West Yorkshire, c. early third millennium BC*
*Right – On prehistoric slab re-used for Byzantine grave at ancient Kaukana, Sicily*

similar mandala on a broken cover slab of a Byzantine grave, almost certainly reused from an earlier feature, was found in 2010 at ancient Kaukana, Sicily. (Wilson, R. 2011, p. 43) It suggests that this type of petroglyph, like the contemporary Trojan Maze symbol, had a widespread Atlantic as well as a Mediterranean distribution. Both Swastika stones have an eightfold system, with four stationary points, and four 'moving' points at the end of the arms.

*The Turning of the Wheel*

As with the Trojan Maze, there are two directions that may be turned on the Wheel of Life. The clockwise direction is the Little Turning, symbolising, in this case, four stages - physical, emotional, mental and incipient spiritual development.

More important is the Great Turning, which has an anticlockwise movement and encompasses the Little Turning in its first quadrant, but then moves on to develop more advanced levels of spiritual growth. The Great Turning follows the constellation signs of esoteric astrology, which are twelve in the system devised by the Greek astrologer Berosus but were eight in ancient times. The Swastika stones follow the eightfold system, with four stationary points marking the states of 'Being' (i.e. achievement) and four as the arms marking the states of 'Becoming' (i.e. development), which may take many lives to achieve.

The whole process (symbolised by the four quadrants of the Cross or the Maze) may be described as follows.

1. The coordination of the physical, emotional and mental aspects of the human Personality, which eventually begins to include a certain level of spiritual awareness. This development is encompassed in the

Little Turning and the Jungian concept of 'Individuation'. (Jung 1964, pp. 160 ff.) This marks the *First Initiation*. In their struggle for sheer physical survival, much of humanity in the Third World is at this stage today.

2. The awareness of a spiritual existence and the beginning of a God-centred life, with many set-backs and stretching over many lifetimes. The battle between the Soul and Personality for spiritual ascendancy, which once achieved enables the individual to follow the spiritual path. Many in the West and the older systems of religious life in the East are at this stage, imperceptibly inching their way towards a serious relationship with God. The completed process is marked by the *Second Initiation*.

3. The development of the mental, intuitive faculties involving deep study and experience on the spiritual path as, in the committed spiritual person, the Soul begins to dominate the Personality. The marked expansion of consciousness which is the climax of this phase of development is the *Third Initiation*.

4. The last quadrant is marked by spiritual service of one kind or another by those whom Djwhal Khul terms 'world-servers', or at a higher level 'world-savers', in collaboration with the Higher Beings of our system, often in difficult and testing circumstances. Such people are not necessarily found in the holders of high spiritual office in any religion, let alone those who have closed themselves off from the world in the various religious orders, both East and West, but amongst the humble servers of humanity dealing with poverty, disease and suffering in mankind, and those attempting to support and protect the world of nature. This is climaxed by the *Fourth Initiation*.

It is at this point that the spiritual initiate leaves the planetary 'Wheel of Life', thus forfeiting the pleasures and familiar associations of not only physical incarnation but also the other planetary 'modes of being' beyond death. It is thus the most difficult and testing stage of spiritual training, which is completed by the *Fifth Initiation*. This is not death as we understand it. Indeed there have been many lives and deaths in the states beyond physical death for the human Monad up to this point. It is simply that there is no longer any need for the *Master of Wisdom*, as he is now termed, to be recycled in physical form for spiritual growth: for further development and service lie off-planet.

## THE OCTONARY (EIGHT-SPOKED) WHEEL

The eight-spoked wheel became a prime symbol and mandala of the Celtic peoples. A fine example showing such a wheel is engraved on a bronze scabbard decoration where it is held, I believe, by two deities. (22.10) It was found in a grave of the great Hallstatt cemetery at Salzkammergut, Austria, and dates to c. 400-350 BC. (Megaw R. and V. 1989, p. 80)

So we have the eight-spoked wheel from the Celtic world and the contemporaneous twelve-segment Zodiac, both of cosmic significance. Associated with them are the planetary Beings and the archetypes of the Seven Rays. So what is their significance, how are they linked and how do they relate to mankind?

I introduced the Zodiac in the last chapter with Djwhal Khul's statement that astrology is 'the purest presentation of occult truth in the world at this time.' He adds an important rider, namely that what he is referring to is *esoteric* astrology, that is concerned not with horoscopes, but with the ultimate big picture

in | cm

*22.10 The Octonary Wheel.*
*Scabbard decoration from Hallstatt cemetery,*
*Salzkammergut, Austria, c. 400-350 BC*

for mankind today – 'the destiny of our planet, of the kingdoms of nature and of humanity as a whole ...' (Bailey 1951, p. 6) So, how precisely does the Zodiac function, and what is meant by the statement that esoteric astrology is 'the *science* [my italics] which deals with those conditioning and governing energies and forces which play through and upon the whole field of space?'

*The principles behind the Great Turning*

Even a summary study of the Houses of the Zodiac suggests a certain rational progression if the process is followed step by step, from the House of Aries round to the House of Pisces. It starts with physical incarnation, the development of physical, emotional and mental faculties, and then works through all the stages of spiritual development, step by step until having reached the pinnacle of transcendent enlightenment available in our planetary system, the human Monad is ready to proceed to higher levels leading ultimately to apotheosis. What we are looking

at in a structured rational form is a cosmic blueprint for a cycle of development, not only for the human Monad but for all planetary life forms, to be achieved over a long period of time.

However, this great progression is so ordered not to produce spiritual clones, but as a paradigm of *systemic cosmic variability*, particularly for the human Monad. Only thus can the full benefits be achieved for the development of Deity at every level. These qualities are summed up in Chapter 10 under *the Seven Laws of Soul or Group Life* as selflessness, devotion, sympathy, discrimination, inclusiveness, spiritual freedom and spiritual integration. This indeed is the Plan of God for mankind, whereby 'humanity will act as a transmitter of light, energy and spiritual potency to the subhuman kingdoms ... Such is the high destiny before the race.' (Bailey 1942, p. 112)

This is a difficult, indeed dangerous, process, and not every Spark of God or human Monad who undertakes this monumental undertaking is successful. Indeed I understand that the failure rate is some 40%. Hence there is the utmost urgency for those in spiritual service to ensure that those human beings and those beings of the natural world (whether animal or plant) within our sphere of influence, are given every encouragement to develop and achieve.

In the ancient world this great system of individual and planetary redemption was considered to be an eightfold process.

This was later expanded under the Zodiac to a twelvefold system, in which each of the four quarters of the 'fixed cross' (see above) is provided with an extra stage or phase. The challenge is too great for the life forms including (particularly) humanity to achieve on their own. The initiative is ultimately monitored as far as our own system is concerned by Aion, the Spiritual Being of our Galaxy, but the planning, concepts and management processes are passed down through levels of intermediaries, each of whose components has special responsibilities. Particular stages of the Great Turning are critical and require the input that only an Entity that is specialised in that line of activity (indeed that is on that particular 'wavelength') can provide, hence the input of each of the Seven Lords of our system (the Archangels) at particular points of the process. They in turn are monitored and energised by the 'Seven Heavenly Men' (as Djwhal Khul terms them) or the spirits of the seven sacred planets (see Chapter 15) of our solar system. Beyond Them again are the Seven Lords of Archon, Who monitor this process in our part of the Milky Way galaxy. This system, akin to the changing of gears in a motor vehicle, is stepped down so that the lower levels can cope with the higher energy levels. The method used is that described in Chapter 19, The Triangles of Power in 1990.

Raw power needs to be tempered, or balanced by two controls at the lower level, for 'our solar system is one in which sensitivity to contact is the dominant quality.' (Bailey 1951, p. 493) The two energies which balance the 'Emanating Energy' are in Djwhal Khul's terms the 'Evocative Force' and the 'Magnetic Centre'. We have met these energies before, and indeed they are the keynote of our system: Love-Wisdom. 'Love is response to contact and this – in the human being

– means understanding, inclusiveness and identification. Wisdom connotes skill in action as a result of developed love and the light of understanding; it is awareness of requirements and ability to bring together into a fused relationship the need and that which will meet it.' (Bailey 1951, p. 494) 'These triangles should not be thought of as *placed*, static and eternally the same, or even as three-dimensional. They must be regarded as in rapid movement, revolving eternally in space and ceaselessly moving onward and as of fourth and fifth dimensional extension.' (Bailey 1951, p. 417) Again it should be stressed that the great beauty of this system is that every living element of every planetary life form of ours has the potential of ultimately achieving individuation and spiritual ascension.

## THE WHEEL OF LIFE AS A METAPHYSICAL CONSTRUCT

Let us look at the meaning of the four- and eight-spoked wheel back at the time of its origins in the ancient world.

### The wheel of the Vedas (22.11)

The universe appeared to the Vedic Aryans of Central Asia during the third and second millennia BC in terms of 'spheres of influence or existence' and 'powers' which they called *vasu* meaning 'that which surrounds.' (Daniélou 1985, p. 85) The primal *vasus* were four (the four-spoked wheel) and comprised:

1. The Earth (*Pṛthivī*), the realm of Fire (*Agni*), the principle of Physical Survival

2. The Sky (*Dyaus*), the realm of the Sun (*Sūrya*), the principle of Intellect

3. Space (*Antarikṣa*), the realm of the Wind (*Vāyu*), the principle of Life

4. The Constellations (*Nakṣatra*), the realm of the Moon (*Soma*), the principle of Immortality.

These broad categories are further broken down into eight *vasus* (the eight-spoked wheel), as set out in the *Mālati-mādhava* and the *Kirātārjunīya* and many other works. The names vary slightly, although the principles aimed at are the same.

The ostensible points of reference of this extraordinarily ancient mandala are the features of the heavens. But behind them in a coded form is the cycle of human spiritual development. After three thousand years or more

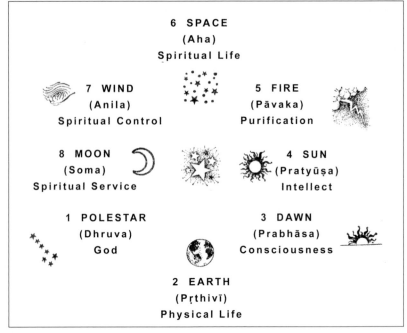

6 **SPACE**
(Aha)
Spiritual Life

7 **WIND**
(Anila)
Spiritual Control

5 **FIRE**
(Pāvaka)
Purification

8 **MOON**
(Soma)
Spiritual Service

4 **SUN**
(Pratyūṣa)
Intellect

1 **POLESTAR**
(Dhruva)
God

3 **DAWN**
(Prabhāsa)
Consciousness

2 **EARTH**
(Pṛthivī)
Physical Life

*22.11 The Vedic Wheel of Life - the eight vasus*

not all the connections can easily be made, but I am sure that the principle holds for all the *vasus*. In some cases the nature of the heavenly body provides the clue, for example that the 'Earth' *vasu* is concerned with human physicality, and the 'Dawn' *vasu* refers to the dawn of human consciousness. Sometimes the ancient word itself has a double meaning. *Soma* for instance means 'Moon', but it also has the connotation of 'offering.'

The eight *vasus* are:

1. *Dhruva*. The Polestar, with the connotation of the 'motionless' or unmovable – a reference to God or the Cosmos, the ultimate source of all Being

2. *Pṛthivī*. The Earth, also categorised as *Dhava* (the flowing) or *Dharā* (the support) – a reference to physical life

3. *Prabhāsa*. Shining dawn. A reference to the 'dawn' of human consciousness

4. *Pratyūṣa*. The luminous or scorching. A reference to the Sun (*Sūrya*) as a symbol of intelligent, human individuation

5. *Pāvaka*. The purifier. Also a reference to fire, the esoteric symbol of spiritual purification

6. *Aha* or *Āha*. The pervading as in 'space' (*Antarikṣa*), or (*Ap*) 'the waters'. At a spiritual level with the connotation of *Sāvitra* (descended from the Sun) it refers to the work of the Holy Spirit of God (*Aha*) transforming the human Personality into a Spiritual Being (*Sāvitra*).

7. *Anila*. 'The One by whom one lives', also the wind (*Vāyu*). Another reference perhaps to the guidance of God in the spiritual life through the Holy Spirit

8. *Soma*. The Moon, but also 'offering,' referring to the spiritual life of service.
This eighth *vasu* (the House of Aquarius) in spiritual terms is concerned with 'service' and the word is thus highly appropriate.

As the spheres of the elements, the *vasus* are the visible images of the laws of the universe in terms of the eight-spoked wheel or Great Turning as set out in this study, and are perhaps the closest that we will ever get to an understanding of the ineffable principles behind that great mandala. With this information we may tentatively envisage the overall structure of the *vasus* or eight-spoked wheel in terms of spiritual development for the human Monad using the anticlockwise motion of the Great Turning. In the process I have reordered the traditional positions of the *vasus* as set out in the *Vishnu Purāna* 1.15.111 or the *Mahābhārata 1.66.19.*

### The Dharmic Wheel of Buddhism

The celestial Bodhisattva, who was born *Siddhārtha* to the rulers of the Sākya tribe in what is now southern Nepal, re-envisioned the function of the four- and eight-spoked wheel after He renounced the world and became the Buddha c. 530 BC.

We will now see how the old Vedic Wheel of Life with its eight states of being or *vasus*, which had hidden spiritual meanings behind its references to the heavens, was replaced by a structure of spiritual belief and practice. The Buddha's first sermon was dedicated to expounding the '*Four* Noble Truths', the discourse being generally described as 'Turning the Wheel of the Doctrine.' This primary exegesis, like that of the four-spoked Vedic wheel, was further elaborated with an exposition of

the 'Eightfold Path', comprising the elements of correct *view, resolve, speech, conduct, livelihood, application, mindfulness,* and *concentration.* The six *Perfections* of Buddhism, *giving, morality, patience, vigour, contemplation and wisdom,* are a restatement of the Eightfold Path, and these, some relating to more than one element of the Path, can be seen to have a sequential progression round the Buddhist Wheel of the Law, which, like the teaching of Jesus Christ five hundred years later, was mainly devoted to bringing about spiritual improvement of life and enlightenment. For the Buddhist the ultimate ascension achievement was *Nirvāna*, or spiritual *salvation* for the Christian Soul.

Within a thousand years the wheel symbolism had largely dropped out of use in the Buddhist areas of India and the Far East, except in Tibet where the Dharmic Wheel continued to be depicted as a ritual diagram (mandala) showing a schematised structure of the Other States of Reality. The basic picture is that of a palace or stupa with entrances at the four points of the compass. (22.12)

The usual Tibetan mandala shows the transcendental Being of the *Yantra* dwelling at the centre and flanked on the quadrants

*22.12 Brass model of Buddhist stupa with the four Heavenly Guardians*

by the other four cosmic buddhas (or kumaras, see Chapter 14). The whole field of the wheel is devoted to images of deities, symbols and attributes illustrating the different nature of every aspect. Thus the Tibetan system relates more to the prehistoric traditions of the Vedic Eight-spoked Wheel than to the original Buddhist Dharmic Wheel with its non-representational moral maxims. In more recent time the Tibetan, Djwhal Khul, (so frequently quoted in this study) has further defined in spiritual terms the significance of the Dharmic Wheel as a symbol of spiritual development: 'Vision the whole of the systemic wheel as in a constant state of circulation, in which the tiny lesser lives are impelled by the force of the central solar life to pass through the extent of the wheel so that they come in contact with all parts of the wheel, and are impressed by all the varying types of "power substance".' (Bailey 1925, p. 1094)

*22.13 The Octonary Wheel*
*Tibetan mandala of Kalachakra Palace (Wheel of Time)*
*eighteenth century. Private collection*

The eighteenth century Tibetan mandala illustrated here (22.13) brings together many of these features in a distinctive manner which is characteristic of the *Kalachakra* or 'Wheel of Time.' Centrally is the eight-spoked wheel set within the *Kalachakra* palace with a gateway on each of the four quarters. The principal components, in terms of figure personifications, may be tabulated as follows:

1. The patron or commissioner of this mandala is shown in the bottom left-hand corner on horseback.

2. In the bottom right-hand corner is a deific personification of the *Kalachakra* who as a protector Deity is trampling underfoot a

pink humanoid. The group is set within a flaming aureole. Kalachakra is represented in a sexual embrace with his Shakti, *Vishramata*. The principle expressed here is important. 'In Buddhist philosophy, the two most important forces in the universe are wisdom (Sanskrit: prajna) and compassion [love] (Sanskrit: karuna). Both must be present for harmony to exist in the universe and for enlightenment to be possible.' (McArthur 2002, p. 109) Every spiritual Being exhibits these two qualities, which are expressed as a duality. 'Compassion' (Love) is represented by the male figure; 'Wisdom' is represented by a female Deity, shown as his consort. The concept is that 'Wisdom' and 'Compassion' are perfect complements, and that the two must be united for enlightenment to be possible. The embrace (*Yab-Yum*) signifies this union. All spiritual Beings are shown in the *Yab-Yum* embrace in this mandala.

3. The other principal Beings depicted are the cosmic Septead. Across the top of the mandala in the 'sky' area are three groups of figures in the *Yab-Yum* embrace. The central figure is *Vairochana*, the supreme Buddha and First of the five *Dhyani* Buddhas, who is set in an aureole of poppies. The figures on either side of Vairochana are the two aspects Whom He unites, the spiritual and masculine Diamond World (Sanskrit: *Vajradhatu*) – right hand figure, and the material and feminine Womb World (Sanskrit: *Garbhadhatu*) – left hand figure. Both *Vajradhatu* and *Garbhadhatu* are surrounded in miniature by four Dhyani Buddhas. In a sense these three cosmic figures relate to the three Rays of Aspect.

4. The four Rays of Attribute relate to the four main Dhyani Yab-Yum figures; two of whom are in the upper, space, register and two in the lower, Earth, register. All are surrounded by an aureole of flame, coloured according to their function:

Top right: Amoghasiddhi – Air – light blue

Top left: Amitabha – Fire – red

Bottom right: Akshobhya – Water – dark blue

Bottom left: Ratnasambhava – Earth – light red.

## THE CHINESE YI JING

The *Yi Jing*, or *Book of Changes* leads us to the last of the great metaphysical symbols to be considered here, the arrangement of eight *bagua* around an octagonal chart. The *Yi Jing* is very ancient, and was millennia old when it became an influence on Lao-Tzŭ, the founder of Daoism. The story of the *Yi Jing* is shadowy and complicated, and there is not space to go into detail here. The version that has survived is the *Zhou Yi*, studied, arranged and edited by King Wen of the Zhou dynasty (eleventh century BC). Its major part contains a list and interpretation of eight basic *trigrams* (three lines stacked one above the other, each line either whole or broken in the middle), and is used as a divination text, although it is much more than that. The eight trigrams (*bagua*) are traditionally arranged around an octagon, and their names and meanings, which can be described as representing the fundamental principles of reality, show extraordinary similarities with the eightfold Wheel of Life of the great Silbury Hill crop formation of 1992, described in the next two chapters. They may be tabulated as follows:

| Silbury Wheel | Yi Jing Trigrams |
|---|---|
| God at the centre of the Cosmos (Pisces/Aries) | Thunder (Zhen) |
| Earth (Taurus) | Earth (Khun) |
| Dawn (Gemini/Cancer) | Mountains (Gen) |
| Fire (Leo) | Fire (Li) |
| Moisture *(Virgo/Libra) | Vapour (Dui) |
| Air (Scorpio) | Heaven (Qian) |
| Wind (Sagittarius/Capricorn) | Wind (Xun) |
| Water (Aquarius) | Water (Kan) |

[*The editor is unable to discern why Michael writes 'moisture' here, unless it be that moisture or vapour is a transitional state between two elements, representing purification such as in the distillation of water, and the House of Virgo, as described in Chapter 24, is a House of purification. The *vasu Pāvaka* is *the purifier*, although related to fire, see above, and the Bagua *Dui* also relates to washing or purifying. (Ed.)]

The positions of the Celtic Wheel of Life, the *vasus* of the Vedic Wheel, the states of the Dharmic Wheel, the Tibetan *Kalachakra Palace* and the bagua chart of the Yi Jing, all of which have a basic octogonary form, are stating a similar truth about the Cosmos and God, namely that God (*Qi* or 'breath' in Chinese) permeates the universe, having created both it and the Earth. *Qi* is binary in the sense that it gives rise to the complementary forces of *yin* and *yang* which reflect, respectively, the qualities of 'Love' and 'Wisdom.' Every physical aspect and change that occurs in the world is seen as a product of *Qi*.

As we have already seen, the Tibetan, Djwhal Khul, sets out in detail (Bailey, *Esoteric Astrology*) the ramifications of the Great Wheel as a symbol of spiritual development, showing how each human Monad is destined in theory to pass through a number of initiations (defined as 'expansions of consciousness') which eventually take the individual off the cycle of reincarnations in our system. How this was set out in symbolic form as a great crop formation in 1992 is the subject of the next two chapters.

# 23. THE DHARMIC WHEEL OF SILBURY HILL: FROM INCARNATION

*For one moment I had stood on another sphere and contemplated from afar, but also from close by, that procession which is both human and divine, wherein I, too, had my place, this world where suffering exists still, but error is no more. Human destiny, that vague design in which the least practiced eye can trace so many flaws, gleamed bright like the patterns of the heavens.*

Marguerite Yourcenar
*Memoirs of Hadrian 1955*

## THE DHARMIC WHEEL OF SILBURY HILL (23.1)

The most important geophysical crop formation of all time, in this writer's opinion, appeared near Silbury Hill, (Avebury CP) Wiltshire in wheat on 18.8.1992 (OS SU094690). All the features were swirled anticlockwise except for the southernmost grapeshot, the larger circle near to it, and the dumb-bell ring. The formation was carefully surveyed by John Martineau, Chris Mansell and Dave Gilfoyle at the time, and extensively studied by the members of Project Argus. Their scientific assessment established beyond any reasonable doubt that this was a true, geophysical formation. (Chorost 1993, p. 23 and 84)

Here I must again declare a personal interest. As a specialist in ancient symbolism I had long been fascinated by the meaning of the eight-spoked wheel of two thousand or more years ago. In *The Crop Circle Enigma* (Green, Michael 1990, p. 145) I explored some ideas about the identity of the eight positions. At a meditation with Beth Davis in a crop formation on Little Trees Hill, Wandlebury, south of Cambridge, in the summer of 1990, I requested that a wheel formation might appear with appropriate symbols on the periphery. Two years later, a hundred miles away, the Silbury Hill formation was put down while I was abroad.

It was not quite what I expected, but clearly represented a symbolic wheel with glyphs round the periphery. The symbols were very strange, although a few of them could be related to magical glyphs from the ancient past. One of the eight symbols was completely missing where there was a modern agricultural cistern in the field. In a short piece in the magazine *Kindred Spirit* (1992-3, p. 40), I tentatively identified the formation to be a statement about the *Great Turning*, as it was known in prehistoric Europe, or the *Dharmic Wheel* in the East.

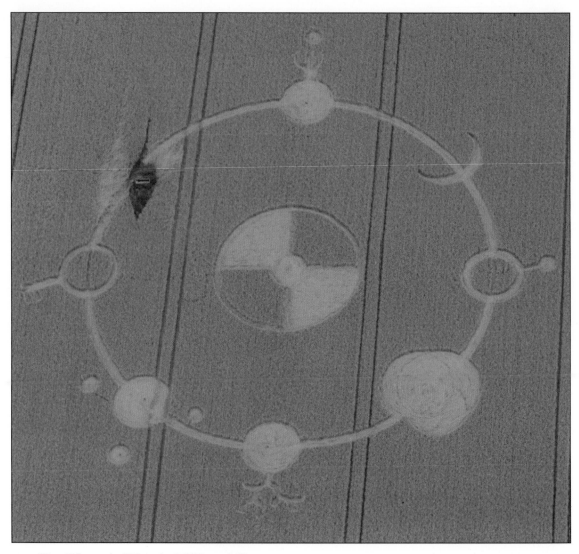

23.1 *The Dharmic Wheel of Silbury Hill*
*Silbury Hill, Wiltshire (OS SU094690), 18.8.1992*

Its importance for us at this time is that it represents a metaphysical statement, in mandalic form, based on the core design of the ancient Zodiac, about the spiritual 'spheres of existence' and their relationship, in particular, to the human Monad. It is indeed about 'those conditioning and governing energies and forces which play through and upon the whole field of space and all that is found within that field.' (Bailey 1951, p. 5)

I have therefore in the detailed assessment of the Silbury Hill Wheel crop formation that follows provided a full page diagram for each 'House', based on the Science of Triangles, showing how this great spiritual process is stepped down from high levels within this, our Universe.

## THE CROSS AND THE WHEEL

We have already seen that the imagery of the Cross as a symbol of spiritual life long predates its Christian associations. The Trojan Maze, dating possibly as early as the fourth millennium BC, has as its central image a cruciform figure of Gaia, or the World Soul, whose four quadrants symbolise successive spiritual stages of possible development for humanity. Djwhal Khul's use of the same imagery is not therefore merely a Theosophical concept introduced in the last century but has much more ancient roots.

In the last chapter we saw what the quadrants of the Fixed Cross and the Trojan Maze comprise in theory for the human Monad in terms of stages of development and initiations, which are the essential stages of physical, psychological and spiritual growth and activity that face humanity at this or any time, and constitute the *Great Turning*. The process is not inevitable in its outcome. Every Personality has free-will, and will not necessarily be prepared to make the sacrifices and committal needed.

Djwhal Khul has reduced the fourfold process to essentially two, with a third lying beyond it: the *Three Crosses*. What he has done is to divide humanity's time on the planet (over many incarnations) into two essential stages, the first of which he defines as the *Wheel of Incarnation*. This is essentially non-spiritual evolution and passes the individual clockwise from *Aries* to *Taurus* through the various stages marked by the energy fields of the Zodiac to a point where the spiritual life is nascent. This is described as the *Common Cross*. For details of the *Wheel of Incarnation* the reader is referred to Djwhal Khul's comments in *Esoteric Astrology*. (Bailey 1951, p. 90 ff.)

The second stage, described as the *Wheel adjusted or reversed*, has an anticlockwise rotation and takes the individual from *Aries* to *Pisces*. This he names the *Fixed Cross*. The key factor is that this is the phase of physio-spiritual development and activity and covers four quadrants of the Wheel of Life. This is the process described in this book.

The third stage, described as the *Wheel controlled or dominated* is not actually part of the rotation of the Wheel of Life at all, but lies off-planet in Initiations 5-7 and beyond, described in Chapter 9 and elsewhere in this study.

Djwhal Khul summarises these three stages as follows:

'1. *The Wheel of Incarnation*

   a. The cycle of ordinary evolution.

   b. The period of captivity, wherein the man is bound upon the wheel.

   c. The fourfold influence of the *Common Cross*.

   d. Life in the three worlds.

   e. The development of personality.

2. *The Wheel adjusted or reversed*

   a. The cycle of discipleship.

   b. The period of emergence, wherein the man alters the revolution of the wheel.

   c. The fourfold influence of the *Fixed Cross*.

   d. Life in the five worlds of superhuman evolution.

   e. The unfoldment of soul through the personality.

3. *The Wheel controlled or dominated*

   a. The cycle of initiation.

   b. The period of liberation from the work of the Great Wheel.

   c. The fourfold influence of the *Cardinal Cross*.

   d. Life in the seven worlds of our seven planes.

   e. Fusion of spirit, soul and personality.'

(Bailey 1951, p. 94)

I have brought together here a number of important aspects connected with the Dharmic Wheel as set out by Djwhal Khul in *Esoteric Astrology*. Under different symbolism I have covered much of this material already, and indeed in many respects the Tibetan's classification set out here may be regarded as an apt summary of the critical stages of the human Monadic development discussed earlier.

It remains to examine in detail each of the symbols of the Silbury Hill crop formation, in terms of the *Wheel adjusted or reversed*, beginning at the equivalent of the House of Aries and proceeding anticlockwise. Each of the positions of the wheel relates either to a single House on one of the four points of the compass or to two Houses (a 'double sign') in one of the quadrants.

Each symbol tells us something about its spiritual source, has a distinct meaning for spiritual mankind at that particular stage of the wheel, and usually there is some numinous echo which serves to make the symbol of special spiritual significance.

For each position of the wheel I have shown in a page diagram the process of stepping down energy from the Virgo Supercluster via the local group of galaxies (*An*), the Milky Way galaxy (*Aion*), and our local solar group (*Archon*), transmitting the galactic Ray system (the Zodiac) through the solar system, using the corresponding Planetary Rays of our Solar Logos (*Bel*), ending up with our Earth Logos (*Ibez*) and ultimately humanity. It should be stressed that these represent to my mind only some of the high-points of the process. In ours the Twelfth Universe or centre (chakra) of God there are many stages beyond the Virgo Supercluster, and indeed within our own Milky Way galaxy. All, however, from the highest to the lowest, are linked by the Holy Spirit of God, in Old Welsh the *Manred*,

described in the Celtic mystic tradition by Iolo Morganwg as 'the smallest of all the small, so that a smaller could not be, which flowed in one sea through all the *Ceugant* [the Cosmos of God] – God being its life, and pervading each atom, and God moving in it, and changing the condition of the manred, without undergoing a change in Himself.' (Williams, J. 1862, p. 262)

The reader is invited to compare the Vedic Wheel of Life in illustration 22.11 with the diagram of the Silbury Hill Wheel in illustration 23.2, when reading this chapter and the next.

I have also provided an illustration showing the Rays, the archangels, and the realms of nature related to them. (23.3)

The governing Houses, planets and Rays for each sign of the Zodiac are discussed in detail by Djwhal Khul in *Esoteric Astrology* to which reference should be made.

## THE SYMBOLS OF THE SILBURY HILL WHEEL (23.2)

### THE HOUSE OF ARIES (23.4)

The south-west quadrant is shared by Pisces and Aries, of which the latter is perhaps the more important, being at the beginning of the spiritual cycle of development on the *Wheel adjusted or reversed*.

However, in another sense: 'Pisces is seen to be at the head of the list of zodiacal signs because it is governing the present great astrological world cycle of 25,000 years.' (Bailey 1951, p. 37) This quadrant is literally the Alpha and Omega of the process, since Pisces 'sees the relinquishing or the death of all the influences which hold the man to the wheel of birth and his release from the control of the Common or Mutable Cross.' (Bailey 1951, p. 96)

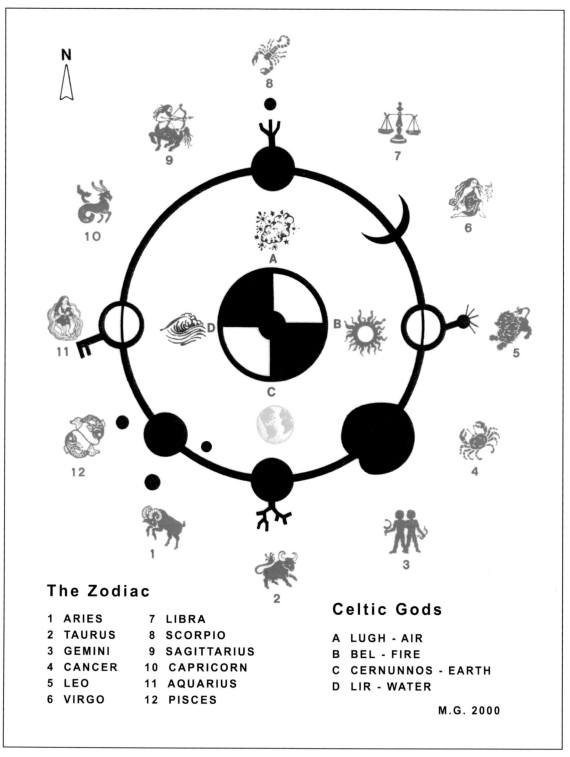

**The Zodiac**

| | | | |
|---|---|---|---|
| 1 | ARIES | 7 | LIBRA |
| 2 | TAURUS | 8 | SCORPIO |
| 3 | GEMINI | 9 | SAGITTARIUS |
| 4 | CANCER | 10 | CAPRICORN |
| 5 | LEO | 11 | AQUARIUS |
| 6 | VIRGO | 12 | PISCES |

**Celtic Gods**

A  LUGH - AIR
B  BEL - FIRE
C  CERNUNNOS - EARTH
D  LIR - WATER

M.G. 2000

*23.2 The Dharmic Wheel of Silbury Hill*
*Occult Correspondences*

**1-7 MICHAEL**
**Lord of Earth**

**4 HANIEL**
Bird life

**7 SANDALPHON**
Plant life and other
planetary life forms

**3 KHAMAEL**
Sea life

**GOD**

**6 GABRIEL**
Humanity

**2 (1) TZADKIEL**
Life

**5 URIEL**
Devic life

**7(2) RAPHAEL**
Animal life

*23.3 The Dharmic Wheel of Life*
*The Rays, the Archangels and the Realms of Nature*

In the words of Djwhal Khul:

'Aries initiates the cycle of manifestation ... the first impulse is awakened in Aries, for Aries is the place where the initial idea to institute activity takes form. ... There originates the response of the soul to the highest aspect or quality of Deity because there appears the "will to incarnate." The first ray aspect of the Monad, responding to the first aspect of Deity, evokes response from the first aspect of the soul and the first step towards incarnation is taken ... Aries "awakens the will to reach the lowest and there control, to know the uttermost and thus to face all experience".' (Bailey 1951, p. 92) 'Aries is also the purveyor to our solar system of Fire (Electric Fire) and

of the dynamic nature of God which has in it the qualities of fostering and nourishing heat and also of the fire which burns and destroys.' (Bailey 1951, p. 95)

I summarise here the Tibetan's teaching on the human Monad and Aries and the four different cycles of progress upon the Path in its various stages of individualisation to initiation (the reader is invited to refer to page 107 of Bailey's *Esoteric Astrology* for the full wording):

1. *Re-creation* ... which produces the pull into incarnation.

2. *Re-generation* ... which produces those interior changes which eventually lead to:

**ARIES**
(PISCES)

**TZADKIEL**

**LOCAL
SUPERCLUSTER**

VIRGO
Supercluster

**LOCAL GROUP
OF GALAXIES**

Local Group Logos
**AN**

Andromeda ◇ Triangulum

Milky Way

**The Galactic Logos
AION**

Alcyone ◇ Merak

Sirius

**MILKY WAY
GALAXY**

**LOCAL SOLAR GROUP**

Local Solar Group Logos
**ARCHON**

**ZODIAC HOUSES**

Libra ◇ Aquarius

Aries

**The Solar Logos
BEL**

Mars ◇ Mercury

Uranus

**SOLAR SYSTEM**

**The Planetary Logos
IBEZ**

**PLANETARY
RAYS**

6 ◇ 4

7

**Lord of Planet Earth
Archangel MICHAEL**

World Soul ◇ Spiritual Will

The Seven
Hierarchies

**PLANET
EARTH**

**Humanity**

*23.4 The stepping down of divine energy from the Virgo Supercluster to humanity, with reference to the Dharmic Wheel of Silbury Hill, Wiltshire, 18.8.1992*

23.5 *'Aries', satellite 2*

23.6 *'Aries', satellite 4*

3. *Re-orientation* or the great cycle of repolarisation (the "swerving of the Bull in mid-career") on the Cardinal Cross around the Wheel, in which the inner subjective man comes into outer manifested expression and the Personality recedes into the background.

4. *Renunciation.* The disciple or initiate renounces all for the love of humanity and its service, and lays himself upon the altar of sacrifice. He achieves as a result the final liberation.

*The crop circle symbol in Aries* (23.5 and 23.6)

The symbol in the south-west corner consists of a circle (24 ft diameter) on the wheel ring, with three smaller circles of diminishing size (9 ft, 7 ft 6 in, and 6 ft diameters) arranged round it as satellites. (Dimensions are approximate.) As with all the seven surviving symbols around the Wheel, this apparently simple diagram is multi-faceted in its meaning.

'We have seen that Aries is the sign of beginnings – the beginning of the creative process, the first step of the soul ... towards incarnation, the beginning of recurring and constant cycles of experience, the beginning of the period wherein the soul changes its direction, its purpose and its method, and finally enters upon that definitely defined process which we call spiritual regeneration and initiation.' (Bailey 1951, p. 106)

So Aries is pre-eminently the House of the beginning of the creative process, and thus of Ray 1. The symbol thus shows the large undifferentiated circle representing Spirit (First Cosmic Logos), broken down into the threefold Trinity (Second Cosmic Logos) of Spirit, Soul and Personality (Father, Son and Holy Spirit), shown as the three satellites of increasing size. So far as humanity is concerned the symbol relates in the East to *Shiva*, who appears on a seal of the Harappan culture from Mohenjo-daro (c. 2300-1750 BC) seated in the lotus position, horned, priapic and with three faces, Birth, Life and Death. (23.7) On the Vedic Wheel of Life (22.11)

*23.7 Shiva*

this is *Dhruva*, the Polestar, symbolising God at the centre of the Cosmos. In the West this is the position of the Archangel Tzadkiel, Ray 1 of the Esoteric Kumaras of the Great Council of planet Earth [In Chapters 12 and 13 Tzadkiel is at Ray 2. The reader is invited to consider the conundrum, which has defeated the editor. (Ed.)]. The numinous quality of this symbol relates it to the core principle of energy transmission on which the whole system operates, namely the Science of Triangles, discussed in detail in Chapter 19.

It is indeed a neat diagram showing the four elements of Triangles of Power:

1. Emanating Energy (large circle)

2. Evocative Force (smallest satellite)

3. Magnetic Centre (second smallest satellite)

4. Distributing Centre (largest satellite).

In Aries, the quintessential pressures that are brought to bear upon the human Monad are the purifying processes required during incarnation alongside the parallel aspects of spiritual illumination. Both the planets and the Rays dominating Aries reflect this. 'Through the fiery processes of war and strife, brought to the individual through the influence of the planetary ruler, Mars, the God of War, a needed purification takes place. The same purification, but this time through vision, comes to the [spiritually] developed man through the activity of the subjective ruler of the planet, Mercury, who is

the illuminating principle which releases the mind, directs the way of man through life and enables him to become aware of the divine Plan which underlies all his fiery experience.' (Bailey 1951, pp. 95-96) In the case of the Rays, Aries' primary agent is Ray 1 of Will or Power, with reference to the hidden planet, Uranus (Ray 7). Mars embodies the Ray 6 force and Mercury Ray 4. (Bailey 1951, pp. 99-100)

In all this Aries represents the beginning of the spiritual developmental process for the Soul, where the Personality has perfected self-consciousness and developed a rounded-out character. Spiritual light begins to pour 'through dense fogs of illusion and [the human Monad] is preparing for the major tests in Scorpio, to be followed by initiation in Capricorn. (Bailey 1951, p. 103)

## THE HOUSE OF TAURUS (23.8)

The next House on the Wheel is Taurus, the Bull. 'This sign ... brings expression of an inner urge of some definite nature upon the physical plane. This it does, because its basic quality demonstrates *as desire* in the mass of men and *as will* or directed purpose in the disciple or the initiate. ... It manifests ... as intelligently expressed will – actuated by the impulse of love ... This connotes adherence to soul purpose.' (Bailey 1951, p. 375)

In a communication from the Archangel Michael channelled by Isabelle Kingston on 27.10.1991 the functions of various archangels were discussed:

Michael Green: "What about the One Who is responsible for the Animal World?"

The Archangel Michael: "Ceres, Sirius, Sorpah" (phon.). [Possibly *Sopet*, the Graeco-Egyptian vernacular for Sirius]

Michael Green: "Is there a classical name one could equate with that Being?"

# TAURUS

# RAPHAEL

**LOCAL
SUPERCLUSTER**

**VIRGO**
Supercluster

**LOCAL GROUP
OF GALAXIES**

**Local Group Logos
AN**

Andromeda ◇ Triangulum

Milky Way

**The Galactic Logos
AION**

**MILKY WAY
GALAXY**

Alcyone ◇ Merak

Sirius

**LOCAL SOLAR GROUP**

**Local Solar Group Logos
ARCHON**

**ZODIAC HOUSES**

Capricorn ◇ Virgo

Taurus

**SOLAR SYSTEM**

**The Solar Logos
BEL**

Venus ◇ Vulcan

Vulcan

**The Planetary Logos
IBEZ**

**PLANETARY
RAYS**

5 ◇ 1

1

**Lord of Planet Earth
Archangel MICHAEL**

**PLANET
EARTH**

World Soul ◇ Spiritual Will

The Seven
Hierarchies

**Humanity**

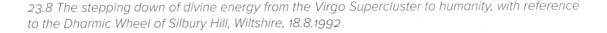

*23.8 The stepping down of divine energy from the Virgo Supercluster to humanity, with reference to the Dharmic Wheel of Silbury Hill, Wiltshire, 18.8.1992*

The Archangel Michael: "The angel is the angel of healing, Raphael, but also Ceres."

This valuable communication, as in all the discussions with the Archangel Michael, raises important issues.

The House of Taurus, the southernmost of the Silbury Hill Wheel, is concerned with the physical plane of the human Monad, the incipient beginnings of spiritual life (for the ordinary man), and spiritual direction in the case of the more advanced one. In more general terms it is concerned with (land) *animal life* on the planet, and the nutritional support of that life. (23.3)

The House is on Ray 2 of Love-Wisdom and hence the connection with *Sirius*. As we have seen (Chapter 16), the star system of Sirius is Ray 2 of the local solar group of Archon. *Ceres* is the Roman name for the Greek goddess Demeter, 'even if it is etymologically true that Ceres was a very early vegetative force (the name is related to a root-word meaning 'growth') worshipped by the Romans, this very early goddess was completely eclipsed by the other.' (Grimal 1986, p. 97) Demeter, the Greek Mother Goddess of the Earth, is the divinity of agriculture and essentially the Corn Goddess.

The Archangel Raphael leads the five Buddhas of Activity in the hands-on management of *physical aspects* of life on the planet (Chapter 14), under

the aegis of the Archangel Michael, the Soul and Lord of planet Earth.

I have in earlier chapters related the Archangel Raphael to the devic Lord Kshiti, Lord of Earth (matter as opposed to the planet). Djwhal Khul describes Him as the 'Life of the physical plane' (Bailey 1925, p. 636), or again 'He is a deva of rank and power equal to a Chohan [i.e. an adept who has taken the sixth Initiation] of a Ray; He presides over everything outside the human kingdom upon the physical plane, and He has for His council the four subordinate deva lords of the four etheric levels. He, with these subordinate devas … who handle all that concerns the deva evolution, and the work of the greater and lesser builders.' (Bailey 1925, p. 911)

As regards Triangles of Power, Djwhal Khul states: 'The earthly triplicity of Capricorn, Virgo and Taurus form a triangle of material expression … Capricorn marks the point of greatest density and concrete expression and shows the life divine as deeply imbedded in substance. … In Virgo, however, … the hidden

*23.9 **'Taurus'** symbol, looking South East. Silbury Hill in the background*

[spiritual] life begins to pulsate within the concrete form, producing in Taurus that reaction to desire ... and powerful movement which distinguishes the evolutionary progress of the individual, working under the impulse of desire.' (Bailey 1951, p. 379) In terms of the planets and the Rays, Taurus is 'governed by only two planets. Venus [Ray 5] is its exoteric ruler and Vulcan [Ray 1] is its esoteric and hierarchical ruler.' (Bailey 1951, p. 382)

*The crop circle symbol in Taurus* (23.9)

Here we have one of the strangest symbols found at Silbury. As with Aries, a simple circle, some 23 ft in diameter, cuts the wheel ring of the formation. Sprouting from a short 3 ft stem are two antlers, each with three tines. This extrusion on the south side extends some 15 ft.

Although, as we will see, this symbol has multiple possible meanings, one of the most evident is that it refers to the ancient Indo-Aryan horned god *Cernunnos*, Lord of Nature. (23.10) An image of this Deity appears as Magdalenian rock art at Les Trois-Frères cave (Ariège, France) around 15,000 BC, and much later as a rock carving from Val Camonica in northern Italy, possibly in the first millennium BC. This figure carries a torque on its right arm and a snake on its left, symbolising lordship and relationship with the Earth Goddess symbolised as a snake. The same attributes are found in the same positions on the squatting Cernunnos depicted on the Gundestrup Cauldron (second to first century BC, National Museum of Denmark) from Northern Jutland. In this case he also is surrounded by the wild animals, over whose realm he rules.

Cernunnos is closely related to the devic Beings Pan and *Faunus* whom I encountered at the temple of the *Magna Mater* on the Palatine Hill in Rome. Sixty years ago I was

23.10 *Cernunnos*

Les Trois-Frères cave, Ariège, France

Rock carving from Val Camonica

From the Gundestrup Cauldron

in the Palatine Gardens leaning against the podium of this, the oldest temple in the city. It was mid February and the New Moon was in the sky. It was, I realised later, the date of the ancient *Lupercalia*, whose early fertility rites were celebrated in Rome. Nobody else was around. I saw in a visionary state the *Faunus Lupercal* moving amongst the trees. He reminded me of the dancing faun statue from Pompeii, and was laughing when he came towards me. At his touch I experienced all the beauty and horror of that sacred place in that ancient world he personified. I realised that I must be standing near the lost cave where the Roman mythological story began, and Romulus and Remus were suckled by the wolf.

Viewed from the inside of the circle this symbol is reminiscent also of another potent image of the physical plane, this time in connection with the ancient Indo-Aryan *Tree of Life*. An inverted oak tree buried in the sand with its roots in the air was discovered at Holme-next-the-Sea on the Norfolk coast in 1998. The tree was surrounded by a ring of 54 wooden posts in a ritual setting, and appears to date to the Early Bronze Age (c. 2000 BC). This strange arrangement has been described as 'the image of the dispersion of the Divine Life through the thousand-branched tree of life, whose roots, high above, are deeply imbedded in heaven and whose branches come down to our earthly realm bringing the divine life to all.' In other words it represents Deity in manifestation, drawing on the resources of the Unmanifest from above, and whose fruit is the myriad forms of cosmic life in the universe below. (See Green, Michael 1999a, p. 23.)

Turning to the distinctive human component of this symbol, a metaphysical paradigm is indicated by the six tines of the horns of the crop formation. Mankind has animal antecedents but needs to reorganise the raw components of the human metabolism before the spiritual journey can properly begin. These components (*skandha*) were categorised in the ancient Indian world as physicality (*rūpa*), feeling (*vedanā*), perception (*saṃjñā*), intelligence (*saṃskāra*) and consciousness (*vijñāna*). To these might be added at a slightly higher level the concept of obligation or duty (*vrata* = vow) operating at a family or social level: i.e. the group consciousness.

Finally there are two mystical components implied in this symbol, whose significance has been stressed earlier. This House is on Ray 2 of Love-Wisdom: the ultimate principle on which all manifested life is planned and co-ordinated – hence the *two* antlers of the symbol. Lastly the six tines can also be interpreted as symbolic of Ray 6, among other things that of emotion, feeling and *desire*, producing that powerful motion that ultimately moves the physical state to that of the spiritual in all life forms.

### THE HOUSE OF CANCER (23.11)

There are two Houses in this quadrant, Gemini and Cancer, of which Cancer is the more important for our purposes. We first consider Gemini, the House after Taurus. 'This sign is sometimes called the "constellation of the resolution of duality into a fluid synthesis." Governing as it does all the pairs of opposites in the Zodiac, it preserves the magnetic interplay between them, keeping them fluid in their relations, in order eventually to facilitate their transmutation into unity, for the two must finally become the One.' (Bailey 1951, p. 347)

Cancer represents a critical stage not only of the individual's psycho-spiritual development,

# CANCER
## (GEMINI)

# URIEL

## LOCAL
## SUPERCLUSTER

**VIRGO**
Supercluster

**Local Group Logos**
**AN**

## LOCAL GROUP
## OF GALAXIES

Andromeda ◇ Triangulum

Milky Way

**The Galactic Logos**
**AION**

## MILKY WAY
## GALAXY

Alcyone ◇ Merak

Sirius

**Local Solar Group Logos**
**ARCHON**

## LOCAL SOLAR GROUP

## ZODIAC HOUSES

Aquarius ◇ Virgo

Cancer

**The Solar Logos**
**BEL**

## SOLAR SYSTEM

Moon ◇ Neptune

Saturn

**The Planetary Logos**
**IBEZ**

## PLANETARY
## RAYS

4 ◇ 6

3

**Lord of Planet Earth**
**Archangel MICHAEL**

World Soul ◇ Spiritual Will

## PLANET
## EARTH

The Seven
Hierarchies

**Humanity**

*23.11 The stepping down of divine energy from the Virgo Supercluster to humanity, with reference to the Dharmic Wheel of Silbury Hill, Wiltshire, 18.8.1992*

but also that of humanity as a whole. Djwhal Khul states that 'a fairly large minority are becoming *group conscious*, whilst the majority [of humanity] are emerging out of the *mass conscious* stage and becoming *self-conscious* individuals.' (my italics) (Bailey 1951, p. 311)

'In Cancer, God breathed into man's nostrils the breath of life and man became a living soul ... *In Cancer* this living substance assumed a triple differentiated relationship to which we give the names of Life (Aries), of Consciousness (Taurus, the next sign to Aries) and manifested duality (Gemini, the sign preceding Cancer) and these three, blended together, came into outer manifestation in Cancer.' (Bailey 1951, pp. 313-4) 'Cancer ... is the Door to the physical plane expression of spirit.' (Bailey 1951, p. 316) In Capricorn the fifth aspect comes into operation, namely that of spiritual immortality which is 'the divine aspect of self-preservation' (Bailey 1951, p. 316) at the Third Initiation. As we will see the number five has great importance in this House.

For the spiritual initiate the process towards apotheosis only really starts in *Cancer*, for under Cancer the conscious personality achieves Individuation. Later in *Virgo* dormant spirituality becomes in *Scorpio* a process of spiritual committal where the claims of personality are subsumed to that of the Soul. In *Capricorn* spiritual development becomes in *Pisces*, spiritual service. 'Such is the way of the Initiate.' (Bailey 1951, p. 320)

Since in Cancer so much of the human Personality is brought to fruition, ready for the spiritual process to begin, it is very much the sphere of the Devic world (23.3), which in many capacities equips the human Monad at this stage of development. In my discussion

with the Archangel Michael in 1991, He comments on this House and this writer's connection with it:

The Archangel Michael: "At present the One known within the Christian teaching as Uriel is very much in evidence at this time. Uriel linked specifically with those entities [with] which you have a great affinity, with those energies you hold in your heart and whom you understand. I have told you before you are the 'Green Man' linked with the Devas and Nature Spirits."

Michael Green: "This I think we link with Saturn in our system. Is that correct?"

The Archangel Michael: "This is true. Sometimes depicted differently from what we would consider correct."

The Houses which form a Triangle of Power with Cancer: 'are Cancer-Virgo-Aquarius. In this combination, you have the sign of mass-consciousness, the sign of the Christ-consciousness and the sign of universal consciousness very closely related to each other and all of them through the medium of the influence of Neptune, which the Moon veils.' (Bailey 1951, p. 321) 'Cancer ... is ruled by only one planet ... Neptune because it is the form nature which is dominant in the longest stage of human unfoldment, just as esoterically, it is the feeling-sensitive nature which dominates the average man.' (Bailey 1951, p. 321)

However, as noted above in the Archangel's comment, *Saturn* is also a planetary influence. Saturn has a profound impact on all spiritual life in physical manifestation. 'Saturn is the lord of Karma, the imposer of retribution and the one who demands full payment of all debts and who therefore condemns us to the struggle for existence, both from the form side and from the soul side ... Saturn's power is completely ended and his work accomplished when man (the spiritual man) has freed himself from Karma' (Bailey 1951, p. 105) and has taken the Fourth Initiation. (See Chapter 9.) Saturn is therefore an essential planetary influence at this stage of the human Monad's development.

However, in the case of the *Wheel adjusted or reversed*, 'when a man is an initiate ... the watery life of emotional reaction [i.e. Neptune's influence] is superseded by the life of true and of inclusive love. [But] without the form and without the ability to bear in mind the need to respond sensitively to the environing conditions and circumstances, the soul would never awaken to knowledge in the three worlds and, therefore, would never know God in manifestation.' (Bailey 1951, pp. 322-323)

*The crop circle symbol in Cancer* (23.12 and 23.13)

23.12 *'Cancer' symbol, looking South West*

23.13 *'Cancer' symbol, looking North East*

The symbol here consists of an irregular heart-shaped formation some 40 ft wide straddling the wheel ring. The researcher Stanley Morcom noted that the slightly irregular outline of the figure was due to its being constructed as a group of five circles of diminishing area: 29 ft, 27 ft, 22 ft 6 in, 21 ft and 17 ft in diameter. There is clearly some numerical, indeed symbolic, significance in these varying sizes and their placement. There are *five circles* and their strange grouping suggests that there is a clear reference here to the Buddhas of Activity, concerned with the hands-on management of planet Earth.

Thus the symbol here refers to planet Earth in her archetypal role as the nurturing mother (*Gaia*) of all life within her sphere. The cardiac shape is a direct reference also to symbols (11.3) which first appeared eleven thousand years ago at Mas d'Azil, France, painted on pebbles, showing the squatting Earth Goddess. As a crop formation symbol it has occurred at Chilcomb, Hampshire in 1990 (11.1) and elsewhere in Wessex and notably at Ickleton, Cambridgeshire in 1991 (11.10), see Chapter 11.

The Archangel Raphael constitutes the intelligence factor of the creative force of

Deity, which transforms spirit into matter and energises it as a living organism. In this capacity He presides over the devic lords of Air, Fire, Water and Earth. The functions of these departments are extensively discussed in Chapter 14 and elsewhere in this study. It may be felt that this body of teaching about the management of this planet is an exclusively Eastern or Theosophic paradigm. However this is not the case, for Jesus Christ himself indirectly refers to them in allegorised terms as 'trees' in one of the lesser known parables: 'for you have five trees in Paradise which are unmoved in summer (or) in winter and their leaves do not fall. Whoever knows them will not taste death'. (Brill 2001, pp. 13-14) This is yet another example of the emphasis of the incarnatory experience as an essential ingredient of spiritual life.

In this quadrant of the Wheel, humans, as physically coordinated and sentient beings, begin to relate to their fellows and other forms of life. The person becomes aware of his and their limitations, and in this sense experiences *suffering*, the First of the Noble Truths of Buddhism. There is also a dawning sense of the presence of God and the need for ethical behaviour towards others. This is the place of the *Five Precepts* of the Buddhist Perfection of *morality* (*Sila*), the prohibitions against taking life, theft, unchastity, lying and intoxication. When the human person is aware of God, the First Initiation has been achieved. This is the *vasu Prabhāsa*, a reference to the dawn of human consciousness.

Lastly the mystical symbolism of the 'heart' shape of this crop formation symbol should not be overlooked. It may not have much significance in the East, but in the West it has the connotation of 'love'. The somewhat negative directives of the Five Precepts of Buddhism should be viewed as wrapped in the positive quality of unqualified love or compassion for others.

## THE HOUSE OF LEO (23.14)

Of all the twelve Houses of the Zodiac or the eight *vasus* of the Vedic Wheel of Life, that of the eastern quarter is of the most immediate importance to the majority of humanity. It relates to mankind at its most developed, where the intellect is fully formed and individuation as a self-conscious entity has been achieved. The corporate aspects of the emotions and physicality are coming under control, and man has become a living Soul. In the words of Djwhal Khul: 'The keynotes of this sign are exceedingly well known. They sound out the note of individuality and of true self-consciousness. ... Yet the only truly self-conscious person is the man who is aware of purpose, of a self-directed life and of a developed and definite life plan and programme.' (Bailey 1951, p. 288)

On the Zodiacal Houses which influence Leo: 'In the relationship of Taurus-Leo-Aquarius, you have a significant and important zodiacal triangle as far as man is concerned and it is peculiarly significant to the fourth Creative Hierarchy, the human Hierarchy. You have, therefore:

1. Taurus - The incentive towards experience in order to gain knowledge.

2. Leo - The expression of experience in order to justify knowledge.

3. Aquarius - The use of experience in order to make the gained knowledge a factor in service.

This triangle expresses the life of humanity and it demonstrates finally the perfection or consummation of the human way.' (Bailey 1951, pp. 289-290)

# LEO

# GABRIEL

**LOCAL
SUPERCLUSTER**

**VIRGO
Supercluster**

**LOCAL GROUP
OF GALAXIES**

**Local Group Logos
AN**

Andromeda ◇ Triangulum

Milky Way

**MILKY WAY
GALAXY**

**The Galactic Logos
AION**

Alcyone ◇ Merak

Sirius

**LOCAL SOLAR GROUP**

**Local Solar Group Logos
ARCHON**

**ZODIAC HOUSES**

Aquarius ◇ Taurus

Leo

**SOLAR SYSTEM**

**The Solar Logos
BEL**

Sol
(h.s.) ◇ Sol
( s.)

Sol
( f.)

**The Planetary Logos
IBEZ**

**PLANETARY
RAYS**

3 ◇ 2

1

**Lord of Planet Earth
Archangel MICHAEL**

World Soul ◇ Spiritual Will

**PLANET
EARTH**

The Seven
Hierarchies

**Humanity**

*23.14 The stepping down of divine energy from the Virgo Supercluster to humanity, with reference to the Dharmic Wheel of Silbury Hill, Wiltshire, 18.8.1992*

Leo is a unique House since it has only one cosmic ruler, the Sun: 'the Sun is the ruler of all the three conditions of Leo – exoteric, esoteric and hierarchical. It is a correct surmise that the purpose of this solar system is the unfoldment of consciousness, and if for the strictly human being self-consciousness is the goal, then the Sun must obviously rule, for it is the source of physical consciousness (exoteric and symbolic of the personality), of soul awareness (esoteric), and of spiritual life (hierarchical).' (Bailey 1951, p. 294) We are obviously not looking at the undifferentiated Solar Logos here, but three distinct aspects:

Ray 3  – 'exoteric' – the Holy Spirit (form aspect)

Ray 2  – 'esoteric' – the Son (soul aspect)

Ray 1  – 'hierarchical' – the Father (spirit aspect).

'The outstanding theme of Leo is the activity of the self-conscious unit [i.e. man] in relation to its environment or *the development of sensitive response to surrounding impacts* by the one who stands – as the Sun stands – at the centre of its little universe. The whole story and function of Leo and its influences can be summed up in the word *"sensitivity"*.' (Bailey 1951, p. 294)

In a discussion with me in October 1991, the Archangel Michael made some passing but important references to this House: "We have a Ray Who is known as the Master Ray – terminology perhaps different – but the great mystical entity now coming closer to the Earth linked closely with your Gabriel, who, in the 'great communicator', is also part of the formulae you seek."

I believe that the 'Master Ray' spoken of here is One of the three Lords of Liberation spoken of in Chapter 1, where They were invoked at the Sirius Rite in 1989. In Chapter 12 I quote Djwhal Khul in his comment that 'one of Them is closer to the Earth and to humanity than are the other Two', and identified this seraph as the Archangel Metatron.

The Archangel Gabriel, famous in Christian hagiology as the herald of the birth of Christ to Mary (*Luke* 1:26), occurs as One who brings spiritual 'wisdom and understanding' to mankind. (*Daniel* 9:22) 'In Scripture he is set forth only as a representative of the angelic nature in its ministration of comfort and sympathy to man.' (Smith, W. 1875, p. 275) Gabriel is thus peculiarly suited to preside over the House of Leo, concerned specifically with the development of mankind.

'The *formulae* I seek' mentioned by the archangel is, of course, the spiritual *causus vitae* for mankind, set out in great detail throughout this study!

*The crop circle symbol in Leo (23.15)*

The symbol illustrating this House has three simple components: a large ring 23 ft in

23.15 *'Leo'* symbol, looking North

diameter and 5 ft wide cutting the wheel ring, connected on the outer side by a path 2 ft 6 in wide to a small circle, 7 ft 6 in in diameter, set at an angle to the formation. The setting-out line of the bisected wheel ring, about 1ft 6 in wide, can be seen running across the centre of the symbol, a feature that occurs also in the House of Aquarius on the opposite side.

When discussing this symbol in 2000, I described it as the 'Mahadiva' symbol of sexual and creative energy. The epithet of Agni, 'Light through knowledge' emphasises the intellectual component of the creative process as an aspect of the Lord of Fire. The symbol also brings into focus another aspect of creation, the infusing of form or matter by spirit. This is brought out in the Etchilhampton Hill formation, Wiltshire (29.7.1990) which also has the circle and ring dumb-bell. (15.5 and 15.6) That formation is clearly delineated as a solar power by rays. (See Chapter 15.)

In Chapter 15 I described the Etchilhampton formation as an aspect of the Solar Logos, with the five ray penumbra symbolising intellectual achievement. There is a truth in my earlier identification of the Silbury Leo symbol with the Eastern *Mahadiva* symbol, but careful examination of the extant photos would suggest a simpler interpretation. They indicate a feature not picked up at the time by the original surveyors. Branching out of the circle near the field tramline (the route made by tractor wheel marks) are two spurs on either side of the circle, all that remains, I believe, of five such spurs, the other three being obliterated by the tramline. (23.1) This missing feature, I believe, indicates that this dumb-bell symbol was originally planned to have the solar rays characteristic of the Etchilhampton formation. It will be noted however that the ring and the circle have been reversed in the Silbury formation. If this is correct we appear to have a five-rayed Solar Logos, as at Etchilhampton, symbolising a Divine *Manasputra* or Son of Mind, which would make excellent sense of a House with the vitalising, energising effect of Solar intelligence.

In Buddhism this particular Perfection is that of *vigour* (*Virya*). This energy brings into play an essential ingredient of spiritual life, namely that of creative activity. There really is no room for bystanders. World religions and belief systems, including the New Age, tend to be overwhelmingly patronised by sedentary 'believers' only interested in receiving their regular religious 'fix'. In the words of the Apostle James: 'What good is it, my brothers and sisters, if you say you have faith but do not have works? Can faith save you? If a brother or sister is naked and lacks daily food, and one of you says to them, 'Go in peace; keep warm and eat your fill', and yet you do not supply their bodily needs, what is the good of that? So faith by itself, if it has no works, is dead.' (*James* 2:14-17). As Christ's message was to the 'supine churches' of Asia Minor: 'Wake up ... you are lukewarm ... I am about to spit you out of my mouth' (*Revelation* 3:15); or as Krishna states in the *Bhagavad Gita*, 'Action is greater than inaction.' This House, therefore, is that of active spirituality, and marks the achievement of the First Initiation.

# 24. THE DHARMIC WHEEL OF SILBURY HILL: TO APOTHEOSIS

*'What no eye has seen, nor ear heard,*
*nor the human heart conceived,*
*what God has prepared for those who love Him' –*
*these things God has revealed to us*
*through the Spirit; for the Spirit searches*
*everything, even the depths of God.*

*1 Corinthians 2:9, 2:10*

In the previous chapter we studied the Houses which have led up to the First Initiation, and the effective beginning of the spiritual process. Now we examine the Houses and spiritual process which lead to the Fifth (Planetary) or First Cosmic Initiation and the beginning of the great transformation of the human Monad to advanced deific service.

The reader may wish to refer to the first illustrations for the Silbury Hill Wheel, from the last chapter. (23.1, 23.2, 23.3)

## FOURFOLD SPIRITUAL DEVELOPMENT

But first, a reminder about the fourfold nature of the Wheel. The apparent confusion and complexity of the traditional structure of the Zodiac hides an essentially fourfold framework of spiritual development. It is the reason why the earliest mandalas of the Dharmic Wheel take the form of a cross (Chapter 22), which develops successively as an eightfold and then as a twelvefold structure. The four procedural steps, as we have traced them in this study, are effectively 'incarnation', 'individuation', 'spirituality', and 'apotheosis', each one of which, I believe, refers to a particular quadrant of the Dharmic Wheel of Life, the life crises or challenges which have to be surmounted by the human Monad.

It is in this light that the Twelve Houses of the traditional Zodiac should be seen. The three Houses of each quadrant each reflect a particular stage of growth peculiar to that quadrant.

First there is a period of conflict where the new emerging Personality confronts the old, so that the transmutation process may take place. The Archangel Michael has often described it as a process where the higher aspects battle with the lower, not always successfully. On the Zodiac each quadrant contains a House which is a statement about this duality:

South-west quadrant of 'incarnation'
– *Pisces*

South-east quadrant of 'individuation'
– *Gemini*

North-east quadrant of 'spirituality'
– *Libra*

North-west quadrant of 'apotheosis'
– *Sagittarius*.

Usually this House of Conflict is found at the beginning of the process, but when a spiritual Being is born (like the human birthing process itself), this trauma is at the end of a process of natal growth, as in the case of the House of Libra.

The second type of House in each quadrant represents the core of the transformative process of that phase. This House, which should be equated with the appropriate *vasu* of the Vedic Wheel, is the aspect which is given greatest attention in this study. They are in Zodiacal terms:

South-west quadrant of 'incarnation'
– *Aries*

South-east quadrant of 'individuation'
– *Cancer*

North-east quadrant of 'spirituality'
– *Virgo*

North-west quadrant of 'apotheosis'
– *Capricorn*.

The third type of House marks the final aspect of each quadrant, and, except in the case of the first, is registered by an initiation of increasing importance. It does of course register the beginning of a new phase of development, but more importantly it marks the end of a transformative process which has been active as an undercurrent in the previous quadrant.

Southern quarter of 'incarnation'
– *Taurus*

Eastern quarter of 'individuation'
– *Leo* – First Initiation

Northern quarter of 'spirituality'
– *Scorpio* – Second Initiation

Western quarter of 'apotheosis'
– *Aquarius* – Third/Fourth Initiation.

## THE HOUSE OF VIRGO (24.1)

Although our main consideration will be the House of Virgo, something should be said in passing about the succeeding House, Libra. 'The sign Libra is one of peculiar interest, but in a most paradoxical manner, for most of its interest is based upon the fact that it lacks spectacular interest of any kind – except in the case of disciples or those nearing the Path. It is a sign of balancing, of careful weighing of values, and of achieving values, and of achieving the right equilibrium between the pairs of opposites. It might be regarded as the sign in which the first real vision of the Path appears and of the goal towards which the disciple must ultimately direct his steps.' (Bailey 1951, pp. 226-227)

'The sign Virgo is one of the most significant in the Zodiac for its symbology concerns the whole goal of the evolutionary process which is to shield, nurture and finally reveal the hidden spiritual reality. ... The keynote which embodies the truth as to the mission of Virgo most accurately is "Christ in you, the hope of glory".' (*Colossians* 1:27) (Bailey 1951, pp. 251-252)

This most ancient of symbols on the Babylonian Zodiac Compilation Tablet 2 (Chapter 21) started life as that seminal totem of the Neolithic world, the *barley stalk*, held by a Mesopotamian agricultural goddess, *Sala*. (21.5) By the second century BC attention has shifted from the barley stalk to the woman herself, who has become Virgo the Maiden. Djwhal Khul has much to say about the numinous feminine aspect of the House of Virgo, and of its importance to mankind, but rather less about its significance to the natural world. In discussion with the Archangel Michael in 1990 an attempt was made to identify which of the Great Beings of

# VIRGO
(LIBRA)

# SANDALPHON

**LOCAL SUPERCLUSTER**

**VIRGO**
Supercluster

**LOCAL GROUP OF GALAXIES**

Local Group Logos
**AN**

Andromeda ◇ Triangulum

Milky Way

**MILKY WAY GALAXY**

The Galactic Logos
**AION**

Alcyone ◇ Merak

Sirius

**LOCAL SOLAR GROUP**

Local Solar Group Logos
**ARCHON**

**ZODIAC HOUSES**

Capricorn ◇ Taurus

Virgo

**SOLAR SYSTEM**

The Solar Logos
**BEL**

Mercury ◇ The Moon

Jupiter

**PLANETARY RAYS**

The Planetary Logos
**IBEZ**

4 ◇ 4

2

**Lord of Planet Earth
Archangel MICHAEL**

World Soul ◇ Spiritual Will

The Seven
Hierarchies

**PLANET EARTH**

**Humanity**

*24.1 The stepping down of divine energy from the Virgo Supercluster to humanity, with reference to the Dharmic Wheel of Silbury Hill, Wiltshire, 18.8.1992*

our system (as represented by their classical or Eastern counterparts) were responsible for particular areas of nature. (23.3)

Michael Green: "Now the plant world. What Great Energy is responsible for their care?"

The Archangel Michael: "Sol."

Michael Green: "Venus is sometimes associated in the systems which I work with. To what extent is this correct?"

The Archangel Michael: "Venus is the planet and the Deity most closely associated with all life forms, with the nurturing of the planet."

24.2 *'Virgo' symbol, looking North West*

Venus and Virgo are closely linked. 'Venus, pure love-wisdom, falls into generation in this sign and occultly "descends to earth" and stands ... for the gift of mind and of divinity, embodied in the Son of Mind and thus for the descent of the Christ principle into generation or into matter. Virgo and Venus are together two aspects of intelligence.' (Bailey 1951, p. 281)

In terms of the Houses related to Virgo, to quote Djwhal Khul: 'Virgo belongs to the earthly triplicity ... Taurus-Virgo-Capricorn and they are related to each other in a peculiar way in connection with the non-sacred planet, our Earth.' (Bailey 1951, p. 259)

To condense Djwhal Khul:

1. Taurus – Incentive behind evolution
   Aspiration for the Light of Knowledge

2. Virgo – Incentive behind discipleship
   Aspiration for the Hidden Light of God

3. Capricorn – Incentive behind Spiritual Service
   Aspiration for the Light of Life.

'All these express desire as it merges into aspiration, and in the process bring light and life to man.' (Bailey 1951, p. 259)

There are three rulers of Virgo. Mercury 'is the orthodox ruler. It signifies the versatile energy of the Son of Mind, the Soul. ... The Moon ... is the esoteric ruler. ... The Moon rules the form and it is the will of God to manifest through the medium of form. ... Jupiter ... is the hierarchical ruler and rules the Second Creative Hierarchy, that of the Divine Builders of our planetary manifestation. ... This is the seventh Creative Hierarchy as well as the second, if the five unmanifesting Hierarchies are counted.' (Bailey 1951, p. 263) (See Chapter 14, the Borstal formation of 1999.) (14.7)

'Through these three planetary rulers the energies of the fourth ray pour, governing the mind through Mercury and the physical form through the Moon; the energies of the first ray, expressive of the will of God, begin their control of the self-conscious man (unfolded in Leo) and the energies of the second ray, embodying the love of God, pour through into manifestation.' (Bailey 1951, p. 263)

Djwhal Khul sums up the maternal aspect of this House as follows: 'Virgo symbolises depths, darkness, quiet and warmth; it is the valley of deep experience wherein secrets are discovered and eventually "brought to light"; it is the place of slow, gentle and yet powerful crises and periodic developments which take place in the dark and yet which lead to light. ... Virgo stands for the "womb of time" wherein God's plan (the mystery and the secret of the ages) is slowly matured and – with pain and discomfort and through struggle and conflict – brought into manifestation at the end of the appointed time.' (Bailey 1951, p. 260)

The archangel of the House of Virgo is, I understand, Sandalphon, Who is one of the Buddhas of Activity, an aspect the Archangel Raphael, and a key figure of the Executive Council, since, under the Archangel Michael, He helps to preside over planet Earth as its etheric body. (See Chapter 14.)

This House and *vasu* is of critical importance for the beginning of the spiritual process for mankind, one of the key reasons for the existence of our solar system. I suspect that Sandalphon is an emanation of that great seraph, Metatron, and has been drafted in to ensure that the critical aspects of Love-Wisdom (Ray 2) are carried through into the spiritual formulation of mankind. These two archangels, I believe, are emissaries from Archon.

*The crop circle symbol in Virgo* (24.2)

In the light of the rulership of this House, it is hardly surprising that its symbol should be the waxing crescent moon viewed from the interior of the formation (the diameter of the 'full' crop circle moon would have been about 28 ft). As usual with such symbols at Silbury, it has a multiplicity of meanings.

The Tibetan provides a succinct definition of the spiritual, symbolical importance of the moon: 'The Moon ... stands for the glorification, through purification and detachment, of matter, and Venus stands for the emergence of the love principle through the directing power of the mind.' (Bailey 1951, p. 126)

The crescent moon is found as the symbol of many deities in the ancient world, mostly feminine, but in a notable case relating to a male god, the moon-god, *Nanna-suen* or *Sin* in the Sumerian pantheon. He was symbolised by the crescent moon in Mesopotamian art right through to the Neo-Babylonian period (625-539 BC). The Sumerian goddess *Inanna, Ištar* to the Akkadians and *Astarte* in the Levant (Hebrew, *Ashtoreth*) was sometimes equated in the Phoenician world with *Tanit*, who in turn was identified with the Roman Deity, *Juno-Caelestis*, whose queenly and matronly aspects predominated over those of fruitfulness. (See Harden 1971, p. 79.)

Inanna's symbol was the crescent moon supporting a disk, a symbol which can be seen on a probable incense burner, from the temple of Waddum-dhū-Masma'im (eighth to seventh century BC) in the kingdom of Saba in southern Arabia, modern day Yemen. In Arabia it was, inter alia, that of the Moon god Wadd. The symbol is illustrated here by a strikingly similar incense burner from a later period. (24.3)

Amongst the tribal peoples of southern Arabia the worship of lunar deities continued until the symbol became eventually the totem of Islam. In the classical world the crescent moon is associated with all moon goddesses like Luna, Selene and Artemis (Diana).

The essential distinction between the Babylonian Ištar and the Phoenician Tanit is that Ištar's attributes are primarily sexual and aggressive, as befits a tutelary Deity. In many respects the Hellenistic Artemis shared the same non-maternal qualities. Tanit however follows in the long prehistoric Mediterranean tradition of fertility and mother goddesses, whose images as crop formations have already been noted in Chapter II. This brings us to an interesting dichotomy which is evident in the House of Virgo, which links uneasily, in its symbol the crescent moon, the female chaste quality characteristic of Virgo, and the female physicality of Venus, goddess of love and sex.

In fact the presence of this crescent moon, chosen by the geophysical crop circle makers as an appropriate image for this House, reminds us that there should not be a conflict here, since Virgo is essentially concerned

24.3 South Arabian limestone incense burner with the symbols of the crescent moon and disk. C. first century BC - first century AD. Private collection

with femininity in all its aspects. The eternal woman combines the beauty and modesty of the maiden, the passion of the lover, the love of the mother and the wisdom of the matriarch – all to be encompassed in the ideal life of the female, human Monad.

And what of the numinous quality of this symbol? The crescent moon shows the light of the spiritual Sun beginning to illuminate the dark physical form of the Moon, as innate spirituality begins to illumine the Personality of the human Monad in this House. In the words of Djwhal Khul:

'Ponder upon the beauty of this synthesis and know that you yourself have said the first word as the soul, descending into the womb of time and space in a far distant past. The time has now come when you can, if you so choose, proclaim your identity with both divine aspects – matter and Spirit, the Mother and the Christ.' (Bailey 1951, pp. 284-5)

Although I believe my interpretation of this symbol as the New Moon (viewed from the centre of the formation) to be correct, it can also (viewed from outside) be regarded as the Old Moon. Now we have seen that the Moon, in esoteric terms, stands 'for the glorification, through purification and detachment, of matter.' (Bailey 1951, p. 126) The Old Moon in this context would suggest the gradual phasing out of those elements of the Personality which act as a bar to spiritual development. The key words here are *purification* and *detachment*, for this *vasu* (*Pāvaka, purification*) and House represent a phase of nascent spirituality, where the inbuilt barriers to spiritual development begin to be dismantled. This is a painful process. The process of purification requires *patience* (*Kṣānti*) which is the essential quality of the Buddhist Perfection of this quadrant. Vishnu is connected to this House also, which is the equivalent in the East of the Christ Consciousness. Christ Himself, in the parable of the sower, commanded that the believer should "bear fruit with patient endurance." (*Luke* 8:15)

## THE HOUSE OF SCORPIO (24.4)

For anyone on the spiritual path, this stage of the Ascension Process is a major challenge. Djwhal Khul has described Scorpio as being 'of paramount importance in the life of evolving man' (Bailey 1951, p. 193), and again: 'Scorpio, at this particular stage of human evolution, governs the Path of Discipleship' (Bailey 1951, p. 195), for: 'It is here that the divine necessity of achieving *alignment* is portrayed for us in the symbolism of the sky and when it has been achieved then there is a direct inflow of divine energy and man is linked up in a new and creative manner to sources of divine supply.' (Bailey 1951, pp. 196-197)

'In Scorpio ... the disciple undergoes those tests which will enable him to take the second initiation and demonstrate that the desire nature is subdued and conquered ... and that from the "earthy" foundations of Scorpio the personality can be so tested that it shows fitness for the world service demanded in Aquarius.' (Bailey 1951, p. 143) 'At this time the Ego [Soul] grips afresh the two lower vehicles [the physical and emotional bodies] and bends them to his will ... We must not make the mistake of thinking that all this follows in the same invariable consecutive steps and stages. Much is done in simultaneous unison, for the labour to control is slow and hard, but in the interim between the first three initiations some definite point in the evolution of each of the three lower vehicles [the physical, emotional and mental bodies] has to be attained and held, before the further expansion of the channel can be safely permitted. Many of us

are working on all the three bodies, now as we tread the Probationary Path.' (Bailey 1922a, p. 85)

'The three ruling constellations are Scorpio, ... Taurus, ... and Pisces ... This would necessarily be so because testing, trial, desire, illumination, matter, form and salvation are the keynotes of our solar system and of our Earth in particular. This solar system is a system which is expressing the second aspect of divinity [Love-Wisdom] and hence the emphasis upon the forces pouring through Scorpio, Taurus and Pisces.' (Bailey 1951, pp. 486-7)

'We come now to a consideration of the Rulers which govern the sign, Scorpio ... Mars and Mercury control and Mars is particularly active ... Mars is the dominating factor in the tests and trials of the disciple ... the planet which rules and controls the physical vehicle.' (Bailey 1951, pp. 209-210) 'Through the influence of Mercury and Neptune the group consciousness of the individual is developed, so that through the tests in Scorpio and the experience in Aquarius the disciple emerges *on the physical plane* into the position of a world server.' (Bailey 1951, p. 219) Mars is both the orthodox and the esoteric ruler of this House, and Mercury its hierarchical ruler.

The third ruler of this House is *Uranus*, the planet 'whose characteristics are the scientific mind ... [where] the way of divine knowledge can take the place of the mystic way of feeling.' (Bailey 1951, p. 224) For the disciple a new order of life is initiated accompanying spiritual reorientation. It produces an understanding of the causes of things as they are, and the desire to change the old order and the old alignment into the new. 'Carried forward to its logical conclusion, the influence of Uranus finally produces an unfolded spiritual consciousness

**SCORPIO**  **MICHAEL**

**LOCAL
SUPERCLUSTER**

VIRGO
Supercluster

**LOCAL GROUP
OF GALAXIES**

Local Group Logos
**AN**

Andromeda ◇ Triangulum

Milky Way

**The Galactic Logos
AION**

**MILKY WAY
GALAXY**

Alcyone ◇ Merak

Sirius

Local Solar Group Logos
**ARCHON**

**LOCAL SOLAR GROUP**

**ZODIAC HOUSES**

Taurus ◇ Pisces

Scorpio

**The Solar Logos
BEL**

**SOLAR SYSTEM**

Mars ◇ Mercury

Uranus

**The Planetary Logos
IBEZ**

**PLANETARY
RAYS**

6 ◇ 4

7

**Lord of Planet Earth
Archangel MICHAEL**

World Soul ◇ Spiritual Will

**PLANET
EARTH**

The Seven
Hierarchies

**Humanity**

*24.4 The stepping down of divine energy from the Virgo Supercluster to humanity, with reference to the Dharmic Wheel of Silbury Hill, Wiltshire, 18.8.1992*

... for this reason, Uranus is exalted in this sign.' (Bailey 1951, pp. 224-225)

The archangel Who is particularly associated with this House is Michael. He is especially concerned with the physiological, psychological and spiritual development of mankind, and thus is deeply involved with the processes of spiritual transformation characteristic of Scorpio. As we have seen, He is the 'Soul' of planet Earth, and He alone of the planetary hierarchy is 'self-sustaining and self-sufficient'. He combines all the Rays in His make-up; necessary for 'controlling each unit and directing all evolution.'

The Silbury formation was produced under His direction, with new symbols entirely different from those of conventional astrology. They appear to have been designed to illustrate the processes necessary for the spiritual development of mankind at this time.

*The crop circle symbol in Scorpio* (24.5 and 24.6)

The symbol that appeared at the northern point of the formation is one of the most mysterious of the group. In October 1992 I discussed its significance with the Archangel Michael. The recorded conversation ran as follows:

Michael Green: "The symbol on the north which is the claw, the hand ... it is one of the symbols of the crop circle makers. It is one of the more puzzling ones."

24.5 *'Scorpio'* symbol, looking South

24.6 *'Scorpio'* symbol, looking North

The Archangel Michael: "My dear friend, you understand the basis. You question the separate circle. It is an indication of Life ... of Spiritual Life ... It is the giving of Life."

Michael Green: "This is the position, of course, of the Second Initiation. The confrontation of Personality and Soul: in fact of Spiritual Life."

The Archangel Michael: "It is."

The act of offering relates this symbol to the Buddhist Perfection of *giving* (*Dāna*), which, at its most significant level, as the Archangel

Michael makes clear, is the giving of eternal life to the human Monad by God. However, viewed in another way, it should reflect at the human response level a generosity of spirit, an expression of that most desirable of spiritual qualities, compassion.

At a numinous level this strange three-fingered hand has a deeper meaning. 'The wheel of fire turns and all within that wheel is subjected to the threefold flame, and eventually stands perfected.' (Bailey 1925, p. 97) The Second Initiation is of critical importance, for it represents for the human being direct contact with Deity. The three-fingered hand, therefore, also symbolises the 'threefold flame' of purification and the consequent offer of spiritual life from the hand of God.

## THE HOUSE OF CAPRICORN (24.7)

The fourth and last quadrant on the north-west is for those on the spiritual path the most important. It also contains two Houses, Sagittarius and Capricorn, of which the latter is the more important for our purposes.

Sagittarius, the archer, is a duality, a House of Conflict as already noted, half animal and half human. The devout disciple in this House is split between growing spiritual aspiration with awareness of initiatory targets to be achieved (the archer aspect) and the pull of the physical and emotional natures, as yet not fully under control.

'In studying Sagittarius, it becomes obvious that one of the major underlying themes is that of *Direction*. The Archer is guiding his horse towards one specific objective; he is sending or directing his arrow towards a desired point; he is aiming at some specific goal. This sense of direction or guidance is characteristic of the enlightened man, of the aspirant and disciple, and this is a growing recognition; when

this faculty of sensitive direction is rightly developed it becomes, in the early stages, an effort to identify all soul and personality activity with God's Plan, and this is, in the last analysis, the ordered direction of God's thought.' (Bailey 1951, p. 190)

Capricorn, the goat, is a House of *transformation* under the great creative plan of God. It opens the door to the spiritual community of planet Earth (the Hierarchy) where the last three initiations can be undergone (Initiations 5 to 7). Djwhal Khul identifies three characteristics of Capricorn.

1. First it is an *earth sign*, and in it the human Monad expresses 'the densest point of concrete materialisation of which the human soul is capable.' (Bailey 1951, p. 158) This represents the outer limit of *devolution* and the furthest point of intellectual development. On the Trojan Maze for example (see Chapter 22) it is represented by the third or outer ring of the Little Turning, and its achievement is marked by the Third Initiation.

2. Second, it is the sign of conclusion, and of this the mountain top is frequently the symbol.

3. This process of spiritual *evolution* now begins as a consequence of the above, in which is inaugurated a new cycle of effort. Indeed, 'effort, strain, struggle, the fight with the forces native to the underworld, or the strenuous conditions entailed by the tests of discipleship or initiation – these are distinctive of experience in Capricorn.' (Bailey 1951, p. 159) 'In Capricorn we have the triumph of matter; it reaches its densest and most concrete expression; but this triumph is followed by that of spirit.' (Bailey 1951, p. 171)

Spiritual initiates in this quadrant are

# CAPRICORN
(SAGITTARIUS)

# HANIEL

**LOCAL
SUPERCLUSTER**

**VIRGO
Supercluster**

**Local Group Logos
AN**

Andromeda ◇ Triangulum

Milky Way

**LOCAL GROUP
OF GALAXIES**

**The Galactic Logos
AION**

Alcyone ◇ Merak

Sirius

**MILKY WAY
GALAXY**

**Local Solar Group Logos
ARCHON**

**LOCAL SOLAR GROUP**

**ZODIAC HOUSES**

Pisces ◇ Scorpio

Capricorn

**The Solar Logos
BEL**

Saturn ◇ Venus

Mercury

**SOLAR SYSTEM**

**The Planetary Logos
IBEZ**

3 ◇ 5

4

**PLANETARY
RAYS**

**Lord of Planet Earth
Archangel MICHAEL**

World Soul ◇ Spiritual Will

The Seven
Hierarchies

**PLANET
EARTH**

**Humanity**

*24.7 The stepping down of divine energy from the Virgo Supercluster to humanity, with reference to the Dharmic Wheel of Silbury Hill, Wiltshire, 18.8.1992*

subjected to the impact of energies from Scorpio, Capricorn and Pisces. They are 'brought into relation to the world disciples through the constellation Scorpio, to the hierarchical centre through Capricorn, and to the mass through Pisces, the sign of all world saviours.' (Bailey 1951, p. 163)

'The exoteric and the esoteric planetary rulers of Capricorn are the same. ... Saturn forces man to face up to the past, and in the present to prepare for the future.' (Bailey 1951, pp. 163-164) 'Venus ... is the source of the intelligent mind, acting either through desire (in the early stages) or love (in the later stages).' (Bailey 1951, p. 244) The third planet that governs Capricorn is Mercury. 'Mercury, the Messenger of the Gods, carries to humanity a certain type of force and precipitates a point of crisis; it brings about the next great revolution which will lead mankind on to new experience, and to the revelation of the divinity which it is the destiny of man to reveal.' (Bailey 1951, p. 549)

The archangel of this House and *vasu* is Haniel (Ray 4), whose name means 'the grace of God.' Traditionally this Being is said to be in the likeness of a woman, and is 'appointed on all manner of love.' (Tyson 1995, p. 534) Venus is a planetary ruler of this House and it is particularly appropriate therefore that the powerful energies of Love-Wisdom are available to the disciple passing through this difficult stage of his spiritual development, which culminates in the Fourth Initiation. It is this initiation which results in the absorption of the 'perfected Personality' by the Soul or Ego. (See Chapter 9.) The Greater Master describes Haniel

as being the archangel of harmony and beauty. The archangel presides over interrelationships whether of spheres, planets, plants or animal and human life: He is 'the great archetype of sympathetic vibration.' (Fortune 1976, p. 151) It is this House and its archangel that are responsible for the bird kingdom: 'Birds ... are closely connected with Wisdom, and therefore with the psychic nature of God, of men and of devas.' (Bailey 1925, p. 896)

[I believe Michael associated the House of Capricorn with the Buddhist Perfection of *contemplation* (*Dhyāna*) (Ed.)]

*The crop circle symbol in Capricorn* (24.8)

The notable feature on the ground in this House was a modern water tank. Apart from an area of grass around the tank, the crop had been disturbed on both sides of the wheel ring. This anomaly was discussed with the Archangel Michael in October 1992.

The Archangel Michael: "The first question I would give you is your questioning of the water trough. As to why it was necessary with all the expanse (of field) to position this information (here). It is because that at that point the energies needed to enter into the

*24.8 'Capricorn', and 'Aquarius' (behind) symbols, looking South West*

Earth – into what you call the fiery centre. Give it thought and we will channel into your mind an understanding of that. There was purpose."

Michael Green: "Did it in fact spoil the symbol that had been intended for that position?"

The Archangel Michael: "That symbol had to be disintegrated – to be in another way of Being, if you understand me."

Michael Green: "It had obviously puzzled me as to what that symbol had originally to be ... Can you tell me what the symbol was?"

The Archangel Michael: "The circle ..."

Michael Green: "Formed with the moon crescent on top?"

The Archangel Michael: "That is correct."

Michael Green: "Which is the sign of Mercury."

The Archangel Michael: "That is correct."

The immediate question is why it was necessary to disintegrate the symbol of this House. In our survey of the Wessex Triangles of Power, described in Chapters 19 and 20, a number of major crop formations were identified as Distributing Centres, the culminating points of an outgoing ray energy described as Emanating Energy. The recipient of the cosmic energies was the Michael-Mary Line running SW to NE across southern England. It is effectively an artery or meridian of planet Earth, and such an energy field conveys information and stimulates the etheric body of the planet.

Despite the importance of the crop formation Distributing Centres in 1990-91, at no point was it found necessary to disintegrate the symbols. What then was the special nature of the Silbury formation in 1992 that made this necessary? In His communication

of October 1992, the archangel promised to reveal the significance of this occurrence, which in due course happened.

*Mercury: the astrological symbol*

As we saw in Chapter 20, the crop circle makers took trouble to duplicate certain important crop formations where the information was in danger of being lost. This was such a case. The symbol had to be removed from its position on the Silbury Hill Wheel, as was explained by the archangel, but in fact it was duplicated nearby in Wiltshire shortly before the Wheel

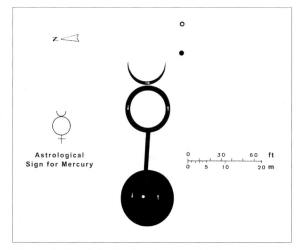

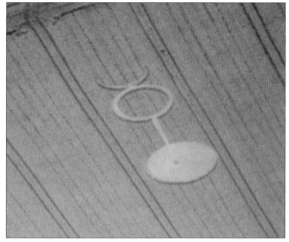

24.9 **The Sign of Mercury**
*Draycot Fitz Payne, Wiltshire*
*(OS SU132629), 2.8.1992*

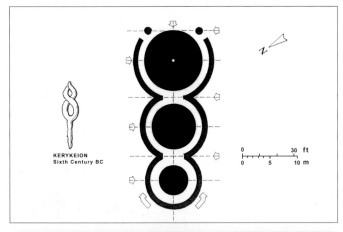

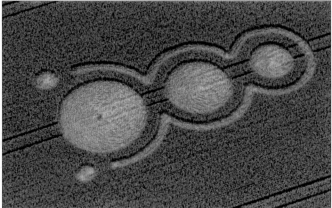

24.10 **The Kerykeion**
*Upham, Hampshire (OS SU545198) on 14.6.1997*

was put down on 18.8.1992.

The geophysical crop formation (24.9) appeared near *Draycot Fitz Payne, Wilcot CP, Wiltshire* (OS SU132629) on 2.8.1992. It was surveyed by Nigel and Paul Mann (and separately by this writer). John Martineau produced a drawing and aerial photos taken by several photographers. The design is clearly that referred to by the archangel, and bears a sufficient likeness to the astrological symbol of Mercury (24.9, inset) for a confident identification. However there is an important difference. Instead of a cross on the conventional symbol, the lower part of the formation has been replaced with a dumb-bell design with a ring at the top and

a connected circle. Such designs have been identified elsewhere in this study as 'Logoi formations': symbols for a Cosmic Entity where the ring represents Spirit, and the circle Form. The significance of the New Moon is essentially dawning spiritual life, and is discussed above under the House of Virgo. The 'signature' circles were sited in the tramlines and may be man-made.

*Mercury: the deific communicator*

Even if the case for the identity of this symbol is reasonably secure, it still does not explain why Mercury (Hermes in Greek) should have been considered of sufficient importance to have been transferred into the Energy Field of the Michael-Mary Line as described by the archangel. To understand this problem we need to look not at the astrological symbol, but at the symbol of the Caduceus sceptre (Kerykeion in Greek) always carried by this Deity from earliest times. Mercury/Hermes as a Cosmic Being appears to have been downgraded from a more important early role as a Deific Communicator to mankind – a point made by Jane Harrison. (Harrison J.E. 1963, p. 296 and its fn. 1)

The symbol of his primary message is the Kerykeion and is depicted as early as the sixth century BC. (24.10, inset) So important is this message that it appeared as a major crop formation in 1997.

*The Kerykeion: symbol of Love-Wisdom* (24.10)

The formation appeared near *Upham, Bishops Waltham CP, Hampshire* (OS SU545198) on 14.6.1997. It was studied and recorded by Richard Andrews. He stated that it was

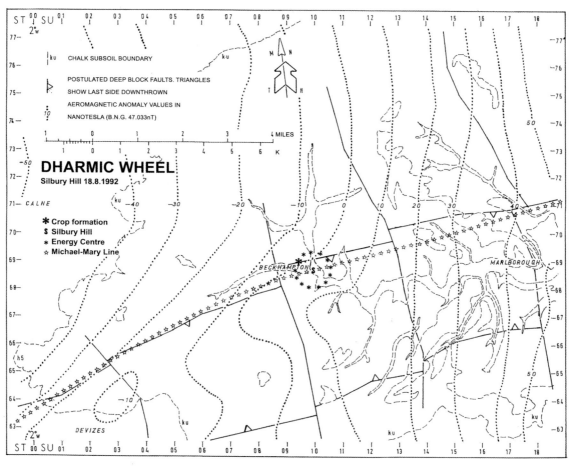

*24.11 Map of Central Wiltshire, showing Silbury Hill with the Michael-Mary Line passing through, surrounded by energy centres, with the Silbury Wheel crop formation on one of them*

in pristine condition with no broken or scraped stems (characteristic of man-made formations). The small circles had stalks bent horizontally at the nodes to follow the curve of the circle. There was a central geodetic energy path running from top to bottom of the formation, which returned up the linked rings on either side. Across the formation ran six energy lines flowing alternately. The two small circles were strong foci of geodetic energy. The top of the outer pathway was terminated by the two small circles mentioned above. The serpentine path entirely enclosed the three linear circles of decreasing size, which I interpret as symbolising the Trinity

of Deity.

In 1998 I published a paper 'The Trinitarian Caduceus of Upham' in *The Circular* # 31, pages 55-57. (Green, Michael 1998b) It traced the symbolism of the Kerykeion in Early Christianity in the British Isles. However I failed at the time to grasp the core significance of this beautiful mandala.

The absolutely critical point about this symbol, and indeed all representations of these entwined serpents from the earliest periods of recorded history, is that the 'two' serpents are engaged in sexual intercourse. They are the exact parallel of the Eastern Embracing Posture (Tibetan *Yab-Yum*) where a god (representing *compassion* (love)) and his female consort (representing *wisdom*) are eternally linked. They are effectively one divine unit and are represented as such. (22.13) This is symbolised in the crop formation by the linking of the two serpents at the base to be effectively a single Entity with two heads. Furthermore the Cosmic Trinity of the crop formation is entirely wrapped in this dual concept of Love-Wisdom, so often mentioned in this book. It is this quality above all else that was being infused into the geodetic structure of the planet in this way in 1992.

*The Dharmic Wheel: agent of the deific purpose*

The area of Silbury Hill (24.11) has been an important centre of geophysical crop formation activity from 1988 onwards. There are three geodetic elements involved here:

1. The geophysical meridian, the Michael-Mary Line.

2. The great Energy Centre, whose diameter is about 985 yards, centred on Silbury Hill, on this meridian. This indeed was the reason for prehistoric concentration on the site as a sacred centre in the first place.

3. The geological structure of the area, which includes deep block faults, described under the heading: 'The Geophysical Connection' in Chapter 19.

The purpose of the Silbury formation was twofold: first, to convey a detailed diagram of the stages of human development along the line of symbols on the ancient Dharmic Wheel; and second to convey information and stimulus about Love-Wisdom, the human, culminating spiritual achievement, to the 'fiery centre' of the planet, to use the Archangel Michael's expression. Indeed much of the purpose of the crop circle phenomenon generally appears to have been

the interchange of information between spheres of activity (not necessarily human) in connection with planet Earth.

The problem with Silbury from the geophysical crop circle makers' point of view was that there was only a very limited number of locations available where this process could take place, and combine all the elements listed above. In the event the Silbury formation lay just within the Energy Centre zone around Silbury Hill and thus also made use of the Michael-Mary Line. More importantly it lay right on top of a geological block transform fault providing access to deep within the mantle of the planet.

It would be a mistake to think that devic activity is confined to the surface of the planet. The abysmal depths of the Earth from the crust to the inner core are full of entities and geodetic activity, all at different levels of being (and indeed scale). They maintain the system to ensure that optimum conditions exist on the surface for the development of various life forms and, in particular, humanity. The organisational structure and interrelationships are set out in Chapter 14, and all are responsible to the Archangelic Executive of the Great Council of the planet, under the *aegis* of the Archangel Michael, Lord of planet Earth.

## THE HOUSE OF AQUARIUS (24.12)

This is the last *vasu* of the Vedic cycle (*Soma, the Moon or offering*), although in terms of the traditional Zodiac in the case of the *Wheel adjusted or reversed*, the last House is Pisces. By this stage the initiate has taken the Fourth or 'liberating' Initiation, and is working for the Fifth (Planetary) or First Cosmic Initiation which can take him out of

# AQUARIUS                    KHAMAEL

**LOCAL**
**SUPERCLUSTER**

**VIRGO**
Supercluster

**LOCAL GROUP**
**OF GALAXIES**

**Local Group Logos**
**AN**

Andromeda ◇ Triangulum

Milky Way

**The Galactic Logos**
**AION**

**MILKY WAY**
**GALAXY**

Alcyone ◇ Merak

Sirius

**Local Solar Group Logos**
**ARCHON**

**LOCAL SOLAR GROUP**

**ZODIAC HOUSES**

Pisces ◇ Aries

Aquarius

**The Solar Logos**
**BEL**

**SOLAR SYSTEM**

Uranus ◇ Jupiter

The Moon

**The Planetary Logos**
**IBEZ**

**PLANETARY**
**RAYS**

7 ◇ $\frac{2}{(3)}$

4

**Lord of Planet Earth**
**Archangel MICHAEL**

World Soul ◇ Spiritual Will

**PLANET**
**EARTH**

The Seven
Hierarchies

**Humanity**

*24.12 The stepping down of divine energy from the Virgo Supercluster to humanity, with reference to the Dharmic Wheel of Silbury Hill, Wiltshire, 18.8.1992*

our planetary system altogether.

The keynotes of the Sign are three:

1. Concentration on personal development transmutes itself into service for humanity.

2. Superficial and selfish activity changes into a deep and serious intention to be active on behalf of the spiritual Hierarchy of the planet.

3. Self-conscious living changes finally into a sensitive humanitarian awareness.

(See Bailey 1951, p. 135 which I have slightly reworded.)

Turning to the governing Houses, there are three that form the end of the cycle of expression upon the *Wheel adjusted or reversed*:

'1. Aquarius ... Consecration to the service of the Whole. The death or negation of all personality selfishness. ...

2. Pisces ... Emergence of a world saviour. Death of all separative desire and love, even spiritual longing and aspiration. ...

3. Aries ... Appearance of the will to cooperate with the Plan [of the Hierarchy]. The death of Self-will.'

(Bailey 1951, p. 151)

The planetary rulers of this House reflect this process of spiritual dedication and service.

1. *Uranus*, that mysterious and occult planet, stimulates innate spontaneous activity, indeed leadership qualities, and this produces evolutionary development – both natural and spiritual. It is the urge to better conditions.

2. *Jupiter* stimulates the fusion of heart and mind, which is the subjective purpose of manifestation. The achievement of ultimate synthesis is inevitable.

3. *The Moon* brings about the inclination to create those conditions which lead to the great and critical transformation of instinct and intellect. Uranus, however, stimulates the great transference from intellectual perception to intuitive knowledge. (See Bailey 1951, pp. 137-139.)

Aquarius is a water sign, water being the symbol of substance and of material expression plus emotional motivation. Aquarius is consequently dual in its activity, and Ray 3 expresses itself powerfully through it. In classical tradition Neptune was the brother of Jupiter. In a communication in October 1991, the Archangel Michael linked Jupiter with the protection of the sea and its life forms, which I believe to be the characteristic feature of this House. (23.3)

The archangel of the House of Aquarius is *Khamael*, operating on the underlying Ray of Aquarius. This great seraph is described by the Greater Master as 'the Protector of the weak and wronged; He is also the Avenging Angel who punishes the breakers of Law.' (Fortune 1976, p. 151) He is traditionally associated with

24.13 *'Aquarius', and 'Aries' (behind) symbols, looking South*

the Kabbalistic *Geburah* meaning strength, and *Din* meaning judgement or severity. It is in this last stage of the human Monad's planetary journey that the final aspects of personal Karma (the law of retribution) have to be worked through and resolved, the consequences of activities extending perhaps over many previous lifetimes. Karma is the power that controls all things, sometimes the result of good moral action (the Karma of merit); more often it is the moral consequences of personal, selfish behaviour (the Karma of demerit). It is essential that the human Monad enters the realms beyond the Fifth Initiation with a clean bill of spiritual health. It is the responsibility, indeed concern, of Khamael that this happens.

*The crop circle symbol in Aquarius* (24.13)

The symbol on the Silbury formation is a ring some 26 ft 7 in in diameter, cutting the wheel ring, with a 14 ft 9 in outer extension (approximate dimensions) with two tines, clearly indicating a key of the old-fashioned, slide-key type. As the archangel confirmed in a communication of October 1992, this is symbolic of the unlocking of the door to spiritual life: "– a representation of all that we are hoping to achieve with you, dear friends" (The Archangel Michael). In the words of Djwhal Khul this stage of spiritual development 'leads through the Hall of Wisdom, and puts into a man's hands *the key* [my italics] to all information, systemic and cosmic, in graduated sequence.' (Bailey 1922, p. 14) In Buddhist terms it constitutes the achievement of the Sixth Perfection, *wisdom (Prajñā)*, which as a summation of the previous five (*morality, vigour, patience, giving and contemplation*) also looks forward to a higher spiritual state while deriving its energies from a lower. As *The Perfection of Wisdom* puts it, 'the perfection of wisdom

is neither form nor other than form.' (Jamieson 2000, p. 28)

The House of Aquarius represents the state between the Fourth and Fifth Initiations, the achievement of the *Hall of Wisdom*, when the Personality of the individual (a composite of the physical, emotional and mental aspects) has begun to merge with its higher aspect, the Soul, and is in regular contact with the highest aspect, the Spirit. A great expansion of consciousness takes place with a vision of the Divine as an expression of cosmic Love and Wisdom. This I believe is the significance of the *two* tines on the crop glyph, the *Key of Life*.

**THE CENTRE**

We now turn to the central symbol of the Silbury formation, indeed the most important of the Dharmic Wheel. If the other symbols round the periphery have at times seemed obscure, this is the strangest and most impenetrable of all, for it is a symbol of the Solar Logos, and indeed the states of Deity beyond.

*The symbol at the Centre* (24.14)

The outer ring is 59 ft in diameter with a ring width of 3 ft 3 in. The inner circle has a diameter of 15 ft 7 in – all dimensions are approximate. The symbol is quartered with alternating standing and flattened quadrants (those on the NW and SE). Each of the flattened quadrants is swept from east to west.

The symbol thus consists of two elements, the first being the *Bi* symbol used throughout the crop formations for an expression of Deity in its simplest of terms. The inner circle represents the Spirit or Unmanifest state of Deity, the broad outer ring symbolises Manifested Form. The second element consists of the alternating flattened and standing quadrants of crop.

*24.14* **The Centre** *of the Dharmic Wheel of Silbury Hill, looking North East*

In its simplest, lineal, state the symbol represents the Indo-Aryan four-spoked wheel with a history reaching back to the fourth millennium BC. A crop formation of exactly this type appeared in 1997 in Southern England at Haselbury Plucknett. (22.8)

Here I wish to record remarks made by the Archangel Michael concerning the central symbol of the Silbury formation, and more generally about the One Who is All – "In Him we live and move and have our being." The material was channelled by Isabelle Kingston at Ogbourne St Andrew, Wiltshire on 27.10.1991 and 16.10.1992:

Michael Green: "We come ... to the moving off the Great Wheel, the coming together of Spirit and Soul. Death and transformation – the last of the (symbols)."

The Archangel Michael: "And I would use the term 'freedom'."

Michael Green: "I have spoken ... about the Centre – the dark and the light – the Sun – the Light behind the Light."

The Archangel Michael: "And the Balance, that of Progress and the Whole."

16.10.1992

Michael Green: "Is there any other Great Being who you would like to mention?"

The Archangel Michael: "It is the One Who is All: Yahweh, Shiva ...God."

Michael Green: "Who stands at the centre."

The Archangel Michael: "It is true. Who holds all the Cosmos, all the Universe and all dimensions."

27.10.1991

## CONCLUSION

Finally I wish to record the concluding remarks by the Archangel Michael in connection with the crop circle phenomenon generally, its energies and purpose – again channelled by Isabelle Kingston on 27.10.1991.

"You are dealing with a universal energy, a cosmic energy, an energy far greater than perhaps humankind can understand. You are not dealing with the simplistic human form. You are dealing with an Intelligence, a knowing far greater than perhaps the human mind can conceive. The human mind and heart can grasp, and will in time understand, what is being given is a great power. What is being given is great guidance. However, the separate formations and shapes are part of a great plan and certain formations have certain information whereas others will be linked to different levels, a different understanding. You are dealing with what your people might call science, you are dealing with heart, you are dealing with nature, in fact you are being given information in separate ways that have different purposes and from different entities or energies. It does not in a sense have to be separated, it all comes from one source but you will find there are different energies playing in the different formations. In some cases there is a communication of Gaia. This is a certain type of formation. There are some formations where Gaia is allowing this to happen for the spiritual benefit of the humankind."

# 25. CONCLUSION

*When I look at your heavens, the work of your fingers,*

*the moon and the stars that you have established;*

*what are human beings that you are mindful of them,*

*mortals that you care for them?*

*Yet you have made them a little lower than the Divine Beings*
*(Heb. elohim),*

*and crowned them with glory and honour.*

*Psalm 8:3-5*

## THE COSMIC DIMENSION

I began this book with a challenge and a commission. The challenge was to remember what I once knew in other existences; the commission was to commit this knowledge to paper in an accessible form for this generation of humanity. The *aide-mémoire* for this exercise was the crop circle phenomenon with which I had been involved. Whether I have been successful is not for me to judge, but some of the material of this book relating to the *Big Picture* has not, I think, been assembled in quite this form before.

What has emerged from this communication process, and has been discussed in detail in this book, can be summarised as follows.

The human individual is a sum of parts – living intelligent entities presided over by a Higher Spiritual Being (the Spark of God) who has the responsibility of raising the spiritual consciousness of this living form within a finite period.

Humanity in its totality forms part of the living structure of planet Earth, which is also on a path of spiritual development through the exercise of loving service, as are all Cosmic Beings. A human being is a cell of greater or lesser significance within this corporate form. The planet in its turn is one of the energy centres of the Solar Logos, that great Triune Spiritual Being who is the God of our system. (The Christ Spirit is the Second Person of the Solar Trinity as evidenced by such statements as, 'I am the Light of the World' or 'I am the light that lighteth every man that cometh into the World' – meant both literally and figuratively.) A human is smaller in structure than an atom to such a Being, but of course of infinitely greater importance, as made 'in the image of God', in terms of its spiritual potential.

The solar system is one of a group of star systems all moving together as an Entity in our part of the galactic spiral arm. They form one of teeming millions of such groups which comprise our galaxy, which in turn forms part of the local group of galaxies. The billions of such living, intelligent structures comprise our universe which operates at a particular vibrational level, but of which we are only aware of the gross physical components. There are twelve such universes, coeval but separate, infinite but bounded, which form the centres of the One, the God, the All that Is, Who thus lovingly and intelligently pervades every aspect of His created Cosmos. The system is vast and complex beyond our imagining.

The really important point to appreciate is that the One God, although 'Perfect' in our terms, has planned for Himself a Path of Development, for which (and this is the really critical aspect) He relies on all His component parts *developing* and *achieving* to carry the dynamic process along. At our minuscule level Humanity is a part of this awesome project, and hence the emphasis in this book on *Spiritual Ascension*, through the operation of what is termed here the *Initiation Process*, to steadily higher levels of being.

All component holons of this great system of Life and Intelligence have active life cycles of variable length, interspersed by inactive periods during which the experiences of the past are digested and future development is planned – the 'days and nights of Brahma.'

At a certain level of spiritual development such spiritual Beings achieve eternal life, though that life may take different foci even within a single cycle. At a lower level there are regular extinctions of life forms and their environments whose useful span of activity has passed, to be replaced by others of greater potential growth. For example, there have been five significant mass extinctions in the Earth's history, around 440, 360, 250, 200 and 66 million years ago.

Humanity is not essentially different from the earlier life forms, except of course that it has far greater potentiality for spiritual development.

As I understand it, within any cosmic scheme or life cycle there is a process of descent into incarnation and then back again, all in basically seven stages. We, on planet Earth, are now passing through the fourth stage of experience, the most dense as far as our Earth Logos is concerned. The Archangel Michael, as Guardian and Soul of planet Earth, is responsible for this phase of activity at this time.

The process provides the human Soul or cell within the Planetary Being with a discrete number of incarnation experiences for its spiritual development within each cycle. Those human entities who negatively and consistently reject this process (and have consequentially broken the link with their Soul, although continuing to function as an intelligence) during the fourth stage have their constituent parts dissolved back into the Cosmos at the end of this cycle. Those human entities which have failed to make any progress, but are still linked to their Soul, are put into cold storage and held over for another chance in the next cycle. Those human Personalities, on the other hand, who have made spiritual progress, are absorbed within their Soul and higher Spirit, and move on for further service both on and off planet.

However, at the end of all seven planetary cycles, when the complete Mahamanvantara has been passed through: 'All will be reabsorbed within the Absolute ... the cosmic heaven of rest will then ensue ...' (Bailey 1925, p. 87) Those who have wholly failed to develop and achieve spiritual individuation during many incarnations over aeons of time will be dissolved back into the components of the Cosmos.

In a situation where fallible humanity could so easily fail to achieve the Spiritual Ascension Process, one might consider the case of the Jewish ruler two thousand years ago, who asked Jesus Christ: '... what must I do to inherit eternal life?' (*Luke* 18:18) Jesus replied: 'You know the Commandments.' In another passage He identifies the two critical commandments in this context: '*"You shall love the Lord your God with all your heart, and with all your soul, and with all your mind."* This is the greatest and first commandment. And a second is like it: *"You shall love your neighbour as yourself."* On these two commandments hang all the Law and the Prophets.' (*Matthew* 22:37-40)

## THE MESSAGE TO HUMANITY

Thus the overwhelming message of Jesus Christ and, two thousand years later, I believe, the crop circle phenomenon also, is that we are being urged as individuals to communicate directly and lovingly with our own Higher Consciousness, which is an aspect of Deity, and indeed with God Himself. Our success in doing so is to be judged quite simply by the extent to which we treat those around us with consideration and kindness. Given this basic attitude, our Spiritual Mentors then wish us to pursue lines of activity in connection with the well-being of our planet and its inhabitants. It is my personal belief that what is being spelt out is nothing less than the nature of the New Spirituality for humankind in the twenty-first century and beyond.

## THE SON OF MAN

'I heard behind me a loud voice like a trumpet saying, ... '*Write in a book* what you see ... Then I turned to see whose voice it was that spoke to me, and on turning I saw ... one like the Son of Man, clothed with a long robe ... His head and his hair were white as white wool, white as snow; his eyes were like a flame of fire ... he held seven stars ... and his face was like the sun shining with full force.'

(*Revelation* 1:10-16)

# Glossary

For Theosophical terms the reader is referred to the glossary in *Initiation Human and Solar*, pages 215-225. (Bailey 1922a)

**ADAS.** The Agricultural Development and Advisory Service, a group of scientific agricultural advisers, formerly part of the British Ministry of Agriculture, Fisheries and Food

**Anisotropic.** Having different physical properties in different directions

**Bi disc.** Ancient Chinese amulet symbolising deity, having a stone disc representing the manifest state of God, with a hole in the centre alluding to its Unmanifest state

**CCCS.** The Centre for Crop Circle Studies

**Centre.** See chakra

**Chakra.** An etheric centre of force, one of seven or more found in all sentient cosmic beings, and responsible for the evolution of the body and psyche. The alternative word 'Centre' is generally used in this study.

**Granodiorite.** A coarse-grained plutonic rock containing quartz and plagioclase, between granite and diorite in composition

**Great cycle.** See manvantara

**Kumara.** In Theosophy the four Kumaras under their leader, Sanat Kumara (the Eternal Youth) consititue the Ray of Activity and the four Rays of Attribute.

**Kabbalism.** The esoteric, mystical teaching of Judaism

**Lemuria.** A modern term first used by some naturalists and now by Theosophists to indicate a continent which, according to the Secret Doctrine of the East, preceded Atlantis. It was the home of the third root race. (Bailey 1922a, pp. 219-220) Lemuria should perhaps be regarded as a state or stage of human development from 'animal man' to 'Homo sapiens' rather than a discrete land-mass. That said this development almost certainly took place in a physical location, i.e. Africa between 150,000 – 100,000 BC. A major world interglaciation c.115,000 BC led to the desiccation of the humanoid habitat and the subsequent dispersal of the human and sub-human species into Europe and Asia in the following millennia. Blavatsky's channelled material speaks of the destruction of Lemuria by 'fire' perhaps referring in metaphysical terms to the global heating of the continent, followed by 'water' or submergence of the coastal plains as a consequence of the associated rise in sea level through the melting of the ice.

**Logos.** The outward expression of any 'Emanation' of Deity, or an outer 'effect' of the Cause which is ever concealed. Thus, speech is the Logos of thought, aptly translated by the Latin *verbum* or 'word' in its metaphysical sense.

**Manas.** Intelligence

**Manasputra.** Son of Mind

**Mandala.** A Tibetan term meaning a picture illustrating in symbolic terms the spiritual structure of the Cosmos

**Manvantara or 'great cycle'.** A period of activity or manifestation

**Michael-Mary Line.** The energy line or 'ley line' which runs SW-NE across southern England from Cornwall to Norfolk, connecting energy centres of our living planetary ecosystem. It links with other energy lines to make up the geomorphic energy body of the Earth.

**Monad.** The One. The threefold spirit on its own plane. In occultism it often means the unified triad – Atma, Buddhi, Manas: Spiritual Will, Intuition and Higher mind. – or the immortal part of man which reincarnates in the lower kingdoms and gradually progresses through them to man and thence to the final goal (Bailey 1922a, p. 222). In this study, 'Human Monad' denotes sometimes the whole human entity, and, where appropriate, its highest element.

**Pitr (pitris).** Sanskrit – 'fathers', spirits of departed ancestors. See Chapter 5 for the meaning developed in this book.

**Plane.** As used here, the term denotes the range or extent of some state of cosmic consciousness.

**Quaternio.** The four Rays of Attribute

**Ray.** One of the seven streams of force or energy of deity. Each of them is the embodiment of a great cosmic Entity. The three Rays of Aspect (Will or Power, Love-Wisdom, Intelligent Activity), and the three Rays of Attribute, subdivisions of the Ray of Intelligent Activity

**Ring-pass-not.** The periphery of the sphere of influence of any central life force

**Sefirah (Sefirot).** A centre of force or being, Ten of which comprise aspects of deity in Kabbalistic teaching and form the Tree of Life

**Septead.** The seven Rays

**Septenate.** The Angelic members of the Great Council of planet Earth

**Swastika.** Sanskrit – ancient symbol of divinity and spirituality in Hindu religions

**Telluric.** Of, relating to, or originating on or in the earth or soil; terrestrial, especially in reference to natural electrical or magnetic fields

**Temenos.** A place dedicated to a God, a precinct

**Vedas.** Indo-Aryan poetry (originally an oral tradition) from India predating the Hindu cultures

**Vesica piscis.** A fish bladder symbol

**Yantra.** A sacred geometrical diagram

# Illustration Credits

By Michael Green except as below. Every effort has been made to identify the authors of illustrations listed as 'unknown'. Please inform the publishers if you have any information.

**FRONT COVER**

Unknown. See page 172

**FRONTISPIECE**

Richard Wintle. www.calyxpix.com

**BENEATH DEDICATION**

Unknown

**INTRODUCTION**

0.1. Bob Croxford

**CHAPTER 1**

1.1.    Beth Davis

1.3.    James Green

1.4.    Nicholas Shea

1.5.    P. Ryder

1.6.    Caroline Martens — Musées d'Avignon, CC BY-SA 4.0, https://commons.wikimedia.org/w/index.php?curid=74483350

1.7.    Drawing after J. Granier. Star map, public domain, NASA

**CHAPTER 2**

2.1.    Robert Plot

2.3, 2.4, 2.5, 2.6. Michael Green and Jim Lyons

2.7.    Lucy Pringle, www.lucypringle.com

2.8, 2.9 Jim Lyons

2.10.    Richard Beaumont

2.11.    Photograph Steve Alexander, www.temporarytemples.co.uk. Diagram Tony Crerar

2.12.    Jim Lyons

**CHAPTER 3**

3.1.    Photograph Andrew King

**CHAPTER 4**

4.2.    Le Men 1868. Figure 'e' by Paulii 1734 (after Oxenstierna). Annotations by Michael Green

4.4.    Photograph courtesy of Alec Down

4.6.    George Wingfield

4.8.    Photograph Beth Davis

4.9.    After Wolfgang Schindler

4.11.    After Wolfgang Schindler

**CHAPTER 5**

5.1.    Jean-Charles Guillo, public domain, wikimedia

5.4.    Christine Green

5.6.    Anthony Cheke

**CHAPTER 6**

6.1.    Steve Alexander

6.3, 6.4. James Green

6.5.    Lucy Pringle

**CHAPTER 7**

7.1.    Steve Alexander

7.3.    Andrew King

7.4.    Information from Joyce Galley and Ralph Lovegrove

# Bibliography

Acts, see Holy Bible

A.E. (George William Russell) (1918). *The Candle of Vision*. London: Macmillan

BAILEY, A.A. (1922a). *Initiation, Human and Solar*. 4th paperback ed. New York: Lucis Publishing Company

BAILEY, A.A. (1922b) *Letters on Occult Meditation*. 5th paperback ed. New York: Lucis Publishing Company

BAILEY, A.A. (1925). *A Treatise on Cosmic Fire*. 3rd paperback ed. New York: Lucis Publishing Company

BAILEY, A.A. (1927). *The Light of the Soul*. 4th paperback ed. New York: Lucis Publishing Company

BAILEY, A.A. (1934). *A Treatise on White Magic*. 4th paperback ed. New York: Lucis Publishing Company

BAILEY, A.A. (1936). *Esoteric Psychology Vol 1*. 4th paperback ed. New York: Lucis Publishing Company

BAILEY, A.A. (1942). *Esoteric Psychology Vol 2*. 3rd paperback ed. New York: Lucis Publishing Company

BAILEY, A.A. (1944). *Discipleship in the New Age Vol 1*. 3rd paperback ed. New York: Lucis Publishing Company

BAILEY, A.A. (1950). *Telepathy and the Etheric Vehicle*. 4th paperback ed. New York: Lucis Publishing Company

BAILEY, A.A. (1951). *Esoteric Astrology*. 5th paperback ed. New York: Lucis Publishing Company

BAILEY, A.A. (1953). *Esoteric Healing*. 1st paperback ed. New York: Lucis Publishing Company

BAILEY, A.A. (1954). *Education in the New Age*. 4th paperback ed. New York: Lucis Publishing Company

BAILEY, A.A. (1955). *Discipleship in the New Age Vol II*. 3rd paperback ed. New York: Lucis Publishing Company

BAILEY, A.A. (1957). *The Externalisation of the Hierarchy*. 3rd paperback ed. New York: Lucis Publishing Company

BAILEY, A.A. (1960). *The Rays and the Initiations*. 3rd paperback ed. New York: Lucis Publishing Company

BAILEY, D.W. in ANTHONY, D. W. and CHI, J. Y., eds. *The Lost World of Old Europe – The Danube Valley, 5000-3500 BC*. New Jersey: Institute for the Study of the Ancient World at New York University and Princeton University Press (2010), 113-127

BARTON, T. (1994). *Ancient Astrology*. London: Routledge

BATES, O. (1914). *The Eastern Libyans*. London: Macmillan

BECKJORD, J.E. (1991). 'Having a go at decoding' in *The Circular* #2.2, 1991, June, 13-15*

BETZ, H.D., ed. (1996). *The Greek Magical Papyri in Translation*. Chicago: The University of Chicago Press

BLACK, J. and GREEN, A. (1992). *Gods, Demons and Symbols of Ancient Mesopotamia*. London: The British Museum Press

BOARDMAN J., GRIFFIN J. and MURRAY O., eds. (1986). *The Oxford History of the Classical World*. London: Guild Publishing

BOYCE, M., ed. and trans. (1984). *Textual Sources for the Study of Zoroastrianism*. Manchester: Manchester University Press

BREUIL, H. and BURKITT, M.C. (1929). *Rock Paintings of Southern Andalucia*. Oxford: Clarendon Press

BRILL, E.J. (2001). *The Gospel according to Thomas*. Leiden: Brill

BROWN, K. (1992). 'The Fake that Grew a Ring' in *The Cereologist #7*, 1992, harvest, 13-14*

BUDGE, E.A. WALLIS, ed. (1899). *The Book of the Dead* (1989 Arkana edition). London: Penguin

BURA, P. (2000). *Stepping to the Drummer: The Extraordinary Tales of a Psychic Man*. Instow: Honeytone Promotions

BURL, A. (1985). *Megalithic Brittany*. London: Thames and Hudson

CANNON JOHNSON, P. (2005). 'The Neoplatonists and the Mystery Schools of the Mediterranean' in MACLEOD, R., ed. *The Library of Alexandria*. London: I.B. Tauris, 2005, 145-6, 159

CASTLEDEN, R. (1987). *The Stonehenge People: an exploration of life in Neolithic Britain 4700-2000 BC*. London and New York: Routledge and Kegan Paul

CAUVILLE, S. (1997). *Le Zodiaque d'Osiris*. France: Peeters

CHADWICK, N.K. (1966). *The Druids*. Cardiff: University of Wales Press

CHOROST, M., ed. (1993). *Report on the Results of Project Argus: An Instrumented Study of the Physical Materials of Crop Circles*. North American Circle, P.O. Box 61144, Durham NC 27715-1144

Circular, The, #19, 1994-5, 1995, winter, 21*

Colossians, see Holy Bible

CONWAY, D. (1985). *Secret Wisdom: The Occult Universe Explored*. London: Jonathan Cape

CONYBEARE, F.C., trans. (1912). *Philostratus: the Life of Apollonius of Tyana*. London: William Heinmann

Corinthians, see Holy Bible

CUMMINS, G. (2012). *The Road to Immortality*. Guildford: White Crow Books

CUMONT, F. (1956). *The Mysteries of Mithra*. New York: Dover Publications Inc.

CUNLIFFE, B. and KOCH, J.T., eds. (2010). *Celtic from the West: Alternative Perspectives from Archaeology, Genetics, Language and Literature*. Oxford: Oxbow Books

Daniel, see Holy Bible

DANIÉLOU, A. (1985). *The Gods of India: Hindu Polytheism*. New York: Inner Traditions International

DAVIS, B. (1991). 'The Cambridgeshire Mandelbrot' in *The Cereologist #5*. 1991/2, winter, 7-8*

DAVIS, B., ed. (1992). *Ciphers in the Crops: the Fractal and Geometric Circles of 1991*. Bath: Gateway Books

DELGADO, P. and ANDREWS, C. (1989). *Circular Evidence*: London: Bloomsbury

DELGADO, P. and ANDREWS, C. (1990). *Crop Circles: the Latest Evidence*. London: Bloomsbury

DE MAILLY NESLE, S. (1981). *Astrology, History, Symbols and Signs*. Translator Lawrence Lockwood. Leon Amiel

DOE, B. (1971). *Southern Arabia*. London: Thames and Hudson

DOWN, A. (1979). *Chichester Excavations*, Vol. IV. Chichester: Phillimore

ELIOT, T.S. (1936). *Usk*, in Collected Poems. 1909-1935. London: Faber and Faber

EOGAN, G. (1986). *Knowth and the Passage-tombs of Ireland*. London: Thames and Hudson

ERIM, K.T. (1986). *Aphrodisias: City of Venus Aphrodite*. London: Muller, Blonde and White

Exodus, see Holy Bible

FAULKNER, R.O. (1969). *The Ancient Egyptian Pyramid Texts*. Warminster: Aris and Phillips

FINKEL, I.L. and SEYMOUR, M.J. (2008). *Babylon, myth and reality*. London: The British Museum Press

FORTUNE, D. (1976 edition). *The Cosmic Doctrine*. The Society of the Inner Light. York Beach, Maine: Samuel Weiser Inc.

FORTUNE, D. (1995). *The Cosmic Doctrine*. London: S.I.L. Trading Ltd

GAGNIÈRE, S. and GRANIER, J. (1963). 'Les stèles anthropomorphes du musée Calvet d'Avignon'. In: *Gallia préhistoire, tome 6, 1963*, pp.31-62. Paris: CNRS Editions and open access at:
doi : https://doi.org/10.3406/galip.1963.1221

https://www.persee.fr/doc/galip_0016-4127_1963_num_6_1_1221

GAUR, A. (1992). *A History of Writing*. New York: Cross River Press

GELLING, P. and DAVIDSON, H.E. (1969). *The Chariot of the Sun*. London: J.M. Dent and Sons

Genesis, see Holy Bible

GIMBUTAS, M. (1982). *The Goddesses and Gods of Old Europe, 6500 to 3500 BC: Myths and Cult Images*. London: Thames and Hudson

GIMBUTAS, M. (1989). *The Language of the Goddess: Unearthing the Hidden Symbols of Western Civilisation*. New York: Harper and Row

GIMBUTAS, M. (1991). *The Civilisation of the Goddess: The World of Old Europe*. San Francisco: Harper San Francisco

GLEICK, J. (1987). *Chaos: Making a New Science*. London: Cardinal by Sphere Books

GODWIN, J. (1981). *Mystery Religions in the Ancient World*. London: Thames and Hudson

GOMEZ-MORENO, M. (1962). *La Escritura Bastulo-Turdetana (Primitiva-hispanica)*. Madrid: Ediciones de Revista de Archivos, Biblioteca y Museos

APULEIUS, LUCIUS. GRAVES, R., trans. (1950). *The Transformation of Lucius, otherwise known as the Golden Ass*. Harmondsworth, Middlesex: Penguin Books

GREEN, H.J.M. (1986). 'Religious cults at Roman Godmanchester' in Henig M. and King A., eds., *Pagan Gods and Shrines of the Roman Empire*. Oxford: Oxford University Committee for Archaeology Monograph 8, 29-55

GREEN, Michael (1990). 'The rings of time: The symbolism of the crop circles' in Noyes, R., ed., *The Crop Circle Enigma*. Bath: Gateway Books, 1990, 137-171

GREEN, Michael (1991). 'The Language of the Circle Makers' in Bartholomew A., ed., *Crop Circles: Harbingers of World Change*. Bath: Gateway Books, 1991, 126-143

GREEN, MICHAEL (1993). In *Kindred Spirit*. London: Tendertheory, 1992-3, 40

GREEN, Michael (1996). 'Soil Tests by the Agricultural Development & Advisory Service' in *The Cerealogist* #17, 1996, autumn, 6-8*

GREEN, Michael (1997). 'A Metaphysical Interpretation of the 1997 Longstock Formation' in *The Cereologist* #20, 1997, autumn, 6*

GREEN, Michael (1998a). 'Spirals and Rings' in *The Circular* #31, 1998, May, 44-46*

GREEN, Michael (1998b). 'The Trinitarian Caduceus of Upham' in *The Circular* #31, 1998, May, 55-57*

GREEN, Michael (1998c). 'The (Beltane) Torus Formation 1998' in *The Circular* #32, 1998, September, 16-17*

GREEN, Michael (1999a). 'The World Tree' in *The Cerealogist* #24, 1999, spring, 23-24*

GREEN, Michael (1999b). 'Doug, Dave and the Wessex Sceptics', in *The Cereologist* #25, 1999, summer, 20-24*

GREEN, Michael (2000a). 'Who Are the Crop Circle Makers?' in *The Cereologist* #27, 2000, spring, 9-13*

GREEN, Michael (2000b). 'A Basket of Teachings' in *The Cereologist* #29, 2000, autumn, 9-13, 16-17*

GREEN, Michael (2002). 'A Web of Deceit' in *The Circular* #48, 2002, December, 22-24*

GREEN, Michael (2005). 'Sibson: Part 2. The Metaphysical Parameters of the Phenomenon: an Interpretation' in *The Circular* #55, 2005, winter-spring, 79-90*

GREEN, Miranda (1989). *Symbol and Image in Celtic Religious Art*, London: Routledge

GREEN, Miranda (1991). *The Sun-Gods of Ancient Europe*. London: B.T. Batsford

GRIMAL, P. (1986). *The Dictionary of Classical Mythology* (Eng. Ed. Trans. A.R. Maxwell-Hyslop). London: Blackwell

GRIST, B. (1991). 'Alchemy and Chaos at Barbury Castle' in Davis, B., ed., *Ciphers in the Crops: the Fractal and Geometric Circles of 1991*. Bath: Gateway Books, 1992, 45-56

GWILT, J. (1826). *The Architecture of Marcus Vitruvius Pollio in Ten Books. Translated from the Latin by Joseph Gwilt*. London: Priestley and Weale

HALEVI, Z'ev ben Shimon (1985). *Adam and the Kabbalistic Tree*. London: Gateway Books

HALEVI, Z'ev ben Shimon (1976). *Tree of Life: Introduction to the Cabala*. London: Rider

HARDEN, D. (1971). *The Phoenicians*. Harmondsworth: Penguin Books

HARRISON, J.E. (1962). *Prolegomena*. London: Merlin Press

HARRISON, J.E. (1963). *Themis*. London: Merlin Press

HAWKES, J. (1937). *The Archaeology of the Channel Islands, Vol. II The Bailiwick of Jersey*. Jersey: Societé Jersiaise

HELSKOG, K. (1988). *Helleristningene i Alta: Spor etter ritualer og dagligliv i Finnmarks forhistorie.* Norway: Alta Kommune

HINCKLEY ALLEN, R. (1899). *Star Names, their Lore and Meaning*, 1963 edition. New York: Dover

Holy Bible: New Revised Standard Version, Anglicised Edition, 1995, Oxford University Press

Isaiah, see Holy Bible

James, see Holy Bible

JAMIESON, R.C. (2000). *The Perfection of Wisdom.* London: Frances Lincoln

JENSEN, H. (1970). *Sign, Symbol and Script: an Account of Man's Efforts to Write*, 3rd edition. London: George Allen and Unwin

Job, see Holy Bible

John, see Holy Bible

JUNG, C.G. (1964). *Man and his Symbols.* New York: Doubleday

KEEN, M. (1992). *1991 – Scientific Evidence for the Crop Circle Phenomenon.* Norwich: Elvery Dowers Publications

KHALIDI, T. (2001). *The Muslim Jesus.* Cambridge Massachusetts: Harvard University Press

KHYENTSE, Dzongsar Jamyang (2007). *What makes you not a Buddhist.* Boston: Shambhala Publications

KINGSLEY, P. (1999). *In the Dark Places of Wisdom.* California: The Golden Sufi Centre

KIRK, G.S., RAVEN, J.E. and SCHOFIELD, M. (1983). *The Presocratic Philosophers.* Cambridge: The Cambridge University Press

KOLLERSTROM, N. (2000). 'The Heptagon Family', in *The Cereologist* #28, 2000, summer, 3-6*

KRUTA, V. and FORMAN, W. (1985). *The Celts of the West.* London: Orbis Publishing

LAMY, L. (1981). *Egyptian Mysteries: New light on Ancient knowledge.* London: Thames and Hudson

LE MEN, R.F. (1868). 'Subterranean Chambers at La Tourelle, near Quimper, Brittany' in *Archaeologia Cambrensis* 3rd Ser. Vol. XIV, 308-309. Available from archive.org

Luke, see Holy Bible

LYONS, J. (1993a). 'Euclidean or Fractal. Which Geometry Circlemakers?' in *The Circular* #14, 1993, September, 18-20*

LYONS, J. (1993b). 'Arras Hill Formation' in *The Circular* #15, 1993, December, 23-24*

LYONS, J. (1994). 'Circles of Symmetry' in *The Circular* #16, 1994, March, 16-18*

LYONS, J. (1995a). 'The Physics of Crop Circle Formation: New Developments' in *The Cereologist* #14, 1995, summer, 11*

LYONS, J. (1995b). 'Summary Statement of ADAS and other 1995 Crop Circle Tests' in *The Circular* #23, 1995, winter, 6-7*

LYONS, J. (1998a). 'Bubbles and Knots' in *The Circular* #31, 1998, May, 4ff.*

LYONS, J. (1998b). 'Silbury Torus Formation' in *The Circular* #32, 1998, September, 17*

MacCANA, P. (1970). *Celtic Mythology.* London: Hamlyn Publishing Group Ltd.

MALLORY, J.P. (1989). *In Search of the Indo-Europeans: Language, Archaeology and Myth.* London: Thames and Hudson

Mark, see Holy Bible

MASCARÓ, J., trans. (1973). *The Dhammapada*. London: Penguin Books

Matthew, see Holy Bible

McARTHUR, M. (2002). *Reading Buddhist Art*. London: Thames and Hudson

MEAD, G.R.S. (1901). *Apollonius of Tyana, the Philosopher-Reformer of the First Century A.D.* London and Benares: Theosophical Publishing Society

MEAD, G.R.S. (1906). *Thrice Greatest Hermes*. London: Theosophical Publishing Society

MEADEN, G.T. (1989). *The Circles Effect and its Mysteries*. Bradford on Avon: Artetech

MEADEN, G.T. (1991). *Circles from the Sky*. London: Souvenir Press

MEGAW, R. and V. (1989). *Celtic Art: from its Beginnings to the Book of Kells*. London: Thames and Hudson

METROPOLITAN MUSEUM OF ART, THE (1986). *Treasures of the Holy Land*. New York: Metropolitan Museum of Art

MICHELL, J. (1990). 'The Peterborough Rings' in *The Cerealogist* #2, 1990, winter, 5*

MICHELL, J. (1991a). 'Geometry and Symbolism at Barbury Castle' in *The Cerealogist* #4, 1991, summer, 24-25*

MICHELL, J. (1991b). Footnote in *The Cerealogist*, #5, 1991-2, winter, 24*

MILLER, J. (1985). *The Vision of Cosmic Order in the Vedas*. London: Routledge and Kegan Paul

MISTREE, K.P. (1982). *Zoroastrianism: An Ethnic Perspective*. Bombay: Good Impressions

MORCOM, S. (1991). 'Field Work – the Pictogram at East/West Kennett Long Barrows' in *The Circular* Volume 2, Number 1, 1991, March, 9-13*

NASR, SEYYED HOSSEIN (1978). *An Introduction to Islamic Cosmological Doctrines: Conceptions of Nature and Methods Used for its Study by the Ikhwan al-Safa, al-Biruni and Ibn Sina*. London: Thames and Hudson

NASR, SEYYED HOSSEIN (2000). *Ideals and Realities of Islam*. Chicago: ABC International Group

NOYES, R., ed. (1990). *The Crop Circle Enigma*. Bath: Gateway Books

O'KELLY, M.J. (1982). *Newgrange: Archaeology, Art and Legend*. London: Thames and Hudson

O'RAHILLY, T.F. (1984). *Early Irish History and Mythology*. Dublin: Dublin Institute for Advanced Studies

O'DONOHUE, J. (1998). *Anam Cara*. London: Bantam Press

Oxford English Dictionary, The Shorter. (1973). Third edition. Oxford: Clarendon Press

PALGRAVE-MOORE, P. (1991). *Crop Circle Classification*. Norwich: Elvery Dowers

PARKER PEARSON, M. (2005). *Bronze Age Britain*. London: Batsford

PARKER, D. and J. (1983). *A History of Astrology*. London: Andre Deutsch

PARROTT, B. (2002). 'A New Twist to the DNA Formation' in *The Circular* #47, 2002, autumn, 40*

PENNICK, N. (1990). *Mazes and Labyrinths*. London: Robert Hale

PLOT, R. (1686). *The Natural History of Staffordshire*. Oxford: Printed at the Theatre

PRINGLE, L. (1993). 'The Bluffer's Bluff is Called' in *The Circular*, #14, 1993, September, 13-15*

Psalms, see Holy Bible

RAFTERY, B. ed. (1990). *Celtic Art*. Paris: Unesco-Flammarion

REES, A. and B. (1961). *Celtic Heritage: Ancient Tradition in Ireland and Wales*. London: Thames and Hudson

REES, M., gen. ed. (2009). *Illustrated Encyclopedia of The Universe*. London: Dorling Kindersley

RENFREW, C. (1987). *Archaeology and Language: the Puzzle of Indo-European Origins*. London: Jonathan Cape

RENFREW, C. and BAHN, P., eds. (2012). *Archaeology* 6th edition. London: Thames and Hudson

Revelation, see Holy Bible

ROSS, A. (1967). *Pagan Celtic Britain*. London: Routledge and Kegan Paul

ROWELL, G., STEVENSON, K. AND WILLIAMS, R. (2001). *Love's Redeeming Work*. Oxford: O.U.P.

SCARRE, C. (2007). *The Megalithic Monuments of Britain and Ireland*. London: Thames and Hudson

SCARRE, C., ed. (2005). *The Human Past: World Prehistory and the Development of Human Societies*. London: Thames and Hudson

SCOTT, W. (1992). *Hermetica*. Bath: Solo Press

SHAW, R. (1996). 'Circles in Herts' in *The Cereologist* #17, 1996, autumn, 23*

SHERWOOD, J. (1969). *The Country Beyond. The Doctrine of Rebirth*. Saffron Walden: C. W. Daniel

SILVA, F. (2002). *Secrets in the Fields*. Charlottesville, USA: Hampton Roads

SISUNG, K.S., ed. (1996). *Angels A to Z*. Detroit: Visible Ink Press

SMITH, D.G., ed. (1982). *The Cambridge Encyclopedia of Earth Sciences*. Cambridge: Cambridge University Press

SMITH, W. (1875). *A Concise Dictionary of the Bible*. London: John Murray

STEWART, R.J. (1985). *The Underworld Initiation: a Journey towards Psychic Transformation*. Wellingborough: The Aquarian Press

TAYLOR, B. (1992). *Crop circles of 1991*. Marlborough: Beckhampton Books

TAYLOR, J. H., ed. (2010). *Journey through the Afterlife, Ancient Egyptian Book of the Dead*. London: British Museum Press

THOMAS, A. (1996). *Fields of Mystery: the Crop Circle Phenomenon in Sussex*. Seaford: SB Publications

TOYNBEE, J.M.C. (1964). *Art in Britain under the Romans*. London: Oxford University Press

TRUMP, D.H. (1990 edition). *Malta: An Archaeological Guide*. Valletta, Malta: Progress Press

TYSON, D., ed. (1995). *Three Books of Occult Philosophy written by Henry Cornelius Agrippa of Nettesheim*. St Paul MN. USA: Llewellyn Publications

VEEN, V. (1992). *The Goddess of Malta.* Haarlem, Holland: Inanna-Fia

WALKER, B. (1983). *Gnosticism: its History and Influence.* Wellingborough: The Aquarian Press

WARING, J.B. (1870). *Stone Monuments, Tumuli and Ornament of Remote Ages.* London: John B. Day

WHISHAW, E.M. (1997). *Atlantis in Spain.* Kempton, Illinois USA: Adventures Unlimited

WHITFIELD, P. (2001). *Astrology: a history.* London: The British Library

WILKINSON, T. (2005). *Dictionary of Ancient Egypt.* London: Thames and Hudson

WILLIAMS, J. (1862). *Barddas, Vol I.* London: Longman

WILLIAMS, M.H. (2000). 'Philostratus of Athens, the life of Apollonius of Tyana' in VALANTASIS, R., ed., *Religions of Late Antiquity in Practice.* Princeton and Woodstock: Princeton University Press, 2000, 35

WILSON, R. (2011). 'Banquets for the Dead', in *World Archaeology* #44, Dec 2010/Jan 2011. London: Current Publishing, 38-45

WILSON, T. (1998). *The Secret History of Crop Circles.* Paignton, Devon: CCCS

WINGFIELD, G. (1991). 'Towards an understanding of the nature of the circles' in Bartholomew, A., ed. *Crop Circles: Harbingers of World Change.* Bath: Gateway Books, 1991, 27-29

WINGFIELD, G. (1991-2). 'The Doug 'n' Dave Scam' in *The Cerealogist* #5, 1991-2, winter, 3-6*

WINGFIELD, G. (1992). 'The Cipher of Chaos' in Davis, B., ed., *Ciphers in the Crops: the Fractal and Geometric Circles of 1991.* Bath: Gateway Books, 1992, 16-28

WINGFIELD, G. (1990). 'A Carefully Planned Hoax' in *The Cerealogist* #2, 1990, winter, 8-10*

YOURCENAR, M. (1955). *Memoirs of Hadrian.* (Grace Frick trans.) London: Secker and Warburg

ZAMMIT, T. (1980 edition). *The Copper Age Temples of Hal-Tarxien, Malta.* Malta: Union Press


*The Cereologist/Cerealogist*, and *The Circular* (the magazine of the Centre for Crop Circle Studies 1990-2005). Runs of these magazines were deposited in the libraries of *The Society for Psychical Research* and *The Theosophical Society*, London.

# Index

East Dean Formation